THE SILENT VOICES
AND THE CREATION
OF A NEW UNIVERSE

THE SILENT VOICES AND THE CREATION OF A NEW UNIVERSE

Sikh Gurus on Women and Society

PRATIBHA CHAWLA

BOYDELL·MANOHAR

© Pratibha Chawla, 2024

All Rights Reserved. Except as permitted under current legislation no part of this work may be photocopied, stored in a retrieval system, published, performed in public, adapted, broadcast, transmitted, recorded or reproduced in any form or by any means, without the prior permission of the copyright owner

The right of Pratibha Chawla to be identified as the author of this work has been asserted in accordance with sections 77 and 78 of the Copyright, Designs and Patents Act 1988

ISBN 978-81-19953-12-7 (Manohar Publishers & Distributors)
ISBN 978-18-37652-39-6 (Boydell ◆ Manohar)

First published 2024 by
Ajay Kumar Jain for
Manohar Publishers & Distributors
4753/23 Ansari Road, Daryaganj
New Delhi 110 002

First published Worldwide excluding India, Sri Lanka, Nepal, Bangladesh, Afghanistan, Pakistan and Bhutan, 2023 by Boydell ◆ Manohar
A joint imprint of Boydell & Brewer Ltd and
Manohar Publishers & Distributors
PO Box 9, Woodbridge, Suffolk IP12 3DF, UK
and of Boydell & Brewer Inc.
668 Mt Hope Avenue, Rochester, NY 14620–2731, USA
website: www.boydellandbrewer.com

A CIP catalogue record for this book is available
from the British Library

The publisher has no responsibility for the continued existence or accuracy of URLs for external or third-party internet websites referred to in this book, and does not guarantee that any content on such websites is, or will remain, accurate or appropriate

Typeset by
Kohli Print
Delhi 110 051

*To
the loving memory
of my parents*

Contents

Acknowledgements	9
Introduction	13
PART I: BACKGROUND AND DEVOTIONAL MOVEMENTS	
1. The Land and its People	57
2. Guru Nanak and *Bhakti Sant*s on Women	102
PART II: CONTEXTUALIZING WOMEN IN MEDIEVAL PUNJAB	
3. *Stri Svabhav, Stri Dharam* and Prevailing Realities	145
4. Aspects of the Marital Bond	159
5. Women in the Social Sphere	212
6. Discrimination and Social Evils	269
7. The Sikh Panth and Women's Identity	300
Conclusion	335
Glossary	347
A Note on Primary Sources	357
Bibliography	395
Index	425

Acknowledgements

This work has finally come to the stage of publication with the immense support, encouragement, and guidance of a number of people.

Prof. Dilbagh Singh, my doctoral supervisor at the Jawaharlal Nehru University, New Delhi, India for his rigorous analytical skills and guidance. I owe him my enduring gratitude. His unfaltering encouragement and faith in my work despite long spells of interruptions and self-doubt was pivotal. I am grateful to Prof. Singh and Mrs Satyender Kaur for their patience through the long discussions in the course of my dissertation. Their feedback was extremely valuable. I could not have done without their immense support.

Prof. Jaswinder Singh, Principal Sri Guru Tegh Bahadur Khalsa (S.G.T.B.) College, University of Delhi, despite his many administrative responsibilities, has been consistent in his encouragement and abiding assistance to get the work published, and his generous spirit has been inspirational. Foremost, he has been instrumental in driving me out of my hibernation and furthering my research interests in Sikh history.

I must express my sincere gratitude to Prof. Indu Banga, who was the first person, as the external examiner of my thesis, to encourage me to research further and get the work published.

My gratitude is on record to Prof. Gurinder Singh Mann, Director, Global Institute for Sikh Studies, New York for being a consistent source of encouragement and inspiration.

I must express my gratitude to Dr (Late) H.S. Chawla who ignited my interest in Sikh studies and was always more than willing to share his knowledge as well as his treasure trove of rare books with me. I am especially indebted to Sardarni Surinder Kaur who helped me in sharpening my linguistic skills and with the transcription of sources in a limited time span.

I owe a great deal to the staff of S.G.T.B. Khalsa Library, as well as Mr Anand and Alka Madan of Bhai Vir Singh Sahitya Sadan Library, Punjabi University Main Library, Patiala and the Teen Murti Library, New Delhi. The functionaries of all these institutions were always very helpful and went out of their way in finding the reading material with a smile. I must express my gratitude to Mr Jyotirmoy Chaudhuri and Dr Mushtaq Hussain for their valuable inputs as well as editorial skills.

Amongst my family members, I would like to especially remember and pay homage to my parents Mrs Kamal Kaushi and Mr Amar Nath Gyani, both of whom, with their struggles in their lives exemplified the Sikh values and the grace of Kirat Kar, Wand Khaana. They highlighted the importance of hard work, honest living and setting the goal of self-growth—growth of the family through pursuits of education. I am indebted to both of you for making us what we are despite the challenges posed before both of you by traumatic adversities like the Partition of India.

Besides, I am thankful to my parents-in-law Mr (Late) V.P. Chawla and Mrs Anjana Chawla for their support and encouragement for pursuing my professional growth. I must make special mention of Mr (Late) Harish Sachdeva and Smt. Raj Bhutani who have inspired me by their trait of personal generosity and humility. I should also take this opportunity to thank Mr Pankaj Sachdeva and Dr Anupama Sachdeva.

Special mention must be made to my elder brothers and sisters-in-law, Mr Vijay Pratap, Prof. Ritu Priya, Mr Jawahar, Mr Vidya Bhushan and Dr Prabha, and my doting sister and brother-in-law Prof. Mridula Arora and Dr Ajit Jha who have been consistent pillars of support and inspiration for me. My siblings being older to me, have not only been my academic mentors but have made the journey of life a much smoother and pleasant one for me. I owe special thanks to my sister Mridula who has inculcated a love for history and has been a great friend, mentor and moral support for all these years. I don't say it enough, but I am so thankful to have you all in my life.

I owe thanks to my dear friends, Dr Bhawna Goel, Dr Deepali Sharma, Dr Nachiketa Singh, Dr Devika Rangachari, Dr Nimmi Singh, Dr Jasneet Kaur, Dr Vinayneet Kaur and Dr Inderpreet Kaur for their support and friendly inputs and encouragement during the course of this work.

I must also acknowledge S. Jarnail Singh's guidance and ever readiness to assist me in my administrative responsibilities towards the institution.

I am thankful to my daughter Snigdha who was a child when I began my work and has grown up to be a committed feminist and sensitive human being. She often pushes me to review my juxtapositions and contributes in my thought process. Thank you Snigdha for being my lifeline and for always supporting my dreams! I am so grateful to have you in my life and cherish our warm and lovely telephonic conversations! You are the most amazing daughter Satyakam and I could have asked for! I must make a special mention of my nephew Kartikeya who has always been very caring and protective. Being a prolific reader and a lawyer by training he has provided me support and helped me refine my thought processes at critical junctures. Both Snigdha and Kartikeya along with Manvi Priya, Raghav and Ikshula have graced me with their love and wisdom.

Lastly, my enormous debt and gratitude goes to my rock and partner, Satyakam who has provided loving support and faith in me. He has been a great partner having inherent qualities of being generous, supportive and truly encouraging in thought and action. He has often lovingly reprimanded and reminded me of what one is capable of due to rigorous academic training. I have been a silent admirer of his focus, hard work and time management and the biggest beneficiary of it all.

Admittedly, this book would never have been published without the unceasing encouragement and support of my lovely family, friends, colleagues, respected teachers and the University of Delhi that granted me study leave.

I must make a special mention of Mr (Late) Ramesh Jain, Proprietor, Manohar Publishers & Distributors who took a special interest and pains in the publication of the work. Thanks to you, Mr Jain, for your guidance and patience. I owe gratitude to Mr Ajay Kumar Jain and Mr Ananya Jain for their professionalism and due encouragement. I must express my gratitude to the entire editorial team, especially Mr Sanjay Kala. I take full responsibility for its final form and all the mistakes inadvertently committed.

Pratibha Chawla

Introduction

> [Religion is] 'a system of symbols which acts to establish powerful, pervasive and long-lasting moods and motivations in men. . . .'
>
> CLIFFORD GEERTZ[1]

> Religion is among the foremost of institutions which conserve society, encoding stabilizing world views and values and transmitting these from generation to generation. Religion has been an instrument of liberation for women. But religion has just as often become an instrument of women's social oppression.
>
> NANCY FALK AND RITA M. GROSS[2]

The above lines are a gist of the complex relationship between religion and the sociocultural aspects of society. Its role becomes still more significant in the context of its overarching influence on social values, norms and ethos of the time, especially in relation to women.

The feminist historian, Joan Wallach Scott, argues for a shift from 'women's history' to a 'history of gender'. According to her, the category of gender not only illuminates the unequal relations of power between males and females, but also helps clarify that such unequal relations are extended to diverse areas of social life. The category of gender is fluid, always evolving and transforming. Scott insists that a radical feminist epistemology is necessary in the study of history. She advocates a post-structuralist approach, one that can address the theory and the status of knowledge, thereby linking knowledge and power. Scott writes:

> The emphasis on 'how' suggests a study of processes, not of origins, of multiple rather than single causes, of rhetoric rather than ideology or

consciousness. It does not abandon attention to structures and institutions, but it does insist that we need to understand what these organizations mean in order to understand how they work.[3]

It is an accepted conceptual assumption that gender relations cannot be studied in isolation. Gender relations has to be looked at in the context of structures and processes in which such relations are embedded. It has often been argued among feminist scholars that the results of an exclusive focus on women will be disastrous, as the male bias of the past will be replaced by a female bias. Can we then assuredly comprehend social reality? What is advocated, therefore, is a bifocal analysis, looking at social relations from the perspectives of both men and women. Based on the same premise, in the last few decades, extensive 'women's studies in religion' have been undertaken. The scholarship is distinguished from other approaches to the study of religion by a fundamental concern for gender as the critical variable in religion. Taking 'gender' as a primary category of analysis, women's studies in religion examine the function of gender in the symbolization of religious traditions – the institutionalization of gender confirming roles in religious communities and the dynamics of the interaction between systems of religious belief and the personal, social and cultural conditions of women. Under the rubric of women's studies in religion, feminist scholars can pursue one of their main purposes, which is the recovery of women's distinctive historical and contemporary experiences on the basis of the recovered experience and perspectives of women. Women's studies offer a critique of religion and cultural traditions, while making the experiences and the perspectives of women the starting point for the feminist re-interpretation and reconstruction of both religion and culture.

The close connection between religious and societal norms is well evinced by our values, religious beliefs and social behaviour. Institutionalized religion has been at the forefront of conserving and stabilizing societal values and world views and transplanting them from generation to generation.

Religious ideology very often plays a crucial role in legitimizing and sustaining the subordination of women. It is in context of this close connection between religion and social norms that I decided to study the impact of the Sikh Gurus on issues concerning women. In sharp contrast to the general social perception and ethos of the sixteenth and seventeenth centuries, Sikhism advocated an egalitarian society. For Guru Nanak, men and women were equal not only before God, but also before one another. Under Sikhism women are considered an integral part of society who must not be excluded by a ritual or doctrinal consideration. Thus, I was inclined to study as to how the Sikh Gurus perceived gender. In this book, I raise several related questions: How did these perceptions and ideals make an impact on social relations? How did these ideals affect the evolution of the Sikh Panth? Was there a difference in Guru Nanak's perception of women and their position from that of the contemporary Bhakti saints as well as subsequent Sikh Gurus? At a more abstract level, was there a difference in the focuses and emphasis of their teachings? What impact did they have on the social milieu and how were their ideals furthered?

The study of the impact of the Sikh Gurus on the dominant patriarchal ideology of the Punjab of the sixteenth and seventeenth centuries cannot be oblivious to the fact that the Punjab region has been an unusually fluid land, not just geographically but socially and culturally as well. The boundaries of present-day Indian Punjab are a little less than 15 per cent of the total geographical area of pre-Partition colonial Punjab. The boundaries have been redrawn several times over the last few centuries. Socially and culturally too, Punjab has seen many changes. In the course of this study, the myth of a homogeneous region, that is, Punjab and the community was clearly demolished. In Punjab, Hindus and Muslims have coexisted and shared a common culture. In the early decades of the sixteenth century, Sikhism in its nascent stage had not evolved as a distinct community. There was no collective urge either on the part of the Sikh Gurus or their followers to evolve a distinct identity of their own. In the context of Punjab, multiculturalism is not just a statement of fact, it is also a practised value. It is a society characterized not by multiple cultural exclusivities or endemic cultural strife, but by communities living in harmony and sharing a common culture. The society of Punjab, at that point of time, was marked by the fusion of traditions where Hindus, Muslims, and Sikhs (if we may use the term) shared the aspirations of their lives, social values, cultural ethos and social expressions which were articulated in myriad rituals and rites. When historians and political analysts look back at the period, they need to evaluate the sociocultural, political, and economic significance of events during the times. The cumulative effects of these events cannot be immediately gauged at one go as society in the Punjab was continuously affected by frontal attacks from the eleventh century onward.

In the field of gender studies, it is difficult to account as to how women's identities were formed and what they signified in such a distant past. It becomes still more significant as the past has an uneasy relationship with the modern Indian woman. It is an apparent limitation of this study as the period under review is the sixteenth and seventeenth centuries where it was unimaginable that women could have an identity of her own. However, it is crucial to understand the processes by which women become the sites for the construction of group identities. In this context, the social milieu of the period provides a context to study the social institution of marriage, child marriage, relationship between marriage and caste, and the underlying logistics of ritual purity of varied forms of widow remarriage – *karewa* and *chadar pauna*. This study will also discuss the still prevalent, if not predominant, ideology of domesticity and seclusion.

This work attempts to tap the different and often contentious issues concerning women, the gender negotiations that take place between men and women of the household, and how the patriarchal forces (the society at large) tried to resolve them. Did the Sikh Gurus have any impact on the dominant patriarchal ideologies? Could they succeed in formulating or even modifying the formulations of the dominant ideological current and evolving a new social ethos? With this goal, a variety of primary sources – *Sri Guru Granth Sahib*, hagiographic sources known as *janamsakhis*, the contemporary or near-contemporary sources ranging from *Prachin Panth Parkash* and the more propitiatory *Gurbilas Patshahi Chhevin* and *Gurbilas Patshahi Dasvin* to works focusing on genealogy like *Bansavali-namah*, besides *Sau Sakhi* and *Dasam Granth* – have been analysed from a gender perspective to come to an understanding of the discourse surrounding gender during the initial phase of the formation of the Sikh traditions. Due attention has been paid to popular folklore tradition of *Hir-Ranjah*, ranging from Damodar Gulati and Waris Shah to the mystical verses of Shah Hussain. The aim is to come to an understanding of gender themes within the earliest sources, both historical and scriptural.

WHY PUNJAB?

The foremost reason for choosing the Punjab region is that I am a Punjabi myself and therefore I have been brought up on a value system emphasizing equality between men and women. The Sikh faith has always espoused an egalitarian approach to gender relations. This understanding being subjected to the hard blows of present-day realities, I was pushed to look for contradictions in the past narrative. Apart from my familiarity with the culture and traditions of the land, a closer academic scrutiny of the region further enhanced my interest in the subject.

Geographically and geo-politically, Punjab occupies an area of north India which has had to bear the brunt of several frontal challenges. In Muhammad Akbar's words,

The Punjab was overwhelmed by the intermittent waves of the immigration of hordes of the Aryans, the Scythians, the Greeks, the Arabs, the Turks, the Afghans, the Persians, and the Mughals. These groups appearing at intervals and advancing into the peninsula left something to be assimilated by the people already in the province.[4]

In sum, ethnically and culturally, Punjab has been home to people of different ethnicities that constantly interacted with one another. Moreover, the region of Punjab has been a hub of the Bhakti ideology, where Guru Nanak emerged as an iconic figure. There were great similarities in the teachings of Guru Nanak and the other fifteenth-century poet saints like Kabir on caste, idol worship, and perfunctory rituals. However, when I compared Guru Nanak's position on women and their place in society, I discerned a subtle difference in his teachings from those of Kabir.

Guru Nanak's position on women was in great contrast to the predominant social and cultural ethos of the times. For the Nath *yogi*s,[5] whose primary objective was the suppression of desires, particularly the sexual urge, women were perceived as great obstacles in the path of salvation and therefore they needed to be conquered. Kabir viewed women as seductive beings, who tempted men away from their spiritual inclinations. Kabir asked men to shun the company of women. He questioned the misery of men, who cohabited with women every day (*kabira tin ki kya gat jo nit naari ke sang*). Sant Tulsidas, the revered fifteenth-century Hindi poet and author of *Ramcharitmanas*, placed women at par with *shudra*s and animals (*dhol gawar shudra pashu naari, sakal taran ke adhikaari*). Guru Nanak, on the other hand, criticized the *yogi*s for their solitary spiritual search and furthered the ideal of the householder. He saw marriage as a sacred institution, a spiritual bond between two equal partners, not merely a physical union between two individuals. He asserted that one attains salvation living within the family.[6] A strict moral code of conduct was prescribed for men and women in Sikhism, where the duties of both husband and wife were well defined.

This contrast between the social ethos and norms prevailing at that time and Guru Nanak's perceptions made me curious about the extent it might have affected the dominant ideologies of patriarchy. Did it actually manage to formulate a new social ethos on gender relations or did it bring about only a limited modification in attitudes?

FUSION OF TRADITIONS

Punjab, during the period of our study, was home to Hindus, Muslims and Sikhs. In fact, Muslims outnumbered Hindus and Sikhs. There is a complex interplay between religion and social change. Religious traditions have been important players in the transformation of societies and have always been of utmost importance in determining the status of women, since such factors exert a powerful influence on the thought processes, cultural values and social behaviour of people. This analysis becomes even more complex because in the sixteenth and seventeenth centuries, the Sikhs had not emerged as a distinct community. Nor was there any collective urge within the community to distinguish themselves from the predominant Hindu culture, traditions, rituals, or religion. Consequently, the two communities shared intercutting and intersecting relations among themselves. In other words, the fortunes of Sikh women were inextricably linked with that of Hindu women in this region. Sikhism was itself in an evolutionary stage with its changing ideological focuses during the period under study. In the course of its evolution, a number of dissenting or deviant sects emerged such as Sangatshahis, Udasis, Kukas and Namdharis. This study is further complicated by the fact that initially there were at least eleven known traditions. Therefore, it would be inappropriate to presume any kind of homogeneity within Sikhism. In fact, the culture of Hindus and Sikhs was somewhat co-terminus. Thus, it would be improper to presume them as two separate communities having distinct traditions, cultural values, and norms. Harjot Oberoi puts it very succinctly when he writes,

Sikh notions of time, space, corporeality, holiness, kinship, societal distinctions, purity, pollution, and commensality were hardly different from those of the Hindus. Also, the two shared, the same territory, language, rites of passage, dietary taboos, festivals, rituals, and key theological concepts. The concept of personhood within the two traditions and their solutions for existential problems were quite alike.[7]

This kind of common culture is further attested by the heterodox textuality of the contributors of the *Sri Guru Granth Sahib*, which combined elements from Muslim, Sufi, Hindu and Bhakti traditions. In a similar spirit, the inclusion of Hindu deities and iconographic features in the premises of the Golden Temple is another reflection of common culture.

This fusion of tradition did not leave the Muslim component of population untouched. Kinsley puts it very appropriately when he says

Religion was primarily a localized affair, often a matter of individual conduct and individual salvation. For much of their history, the people of the subcontinent practised their rituals, pilgrimages, and acts of religious piety without objectifying religion into an exclusive entity. Religious traditions were based on local traditions and not on pan-regional organization of communities. Islam may have been the only exception to this, but then, Indian Islam, heavily coloured by Sufism, is of a radically different genre from its counterparts elsewhere.[8]

This holds true in the context of Punjab as the presence and influence of Sufi shrines is clearly discernible. Inclusion of poetry of Baba Farid in *Sri Guru Granth Sahib* and the fact that one of the four persons who laid the foundation stone of Golden Temple, was the esteemed Miyan Mir cannot be ignored. Similarly, the remarkable influence of the Sufi poets Shah Hussain, Sultan Bahu, Bulleh Shah, Waris Shah and others on the popular culture of Punjab is more than evident. The imprint of their verses on the culture of the land is still apparent after centuries. For instance, a Muslim girl named Kaula, being influenced by the Sikh discourses, accompanied Guru Hargobind and stayed in his hometown for the rest of her life. This fusion of diverse traditions makes the present analysis even more complex.

LITERATURE REVIEW: A FEW CONCERNS

An attempt has been made at a nuanced study from a gender perspective of different genres of literature, ranging from the historical to the hagiographical as well as popular literature and folk songs. Yet one must admit the limitation posed by the sources. First, S. Nurul Hasan argues that the destiny of the Punjab, being so closely linked with the rest of the country, there is no worthwhile medieval history or chronicle dealing exclusively with the region.[9] The historical data regarding the Punjab has therefore to be culled from the general medieval chronicles. With the evidence widely scattered, bits of pieces of information have to be collected and inferences drawn. Thus, it becomes difficult to collect evidence. In the context of gender studies, the problem gets magnified many times. It is like studying the position of women through men's eyes. Second, the available sources are hagiographic in nature, associating legends and miracles with the Gurus. At best, they deal with battles, administrative concerns, economic transactions, struggle with the Mughals and genealogies, wherein women had little place other than as wives and mothers of the Gurus. Extraordinary women do find their way into oral traditions, but here one must avoid falling into the trap of treating exceptions as common reality. These exceptional women cannot be held up as examples by which to measure gender egalitarianism in any society. It reminds one of Simon Digby's opinion that every source has a discursiveness of its own kind.[10] While examining and exploring the past of a society, we cannot afford to ignore either the sphere of ideas or the socio-economic and political processes that influenced people at a specific time. Gurevich, a distinguished Soviet scholar of modern European history, has rightly observed that historical research is a dialogue between two cultural backgrounds, that is, between the culture of the research epoch and that of the researcher.[11] It becomes still more critical in the context of medieval society and thus needs to be dealt with caution.

It must also be underlined that, given the fact that women have not generally written their own histories, historical accounts were written through the lens of the male gender. What was and is important to men thus becomes the thrust of the sources and focus of historical analysis. Man, as a social instrument, is responsible, if not solely then quite substantially, for the fate of women. Most textual sources are either silent on women or at best prescriptive with an inherent gender bias. In other words, they represent the perspectives of men belonging to the upper echelons of society. Whatever the source material handed down to us from the historical past, they were considered worthy of being preserved by men and have come down to us with the inherent gender bias. In this entire process, there are treasures of knowledge that might have been lost. There are rare instances of women writers in Sikh history. When they do appear, their contributions have often been interpreted as mere guises for the men who were the 'real' voices of history. For instance, the *hukamnama*s of Mata Gujri, wife of Guru Teg Bahadur, are regarded as binding on the whole Sikh community. Yet credit is given to her own brother Kirpal Singh. These *hukamnama*s are not unanimously accepted as written by Mata Gujri. Scholars such as Ganda Singh believe that they were written by Mata Nanki, mother of Guru Teg Bahadur.[12] However, the net result is that the value attached to a particular source suffers a setback putting a question mark on its authorship.

The histories of the Gurus, by and large, are silent about their wives. From Guru Nanak to Guru Gobind Singh, the wives have been treated as part of the historical background and not as individuals in themselves. Needless to say, the overwhelming impression we receive from reading the works on Sikh history is that women do not have a history or presence of their own. From the silences surrounding the women, their lives and experiences can be perceived only as inconsequential. Yet, we know that besides the history composed by men, there exists a 'her story'. Many aspects of this narrative have been wiped out, so it is quite difficult to reconstruct its basic elements.

Another major limitation is that whatever little information is furnished by the sources, it is more often than not about the upper echelons of the society. We can easily presume that as wives, sisters, or daughters of the Gurus or Rajas, they certainly did not lead lives that were akin to their common, contemporary sisters. In many ways, they conjure up false images as to the roles and status of women in society. Adding up to our challenges, in the words of Clarence McMullen, is the gap between the normative and operative beliefs. Though his analysis is placed in the context of contemporary society, it holds still more true for any medieval society. According to his definition,

Normative beliefs and practices are those which are officially stated and prescribed or proscribed by a recognized religious authority, which can be a person, organization, or an official statement. Operative beliefs and practices, on the other hand, are those actually held by the people.[13]

One tends to tap information from the oral traditions with the twin intention of a closer glimpse of the common masses, their concerns and aspirations and to overcome the lacunae embedded, at least to an extent, of the sources emanating from the upper echelons of society. This exercise has inherent limitations of its own kind. The written texts assembled from oral traditions are part of a collective oeuvre. Certain parts must have been reaccentuated, certain potentials from the images actualized, others allowed to fade over time. In this sense, the works are inscribed in an extended rather than a discrete moment of production. They represent intentions, beliefs, desires which stretch beyond the individual and, thus, need to be used with caution when designated as a definable mode of social perception.

To expect homogeneity in terms of culture, values, rituals, rites, taboos in any society are not only inappropriate but it threatens the very nature of human society. The coexistence of multiplicity of traditions becomes more apparent in the context of Punjab, where the three communities, the Hindus, Muslims, and Sikhs not only coexisted but to a great extent shared a cultural fusion. Thus, one has to be consciously alert of the attempt of the sources to flatten out the diversity. Diversity, especially in context of the Indian sub-continent is a pre-eminent reality. This brings us to important aspects of social institutions, particularly the caste system and the class structure, which play a pivotal role in the day-to-day functioning of social relations. The caste system, in context of medieval India, is inextricably linked to gender relations. In fact, the diversity of cultural practices among different castes become apparent in case of gender relations, for instance the forms of marriage or even marriage rituals.

In sum, this entire question of position of women in Punjab needs to be placed in the context of caste, class, and community and at the same time the fusion of traditions needs to be acknowledged. To see 'Hindus', 'Sikhs' or 'Muslims' as exclusive watertight social categories would be misleading. We also need to recognize the fact that any human society cannot be homogeneous. There is need to place social and economic institutions in their ecological and physical settings. Any attempt to overlook the diversity by the primary sources or to 'idealize' by the successive writings goes against the basic reality of any human society, which is imbued with heterogeneity and multiplicity of cultural practices coexisting with each other. According to Nita Kumar, we have to look for 'fault-lines' in our sources to understand the complexities, the struggles and turmoil of the age.[14] Given this understanding, it would be appropriate if we make a brief survey of different genres of literature and the information they yielded on our subject. For a detailed discussion on the content and thrust of the primary sources, one may refer to Annexure I.

SECONDARY LITERATURE

In this section, I am led by two primary objectives. First, it is an attempt to map the major analytical positions that dominate the historical work produced within the sub-discipline of Sikh Studies in specific, and in a larger framework of the Punjab in general. This exercise is undertaken with the hope that both the common ground and points of conflict within the field can be brought out. In other words, an attempt has been made to identify the most important ways in which the Punjab of the past has been dealt with. Second, it attempts to underline a series of epistemological and methodological problems that has influenced the historiography over the past few decades. It insists on the inherent need to acknowledge the heterogeneity of Punjabi society. Instead of attempting an oversimplified, homogeneous and linear presentation of Punjabi society, we need to remember that the region's inherently diverse and hybridized population reflected a stark reality, that is Punjab has long stood at the confluence of the Islamic and the Indic worlds and the cultures of Central and South Asia. However, this section also discusses a few earlier authors on the Punjab and their academic contributions. In the ensuing discussion of secondary literature, one becomes conspicuously aware that the tradition of historical writings on the Sikhs at any rate has been longer and stronger than historical writings on the Punjab. Consequently, very often Sikh history is equated with the history of the Punjab. However, the history of a part cannot be equated with the history of the whole. Nor can the part, especially an important part, be ignored in a history of the whole.

EARLY SCHOLARS

Modern historical writings on the Sikhs are a legacy of the British. Indian historians in the past half a century have written largely with reference to British historians. For instance, the works of later authors revolved around J.D. Cunningham's *History of the Sikhs* published in 1849.[15] However, the first attempt at a real study of the Sikhs was that of John Malcolm, *Sketch of the Sikhs* (1812), though he himself admits that the information available to him was limited and often unreliable.[16] H.H. Wilson's *Civil and Religious Institutions of the Sikhs* (1848) is based largely on Malcolm.[17] The same is a little less true of Cunningham's monumental work, which was claimed as the first open-minded attempt 'to give Sikhism its place in the general history of humanity'.[18] For his impartial discussion of the Anglo-Sikh War (1845-6) and the British responsibility for it, Cunningham lost his political appointment in Bhopal, but won the hearts of the people of the Punjab. Presenting Guru Nanak's movement as a faith that was meant not merely to reconcile but to transcend Hinduism and Islam, Cunningham postulated a close connection between the Sikh polity and Sikh faith through the mediation of Guru Gobind Singh. According to Grewal,[19] Cunningham's attempts at discerning a thread of continuity amidst change lends to the treatment of Sikh history a dimension that is altogether missing in the works of other British historians of the Sikhs. In fact, this perspective on Sikh history in Cunningham's treatise is rather rare in the entire range of historical writings on the Sikhs. However, Cunningham's treatment of Sikh history, Grewal points out, does not take into account the complexity of the historical process under discussion.

Ernest Trumpp, an oriental specialist who was sent to Punjab by the India Office to translate Sikh scriptures, produced the first English version of the *Adi Granth* (1877). Trumpp's insensitive handling of the religious verses, especially his caustic comments on Sikhs in the introduction, offended the community. For instance, he wrote,

The Granth is a very big volume, but I have noted incoherent and shallow in the extreme, couched at the same time in dark and perplexing language, it is for us Occidents the most painful and stupefying task to read even a single *raga*.[20]

Fifteen years later another European, Max Arthur Macauliffe, a British administrator posted in Amritsar, began a similar project, designed to over-turn Trumpp's treatment. He called Trumpp's attempt as highly inaccurate and unidiomatic. Macauliffe's six volume work, *The Sikh Religion: Its Gurus, Sacred Writings and Authors* (1909), created a vision of the Sikh scripture and history that has remained tremendously influential within the Sikh Panth. Macauliffe insisted that

Sikhism was a distinctive religion, and its history was characterized by a constant battle against Hinduism. Popular Hinduism, he argued, was like a 'boa constrictor of the Indian forests . . . it winds round its opponents, crushes it in its folds, and finally causes it to disappear in its capacious interior.' He was apprehensive that Sikhism was threatened with the same fate, as 'the still comparatively young religion' was 'making a vigorous struggle for life', its 'ultimate destruction inevitable without State support'.[21] Khazan Singh's *History and Philosophy of the Sikh Religion* (1914) offered a philosophical exposition of the Sikh concepts on God, Guru, Soul, Karma and Khalsa. In the same year, Dorothy Field came out with *The Religion of the Sikhs*. A sympathetic study in the tradition of Macauliffe, it showed both understanding and appreciation of the Sikhs, as she had personal contact with many Sikhs.[22]

During the nineteenth century, the major scholars of Sikh history were Europeans such as Cunningham, Trumpp and Macauliffe. In the twentieth century, the field has mainly belonged to Indian scholars. Bhai Vir Singh, Bhai Kahan Singh Nabha and Principal Teja Singh being perhaps the most outstanding Punjabi scholars. The non-Punjabi nationalist historians too wrote on the Sikhs. The leading figures were Indubhushan Banerjee and N.K. Sinha. Hari Ram Gupta's voluminous work on Sikh history belongs to the category of 'nationalist' historiography. These were individual scholars who worked virtually on their own. Khalsa College in Amritsar, where Bhai Jodh Singh and Ganda Singh were noted scholars, seems to have been the only place, which provided a broader institutional base for the development of this field of study.

The second phase of Sikh Studies can perhaps be dated from 1962 when Punjabi University was established in Patiala. With the establishment of the Guru Gobind Singh Foundation in Chandigarh and the Guru Nanak Foundation in Delhi in 1965, Sikh Studies gained a fresh momentum.

The normative tradition of historical writing, evoking ideal types of historical role models who embodied the ideals of the Khalsa, looked back to a more distant Sikh past. The heroic martyrdom of the ninth Guru, Guru Tegh Bahadur and the martial spirit of Guru Gobind Singh, served as exemplary models, as did the great protector of the fledgling Khalsa, Banda Singh Bahadur. Bhai Kahan Singh Nabha's pamphlet *Hum Hindu Nahin* (1898) was an attack on the power of the Hindu reformers of the Arya Samaj in Punjab and a response to the Sanatan tradition that remained popular with Punjabi aristocrats and the rural masses. This normative tradition of historical writing was consolidated in the early twentieth century by the likes of Bhai Vir Singh and after Partition, it was increasingly professionalized by a new generation of scholars, most notably Teja Singh, Ganda Singh and Harbans Singh. Teja Singh's early works are booklets titled *Guru Nanak and His Mission* (1918) and *The Sword and Religion* (1918). However, his more important works *Essays in Sikhism* (1944) and *Growth of Responsibility in Sikhism* (1948) came later. The reason for these publications was that the third and the fourth decades of the twentieth century were imbued with struggles for *gurdwara* reform and non-cooperation with the colonial government.[23]

In 1944 appeared an important publication by Sher Singh titled *Philosophy of Sikhism*. This scholarly work became a pacesetter for later researchers in Sikhism. Sher Singh's exposition of ideological identity and of Sikh philosophical concepts like *wismad* was quite remarkable. Another important work of this period was Kapur Singh's *Parasharprasan* or *The Baisakhi of Guru Gobind Singh* (1959). This book contains a valuable exposition of the Khalsa Panth and the rationale of its distinctive features and symbols.

After the Independence of India, Sikh Studies tended to be more critical than philosophical. Both Ganda Singh and Harbans Singh wrote that we might term 'corrective histories' works that challenged interpretations of Sikhism popular outside the community (such as the belief that Nanak's teachings were essentially syncretistic) and disputed evidence that indicated diversity in Sikh identity and practice within the historical record. This corrective approach is most obvious in Ganda Singh's collection of European accounts of Sikhism, where his glosses and footnotes not only correct European misapprehensions, but also rebut European claims that Sikhs engaged in practices that contravened the injunctions of the *rahit*. In short, this framing of the Sikh past became the dominant vision both within the Panth and at least within the Khalsa and was increasingly regarded by informed non-Punjabi South Asians and British commentators as the vision of the Sikh history.[24] To use Ballantyne's terminology, the 'internalist' approach attempted to correct the way of framing the Sikh past that dominated the Sikh historiography over the last century. He further points out that despite significant methodological, epistemological and political differences that we can identify as marking four different versions of the internalist scholarship (normative, textualist, political and cultural), those working within the internalist tradition are united by a common analytical orientation. Internalist scholars prioritize the internal development of Sikh 'tradition', rather than the broader regional, political and cultural forces that shape the community from the outside.[25]

The second phase of Sikh Studies, as already pointed out, can be dated from 1962 and gained momentum from 1965 onwards. This phase is marked by the tercentenary of Guru Gobind Singh's birthday in 1966. The quincentenary celebrations of Guru Nanak were held in 1969 and then came the tercentenary of Guru Tegh Bahadur's martyrdom in 1975. All these occasions were celebrated on a large scale. A number of seminars and conventions were organized along with the publication of many important works. The major works on Guru Gobind Singh's tercentenary were produced by Harbans Singh, R.S. Ahluwalia and G.S. Talib. The quincentenary celebration of Guru Nanak at the Punjabi University, Patiala, resulted in a collection of 54 papers. Works on Guru Nanak emanated from the pens of S.S. Bal, Surinder Singh Kohli, Gurmukh Nihal Singh and Gobind Singh Mansukhani. On the tercentenary of Guru Tegh Bahadur's martyrdom, books were brought out by Fauja Singh, G.S. Talib and Tarlochan

Singh. Satbir Singh and Ranbir Singh brought out a commemoration volume for the ninth Guru. In 1977, four centuries of the foundation of Amritsar resulted in a number of books on the city, Golden Temple and Guru Ramdas. On the same lines, the quincentenary celebrations (1979) of Guru Amardas culminated in publications by Narain Singh, Fauja Singh and G.S. Talib. In 1980, 200 years of Ranjit Singh's birth anniversary became the occasion for books from Fauja Singh and J.S. Grewal.

After a brief discussion about the centennial celebrations and the academic work generated through the combined efforts of the academic fraternity, the broad inference that emerges from most of these works, if not all, is somewhat perplexing. While these internalist models often recognize that the Sikh community has been moulded by the broader structures, institutions and cultural patterns of Punjabi life, they share a tendency to abstract Sikhism from this crucial sociocultural background. It is true that this tendency varies between approaches and individual historians. Yet, one can observe that this internal scholarship tends to privilege religious identity over social and commercial affiliations. Alternatively, regional identity and Sikhism are extracted from the dense webs of economics, social relations, and political structures that have moulded its development in Punjab and beyond.[26]

Several historians depart from the internalist tradition through their explicit emphasis on the importance of the regional context. The most important among them is J.S. Grewal. His works cover a wide spectrum of issues ranging from the history of Punjab, Sikh Gurus and social history. His works are commendable as he takes care of the sensibilities of the community, cultural history and its nuances. He has consistently grounded his exploration of Sikhism in the history of the Punjab. Of all the historians working on Sikhism, Grewal has published most widely on Punjab history more generally and his research consistently foregrounds the importance of the region's geography, its institutions, and political structures, economic fortunes, and cultural ethos. In the light of this insistence, his work typically uses a broader range of sources and deploys a range of approaches – from literary analysis to discussions on political economy – in picking out the nuances of the multifaceted nature of Sikh history. For Grewal, Sikh history is a dynamic story of the shifting relationship between the community and its regional environment. It is commendable that Grewal's works are equally well received in 'traditionalist' as well as 'sceptical' circles. He has mastered the craft of making a nuanced, analytical study of his sources and putting across his sources in a manner that is very difficult to disagree. It is telling that the recent festschrift for Grewal was titled *Five Punjabi Centuries: Polity, Economy, Society and Culture*.[27]

Indu Banga's writings primarily covering the late eighteenth through twentieth century, have consistently foregrounded the importance of Punjab as a context. In part, Indu Banga's significant work on Ranjit Singh's kingdom, a state that is frequently imagined as being explicitly Sikh yet rested upon the Maharaja's skilful balancing of different faiths and ethnicities in both his administration and military establishments. Banga's emphasis on the importance of the regional context also reflects her strong interest in the economic and agrarian history of the region, the crucial milieu within which Sikhism emerged and developed.

The main thrust of the socio-religious evolution of the Sikh Panth in the sixteenth century and its socio-political evolution in the seventeenth century forms the major themes of Sikh history from Guru Nanak to Guru Gobind Singh. The religious tradition of the Sikhs is historical and scholars in the Punjab have paid considerable attention to the historical development of their tradition. The works of Ganda Singh, J.S Grewal and Khushwant Singh have made scholarly impact and have enjoyed wide usage.

Another trend in studies on Punjab at large and Sikhism in specific is associated with Western scholars. The idea to use this categorization is not based on any presupposition of any kind of ideological homogeneity among them, but for the convenience of discussion. The most important pioneer among them is W.H. McLeod whose works have always managed to ignite a strong reaction among 'traditionalists' and a series of works to 'meet his challenge and expose his (McLeod's) distortions . . . effectively rebutted the conclusions of McLeod.'[28] One must here underline that McLeod is not only held responsible for his works, but rather borne to bear the vehement reaction for the works of Harjot Oberoi, Pashaura Singh, N. Gerald Barrier, Doris Jakobsh with the list going on to add those who had joined the 'bandwagon'. He has been blamed to

affix a most damaging brand of Sikh 'academics'. . . . One cannot imagine if anyone has done so much damage to the Sikh image at so high an academic level as Dr Hew McLeod [W.H. McLeod].[29]

However, one must admit that even when one does not agree with McLeod's analysis one cannot dismiss his works which cover a wide spectrum of Sikh history. His works have created a powerful impression on Sikh Studies, ranging from vehement reaction to counter arguments written with an intention to effectively rebut the conclusions of McLeod. For instance, there is Gurdev Singh's *Perspectives on the Sikh Tradition* (1986), Daljeet Singh's *Sikhism* (1979), *The Sikh Ideology* (1984) and a later book titled *Advanced Studies in Sikhism* (1989) in response to McLeod's work *The Evolution of the Sikh Community* (1976). At the same time, there are more positive opinions as well like that of J.S. Grewal when he writes,

The life of Guru Nanak presents serious difficulties due to the lack in our understanding of his environment. Nearly every book written on the life of Guru Nanak is based primarily and almost exclusively on the testimony of the *janamsakhi*s. There is one exception: *Guru Nanak and the Sikh Religion* (1968) by W.H. McLeod. In this book, the *janamsakhi* traditions are subjected to rigorous analysis.[30]

Grewal further opines that McLeod rightly emphasizes that *janamsakhi*s are not biographies; they tell us much about the age in which they became current but not about the age of which they speak.[31] According to Ballantyne, much of McLeod's work proceeds from the close analysis and discussion of a particular key term or concept. McLeod firmly respected linguistic and cultural differences, highlighting the problem of translation. He frequently argued that Sikhism, where possible, should be understood on its own terms rather than according to a Judaeo-Christian frame-work. He has, for example, been a firm advocate of the use of the term 'Panth' to describe the Sikh community, preferring it to other terms such as 'sect' or 'denomination'.[32] The influence of his domineering works is also apparent in the works of Pashaura Singh, Harjot Oberoi, N. Gerald Barrier and now Doris Jakobsh. All these scholars have written extensively on Punjab in general and in fact Doris Jakobsh has worked on gender.[33] Jakobsh's works is discussed in a successive section. Owing to lack of space, it is suffice to say that all these scholars have added a new dimension to Punjab Studies, per se.

Our discussion of secondary works would be incomplete if we do not bring a set of scholars, who have recently started focusing on the position of women in Sikhism. New studies from the late 1990s on the question of gender have been afforded little attention from scholars within Sikh Studies. What has not caught the imagination within Sikh scholarly exercises will not be recognized as important by those outside this area of study. However, this new academic enthusiasm is well-represented in the works of Surinder Suri, Kanwaljit Kaur, Mohinder Kaur Gill and Manjit Kaur to name a few.[34] Before discussing their works, it is to be acknowledged that they have made a fresh attempt to study Sikh history from a gender perspective.

In most of these works, the respective authors are so highly appreciative of Sikh Gurus and their ideology that they forget that any human society cannot be viewed in black and white terms. It is bound to have shades of grey. In their urge to project the Sikh Gurus as ardent advocates of women's equality and the respectable position of women in Sikh society, they overlooked the distinction between the normative and operative beliefs. Surinder Kaur notes:

The status of women was not an issue in Sikhism. Equality was implicit.... Women are considered as an integral part of society who must not be excluded by any ritual or doctrinal consideration. Since rituals tend to be exclusive, they cannot be made part of true faith. In other words, the position of women could be a touch-stone for the genuineness of a faith.[35]

With regard to inherent egalitarianism between Sikh men and women, Kanwaljit Kaur writes,

Sikh women have enjoyed superior status compared to their counterparts in other communities. She has earned this by showing the ability to stand by the side of her husband in difficult times.[36]

Yet, if women and men are inherently equal in Sikh tradition in terms of roles and status, why are they not given similar representations in the pages of Sikh history?

In these works, one notices an attempt to idealize the aspects of history and scripture as they pertain to women. Glorified examples are presented of Sikh women who lived exceptional lives in different roles as the normal, larger reality. These exceptional women are then typically held up as the standard by which to measure gender egalitarianism of the Sikh tradition. The most obvious examples that come to mind are *Sikh Bibiyan* by Simran Kaur and M.K. Gill's *Role and Status of Women in Sikhism*. Both the titles give out the impression of being a study of the position of common women in Sikhism. However, the former deals with the women – daughters, mothers and wives of the Guru families – and the latter focuses on what they presented as the institution of Guru Mahals or the wives of the Gurus. It would be highly erroneous to imagine the condition of the women of Guru families to be anywhere close to the position and status of common women. The exceptional lives of the women of Guru families or iconic women like Mai Bhago – who led Sikh soldiers against the Mughals – are projected as the ubiquitous reality.

One must acknowledge the painstaking efforts these scholars have made to gather information and formulate biographical notes on all the women related to Guru households in different roles, which form the thrust of most of the works. Although Gill admits that the

> Guru histories are by and large, silent about the wives of the Gurus. From Guru Nanak to Guru Gobind Singh the wives have been treated as part of the historical background, not as individuals in themselves . . .[37]

Yet, Gill chooses to emphasize and make the reader believe that the Guru Mahals were very integral to the development of the fledgling Sikh movement. Regarding the silence in the sources, she comments,

> It is the silence of respect that is accorded to the womanhood in the Punjabi culture and ethos. It helps surround her with an invisible cloak of dignity. . . . The silence that surrounds the Guru's family is an intrinsic feature of Sikh tradition.[38]

Here, one begs to differ with her. To view the life and position of women of Guru Mahals as a mirror of the general 'role and position of women in Sikhism', to use her nomenclature, is a fallacy. As wives and sisters of Gurus, they certainly did not lead the lives that were very much akin to their contemporaries. In many ways, they conjure up false images as to the roles and status of women in Sikh society. To negate the obvious, namely that even the Guru Mahals have not been viewed as consequential in the history of the Sikh tradition and to project the Guru Mahals as integral to the very development of the fledgling Sikh movement is like creating a mirage for our own selves. Unfortunately, it also tends toward oversimplification and, at times, contains an element of wishful thinking.

Nevertheless, there are no two ways about the fact that this set of scholars have opened the arena of feminist studies among indigenous scholars, prepared the life-sketches of women of Guru families and in penning down the contributions of Mata Sundri, gave her some credit, for guiding the Sikh Panth in one of its most crucial phases – for a long span of nearly 40 years. At the same time, I would like to point out that this framework of idealizing the contributions of Gurus does not admit the gap between the normative and operative beliefs. Further, I submit that there is no black and white picture in any human society, and that there are shades of grey, which are in fact closer to 'the reality' of social relations. The earlier framework, somehow in an urge to project, rather 'create' an image of the Sikh Gurus as ardent advocates of women's liberation and of an egalitarian ethos seems to be self-defeating. It hampers the real credit that can be awarded to the Gurus for their ideology. In making it a 'reality' the Gurus might not have succeeded as desired or as projected by these scholars. Admittedly, there are many elements within the Sikh scriptural tradition that are emancipatory. However, in this oversimplified and linear presentation of knowledge, they get lost somewhere in between.

Now, it would be appropriate to discuss a set of scholars who are trained in the modern historical methodology and who applied the same scrutiny of rationally analysing the study of religion as well. Quite often it invites vehement reaction from religious leaders as well as scholars who are of the firm opinion that the question of faith cannot be subjected to any critical analysis. Though there are major differences of opinion among these historians as well, yet they broadly agree in their openness to study religion and its different aspects in a critical manner. This approach is reflected in the writings of Harjot Oberoi, Pashaura Singh, Mark Jurgensmeyer, N. Gerald Barrier and Doris Jakobsh. As mentioned above, Jakobsh has written on gender in Punjab.

In their opinion, the principles of silence, negation, accommodation, and idealization have formed the general framework guiding contemporary or near-contemporary writings on women and the feminine in general in Sikhism.[39] This set of scholars, somehow, tend to over-rationalize and find an explanation or hidden agenda for the Gurus' critical comments, as evident from the following examples. In their urge to highlight what has not been criticized and reprimanded, they tend to almost negate whatever has been commented upon. While Guru Nanak grieved the rape of women during the time of Babur, these scholars feel that he did not censure the social order on the whole. While aware of the social challenges facing the widows of the day, Guru Nanak censured them for their unrestrained desires. As a limitation, these scholars point out that Guru Nanak did not re-evaluate social institutions such as marriage and marital practices to make them more equitable for women. Moreover, his silence regarding *sati*s is rather surprising. There was no critique of female infanticide, a practice closely aligned to the upper castes.[40] His vision of ideal women has been perceived as only limited to procreation, the procreation of souls specifically. Following is an oft-quoted verse:

We are conceived in the women's womb, and we grow in it. We are engaged to women, and we are wedded to them. Through the woman's cooperation, new generations are born. If one woman dies, we seek another; without the women there can be no bond. Why call her bad who gives birth to rajas? The women herself is born of a woman, and none comes into this world without the woman; Nanak, the true one alone is independent of women.[41]

In the opinion of these historians although these words have been lauded as the slogan of emancipation for women in the Sikh tradition, though they had none to do with the rejection of prevailing traditions or ritual purity and support of the social hierarchy of the time. Since women give birth to sons, especially those of noble birth, how then could they be considered ritually impure? The second example concerns Guru Amar Das. During his pontificate, both scriptural and popular sources attribute a shift towards the inclusion of women in the Sikh Panth. The tradition credits a definitive criticism of society beyond that of religious ineptitude. Much of this criticism is directed towards the situation of women in society. With regard to *sati*, the third Guru states, 'They are not *sati*s who are burnt alive on the pyres; rather *sati*s are they who die of the blow of separation (from their husbands).'[42] Later accounts present the Guru as having denounced the custom of *purdah*, as he did not allow visiting queens to remain veiled in his presence.

The Gurus condemned female infanticide. Rather than appreciating their criticism, these historians claim that this practice may well have stemmed from Guru lineage only. According to Punjabi lore, Dharam Chand Bedi, a grandson of Guru Nanak was humiliated at his daughter's marriage by the groom's family. Chand was so incensed that he ordered all Bedis to henceforth kill their daughters as soon as they were born rather than bear such humiliation. In their opinion Guru Amar Das' condemnation of the practice may well have emerged from a need to distance the Sikh Panth under his leadership from the original Guru lineage that was at the forefront of the practice of female infanticide. This kind of reasoning appears to be a blinkered response, and clearly Guru Amar Das' powerful injunctions are negated.

These scholars tend to read the ideology of the Gurus from present-day notions of men-women equality. It is anachronistic to weigh it on the modern scale of equality. In those days, if women were made to command respect for their 'feminine' qualities and to see their role in the smooth functioning of society as a 'contribution', that too needs to be acknowledged. A voice of dissent was raised for evils against women such as female infanticide, *sati*, and *purdah*. She was seen and respected as an equal partner in religious assemblies (*sangat*s) worthy of salvation. Sikhism stresses family values and faithfulness to one's spouse. For example, 'The blind man abandons his own, and has an affair with another woman, he is like a parrot, who is pleased to see the semal tree, but at last dies clinging to it.'[43] The Sikh Gurus declared that marriage is an equal partnership of love and sharing between husband and wife. Married life is celebrated in order to restore to women her due place and status as equal partners in life. Further, 'They are not said to be husband and wife, who merely sit together. Rather they alone are called husband and wife, who have one soul in two bodies.'[44] This statement should not be nullified because it could not succeed in bringing about a dramatic, revolutionary change. Moreover, it is a long-drawn process to change the perceptions and attitudes leading to any societal change. Thus, any such endeavour needs to be contextualized in the existing sociocultural milieu.

In sum, we need to admit that any attempt to idealize the ideology and the behaviours of the Gurus does more harm to the acknowledgement of their contributions. Harjot Oberoi rightly cautions,

> how heterogeneous elements in Sikh history, those labelled deviant, marginal, threatening or unimportant are negated in order to generate homogeneity and represent the Sikhs as a collectivity which shared the same values and movements.[45]

We need to realize that any aspect of human society, whether it is a question of women's position or any other sociocultural dimension, cannot be and should not be projected in black and white. It is bound to have shades of grey. Moreover, as appropriately pointed out by Clarence McMullen, we need to make a distinction between the normative and operative beliefs.[46]

To sum up, it can be inferred that all the primary sources have an intention which determines their content, nature, and thrust. As Simon Digby argues, all the sources are discursive in nature, and they cannot be viewed as authentic just by the virtue of their being contemporary or near-contemporary. Only upon an unveiling of the presuppositions of writers and their writings, a thorough evaluation of the inherent biases and attitudes embedded in these writings, one is hopeful of an analysis somewhat close to reality. If historical research is a dialogue of cultures, it should be held on equal terms. Very often, we face difficulties because scholars sometimes investigate medieval sources only for information and ideas that are interesting for twentieth-century researchers. Medieval authors had different ways of thinking and to comprehend their viewpoint in the right perspective, we must listen to what they say of themselves and, on this basis, try to find answers for our questions. For instance, the very notions of 'progressive' and 'conservative' have a special meaning in the context of medieval society and deserved handling with care.

One term that is in wide currency among Sikh historians and requires careful scrutiny is 'tradition'. This is as a catch all phrase that describes textual corpus, practices, and discourses produced by the Sikhs. Yet, this term is problematic for two reasons. First, 'tradition' frequently stands in contradistinction to modernity representing the authentic essence of a pre-modern community. Second, and following on from this, the use of 'tradition' as a concept tends to imagine a homogeneous and strictly unified community. With reference to Sikh history, 'tradition' means that which is handed down within the Panth. The material thus handed down has not been subjected to rigorous scrutiny. It is known to be true because it is said to be derived from sources which are known by the Panth to be absolutely secure and authentic. Webster analysed five works on Guru Nanak, so as to discover at what points, if any, religious beliefs undermine sound historical judgement and concluded, 'Yet this essay suggests a general reluctance, even among the best historians to question radically their received religious tradition – specifically in this case the *janamsakhi* tradition.'[47]

A very cautious handling of the source material becomes still more relevant as a traditionalist historian (this categorization and nomenclature of 'traditionalist' and a 'sceptical' historian are borrowed from W.H. McLeod[48]) repudiates the authority of disciplines like history, sociology, anthropology, women's studies, and religious studies. G.S. Dhillon, representing the viewpoint of traditional historians, states,

> A proper study for religion involves a study of the spiritual dimension and experience of man, a study which is beyond the domain of sociology, anthropology, and history. Religion has its own tools, its own methodology and principles of study which take cognizance of higher level of reality and a worldview which is comprehensive and not limited.[49]

Sukhmander Singh has argued that methodologies relevant to Christian ideology, where scriptures developed as a result of history and culture, are inapplicable to Sikhism, because it is revelatory and authenticated by the prophet himself.[50]

For a traditional historian, the material handed down is known to be true because it is derived from sources which are known by the Panth to be absolutely secure. Not all historians of the traditionalist school would carry the definition so far as that, but essentially, they would agree with its substance. The general tenor of their interpretation makes this clear. Opposed to it are historians who embrace the sceptical view with its rigorous examination of sources. In an extreme form this approach requires everything to be questioned and nothing is to be affirmed unless there is evidence to support it satisfactorily. Here, one would like to end with a note that it is important to expound on both the positive and the negative messages. To know only the negative message is disempowering; to uphold only the positive images is a naive and superficial empowerment. To proffer both leads to a more accurate and genuine discussion of the feminine dimension within the Sikh tradition. It also enables us to contextualize the role of the Sikh Gurus in the then existing social milieu. After a discussion of the primary sources and the review of the secondary works, it would be appropriate to briefly discuss the thrust and focus of the chapters.

A GLIMPSE OF THE CHAPTERS

The present work is divided into two sections. Part I, 'Background and Devotional Movements' comprises two chapters. Chapter 1 describes the land and its people and is followed by Chapter 2 on Guru Nanak and Bhakti Sants on Women. The former contextualizes the study in terms of the geographical, social, religious and economic background. The latter deals with the different ideological formulations under the aegis of the Bhakti movement

Part II of this work, 'Contextualizing Women in Medieval Punjab' begins with the introductory Chapter 3 that foregrounds the questions discussed in the successive chapters. Aside from this Part II comprises four more chapters. Ideally, this entire section should be read as 'one' as the position of women, its varied determinants, its social aspects and various social institutions are so interconnected and interdependent that they make a complex social web, wherein a holistic approach needs to be followed. For practical convenience and ease of reading, it has been subdivided into four chapters: Chapter 4 on marital bond focuses on varied forms of marriage and their interface with caste; Chapter 5 is devoted to women in the social sphere; Chapter 6 engages with social discrimination against women; and Chapter 7 examines the relation between women's identity and the developing Sikh Panth.

PART I: BACKGROUND AND DEVOTIONAL MOVEMENTS

No ideology can be properly understood without contextualizing it in its specific historical, social, economic, and political milieu, which is the subject of Chapter 1. As is well known, religion plays a pivotal role in social values and social changes, which is the thrust of this study. There can be a gap in the historical context of the message of the exponents and its receivers. How is the message accepted and interpreted by the audience? How popular is it and how is it understood and utilized by the receivers? Milton Singer has aptly described this type of analysis as 'the articulation of textual and contextual studies'.[51] In other words, the context is closely related or to put it more sharply, it is a consequence of the land and its people. Thus, a detailed survey of the Punjab, including its physical features and sociocultural milieu, has been studied. A brief look at the political context is relevant for appreciating the conducive ground for the birth and development of Sikhism. It needs to be recognized that the total number of Muslims in the core region was larger than that of Sikhs and Hindus put together. Moreover, in the Punjab, literally the land of five rivers and a place which geographically and geopolitically bore the brunt of the frontal challenge, it is difficult to undertake any significant social study oblivious of these realities.

Ethnically and culturally, Punjab has been a home to people of many ethnicities. To capture the intricacies of the complex social fabric and to understand the complex process by which it eventually fused into a somewhat homogeneous people and cultivate a 'Punjabi' identity, the context and the sociocultural processes must be accorded due importance. Here, I have tried to discuss the main ideological strands prevalent in the area. What were the ruptures, if any, in the social fabric, which prepared a favourable sociocultural background for the rise and growth of Sikhism? An attempt has been made to see if Sikhism owed its success more to its background or was a consequence of the ideological, moral and ethical yet simple, practical, and progressive ideas right from its inception. A liberal approach, intertwining both religion and society, succeeded in winning over the hearts of the masses.

Chapter 2 bears the title 'Guru Nanak and Bhakti Sants on Women'. In the first section of this chapter, I briefly talk about the role of ideology, besides the relationship of religion and society. It touches upon the existing condition of women, which enabled me to contextualize the ideological position of important *nirguni* and *saguni* saints on women. An understanding of the social context is relevant for appreciating the background, besides identifying the continuum and contextualizing their messages. The next section deals with the perceptions of Bhakti sants like Kabir and Tulsidas about women. These are then compared with those of Guru Nanak and his spiritual successors. One is tempted to undertake the study of the comparative trajectory which emerges from the sharp contrast in their perceptions on women. Kabir and Tulsidas held women in low esteem. Women were perceived as living pictures of lust and greed. Kabir, who otherwise spoke vehemently against the caste system, disparity in society, inequalities, and idol worship, spoke ill of women and her 'deceitful nature'. He asked men to shun the company of women. She was looked down upon as a potential temptress. Tulsidas placed women at par with shudras and animals. Kabir has been accepted as the most significant representation of the ideological underpinnings that viewed women as evil. Though perceptions of other *saguni* sants are included in this chapter, yet Kabir has been dealt in specific as a natural choice, because it was only Kabir who had so many sayings about women attributed to him. Due to his loud and clear opinion, he provides a potent ideological baseline for a comparative trajectory.

Against this backdrop, Guru Nanak made Sikhism conform to enlightened, simple, practical, progressive and humane ideals right from its inception. The comparative analysis showed that Guru Nanak, within the patriarchal framework, created a space for women much larger than other Bhakti sants. Yet, the picture is not so simple and the *Sri Guru Granth Sahib*, at some places, has an ambivalent attitude and includes passages where women are projected in a negative light.

Part II: Contextualizing Women in Medieval Punjab

The discussion in this section on varied aspects of women's life clearly brings out that they are closely interconnected and interdependent. I have tried to examine the position, rights, role, and status of women in the family, wherein her roles varied as a mother, sister, wife, daughter, mother-in-law and her individual identity. I have also dealt with women's role in rituals and spiritual life; public sphere; women and work; her role in economy; property rights; position in the context of institution of marriage. An attempt has been made to contextualize the social customs like *naata* and other forms of widow remarriage. I have evaluated the economic logic operating behind the practice of widow remarriage in context of the division of property. I have examined if the custom of *sati* was rare or widespread in the Punjab. We also have the instances of polygamy in the case of Gurus. If polygamy was the reality and its prevalence extensive, what was the nature of the relationship among co-wives and the kind of tactics they employed to catch the attention of their husbands, besides winning their love and care. I have also discussed the position of a girl child; differences in rituals at the time of birth of a son and a daughter; social position of a woman unable to bear a child or those giving birth to daughters only; female infanticide; responses of society to parents committing female infanticide. I have addressed the question of witchcraft, insanity, and other customs that provided a platform to women to articulate her supressed emotions and discomfiture with the existing social realities.

I have made a constant effort to capture the gap between the injunctions of the Gurus (normative belief) and the existing reality (operative belief). On one hand, we have a set of standard norms represented by the ideals of Gurus and, in contrast, we have the reality in operation that contradicted the norm. One of my emphases would be the position of Gurus on major social evils, again identifying the chasm between the normative and reality. As has been noted, Guru Amar Das was highly critical of female infanticide. Guru Gobind Singh, in fact, instructed the Sikhs to shun the company of the killers of the girl child (*kurrimaar*). However, Guru Gobind Singh's strict prohibition of the killing of female infants pointed to a practice, which had continued largely unchecked since the pontificate of Guru Amar Das.[52] Such an exercise called for a rethinking of historiography as a whole, often necessitating a deviation from the established boundaries and pushing against the well-established boundaries of academic endeavours. Nita Kumar characterizes this process as finding 'fault-lines' in the larger patriarchal structures; the positioning of a spotlight on areas where inconsistencies or cleavages in general activity occur.[53] If there is an attempt to justify this gap between the normative and operative aspects, it irons out the aberrations and construct a homogenized unilateral social fabric.

While dealing with this section, it must be underlined that no human society can be so homogeneous that one can perceive the position of women and her status in different roles and social categories as one general truth. In fact, it cannot and, even attempt to be seen, existing as one generalization. One has to acknowledge the variations at all levels like class, caste, communities and even region playing a pivotal role. Thus, an effort has been made to place the entire question of position of women in the context of caste, class, and community, while recognizing the basic fact that human society cannot be homogeneous and there is need to place social and economic institutions in their ecological and physical setting and accept the multiplicity of cultural practices coexisting with each other. One needs to be careful that the social fabric of the sixteenth and seventeenth centuries, with all its nuances and complexities, are not viewed from the mindset of the present times. To view the then realities from today's yardstick of women's position and her role would be anachronistic as well as self-defeating.

In sources like *Charitro Pakhyan*[54] and folk songs, we get a glimpse of the forms of the protests against male dominance, domestic violence, honour, morality, fidelity and chastity. For instance, seclusion and isolation became a symbol of status in a Brahmanical patriarchal system. It was interesting to examine the virtues associated with an 'ideal-virtuous' woman as there is projection of 32 virtues (*battigunni*) in a woman in *Sri Guru Granth Sahib* that were cherished in normal life. The questions which have been dealt with are, what was the mechanism for regulation of social life at the level of family, interpersonal, inter-caste, and inter-community relationships. What was the role of customary practices in determining the position and rights of women? Did the customary practices manage to give women breathing space or, at times, platforms to vent out their bottled-up anger against the existing system.

With this background and in this framework, it became imperative to divide this section into four chapters. Chapter 4 titled 'Aspects of the Marital Bond' focuses on the institution of marriage in detail and acknowledges its importance as a vital social mechanism, which regulates the social and sexual life of human society. It highlights the perceptions of the Sikh Gurus on marriage, where they termed it so important as to proclaim, 'living within the family, one obtains salvation'. They advocated a position of respect and dignity to women's role as a wife and urged men to be loyal to their spouses. In this chapter, I observe the complex relationship between marriage and caste, besides the expectations of society at large and specifically the in-laws. I also assess the impact of exogamous marriage on women, her social presence and her own understanding of her position. I also write on customs like *karewa* and *chadar dalnaa/pauna*. It strives to understand the economic logistics, if any, behind the system of widow remarriage, which succeeded in keeping the possession of land within the husband's family and different manifestations of patriarchal guardianships. I also discuss the practice of child marriage and polygamy.

Chapter 5 titled 'Women in the Social Sphere' focuses on the social space of women and attempts to study it under the aegis of marriage ceremonies and other life cycle rituals. This exercise enables us to see whether women played a significant role in the rituals, or they were marginalized, or their social position and expectation of subordination was equally manifested in the rituals, or even legitimized and actualized by the element of religion which is well-represented by the rituals. Due attention has been paid to the position of lower caste women, besides the women's role in economy and inheritance. This chapter concludes with a section on weapons of the weak, where many customs like *moh-mahi*, beating up one's husband's younger brother at the time of marriage, have been studied in detail. Folk songs have been examined to assess whether they provided an effective platform to women, often to express her anger against the existing system. In this chapter, an attempt has been made to delve into the complexities of the family as the basic social unit, besides constructing the position of women in her varied roles as a mother, wife, daughter, mother-in-law and her individual social identity, if she had any. It tries to capture the complexities of relationships, bond of love, and dependence on the family.

Chapter 6 titled 'Discrimination and Social Evils' deals with the oppression against women. It discusses the social evils like, female infanticide, *sati*, *purdah*, prostitution, and polygamy. This chapter necessitated a cautious handling of the available material and the approach so as to avoid viewing the then existing social fabric from a modern-day mindset. If polygamy was a reality, then what was the nature of the relationship among the co-wives and the kind of moves and strategies they had to apply attempting to win over the love and care of their husband? This chapter also engages with questions ranging from barrenness and female infanticide to dowry and witchcraft. This chapter concludes with a brief recapitulation of the Sikh Gurus' perception on women.

In Chapter 7 titled 'Women's Identity in the Sikh Panth', I have identified the shift in the dominant concerns of the Sikh community with the passage of time, looking for historical and logical connections between the activity and ideas in the various phases. I have also compared the transformation and the changing face of Sikhism to the women's position and her role in religious pursuits. For instance, the early Gurus lived within or near the Majha area of Punjab, a region that was and is still known as a strong Jat constituency. Given the egalitarian nature of the Jats in the early Indo-Islamic period, it is possible that its women were attracted to the emancipatory message of the Gurus and, consequently, to the full participation in developing the Sikh community. Tradition credits Guru Amar Das for making a definitive criticism of society beyond that of religious ineptitude. Much of these criticisms were directed at the situation of women. He vehemently condemned social evils like *sati*, *purdah* and female infanticide. In brief, women would have had the most to gain from rejecting the restrictions placed upon them by an orthodox Brahmanical system and instead embracing the egalitarian message of the early Gurus. The third Guru's criticism of the societal norms pertaining to women would conceivably have encouraged their movement into the Sikh fold.

It was during Guru Amar Das' time that missionaries were appointed to carry the message of the Sikh Panth beyond the immediate surroundings of Goindwal in the Tarn Taran district of the Majha region. Thus, the *manji* system was created, a word literally meaning 'string bed' and referring to the seat of authority. The *manji*s were leaders of local gatherings who were directly accountable to the Guru and, thus, an extension of his influence. While sources conflict with regard to the actual number of *manji*s as well their gender, there is evidence that women might have been sent out to preach the Guru's message. The possibility of women being included among such esteemed emissaries speaks of a growing concern about women and acknowledgement of her potential. Women missionaries would have proven most effective in the recruitment of other women into the Sikh fold, which would have, in consequence, affected the religious leanings.

During the time of Guru Ram Das, the *manji* system was transformed into the order of *masand*s. The *masand*s had a dual responsibility. They preached the message of the Gurus and collected the voluntary offerings from the followers. Thus, the new order was tailored to suit both the missionary activities and the economic interests of the Gurus. According to all accounts, women were excluded from the new system. Significantly, the fourth Guru was highly critical of women in his writings. Similarly, when the development of militancy among Sikhs reached a pinnacle under the tenth Guru, the role and the share of women also got affected. Doris Jakobsh views the episode of Mata Jito adding sweets to water at the site of initiation as a feminine element that came to be added to this male-dominated rite. With the process of institutionalization, gender differences within the Sikh Panth became increasingly pronounced. In fact, one may conclude that with the increased institutionalization, traditionally established role for men and women became more socially and materially feasible and were thus consolidated.

The present-study attempts to remind of the close connection between the role of religion and social change. The thrust of my research draws its perspective by and largely from Joan Wallach Scott's (1988) appropriate and sharp observation that 'gender is an on-going fluid process whereby sexual differences acquire a socially or culturally constructed meaning'.[55] A historical focus on gender thus goes far beyond the mere addition of women to the pre-existing male-dominated historical narrative. In fact, Scott insists that a study of women must also include an analysis of formation of the male gender; a shift from 'women's history' to 'history of gender'. The category of gender not only illuminates unequal relations of power between male and female, but also helps in understanding that unequal male-female relations are extended via metaphors to varied areas of social life, so as to signify unequal relations of power in general. The study also intends to highlight that in the study of any religion and its role, we need to go beyond traditional methods of exegesis to a 'hermeneutics of suspicion'; Paul Ricoeur defines this 'hermeneutics of suspicion' as 'set(ting) out from and original negation, advancing through a work of deciphering and struggle(ing) against masks, finally... put in the quest of a new affirmation.'[56]

Only upon an unveiling of the presupposition of writers and their writings, only upon a suspicious reading entailing a thorough evaluation of the inherent sexist attitudes and practices within these writings, is one able to go beyond this suspicion to what Ricoeur terms the transformative 'power of affirmation'.

NOTES

1. Clifford Geertz, 'Religion as a Cultural System', in *Anthropological Approaches to the Study of Religion*, ed. Michael Banton, London: Tavistock Publications, 1966, p. 4.
2. Nancy Falk and Rita M. Gross, eds., *Unspoken Worlds: Women's Religious Lives in Non-Western Cultures*, San Francisco: Harper and Row, 1980, pp. xv, xxi.
3. Joan Wallach Scott, *Gender and the Politics of History*, New York: Columbia University Press, 1988, p. 4.
4. Muhammad Akbar, *The Punjab Under the Mughals*, Delhi: Idarah-i-Adabiyat-i-Delli, rpt., 1974, p. 29.
5. The Nathyogis are associated with the Nath tradition, a syncretic Yoga and Vedanta school of Hindu philosophy. They represent the

Shaiva tradition, revere Shiva and Dattatreya. Its ideological foundation is attributed to Matsyendranath and Gorakhnath, furthered by seven other Siddha Yoga Gurus called 'Naths'. The Nath tradition was followed by other Indian traditions such as Advaita Vedanta and in turn influenced the ideological churning within Vaishnavism, Shaktism and Bhakti movement. Meetings between Nathyogis and Guru Nanak are known as 'Siddh-Goshti' and it is recorded in *Sri Guru Granth Sahib* as well as *Janamsakhis*.

6. G.S. Talib, *Sri Guru Granth Sahib*, Eng. tr., 4 vols., Patiala: Punjabi University, 1990, p. 661. (Hereafter referred to as *AG*.)
7. Harjot Oberoi 'From Ritual to Counter Ritual: Rethinking the Hindu-Sikh Question', in *Sikh History and Religion in the 20th Century*, ed. J.T. O'Connell et al., Toronto: Centre for South Asian Studies, University of Toronto, 1988, p. 142.
8. David Kinsley, *Hindu Goddesses*, Berkeley: University of California Press, 1986, pp. 197-211.
9. S. Nurul Hasan, 'Medieval Punjab', in *Punjab Past and Present: Essays in Honour of Dr. Ganda Singh*, ed. Harbans Singh and N. Gerald Barrier, Patiala: Punjabi University, 1976, p. 79.
10. Simon E. Digby was a renowned scholar on South Asia. His research interests included, but not limited to the nuanced explorations of Sufi literature, records of conversations and hagiologies, letters. His approach towards sources was comprehensive, yet unconventional. Irfan Habib writes that it was characteristic of Digby to devote lot of care on what many would regard as a second-rate source: to him its myths and inaccuracies also had a message, for it gave him access to the aspirations and tribulations in the minds of the mystics, disciples and clientele. [*Proceedings of Indian History Congress*, vol. 69 (2008), pp. 1367-9.]
11. Aron Y. Gurevich, *Categories of Medieval Culture*, Oxfordshire: Routledge & Kegan Paul, 1984, p. 8.
12. Ganda Singh was a prolific researcher and historian of Sikh studies. In addition to scores of research papers, booklets and pamphlets, he published over two dozen volumes of high historical value. Through his vast array of publications, he made a formidable impact on the growth and direction of Sikh historiography. For his immense contribution to Sikh studies, he received many prestigious honours and awards from academic institutions, foremost of which was the Padma Bhushan in 1983 by the Government of India.

13. Clarence O. McMullen's, *Religious Belief and Practices in the Rural Punjab*, New Delhi: Manohar, 1989. In this work, McMullen powerfully makes the quoted point, though for the twentieth-century village. But it holds true for any human society; in the context of my study of sixteenth- and seventeenth-century Punjab, it is equally true.
14. Nita Kumar, *Women as Subjects: South Asian Histories*, Charlottesville: University Press of Virginia, 1994, 'Introduction', p. 3.
15. J.D. Cunningham, *A History of the Sikhs*, Delhi: S. Chand & Company, rpt., 1966.
16. Max Macauliffe et al., *The Sikh Religion: A Symposium*, Calcutta: Susil Gupta (India) Private Ltd, 1958, pp. 84-145. (Hereafter cited as *Symposium*.)
17. Ibid., pp. 54-70.
18. Ibid., p. xx.
19. J.S. Grewal, 'A Perspective on Early Sikh History', in *Sikh Studies: A Comparative Perspective on a Changing Tradition*, ed. Mark Jurgensmeyer and N. Gerald Barrier, Berkeley: Graduate Theological Union, 1979, p. 33.
20. Ernest Trumpp, *The Adi Granth*, London: W.H. Allen, 1877, Introduction, p. xxii.
21. Max Arthur Macauliffe, *Sikh Religion: Its Gurus, Sacred Writings and Authors*, vol. I, Delhi: Low Price Publications, rpt., 1990, p. vii.
22. For a detailed understanding on the issue, see Gobind Singh Mansukhani, 'The Origin and Development of Sikh Studies', in *Fundamental Issues in Sikh Studies*, ed. Kharak Singh et al., Chandigarh: Institute of Sikh Studies, 1992, pp. 129.
23. Gobind Singh Mansukhani, op. cit., p. 129.
24. Tony Ballantyne, 'Framing the Sikh Past', *International Journal of Punjab Studies*, vol. 10, nos. 1 & 2, January-December 2003, p. 4.
25. Ibid., p. 2.
26. Tony Ballantyne, op. cit., p. 9.
27. Indu Banga, ed., *Five Punjabi Centuries: Polity, Economy, Society and Culture, c.1500-1900*, New Delhi: Manohar, 1997. For an enumeration of the contributions of J.S. Grewal, see the reference list.
28. Gobind Singh Mansukhani, op. cit., p. 131.
29. A letter of a correspondent to the May 1994 issue of the *Sikh Review* referring to the Editorial in the January issue.
30. J.S. Grewal, 'A Perspective on Early Sikh History', pp. 34-5. Also

see J.S. Grewal, 'W.H. McLeod and Sikh Studies', *Journal of Punjab Studies*, vol. 17: 1 & 2, pp. 115-44.
31. J.S. Grewal, 'A Perspective on Early Sikh History', pp. 34-5.
32. Ballantyne, op. cit., p. 13.
33. See the detailed list of her works in the bibliography.
34. See bibliography for the detailed list of their contributions.
35. Surinder Suri, 'Position of Women in Sikhism', in *The Authority of the Religions and the Status of Women*, ed. Jyotsna Chatterjee, Delhi: Uppal Publishing House, 1990, pp. 103-13.
36. Kanwaljit Kaur Singh, 'Sikhism', in *Women in Religion*, ed. Jean Holm and John Bowker, London: Pinter Publishers, 1994, pp. 107-31.
37. M.K. Gill, *The Role and Status of Women in Sikhism*, Delhi: National Book Shop, 1995, p. 52.
38. Ibid., p. 53.
39. Doris R. Jakobsh, *Relocating Gender in Sikh History: Transformation, Meaning and Identity*, New Delhi: Oxford University Press, 2003, p. 3.
40. Ibid.
41. *AG*, p. 473.
42. Ibid., p. 787.
43. Ibid., p. 1165.
44. Ibid., p. 1788.
45. Oberoi, 1994, p. 34.
46. Clarence McMullen's work *Religious Belief and Practices in the Rural Punjab* powerfully makes the above point though for the twentieth-century village. But it holds true for any human society; in context of my study of the sixteenth- and seventeenth-century Punjab it is equally valid.
47. John C.B. Webster, 'Modern Historical Scholarship and Sikh Religious Traditions: Some Exploratory Remarks', in *Studies in Local and Regional History*, ed. J.S. Grewal, Amritsar: Guru Nanak University, 1974, pp. 135-6.
48. W.H. McLeod, *Exploring Sikhism: Aspects of Sikh Identity, Culture and Thought*, New Delhi: Oxford University Press, 2000, pp. 267-9.
49. Gurdarshan Singh Dhillon, 'A Review of Harjot Oberoi's *The Construction of Religious Boundaries*', in *Sikh Past*, 4.33, 1-15 May 1994, p. 4; also in the *Sikh Review*, 42.7, July 1994, p. 59.
50. Sukhmander Singh, 'A Work of Scholarly Indulgence', in *Invasion*

of *Religious Boundaries: A Critique of Harjot Oberoi's Work*, ed. Jasbir Singh Mann et al., Vancouver: Canadian Sikh Study & Teaching Society, 1995, p. 257.
51. Milton Singer, *When a Great Tradition Modernizes*, New York: Praeger Publishers, 1972, p. 39.
52. J.S. Grewal, *The Sikhs of the Punjab*, New Delhi: Cambridge University Press, 1990, p. 30.
53. Nita Kumar, *Women as Subjects: South Asian Histories*, p. 3.
54. Charitro Pakhyan is a part of the *Dasam Granth*. Its authorship has been a subject of significant academic controversy. It is a collection of 404 stories where the immoral, distrustful, and licentious nature of the women form the core content. Each tale is acclaimed by scholars to have a moral message as to how the Sikhs should live their lives and protect themselves from adverse influence and immoral, licentious conduct, and the 'wiles of women'. But there's more to Charitro Pakhyan than just explicit stories.
55. Joan Wallach Scott, *Gender and the Politics of History*, New York: Columbia University Press, 1988, p. 27.
56. Paul Ricoeur, *Freud and Philosophy*, New Haven: Yale University Press, 1970, pp. 20-47.

PART I

BACKGROUND AND DEVOTIONAL MOVEMENTS

CHAPTER 1

The Land and its People

History is the story of human experience rooted in time and space. The relationship between history and geography is intimate. Geography, concerned as it is with human – environment interaction, represents the spatial dimension of human activity, while history represents the time dimension. Geography is by nature the constant companion of historical studies. The historical record is inextricably linked to the geographic setting in which it develops. In other words, history is concerned with understanding the temporal dimensions of human experience (time and chronology), while geography is concerned with understanding the spatial dimension of human experience (space and place). Key concepts of geography such as location, place and region are tied inseparably to major ideas of history such as time, period and events. As an extension, the historians' preoccupation with contexts allows the practitioners of history to appreciate the nuances and complexities of the social and political milieu.

Human culture essentially springs from the interaction between man and his non-human environment. Logically, a change in environment, whether due to natural causes or human action, can lead to cultural change. A qualitative or quantitative change in such an interaction itself may result in cultural change. A more obvious source of cultural change may be contact with the bearers of a different culture – whether peaceful or violent. Without minimizing the importance of this cultural interaction, it may be safely stated that the non-human environment leaves its imprint on cultural formations, whether we think of environmental influence in terms of 'predetermination' or 'adjustment' or 'exploitation'. Spatial variations in sociocultural formations can thus be seen as the result of environmental as well as cultural interaction. Material and physical condition do certainly influence the nature of society.

Before discussing in detail the geography, that is 'land', it would be worth noting that human beings (in this case Guru Nanak and his successors to the Guru's seat, the *gur gaddi*), their actions and the events of history derive their meaning from political, economic, social and intellectual circumstances. The rise of any new awareness, thus, marks the catalytic element not only in the cultural but social system. In itself, the product of what probably are deep tensions in the existing order and of the elements which are its more recent accretions, this consciousness poses a serious challenge to an existing system and heralds the emergence of new formations. Without a proper understanding of the sociocultural and political milieu, it is difficult to contextualize and to appreciate the message of a certain era – in the case of this study, Guru Nanak, in particular, and Sikhism at large. This work strives to understand the nuances of the sociocultural context, which permitted this kind of ideological fermentation and expression. In other words, in what way did the socio-political and cultural milieu contribute to the growth of Sikhism in its nascent stage?

Admittedly, any such ideological formulation of Guru Nanak is a response or reaction to the existing religious, sociocultural and political milieu. His own predilections owe a great deal to his background. Therefore, to comprehend and to appreciate this new thought, an understanding of its context and background is necessary. Moreover, as often quoted, 'History is a dialogue between the past, present and future'. The ideological crystallization and its myriad articulations are an evolutionary process and it becomes clear when we read the works of David N. Lorenzen, scholar of religious studies. In the words of Lorenzen, ideology is a

> form of discourse, primarily verbal but also behavioural, that directly or indirectly claims to describe the structure and functioning of a society

in such a way as either to justify, or to protest against an unequal distribution of social status, economic wealth and political power among different groups within the society.[1]

We may work on the basic premise that one of the basic functions of a religious tradition is to articulate a social ideology that serves as the psychological glue in generating and preserving harmony within a religious community as well as society as a whole.

PUNJAB: GEOGRAPHICAL UNDERSTANDING

A geographical region by definition is a distinct part of a larger whole. It is generally defined on the basis of criteria involving physical features, climate, drainage, soils and the like. To these are added flora and fauna. We must admit that geographical region is not uniform in terms of criterion evolved to define it. There are 'sub-regions' within regions, each marked by differences in relation to others. No region is marked by cultural homogeneity either. There are cultural sub-regions, each marked by differences in relation to others. There is interaction between the sub-regions just as there is interaction between the regions. It would not be an exaggeration to say that Punjab has been an unusually fluid region, not just geographically, but socially and culturally as well.[2] Regional articulations are the outcome of intra-regional and inter-regional interactions. The relation between this regional articulation and regional identity will be discussed in subsequent sections.[3]

The Persian word 'Punjab' derives its name from two words, *panj* (five) and *ab* (water), meaning 'five rivers' and by implication, the land of five rivers. The Punjab, thus, is a geographical entity loaded with inherent logistic problems. The problem arises when we try to take it literally as 'the land of five rivers'. It is not clear, however, precisely which region is covered by the term. There are six rivers in the so-called 'land of five rivers' and it is not certain whether River Indus, River Sutlej, River Beas is meant to be excluded.

Furthermore, it is not clear whether the term 'Punjab' refers to the valleys of the five rivers or to the area between the five rivers. The Punjab as a geographical entity is not a precise connotation.[4] Nevertheless, it is assumed that the Punjab strictly refers to the area lying between the Himalayas and the confluence of all the six rivers of the Punjab. In other words, Punjab proper consists of the five *doab*s – tracts of land lying between the two rivers – up to the foothills.

The vagueness of the Punjab as a geographical entity is further accentuated by its loose identification with a political entity. For the historian too, the Punjab has carried different connotations. The ambiguity of Punjab as a regional concept has allowed historians the freedom to escape the confines of a geographically delineated area.[5] The first difficulty of a historian is to identify her region at a given time and to be clear about the criteria by which it is actually identified. When dealing with the Punjab and its cultural synthesis and currents one tends to strongly relate to the thought process of D.P. Chattopadhyay, presented in his Introduction of *The History of Science, Philosophy and Culture in Indian Civilization* (vol. VII, Part 2), when he says,

> For the purpose a comprehensive study of India (Punjab in this case) the existing political boundaries of South Asia of today are more of a hindrance than help. Cultures, like languages, often transcend the boundaries of changing political territories.[6]

Anshu Malhotra and Farina Mir add another dimension to defining a region. According to them, the three concepts of territoriality, viz. historical, spatial and the imaginary, melt into one another and precisely produces the complexity of experience.[7]

The term 'Punjab' came into currency during the reign of Akbar. In the documents of the Mughal period, we find the use of the terms *Sarkar-i-Punjab* and *Suba-i-Lahore*. Chetan Singh rightly points out that the Lahore *suba* did not encompass the areas of Multan, Sirhind and Hissar Firuza.[8] The Punjab proper in the Mughal times comprised five main *doab*s, which were formed and named by Akbar by combining the first syllables of the names of the rivers between which they lay.[9] The Bist–Jalandhar Doab, comprising the territory between the Sutlej and the Beas, is a very fertile tract. It contains the important cities of Jalandhar and Hoshiarpur. The Bari Doab includes the tract between the Beas and the Ravi. The two most important cities of the Punjab, Lahore and Amritsar, are situated in this *doab*. This is also known as Majha (or middle tract). The Rachna Doab enclosed by rivers Ravi and Chenab is a fertile tract, comprising the notable towns of Gujranwala and Sheikhupura. The Chaj Doab, lying between Chenab and the Jhelum, has the important towns of Gujrat, Bhera and Shahpur. The Sindh–Sagar Doab: the tract between the Jhelum and the Indus is known as Sindh–Sagar Doab, literally meaning 'Ocean of the Indus'. This area is not very fertile and productive. The important towns of this *doab* are Jhelum, Rawalpindi, Attock and Mianwali.[10] In addition to these divisions, Khushwant Singh also gives a comprehensive list of Punjabi names for different regions that have been [and in some cases still are] used.[11]

Thus, we can see that the region under consideration is bordered by the Yamuna in the east and the Indus in the west. To its north and north-west lie vast mountain ranges, while its southern extremities are contained by the Great Indian Desert which flings out extensions in two directions. The eastern extension included much of the Phulkian (Nabha, Jind and Patiala) states. Chetan Singh's study shows that the introduction of canals here has pushed back the desert and converted it into a fertile agricultural region.[12] The western extension went through Sindh and up the Indus Valley to the south-west angle of the Salt Range. The region enclosed within these natural boundaries is a great mass of alluvial soil brought down by the Indus and the other five rivers.

In sum, the greater part of the Punjab consists of flat alluvial plains which are drained by the Indus River system, thus creating five *doab*s. The easternmost of this Bist–Jalandhar Doab, as already discussed, is formed by the Sutlej to the east and the Beas to the west. By virtue of its proximity to the northern hills, the Jalandhar Doab receives a higher average rainfall than the other doabs. Through it also flows two small rivers, the Black Bein and the White Bein, both of which fall into the Sutlej. The larger part of the other *doab*s, however, consists of uplands known locally as *bar*. The northern portion of these quasi-plateaus receives an annual rainfall which averages around 24 inches. Of these the upper Bari Doab, which includes Lahore, receives the greatest amount of rainfall. Westward the average rainfall decreases steadily. The lower part of these *doab*s (in particular those of the Bari and Sindh-Sagar *doab*s) which include Multan and the districts of Muzaffargarh, included sandy tracts which were some of the driest parts of India.

Spread across the upper regions of the Sindh-Sagar Doab is the Pothuhar plateau upon the southern and south-western fringes of which rises the Salt Range. Its western boundary is marked by the Indus, while to the north it is bordered by the Himalayan foothills. As already noted, in this region are to be found the towns of Jhelum and Rawalpindi as also the medieval fortress of Rohtas. The rainfall in this region varies from 13 to 30 inches annually. Narrow strips of low-lying flood plains (*bet*) ranging in width between 15 and 25 km are found along the main rivers. Their limits are defined by broken chains of sand dunes or by an abrupt rise of land along the riverbanks.[13] Steep bluffs of 50 to 100 m in height frequently separate the higher banks from the adjoining *bet*.[14] The rivers tend to change their course quite freely within these *bets*, while the annual inundation that is witnessed here makes them very fertile.

Though the Punjab largely consists of a vast plain, it has easily differentiated sub-regions. These differences probably were even more obvious in medieval times on account of the absence of modern irrigation facilities. This is a factor of utmost significance for it led to divergent socio-economic conditions within the Punjab. It was from this diversity that much of the dynamism of the sixteenth- and seventeenth-century Punjab arose. It attests the fact that the history of every country or region is shaped to a great extent by its geographical conditions and the Punjab has been no exception to this truism.

Making a brief survey of the geographical features of the region and acknowledging their role in the making of history; it can be asserted that it is the cultural characteristics of the people that are closely related to its geographical features. For instance, clothing is largely influenced by the weather conditions. As noted earlier, the regional articulations are the outcome of intra-regional and inter-regional interactions. The intensity of regional articulation in a particular historical situation may lead to a consciousness in which the people of the region are deemed to be different from others. What the people of sub-regions share may appear to be more important than what they do not share with one another. This consciousness of regional identity springs from regional articulation. It creates a kind of self-image which is related to objective reality, but which may not exactly correspond to it. In this context, it would be worth addressing the usage of the term 'Punjab'. When exactly did it come into currency? Grewal, among others, suggests that we have its prototype in the term *Saptasindhu*, or *Madra Desh*, or *Panchnad*. However, this does not help since precious little is known about these 'regions', assuming for the sake of argument that they represented regions in terms of geography, polity, culture of self-image.[15] The term Punjab does not occur in the compositions of Guru Nanak, although he managed to win over the people's heart and used the language of the people. Nor does the term occur in the *Tuzuk-i-Baburi* or *Baburnama* which, otherwise, contains interesting information on the geography, society and political divisions of northern India. In *Akbarnama*, however, the term is used rather frequently. Thus, it is reasonable to infer that it came into currency during the last quarter of the sixteenth century. The province of Lahore was the only one in Akbar's empire which had five *doab*s. The names used in *Akbarnama*, incidentally, passed into popular usage.

The usage of the term 'Punjab' did not remain confined to the politico-administrative unit created by Akbar. The inhabitants of the province brought in the usage of the epithet 'Punjabi'. In fact, it is the cultural category of Punjabi which would become more flexible and fluid in its concept as well as in its operation. In the reign of Aurangzeb, a chronicler refers to Saadullah Khan, the famous Diwan of Shah Jahan, as a Punjabi.[16] Therefore, it can be asserted that even during Mughal times, some people were conscious of the fact that the inhabitants of certain geographical region called the Punjab were naturally to be called Punjabis; that is the people of the Punjab. Criteria other than the politico-geographical were being unconsciously added to the original considerations of area and administration. Interestingly, the term Punjabi also came to be used for the language of the people of the province. The emergence of the dialects of this language several centuries before the time of Akbar was a great cultural development. Amir Khusrau refers to the language of the common masses of the region around Lahore as 'Lahauri'. When the province came to be known as the Punjab, this language could naturally be called Punjabi and with the expansion of the political boundaries of the Punjab the orbit of the language increased as well.

In the late eighteenth century, Punjabi Sufi poet Waris Shah refers to the Punjab as the beautiful forehead of Hindustan. In him, there was the awareness that the region called Punjab, though distinct, was a part of the larger unit called Hindustan. Ahmad Yaar, a well-known Punjabi poet who wrote *The-Shahnameh-i-Maharaja Ranjit Singh* in Persian, refers not only to the region and the people but also to the language Punjabi. Shah Muhammad, another Punjabi poet writing in the early nineteenth century, refers to Punjabi women explicitly as *panjaban*. Also, the Punjabi sentiment is rather strong in his poem and the term clearly cuts across creeds and communities.

Without negating the importance of the geographical boundaries, one is strongly inclined to agree with Grewal's contention that in the narrative part of their (contemporary or near contemporary chroniclers) history, the boundaries of the Punjab expand and contract with the expansion and contraction of the states established in the region. There is no doubt about the primacy of the politico-geographical criterion for them, but they are also aware of the cultural and social entity of the Punjab. Ganesh Das Vadera projects the consciousness even backwards when he refers to Rai Inderjit of the ancient times as a Punjabi.[17] Taking the argument a little further, one is inclined to comment that even the problems of regional history would arise in the mind of a scholar only as a part of the study of the history of a country as a whole. This is so because the process of social change and the factors motivating it can hardly be observed within the narrow field of a region, that too, in terms of a clearly defined geographical entity. In S. Nurul Hasan's perception, ours is a large country with considerable variations in its different regions. At the same time, the existence of major differences notwithstanding, there is a remarkable unity in the broad patterns of socio-economic development, culture, and administrative institutions.[18]

In sum, as J.S. Grewal and S. Nurul Hasan contended, Punjab, during the medieval period, had developed a personality of its own. It was socially and culturally distinct from the Ganga–Jamuna Doab to the east, Kashmir to the north, the territory of Roh to the west, and Rajputana to the south. It is true that within this region there were variations from place to place and from one social group to the other, but these variations do not militate against the broader historical unity of the Punjab. In fact, no one had ever seriously questioned this unity until the British imperialist decided to partition it on the basis of religion.[19]

A SURVEY OF THE POLITICAL CONDITIONS

This is an attempt at a survey of political conditions in the Punjab. It is an analysis of the facts, factors and forces that went into the making of a society, which provided the characteristic dynamism conducive for the origin and evolution of Sikhism. The period, one would readily note, is all but coterminous with the last days of the Delhi Sultanate and the rise, growth and attainment of the peak of Mughal imperial power and glory. During the sixteenth century, in particular, the region witnessed some of the most significant political developments affecting the entire subcontinent. Babur's invasion of India, Humayun's recovery of his lost kingdom, and subsequently, Akbar's defence of his unstable and uncertain inheritance were all initiated in this borderland. It was during this period that the region's role as the threshold of India exposed it to the pressures of external forces. In other words, geographically and geo-politically, the Punjab occupies an area of north India, which had to bear the brunt of the frontal challenges of all the peoples and cultures that were borne from outside the north-western borders on to the northern plains of India. From the earliest days, this aspect was known to history. Entering through the north-western passes or from across the northern mountains, all foreign elements found in the fertile and tropical plains of the Punjab their first haven where they could settle and spread if they chose to do so.

The Achaemenians conquered and made India, west of the Indus and its tributaries, a part of their sprawling empire. Alexander pushed right up to the Beas. Though he went back with his army, the strongest political and cultural hold of the Hellenistic Greeks, and following them, of the Parthians, was on the Punjab. Almost simultaneously began the southward swoop of the Central Asian pastoral and nomadic peoples, avalanche-like and wave after wave, beginning in the pre-Christian centuries with the Sakas and Kushanas and ending only with the Islamized Turks, Afghans and Mughals in the thirteenth to sixteenth centuries. To these migrants belonged, among others, the Abhiras, the Hunas, the Jats, the Gujjars and the pre-Islamic Turks, to mention only a few. Then there were the Buddhists and Hindushahis of Afghanistan, who have also to be taken into account. Punjab happened to be the land to confront them with all attendant shocks, surprises and disturbances, settle them down, incorporate and integrate them as far as her people could and, in the process, to be transformed by them, before the foreign peoples were themselves transformed and spread further inland. However, as B.D. Chattopadhyaya cautions us with regard to the history of ancient Punjab, a historian should at least make an effort to understand early Punjab in terms of the local cultural evolution, rather than relegating it to one of history's eternal 'march' regions (where the Indo-Greeks, the Scythians, the Parthians, the Kushanas and the Hunas all came and left an imprint of their cultures).[20]

What the effect would be of such continuous challenges and pressures on the land and its people can easily be imagined. Ethnically and culturally, the Punjab became a great laboratory where many ethnic types and cultures became eventually fused into one.[21] This perception of one homogeneous culture needs to be discussed in detail. Yet, it clearly hints at exchange of ideas and interaction between different cultures. In other words, the ethnic plurality in the Punjab was matched by the variety in its cultural tradition.[22] After a cursory glance at the political history of Punjab from earliest times, it is advisable to focus our attention on the political developments from the eleventh century onwards.

From the eleventh century, the Punjab became once again a part of large empires when Mahmud of Ghazni annexed it to his dominions in Afghanistan and Central Asia. His successors ruled over the land of five rivers for over 150 years without extending their territory much beyond river Ghaggar. The last of them was ousted from Lahore by the new rulers of Afghanistan, the Ghurids, before the end of the twelfth century. The Turkish generals of the Ghurids conquered the whole of northern India and three Turkish dynasties ruled over the Delhi Sultanate during the thirteenth century. During the fourteenth century, much of the Punjab was a part of the large empire established by the Khalji Turks and maintained by the Tughlaqs. The western *doab*s, however, had come under the influence of the Mongol successors of Chingiz Khan before Timur, the acknowledged ancestors of the Mughal emperors, who invaded India towards the end of the fourteenth century. The Sayyid rulers came into power at Delhi during the early fifteenth century and tried to extend their influence over the Punjab, but without much success. This position was inherited by the Afghan ruler Bahlul Lodhi in the late fifteenth century. Under his successors, Sikandar and Ibrahim Lodhi, the Afghan governor of Punjab extended his influence up to river Jhelum. Meanwhile, Babur was keen to expand his dominions in the direction of India.[23]

Babur writes in his memoirs,

As it was always in my heart to possess Hindustan and as the several countries had once held by the Turks, I pictured them as my own and was resolved to get them into my own hands whether peacefully or by force.[24]

Babur made five attempts to conquer this country. All his expeditions led into the Punjab and the final and decisive battle was fought in this province on 21 April 1526 at Panipat. However, Babur's first expedition bore no fruit. Within a month of Babur's exit from the scene, his territories were retaken by its old masters, expelling Hindu Beg in September 1519. Babur again entered India through the Khyber Pass. The news of disturbance in Badakhshan obliged him to go back without achieving anything. Bad faith and ill-blood had been created between Ibrahim Lodhi and Daulat Khan Lodhi, the governor of Lahore. Daulat Khan was called to Delhi. In order to avoid the anger of the Sultan he did not go personally and instead sent his son Dilawar Khan. This further annoyed Ibrahim, who treated Dilawar Khan in a shabby manner and made no secret of how he was disposed towards his father.[25] The estrangement between the Sultan and the governor worsened. On the basis of his well-founded apprehensions of Ibrahim, Daulat Khan sent an invitation to Babur for help against the Sultan. However, Daulat Khan, who wanted to be independent of Delhi in the Punjab, did not want to give any superiority to Babur or anybody else for any help received. Babur, on his part, readily accepted the invitation, as he did not like to miss the opportunity of interfering in the affairs of Hindustan.[26]

Ibrahim Lodhi, getting an inkling of the conspiracy between Daulat Khan and Babur, sent an army to Lahore. The imperial army captured Lahore without much difficulty and drove Daulat Khan into exile. Babur reached Punjab in 1524 in response to Daulat Khan's invitation. He captured Lahore and, after a brief stay of four days, occupied Dipalpur. Before returning to Kabul, Babur conferred Sultanpur on Dilawar Khan, the son of Daulat Khan. He assigned Dipalpur to Alam Khan Lodhi, the ambitious uncle of the Sultan. Lahore was placed under Mir Abdul Aziz, a close relative of Babur. Sialkot was placed under Khusrau Kukultash. On Babur's return from Punjab, Daulat Khan snatched Sultanpur from his son Dilawar Khan and Dipalpur from Alam Khan. Alam Khan went to Kabul and offered Babur full sovereignty over the Punjab in return for his help to conquer the throne of Delhi from Ibrahim. Babur agreed to the proposal as he considered 'it would give him a legitimate right to what he had only taken by force'.[27] In the meantime, Ibrahim sent an imperial army to liquidate the rebels in the Punjab, but Daulat Khan got an easy victory over the Sultan's army. Leaving Kabul under the charge of his 16-year-old son Kamran, Babur set out for an expedition to Hindustan. The arrival of Babur unnerved Daulat Khan, who again resorted to conspiratorial manoeuvring. He conveyed to Babur that 'if his own faults were pardoned, he would take service with Babur and surrender Malot'. Daulat Khan was pardoned and was handed over to Kita Beg to be taken to Bhera for imprisonment, but he died on the way at Sultanpur. Having dealt with Daulat Khan, Babur decided on a major action. He writes, 'I put my foot on the stirrup of resolution and set my hand on the reins of trust in God and moved forward against Sultan Ibrahim.'[28] Babur set out his troops in proper military array at the historic battlefield of Panipat. Babur emerged victorious and with it began the long era of the Mughal dynasty with the brief interregnum of the Second Afghan Empire.

It has often been suggested that after Panipat, Babur could not pay his full attention to the affairs of Punjab. Actually, after Panipat the theatre of warfare and political activities had shifted to western and later to eastern India. Moreover, major events such as the battles of Panipat and Chausa had overshadowed the perceptions of the contemporary writers, as well as the modern historians. Hence, we have very little information of what actually happened in Punjab. Grewal argues, on the basis of analysis of the phenomena of rehabilitation, resettlement and urbanization in the Punjab province under the Lodhis, that there were 'long spells of peace punctuated by spasmodic warfare in Punjab during the lifetime of Guru Nanak'. To advance his argument, he states, 'After the battle of Panipat, the Punjab remained virtually free from warfare and internal disorder.'[29]

In addition to the political developments at the time of the rise of the Mughal Empire, the other equally important development, on the social front, was the birth of Sikhism. At this point, we will limit ourselves to a brief chronological parallel drawn between Guru Nanak, the founder of Sikhism, and his nine spiritual successors on the one hand and the Mughal Empire, the most formidable political power of the time, on the other. In other words, 250 years of the life and activities of the ten Gurus witnessed considerable changes in the political situation of north India, that is changes that affected Punjab and the expanding Sikh society.

The emergence of Guru Nanak was coterminous with the disintegration of the Delhi Sultanate. Some modern historians refer to the Punjab of those times as a place of comparative peace and prosperity. McLeod observes, 'It seems Guru Nanak was born into a favoured period, at least as far as security and economic conditions were concerned.'[30] In Grewal's opinion, the western dominions of the Lodhi Sultans enjoyed comparative peace for nearly half a century after Guru Nanak's birth.[31] On the other hand, Indubhushan Banerjee assessed the early history of Guru Nanak as an age of disintegration and an age of almost constant strife.[32] So long as Akbar was on the throne at Agra, Mughal policy of non-interference helped the Sikh Gurus and the Sikh community, both directly and indirectly, to further their socio-religious and socio-economic interests. This explains Akbar's double visit to Goindwal, once to meet Guru Ram Das and a second time, to meet Guru Arjan Dev, and his gift of a tract of land on which was laid the foundation stone of the holy city of Amritsar. This policy of Akbar spans the lives and activities of two Gurus and by far the larger part of those of Guru Arjun, that is, of the great formative period of Sikhism and Sikh society.

By the time of Jahangir's accession to the throne, taking advantage of comparative peace and direct prestige and patronage of the imperial court in the shape and form of more than one imperial visit, the Sikh Gurus could initiate and carry out the policies and programmes that imparted on Sikhism a definite form. This was achieved with a dependable body of texts carefully sorted out and codified, enabling the Sikh community to take a definite shape. This was helped further by the patronage they came to receive from the trading and commercial communities. This support was indeed very important, rather crucial, during the formative period of the faith and the community. The tide turned during the reigns of Jahangir, Shah Jahan and Aurangzeb, with the Mughal imperial policy, especially the policy of these three monarchs towards the Sikhs in general and the Sikh Gurus in particular, having become unfriendly, rather hostile.

GURU NANAK ON POLITICAL MILIEU

To place Guru Nanak's ideological fermentation in the right perspective, we are bound to see the political scenario from his eyes, that is the way he perceived the then existing reality. A rigorous analysis of the compositions of Guru Nanak reveals that there is hardly anything in contemporary politics, society or religion that he finds commendable.[33] It becomes still more relevant because the age of Guru Nanak was not fundamentally or even radically different from the previous or the following few centuries. For a rational conceptualization of his position, it may be suggested that the entire social order had lost its legitimacy in his eyes. His sharp response to Babur's invasions underlines the most important political development during his life, that is, the transition from Afghan to Mughal rule in the Punjab and in northern India. The Guru was an eyewitness to the massacre in the town of Saidpur (now Eminabad in Pakistan) during Babur's third invasion (1521). The Guru protested, 'With the bridal procession of sin, Babur issued forth from Kabul and by force demanded the hand of the bride, Oh Lalo.' What pained Guru Nanak the most was the pitiable sufferings of the womenfolk carried away and dishonoured by the ruthless soldiers of the Mughal army. He lamented,

Those who wore beautiful dresses and had the partings of their hair dyed with vermilion have their locks now shorn with scissors, and dust is thrown upon their heads. Broken are the strings of their pearls. Wealth and beauty have now become their bane. Dishonoured, and with ropes round their necks, they are carried away by soldiers. When Babur's rule was proclaimed, no one could eat his food.[34]

Guru Nanak was thoroughly familiar with the politico-administrative arrangements made by the Afghan rulers, particularly in the Punjab. This familiarity, reflected in the use of the metaphors, is a measure of his preoccupation with this vital aspect of the social situation. Moreover, in Guru Nanak's verses, there is a direct denunciation of contemporary rule. For instance, he said that the rulers were unjust. They discriminate against their non-Muslim subjects by extorting *jaziya* and pilgrimage tax. The ruling class oppressed the cultivators and the common people. In fact, the Turko-Afghan rule is seen equated with the dark age. In the Guru's words, 'The *kaliyuga* is a knife; the Rajas are butchers; *dharma* is fast vanishing; in the dark night of falsehood the moon of truth nowhere seems to rise.'[35] In the Guru's experience, corruption was so rampant in the administration that there was no one who did not receive or gave bribe. 'Even the Raja does justice only when his palm is greased but not in the name of God.'[36] 'They live and die in ignorance of the lord; singed by their own pride, they would burn like the forest reed in a wildfire.'[37]

Here an attempt may be made to sum up Guru Nanak's position in respect of his response to his political milieu. According to him, rulership and riches come not as acquisition of men, but as God's gift. The Guru was vehemently against the rulers who exploited the people and indulged in luxuries – fleet-footed caparisoned horses, colourful harems, tall mansions and pleasures of all kinds – all at the cost of the poor.[38] Guru Nanak does not attach divinity to the office of the king. The king as well as the beggar exist because of divine dispensation. Some God has raised to rulership; others wander about begging and God is the fountain of the whole authority. It is in God's power to degrade the Sultan just as it is in His power to exalt the man. According to Guru Nanak, if the ruler's order was against justice and equity, it was not obligatory on the people to honour him and in that lay the seeds of defiance and challenge to the authority of an unjust ruler and his rule. There is a general comment that the rulers (rajas) are avaricious and full of arrogance – *maya-sanch rajai ahankari maya sath na challai piari*.[39] For instance, there is a general reference to 'blood-sucking Rajas'.[40] Then there is an often-quoted more direct comment: 'The Rajas are lions and the *muqaddam*s dogs; they fall upon the *raiyat* day and night. Their agents inflict wounds with claws (of power) and the dogs lick blood and relish the liver.'[41]

SOCIAL MILIEU

The social situation in the Punjab in particular and in northern India in general during the late fifteenth and early sixteenth centuries was marked with significant changes. These were rooted in the circumstances brought about by the Turko-

Afghan rule in the spheres of politics and administration, urban and rural economy and religious and social culture. The medieval period, not only in India and outside, was an era of politico-social change.[42] The Indian subcontinent was a conglomeration of different entities that led to the fragmentation of political dispensations and the social fabric into diverse traditions. The Punjab was no exception, as it too passed through socio-religious upheavals and phases of political disintegration.

The Hindu kingdoms of India were disturbed by the invasion of Muhammad bin Qasim. It opened the north-western gate for the advent of the Muslims in India. Thus began waves of Muslim influx, the impact of which became manifest by the time of Ghaznavid invasions. The last decade of the twelfth and the first decade of the thirteenth century, in Nizami's opinion, were characterized by the clash of two degenerating and decaying social systems, Turkish and the Rajput.[43] The continuities, however, remained as important as the changes. Sensitive individuals responded to the changed situation according to their perceptions and moral fervour. This social background and their social position were equally relevant to the nature and content of their response. Social change was accompanied by social tensions of various kinds. These tensions were probably the strongest in Punjab. Thus, relatively egalitarian religious movements had begun to appear in the region much before the reign of Akbar. Their protagonists felt the urge to address themselves to the common people. This could be done only by using the language they spoke. Malik Muhammad Jaisi prefaced one of his Hindi works with the remark that the Sufis (*auliya*) had always adopted the languages of the countries in which they settled; he specifically mentions Hindi and Punjabi.[44] In this context, Shaikh Farid acquires great significance as he was writing Punjabi verse. In all probability, he must not have been the only one. Grewal presumes that although no conspicuous writer is known, some of the Sufis composed verses in Punjabi in the thirteenth and fourteenth centuries. Thus, there is hardly any reason to believe that no Sufi of the fifteenth century wrote in Punjabi. The then social situation, marked by social tensions, might also partly explain the distinctive responses of Guru Nanak to the social situation in which he lived and moved.[45] In fact, a detailed study of the *var*s of Bhai Gurdas also seem to communicate that Sikhism arose in the context of religious contention, if not turmoil.

The extensive political changes, already discussed, significantly affected[46] the character of the population in Punjab. Yahya Ahmad Sirhindi in his work *Tarikh-i-Mubarak Shahi* projects the early fifteenth century as a dark age for the people of Punjab for its maltreatment, maladministration, and injustice to the inhabitants. It is projected that the social fabric was decaying due to frequent invasions from outside the boundaries of Punjab. The king-like behaviour of the nobles and political distrust had weakened the political bond of the government and it fell into anarchy, causing civil wars. The governors indulged in intrigues to become independent and it led to the disintegration of the Delhi Sultanate.[47] Guru Nanak, in his compositions, denounces the cruelty and bigotry of the kings and their officials in strong words, 'The Kali age is knife; kings are butchers, and righteousness has taken wings. Where can one find the moon of truth in this dark night of falsehood?'[48]

Guru Nanak is not only aware, but a strong critic of the hypocrisy of the headmen (*muqaddam*s), all of whom could not have been Muslims. The Brahmins and the Khatris must have been copartners in this process of exploitation. 'They who perform *namaaz* eat human beings, they who wear the sacred thread wield a knife.' In Guru Nanak's eyes, the pinnacle of hypocrisy is exemplified by the Brahmin and the Khatris who reads the Quran in public but performs *puja* in his private space; he wears *dhoti*, *mala* and *tika*, but eats the food of those whom he regards as *mlechchha*. Above all, the Brahmins (officials) regard cowdung as sacred but levies taxes on cow and even the Brahmins.[49] As Grewal concludes, Guru Nanak castigates the Khatris as collaborators who went to the extent of adopting the language of the *mlechchha* and also greatly compromised, rather discarded, the traditional *dharma*.[50]

In the same spirit, Guru Nanak is sharply critical not only of the Muslim rulers but also of the Shaikhs. The popularly held belief is that Guru Nanak had an extremely positive outlook towards the Sufi Shaikhs and their contribution to the society. However, the Shaikhs are accused of being an integral part of the ruling dispensation, standing allied with those who tax deities and temples.[51] Indeed, to be a true Muslim, one should adopt the path of Sufis (*auliya*), cultivate detachment and willingly accept what is decreed by God. The Shaikh, however, suffers from *haumai* (self-centredness) as much as the *qazi*.[52] There is still a relative appreciation for the Sufi path, but that should not be confused with his approval of the immoral ways of the contemporary Sufis. If the *qazi*s had their offices, the Shaikhs had their establishments.

They tended to treat the means as ends, forgetting that God alone is everlasting. Presuming to be sure of his own place of honour with God, the Shaikh gave assurances to others as well; he was like the mouse which itself was too big for the hole yet tied a winnowing basket to its tail.[53]

During the sixteenth and seventeenth centuries, there were two main communities in Punjab. However, a third community appeared on the socio-economic stage in 1699, soon after the creation of Khalsa. The dominant tribes of the region during the fifteenth and sixteenth centuries were an important legacy of political changes. Many Baloch and Pathan clans were dominant in the Multan province of the Mughal Empire. The Kharal and Sial tribes were dominant in the lower portions of the Bari and Rachna Doabs. The Ghakkhars, Awans and Janjuas were dominant in the upper Sindh–Sagar Doab. Many Rajput clans held lands along the Shivaliks and the border along Rajasthan.

The ideal norm of the Hindu society was social stratification. In the early eleventh century, Alberuni observed that there were four *varna*s among the Hindus, viz. the Brahmin,

The Land and its People

Kshatriya, Vaishya, and Shudra.[54] He also observed a number of sub-castes in each *varna*.[55] While he accepted that some form of societal division was a common phenomenon in history, the *varna*s did not cover all the people. As is well known, these *varna*s were associated with specific duties. However, it is highly improbable that these classified duties comprehended all the professions followed by these social groups, even in Alberuni's times. There were other people, below the Shudras, who did not belong to any *varna*. They were members of certain crafts or professions such as the sailor, basket and shield maker, fisherman, weaver, fuller and shoemaker. The members of these guilds were forced to live outside the villages and towns. At the bottom of the social hierarchy were the people who did not belong either to a *varna* or a guild. The most prominent among them were the Chandala, Badhatu, Hadi and Dom. Barring the Hadi and Dom, most of them were engaged in 'unclean work'. They were treated as 'degraded outcastes' because of the nature of their work and the belief that they had descended from a Shudra father and a Brahmin mother. There was a widely prevalent gradation even amongst these degraded outcastes who were at the periphery of the social system. It is equally significant that the *varna* system was not acceptable to all the members of the Hindu society.

Nevertheless, the concept of *varna* was widely accepted and advocated throughout the medieval period. At the close of the seventeenth century, Sujan Rai Bhandari described the Brahmins (*ahl-i-brahmana*) as those who subscribed to the *varna* order comprising the four castes, viz. the Brahmin, Kshatriyas, Vaishyas and Shudra.[56] At the same time, one must admit the possibility of absorption, upgrading or downgrading of actual social groups within the framework of the *varna*. The socio-economic position of certain social groups did not always correspond to their ritual status. This would be true, for instance, of the Khatris of the Punjab.

During the late fifteenth century, the Hindus of the Punjab, did not fit completely into the four-*varna* order. This tangible change in social organization could be ascribed to the impact of Turkish conquest and the rule of Delhi Sultans. The Rajput ruling class, along with their political power, was almost vanquished from this region. One may presume that some of them might have accepted Islam or still fewer could have compromised to the position of *zamindar*s, popularly associated with the epithet of Rai. Their presence and role in the then-prevalent political scenario almost decimated. With the loss of the position of the Rajputs, the traditional source of patronage enjoyed by the Brahmins also faced a severe setback.[57] Some Brahmins were fortunate to find an alternate source of patronage in the new rulers. Yet, one can safely deduce that the new rulers were neither interested nor successful in providing a similar level of support to the Brahmins as a class. On a positive side, in all probability, they were exempt from the *jaziya*.[58]

Punjab does not seem to have known and experienced the countless proliferations and ramifications of the vertical *jati*-grades and sub-grades nor the socio-religious rigours of the Brahmanical *jati* hierarchy. In Niharranjan Ray's opinion, according to the *Smarta Pauranik*, early medieval Brahminism does not seem to have had a very strong hold on the people of this region even during the centuries preceding the advent of Islam and the consolidation of Muslim political authority. The reasons he ascribes for the limited hold of Brahminism are the prevalence of Mahayana Buddhism for long; and, more importantly, the changing and challenging fortunes of history. This must have had resulted in relatively quicker changes in the socio-political life of the people, generating more social mobility amongst them than anywhere else in India. Such mobility naturally stood in the way of consolidation of the Brahmanical system of *jati*.[59]

By the close of the fifteenth century, the social situation in the Punjab had considerably changed due to the impact of the Turkish conquest and the rule of the Delhi Sultans. The Rajput ruling classes, the Kshatriyas of the *varna* concept, had been dislodged from power. Some of them might have accepted Islam or migrated to the neighbouring hills or deserts. Their significant remnants could perhaps be seen in a few *zamindar*s called Rais. But even at this level, the chiefs of non-Rajput tribes or clans had come into prominence. To equate the Hindu landed gentry (*zamindar*s, *chaudhri*s and *muqaddam*s) of the Lodi Punjab with the Kshatriyas of the *varna* concept would be the best or the worst way of glossing over a significant social change. The occupation of the old Rajput ruling classes, along with the vital politics of the Punjab, was gone. At the close of the fifteenth century, one could find individuals tilling the soil, but styling themselves as Rajput.[60]

With the loss of Rajput sovereignty, the Brahmins lost their traditional patronage and thus, with few exceptions, the position and the legal and formal powers of the Brahmins underwent a considerable change. Some Brahmins sought refuge and honour in the neighbouring principalities in the Punjab hills. Some others were obliged to seek livelihood in alternate professions (traditionally considered inappropriate for the Brahmins). This was not a peculiarity of the Mughal period or only of regions such as the Punjab. Vasudeva Upadhyay has noticed that even before AD 1200, some Brahmins took to the profession of arms, agriculture, trade, and moneylending.[61] Yet, one cannot discount the probability that the Brahmins as a class appear to have increased their influence over the Hindu masses. Notwithstanding the elimination of the Rajputs from power, the Brahmins consolidated their informal authority and personal influence. Perhaps, this had reasons in the Brahmins' need for seeking an alternate source of patronage. The Brahmins now read the scriptures to more numerous but humbler class of patrons, acted as family priests, and taught in schools (*pathshala*s). The Brahmanical emphasis on the meticulous observance of religious rites and ceremonies must have logically increased. In the early nineteenth century, Ganesh Das observed that the priests (*ahl-i-dharm*) among the Hindus were extremely meticulous about the purity of food and drink. They refused to associate with a Hindu who associated with other religious groups.[62] They, in fact, started working as teachers in educational institutions and acting as family priests of relatively modest households.

In sum, the Brahmins as a priestly class enjoyed a status of honour and prestige, which did not correspond to their economic means. For a nuanced understanding of an enhanced economic position and its correlation to a desire for a corresponding improvement in social prestige, the Kshatriyas of the Punjab, in the period under study, are a good example. They traced their origins to the Epic Age. They were some of the old inhabitants of the area, probably older than the Rajputs. The profession of arms was no longer the only important engagement for them. Besides administration, trade and shopkeeping absorbed their best energies and emerged as a new atraction. Although *Char-Bagh-i-Punjab* is a source of a slighlty later period, yet it clearly reflects the inclinations of the Kshatriyas. Ganesh Das, the author of *Char-Bagh-i-Punjab*, mentions service, writership, trade, shopkeeping, drapery and haberdashery, trade in silken goods and banking or money-changing as some of the old and important occupations of the Kshatriyas of the Punjab.[63] Thus, they emerged as a class that responded favourably to the changing realities of the time.

The Kshatriyas were not, in fact, averse to moneylending and *sahukar*s and acting as bankers, making use of *hundis* and *tamassuk*s. Sujan Rai in his work, *Khulasat-ut-Tawarikh*, mentions insurance (*bima*) as a commendable institution.[64] In brief, much of the urban trade and shopkeeping in the towns was in their hands. Though they could be found in the countryside as well, their concentration was significant in towns and cities where they played the role of significant entrepreneurs. According to K.M. Ashraf and I.H. Qureshi, the state did not deny them the right to own private property.[65] According to Romila Thapar, the Kshatriyas of north India had accepted Vaishya status much before AD 1200.[66] The Khatris of Punjab were among those who showed a considerable adaptability and success. It would not be out of place to mention that the Kshatriyas formed the most important constituent of the Nanak Panth. In fact, many prominent Sikhs as well as some of the Gurus, belonged to Khatri sub-castes, such as Sehgal, Ohri, Vohra, Vij, Kapur, Chaddha, Behl, Kohli, Marwah, Mehra, Sodhi, Nanda, and so on.

The Hindu society in the rural Punjab was marked by a preponderance of Jats, particularly in the upper Rachna, upper Bari and Bist-Jalandhar Doabs and on the left side of River Sutlej. Interestingly, Alberuni refers to the presence of Jats in the eleventh century as Shudras, whereas the author of the *Dabistan-i-Mazahib* acknowledged their presence at the lowest rung of the Vaishyas in the middle decades of the seventeenth century. Does this indicate a significant upward mobility?

The rise of the Jats to prominence is an interesting subject. Irfan Habib traces the history of the Jats over a long span of time. In the seventh century, the Jats inhabited central Sind. A primitive community, they had a pastoral economy and a social structure bereft of inequalities. From central Sind they migrated north to Multan and clashed with the Ghaznavid army on the Indus. They spread across the Punjab and crossing the Yamuna reached as far as the Chambal. During this migration, they settled as sedentary cultivators with the help of the Persian wheel. Many of them attained the *zamindari* rights, though a majority were tax-paying peasants. Having improved their economic position, they refused to accept their low social standing and, therefore, entered the fold of Sikhism.[67] Richard M. Eaton saw the rise of the Jats in relation to the shrine of Shaikh Farid at Pakpattan. Since the death (1265) of the Shaikh, his shrine had evolved as a leading centre of pilgrimage. A number of rituals – death anniversary (*urs*), community kitchen, musical sessions, accession of the spiritual head (Diwan), and passing through the southern door (*bihishti darwaza*) – were institutionalized. The Diwan managed the land grants and brought the pastoral (Jat and Rajput) clans to till the soil. These clans, participating in the rituals of the shrine, underwent a slow process of Islamization. The relation of the clans and the shrine was further cemented, as the clan chiefs offered their daughters in marriage into the Diwan's family.[68] In western Punjab, the twin process of agrarian expansion and Islamization went hand in hand.

Divided into numerous clans, the Jats had their landed headmen (*zamindar*s, *chaudhri*s, and *muqaddam*s). The bulk of the Jats consisted of ordinary cultivators. Since they accounted for the largest adherents of Sikhism, it seems that their mind-set and perception of religion was reasonably satisfied by the focus of nascent Sikhism. They did not generally refuse to pay the ordinary dues to the state. Yet, they resented and refused to accept oppression. Probably this rebellious attitude against oppressive tendencies (of the state) made them appreciate the rebellious heroes of Punjab folklore and motivated them into occasionally taking up arms against their oppressors. As expected, there were gradual shifts in the relative importance of the various clans of the Jats. Presumably, when the socio-economic position of certain social groups did not correspond with their ritual status, there must have been processes of absorption, upgradation, or down-gradation at work.

It may be deduced that the Rajputs, Brahmins, Khatris, and Jats formed, no doubt, the most important social groups of Hindu society in the Punjab. But they did not account for its entire non-Muslim population. Ashraf observes that the popular tradition in Hindustan takes account of at least thirty-six social groups, including the various subdivisions of the higher castes.[69] Among them were occupations of the brewer, goldsmith, weaver, tin-worker, betel-leaf seller, shepherd, milkman, carpenter, smith, bhat, dyer, flower-seller, calico-printer, barber, oilman, musician, juggler, and the mountebank. There is no reason to be sceptical about the existence of these occupational groups in the Punjab, rural as well as urban. In fact, some more occupations were found in the region of Batala as those of the tailor, potter, *thathiar*, and the mason in particular. Below them were the untouchables, the Chandals, who were divided into 'castes' of their own and were basically considered outside the pale of the society. The condition of the Hindu craftsmen was perhaps not much different from

The Land and its People

that of the Muslim ones. They all lived in poverty. 'The introduction of Muslim craftsmen,' says Ashraf,

> may have done something towards removing the social disabilities of the class as a whole, but in the long run Muslim influence succumbed to the older traditions. When Babur came to Hindustan no appreciable modification in the social character of these vocations was visible, for the finds indicate that all the craftsmen were organized in rigid and exclusive castes.[70]

The conditions of the untouchables was obviously the worst. They lived a wretched life under the shadow of contempt, social ostracism, and extreme poverty. And none of the castes can be treated as a homogeneous group. At the individual level, one may safely presume that there must have been a sense of disappointment and aggrandisement against the existing realities. They must have hoped for improvement which, keeping in mind the medieval mentality, could have been in the religious front.

The last three quarters of the sixteenth century represented an era of cultural comingling. Prior to this period, the Muslim soldiers, administrators, traders, scholars, men of letters, and religious elite had been coming to the Punjab from Persia, Afghanistan, and Central Asia. It has already been noted that the Punjab had to bear frontal attacks and it greatly impacted the social composition and tenor of the society at large. During this phase, like earlier periods, some of the low-born Hindus were converted either to Islam or to the Sikh faith. In brief, the Punjab of our period witnessed the emergence of comingling which could be seen in both the communities. It must be noted that the Sufis played a significant role in the evolution of the 'syncretic culture'. The mutual interaction and exchange in manners and ceremonies owed a great deal to the Sufi influence, which contributed to evolving an assimilated culture. According to Aziz Ahmad, the history of medieval India, to a very considerable extent, is a history of Hindu–Muslim religious-cultural tensions, interspersed with movements or individual efforts at understanding, cultivating harmony and even composite developments.[71]

As often noted, none of these communities can be treated as a unified whole, for both formed a part of the much larger entities in the Indian subcontinent. In certain spheres and at certain levels of socio-economic life, a strict distinction between 'Hindu' and 'Muslim' may not lead to a meaningful social analysis. While realizing the problem of conceptualization and the complexity of the social situation in the Punjab around AD 1500, one cannot evade a brief discussion about the 'Hindu' and 'Muslim' community per se, so as to weave a complex fabric of the then social milieu.

Muslim society in the Punjab, as in some other parts of India, was as well marked by sectarian divisions as by racial differences. The sectarian differences – Sunni, Shia, Ismaili, Mulahid, Batini, Ibahati, or Mahdavi – was an issue of consideration for social interaction. The Sunnis formed the largest proportion of Muslim population in the Punjab, but the Shias appear to have been well-represented in proportion to their total number in the subcontinent.[72] Though the Sufi orders can in no sense be treated as 'sect', their differences with the Ulema could not be concealed. Differences on the basis of religious belief and practice lent a measure of diversity to the Muslim society in the Punjab.

From a sociological standpoint, the horizontal stratification was more important than the sectarian divisions of Muslim society.[73] According to Ashraf, an early assumption that an 'Islamic' society was bound to be based on the idea of equality is refuted by the socio-economic facts.[74] In the Punjab, as elsewhere, a broad social stratification in Muslim society is clearly evident. The nobles composed the 'social elite' and enjoyed greater economic advantages than any other section or group. The religious dignitaries such as Ulemas, Sayyids, and Shaikhs too enjoyed a high social status and may be considered as the upper class of Muslim society. The middling class was formed by the peasants, soldiers, traders, scholars, writers, Shaikhzadas, and the administrative personnel. The craftsmen, personal servants, and domestic slaves, both male and female, formed the lowest strata. They were poor and downtrodden, and due to their economic condition, they led a wretched life.

In retrospect, one can comprehend that the influx of Muslims into the land had become virtually inevitable after the annexation of the province to the dominions of Mahmud of Ghazni. In fact, for some time, the Punjab became the core dominion of Mahmud's successors. Then, for three centuries, it formed a part of the dominions of the Ilbari, Khalji, Tughlaq, Sayyid, and Afghan rulers. For nearly 500 years, some Muslim soldiers, administrators, traders, scholars, and pious men had been adopting the Punjab as their home. Some of them had been married with local girls, and after a long stay in the country of their adoption, many of them had come to be 'Indianized' and perceived themselves as 'Indian Muslims'. The dramatic immigration of the Mughals and Persians in the early sixteenth century was more conspicuous because of its rapidity. It was nonetheless a part of an old, albeit gradual, process.[75]

However, the 'immigrants' do not appear to have formed a very large proportion of the Muslim community in the Punjab during the period under study. The proportion of 'native' Muslims was perhaps larger. Their existence may be attributed, obviously, to a long process of conversion. In the first place, one cannot deny the forcible conversion and enslavement of women and children as repercussions of war. Individual Muslims, in public or private positions, thought it meritorious to convert the natives to Islam through material inducement or maybe mere persuasion. In the process of peaceful conversion, the Sufi Shaikhs clearly played a very significant role. For instance, Shaikh Ali bin Usman Hujwiri (d. 1072) had settled in Lahore during the Ghaznavid times. According to a later chronicler of the Punjab, the Hindu Gujjars of Lahore were converted to Islam by Hujwiri.[76] It may be enough to say here that the process of gradual conversion through the Sufis continued through the medieval period. In the early sixteenth century, Shaikh Daud, for instance, established his hospice (*khanqah*) at Shergarh in the Bari Doab, where Badauni was to see him converting Hindus in large numbers.[77]

Probably all the major towns of the Punjab had come to have a considerable proportion of Muslim population by the close of the fifteenth century. The close connection of urbanization with administrative arrangement may also lead us to infer that almost all the major towns of the Punjab contained a substantial proportion of Muslim population. The proportion of Muslims in the urban population of the Punjab appears to have been much larger than their proportion in the rural population.[78]

In the discussion on the social milieu, it must be noted that the cities and towns served as the centres of Indo-Muslim culture in the Punjab as elsewhere. The contribution of pre-Mughal Lahore to literature and culture was by no means negligible. According to the Gazetteer of the Lahore District for 1883-4,[79] during the later Pathan and Mughal dynasties, Lahore was celebrated as 'the resort of learned men'. Grewal in his important work, *Guru Nanak in History*, talks about the importance of urban centres in the then Punjab.[80] Multan was another important centre of learning. Badauni reports that Shaikh Adbullah and Azizullah, both from Tulamba, were believed to have set new standards in the pursuit of logic (*mantiq*) and scholastic theology (*kalam*).[81] Nizamuddin Ahmad notes in the *Tabaqat-i-Akbari* that Sikandar Lodi consulted Shaikh Salih of Sirhind at times. From the major chronicles of Akbar's reign, it becomes evident that several towns of the Punjab – Jalandhar, Sultanpur, Ajodhan, Thanesar, Samana, and Narnaul – were reputed as centres of Muslim learning.[82] It is highly probable that learned men of local repute were to be found in all the important towns of the Punjab.[83]

To sum up, it can be inferred that, for Guru Nanak, the contemporary social order had lost its legitimacy. A new social order committing a more egalitarian society could be created. The significant ruptures in the social organization of the Hindus as well as the Muslims and, to mention the least, among the lowest rung of the social ladder in both the communities, whether referred to as slaves or Chandals or outcastes or untouchables, provided a conducive environment for the propagation of a social order with its emphasis on a more 'equal' society. Guru Nanak identified himself with the common people, related to their agonies and propagated an idiom where all individuals had more humane space. Though Guru Nanak had more to offer regarding the Hindu social order, yet there is no reason to think that Muslims were not included among his followers and adherents. The path of the Guru was open to all, irrespective of caste and creed.[84]

RELIGIOUS MILIEU

The ethnic plurality in the Punjab was matched by variety in its religious and cultural traditions. All Muslims formally subscribe to the belief that there was no other God but Allah and Muhammad were his messengers (*rasul*). However, sectarian divisions had appeared among Muslims even before the advent of the Turks in the Punjab. Imported by the immigrant Muslims, ideological differences were perpetuated by those who came under its influence in India. It is easy to identify three old sects: the Sunni, the Shia and the Ismaili. A parallel interpretation of Islam was cherished, advocated, and developed by the Sufis from the very beginning of the Turkish conquest.[85]

More and more people were coming under the influence of Sufis. Baba Haji Rattan of Bathinda and Ali bin Usman Hujwiri of Lahore were the earliest Sufis. Two major Sufi orders, Chishtis and Suhrawardis, emerged in the early thirteenth century. Shaikh Farid, after staying in Delhi and Hansi, established a hospice at Pakpattan. He laid stress on austerities and kept aloof from the state. Suhrawardis, under Shaikh Bahauddin Zakariya, laid emphasis on orthodox practices and close relations with the ruling class.[86] In the fourteenth century, the Delhi Sultanate, employing the instrument of land grants, brought the two orders under its control. In southeast Punjab, the situation was different. The Chishtis of Hansi and Bu Ali Qalandar of Panipat maintained distance from the contemporary rulers. The Sabiri branch of the Chishtis, which was founded by Alauddin Ali Ahmad Sabir (nephew of Shaikh Farid) at Kaliyar Sharif, made notable progress in south-east Punjab. During the fifteenth and sixteenth century, Abdul Quddus Gangohi led the Sabiris to great heights.[87] In Malerkotla, Haidar Shaikh became the local ruler with the help of powerful landed intermediaries. Shaikh Ahmad Sirhindi, inspired by the onset of the second millennium, made strenuous efforts to bring about an Islamic revival. The legacy of the Sufis was seen in the form of shrines, death anniversaries, miraculous tales, Sufi discourses, and biographical works. Sufi poets, ranging from Shaikh Farid to Khwaja Ghulam Farid, produced Sufi poetry that preached universal brotherhood, criticized the theologians, and weakened religious fanaticism. The pious conduct of the Sufis encouraged people to embrace Islam.

Punjab was characterized by the existence of multiple religious faiths. As noted earlier, Hinduism and Islam were the two main religions during the sixteenth century. There were a number of smaller sects in both religions.[88] Brahmanical religion, the oldest of all the religious traditions of India, was transformed into Hinduism in the early medieval period and with this change came the emergence of Shaivism, Vaishnavism, and Shaktism, which later on developed further into various sub-sects. The medieval Hinduism was not a homogeneous or a compact religious system, but a family of religious tenets. Moreover, it was not completely of Vedic origin, but included many heterogeneous sects of non-Vedic origin.[89] It was a combination of many religious ideologies, including Vedic ritualism, Vedantic thought, Vaishnavism, Shaivism, and primeval cults.[90]

All non-Muslims were not 'Hindus' as the term is used today.[91] There were pockets of Tantric Buddhism in the Punjab hills. In the plains, there were Jain monks with a lay following among traders and shopkeepers of many a town. Niharranjan Ray contends that we have direct and indirect evidence to show that apart from the Jain *sannyasi*s, the Nathpanthi *yogi*s, Avadhutas, and Kapalikas were well-known in the Punjab of the fourteenth and fifteenth centuries. Apart from Guru Nanak, his successors had contacts with them, either as contenders or as part collaborators in an ideological sense.[92]

As noted, 'Hinduism' was represented by Shaiva, Vaishnava, and Shakta beliefs. Temples, dedicated to Shiva as the supreme deity, were looked after by Shaiva Brahmins, who also cultivated Shaiva literature, the Agamas and Puranas. The Shaiva *sannyasi*s were known for their hard penance and austerity. They belonged to different orders, traditionally considered to be ten and, therefore, they were also known as Dasnamis. They generally wore ochre-coloured garments, though some of them went naked. Almost all of them wore a frontal mark (*tilak*) on their forehead. Some used three lines, representing Shiva's trident or his third eye. Some used two horizontal lines with a dot as the phallic emblem of Shiva. The *sannyasi*s wandered from place to place, but they also founded monastic establishments (*math*s). Its head could be nominated by the predecessor or elected by his fellow disciples. Within Shaivism, a new movement arose, probably after the Ghaznavid conquest of the Punjab. Initiated by Gorakhnath, the trend called *Hath-yoga* was a theological system with Shiva as the supreme deity. They rejected ritualism and metaphysical speculation. In accepting disciples, they disregarded the differences of caste. They regarded women as 'the tigress of the night', a great temptation and, therefore, a great danger in the *yogi*'s path.

Turning to Vaishnavism, we notice that the Vaishnava texts – *Bhagavadgita*, *Bhagavata Purana* and *Vishnu Purana* – were known to Alberuni in the eleventh century. Temples dedicated to Vishnu as the supreme deity, as Lakshmi-Narayan or one of his incarnations, were looked after by Vaishnava Brahmins. The ascetics among the Vaishnavas were generally known as Bairagis. They recognized merit in ceremonial ritual and pilgrimage to sacred places. With many other Hindus, they shared the practices of veneration for the cow and the Brahmin. They advocated total abstention from meat and alcohol.[93]

The Shaktas worshipped the Goddess in her various forms, giving primacy to the active principle or cosmic force (Shakti) which sustains the universe and various manifestations of gods. Worship of the Goddess was of two kinds, generally referred to as 'the cults of the right hand' and 'the cults of the left hand'. Animal sacrifice in honour of Durga or Kali, or any other ferocious form of the Great Goddess, was an essential element of the cults of the right. The left-handers (*vamacharis*) performed 'black rites', which, in theory, were meant only for the adept and involved wine (*madya*), fish (*matsya*), flesh (*maans*), parched grain (*mudra*) and coition (*maithuna*). The purpose of this ritual was to attain a state of complete identification with Shakti and Shiva. The practice of this rite was secretive and limited. It made the left-handers disreputable in the eyes of the majority of the people. According to Niharranjan Ray, the religion of the common people of the Punjab plains and hills seems to have been based on the Puranic version of the Shakti cult. He further points out the vast influence of the Shakti cult in deriving many toponyms in these regions. For instance, Ambala is derived from Amba; Chandigarh is named after Chandi; Panchkula is a technical term of Tantrik significance; Kalka is a distorted version of Kalika; Simla is again a distorted version of Syamala Devi. Throughout these regions, one still finds countless small shrines with shapeless icons of crude form placed on their altars, which worshippers and common village folk describe as Mansa, Chandi, Kali and Durga. All these were the manifestations of Shakti, the Mother Goddess par excellence of Puranic Brahminism.

This brief account of the major forms of Muslim and Hindu religious beliefs and practices does not take into account a large mass of the common people and their 'popular religion' which bordered on animism and fetishism. Godlings of nature, disease, malevolent spirits, animal worship, heroic godlings, ancestors, and totems made a conspicuous appearance in popular religion.

As in Shaivism, Vaishnavism gave rise to a new movement

known as Bhakti. This path came to be regarded as a valid path for salvation, like the path of knowledge (*jnana* or *gyaan*) and the path of correct observance of ritual (*karma*). In the eleventh and twelfth centuries, Ramanuja made a significant contribution to this movement in southern India by giving primacy to the path of the Bhakti. In the thirteenth and fourteenth centuries, Vaishnava Bhakti began to be addressed to the human incarnations of Vishnu, Rama and Krishna. The cult of Rama Bhakti was popularized by Ramanand in northern India during the fourteenth and fifteenth centuries. It was meant primarily for the upper or middle castes, though its protagonist made some use of the language of the people and they were more indulgent towards the lower castes.

After a survey of the general religious milieu, it would be interesting to briefly analyse the perceptions of the Sikh Gurus, particularly Guru Nanak, on the ongoing belief and practices. He held high spiritual ideas. It was his conviction that the entire universe is suffused with divine light and all creation is His creation. The only source of light in all human beings is the divine light. God alone is the bestower of life upon all living beings. Caste distinctions and social differentiations did not harmonize with this conviction. None should be regarded high (*uttam*) on the basis of his birth or caste and none should be regarded low (*nich*). Instead of the Brahmins and Khatris, Guru Nanak identified himself with the lower castes and untouchables. In his words, 'Be there the lowest among the low, or even the lower, Nanak is with them.'[94] The social reality did not conform to the ideal norm of the caste-based social order. Guru Nanak invited people to come out of the shells of their castes as individuals in search of the path of truth. The idea of equality and universality of spiritual opportunity are the obverse and reverse of the same socio-religious coin. The Shudra and the untouchables are placed at par with the Brahmins and Khatris. Significantly, woman is placed at par with man. The differences of caste, class, gender, and creed are set aside as irrelevant for salvation.

Guru Nanak's attitude towards the traditional Hindu deities and scripture is intimately linked with his attitude towards the *pandit*. It has an in-built rejection of the traditional authority of the Hindu scriptures. With the rejection of Hindu deities and scriptures went the repudiation of traditional modes of worship and religious practices. There was no merit in pilgrimage to the sixty-eight sacred places, not even to Sangam in Prayag, where the Ganga and Jamuna mingled with a third invisible stream. There was no merit in the worship of images. Ritual reading of scripture is a waste of time. The performance of the fire sacrifice (*hom*) is equally useless. Ritual charities are of no use either. The protagonist of such beliefs and practices, the pandits, naturally come in for denunciation. In Guru Nanak's perception, the *pandit* doles out externalities and he is a 'broker' in false practices. He does it in self-interest. With his intrinsic interest in worldly occupations, his pretence of knowledge increases the inner dirt which keeps on multiplying. The sacred thread of the *pandit*s, the sacred mark on his forehead, his spotless loincloth (*dhoti*) and his rosary are useless without a genuine faith.[95] Guru Nanak gives as much attention to the *yogi* as to the *pandit*. He has no appreciation for the *yogi*'s aspiration to gain supernatural powers or to attempt to attain salvation through psycho-physical or chemico-physical means. Nor does he appreciate their idea of renunciation (*uddas*).

Guru Nanak's attitude towards the *ulema* and the Sufis is similar to his attitude towards the *pandit* and *yogi*. While addressing the Muslims, Guru Nanak shows his preference for the path of the Sufis over that of the *ulema*. Those who wish to become true Muslims should 'first adopt the path of the saints (*auliya*), treating renunciation as the file that removes the rust' of the human soul. This relative appreciation of the Sufi path does not mean, however, that Guru Nanak gave the Sufis his unqualified approval. His basic attitude towards Islam and Hinduism is explicitly stated in the line, 'Neither the Veda nor the Ketab know the mystery'.[96] In the same way the *qazi*, *pandit*, and *yogi* are bracketed.[97] The *qazi* utters lies and eats what is unclean. The Brahmin takes life and then goes off to bathe ceremoniously. The blind *yogi* does not know the way. All three are desolated.

To sum up, the Punjab had to bear the brunt of frequent foreign invasions by the logic of its geographical location. Every such episode initiated a cycle of 'action–reaction'. This process of interaction and assimilation of new cultures affected the traditional sociocultural milieu of society. There was a constant exchange between the existing social values and the newer ones that had entered the social scenario. Due to the recurrent cultural onslaught, the value system of society must have inevitably become more open and flexible in its acceptance of varied cultures and traditions. In other words, this must have resulted in lesser rigidity to resist newer ideas. The acceptance, or at least the non-resistant attitude, of society to the new ideological formulations of Guru Nanak's ideas and value system must have been a great contributing factor in preparing a conducive environment for the birth and evolution of Sikhism.

On the political front, the timespan of the sixteenth and seventeenth centuries witnessed considerable changes in north India. These changes could not but have affected Punjab. It coincided with the demise of Lodhi rule and rise of Mughal rule. The emergence of Guru Nanak was coterminous with the disintegration of the Delhi Sultanate. The Lodhi Sultans and their administration do not seem to have paid proper attention to the political affairs of the Punjab during the first quarter of the sixteenth century. Sikandar Lodhi is known to have remained heavily engrossed in the affairs of Gwalior, which had an adverse impact on the political situation in Punjab. Daulat Khan Lodhi, who had been appointed governor of Lahore in AD 1500, had virtually declared himself the de facto ruler of his dominions that extended from Sirhind in the east to Bhera in the west. Since his relations with the Sultan were far from cordial, he sent an invitation to Babur to invade Hindustan. Another such invitation was sent by Alam Khan Lodhi, an uncle of the Sultan.[98] In the meanwhile, the

Sultan dispatched an army under Bahar Khan to divest Daulat Khan of the governorship. Daulat Khan, instead of putting up a fight, vacated Lahore to retire towards Multan.

In the meantime, Babur had already crossed the Indus and reached Lahore without any resistance. Unfortunately, the Afghan army which had been sent with a limited purpose to subdue Daulat Khan, had to fight the Mughals and check their advance to Lahore. In the ensuing battle (1524), Babur, having defeated the Afghan army, captured the city, and set fire to some of its bazaars. Next, he marched to Dipalpur and put the garrison to the sword. Daulat Khan and Ghazi Khan had a sizeable army at their command and were strongly entrenched in Lahore to engage the Mughals. Yet, they abandoned Lahore and retreated to the fort of Milwat (Malot). At Panipat, a decisive battle took place between Ibrahim Lodhi and Babur. It has often been suggested that, after Panipat, Babur could not pay his full attention to the affairs of the Punjab. Actually, after Panipat the theatre of warfare and political activities had shifted to western and later eastern India. Grewal, on the basis of his analysis of rehabilitation, resettlement, and organization in the Punjab province under the Lodhis, held that there were long spells of peace punctuated by spasmodic warfare in Punjab during the lifetime of Guru Nanak.[99] To advance his argument, he states, 'After the battle of Panipat, the Punjab remained virtually free from warfare and internal disorder'.[100]

So long as Akbar was on the throne at Agra, Mughal policy of non-interference helped the Sikh Gurus and the Sikh community, both directly and indirectly, to further their socio-religious and socio-economic interests. Akbar's policy spans the lives and activities of two Gurus and by far the larger part of those of Guru Arjun, that is, of the great formative period of Sikhism and Sikh society. It must, however, be realized that each region has its own peculiarities and a system of governance which tended to respond to local requirements and changing situations. The Mughal administration in the

Punjab was flexible enough to accommodate its regional peculiarities.

As far as the socio-religious milieu is concerned, the fast-changing fortunes of the Punjab resulted in relatively quicker changes in the socio-political lives and generated more social mobility amongst them than anywhere else in India. Such mobility naturally stood in the way of consolidation of the Brahmanical caste system. The Punjab does not seem to have experienced the countless number of proliferation and ramification of vertical *jati*-grades and sub-grades. Nor did it suffer the socio-religious rigours of the Brahmanical caste hierarchy.

In addition to the mild control of the Brahmanical caste system, the ethnic plurality in the Punjab was matched by the variety in its religious and cultural traditions. Apart from the theological currents of Islam, a parallel interpretation was cherished, advocated, and developed by the Sufis from the beginning of the Turkish conquest of the Punjab. As a result, more and more people came under the influence of the Sufis. In fact, this influence in the Punjab was more pervasive than anywhere else in the Indian subcontinent. This was also the period when the Bhakti saints won over the masses by an appeal to the emotive principle of faith, whereby Bhakti came to be regarded as valid for salvation, like the paths of knowledge and rituals. In Punjab, Guru Nanak became the most prominent exemplar of the Bhakti movement. The socio-cultural environment of Punjab proved to be fertile ground for developing the ideological position of Guru Nanak: *ek onkar, nirankar, nirgune, nirbhey*. In other words, the entire universe is suffused with divine light; God alone is the bestower of life upon all living beings. Caste distinctions and social differentiations were antagonistic to this conviction. None should be regarded superior or rich on the basis of his birth or caste. The Shudras and the untouchables are placed at par with the Brahmins and Khatris. The women were placed at par with men and worthy of spiritual success.

NOTES

1. David N. Lorenzen, *Bhakti Religion in North India, Community Identity and Political Action*, New Delhi: Manohar, 1996, p. 3.
2. See Irfan Habib, *An Atlas of the Mughal Empire*, New Delhi: Oxford University Press, 1982, Map no. 4 A.
3. It is interesting to note that the boundaries of the present-day Indian Punjab are a little less than 15 per cent of the total geographical area of pre-Partition colonial Punjab. The boundaries have been redrawn a number of times over the last few centuries.
4. J.S. Grewal, 'The Historian's Punjab', in J.S. Grewal, *Miscellaneous Articles*, Amritsar: Guru Nanak University, 1974, pp. 1-10. It is a brief survey of the multiplicity of connotations that have been given to the term 'Punjab' from the Mughal times to the present day.
5. Chetan Singh, *Region and Empire, Panjab in the Seventeenth Century*, Delhi: Oxford University Press, 1991, p. 12.
6. D.P. Chattopadhyay, 'Introduction', in *The History of Science, Philosophy and Culture in Indian Civilization* (vol. VII, part 2), Delhi: Centre for Studies in Civilizations, 2009.
7. Anshu Malhotra and Farina Mir, ed., *Punjab Reconsidered: History, Culture and Practice*, New Delhi: Oxford University Press, 2012.
8. Chetan Singh, 'Polity, Economy and Society Under the Mughals', in Indu Banga, ed., *Five Punjabi Centuries*, New Delhi: Manohar, 1997, p. 43.
9. Muhammad Akbar, *The Punjab under the Mughals*, Delhi: Idarah-i-Adabiyat-i-Delli, rpt., 1974, p. 1.
10. L.M. Joshi, ed., *History and Culture of Punjab*, vol. I, Patiala: Punjabi University, 2000, p. 4.
11. Khushwant Singh, *A History of the Sikhs*, vol. I: *1469-1839*, Delhi: Oxford University Press, 1999, pp. 3-4.
12. Chetan Singh, op. cit., p. 25.
13. S.L. Duggal, *Agricultural Atlas of Punjab*, Ludhiana: Punjab Agricultural University, 1966, p. 38.
14. Chetan Singh, *Region and Empire: Panjab in the Seventeenth Century*, p. 17.
15. J.S. Grewal, Inaugural Address, *Proceedings of the Punjab History Conference*, Twenty Seventh Session, 28-30 March 1995, p. 5.
16. J.S. Grewal, 'The Historian's Punjab', p. 2.
17. Ibid., pp. 1-3.
18. S. Nurul Hasan, 'Medieval Punjab', in *Punjab Past and Present: Essays*

in Honour of Dr. Ganda Singh, ed. Harbans Singh and N. Gerald Barrier, Patiala: Punjabi University, 1976, pp. 73-80.
19. It is significant that in the course of the earliest studies conducted by the British administrators, the observation has generally been made that the cultural differences on ground of religion are of a comparatively minor nature. Cf. *Punjab District Gazetteers*, published in the years stated and for the following districts: Dera Ghazi Khan (1883-4), Ferozepur (1883-4), Gurdaspur (1884), Jalandhar (1884), Lahore (1883-4), Ludhiana (1888-9), Rawalpindi (1883-4), Kalsia (1904), Nabha (1904). Also see, S. Nurul Hasan, 'Medieval Punjab', p. 74.
20. B.D. Chattopadhyay, 'Geographical Perspectives, Culture Change and Linkages: Some Reflections on Early Punjab', *Proceedings of the Punjab History Conference*, 27th session, Patiala, 1995, p. 28.
21. Niharranjan Ray, *The Sikh Gurus and the Sikh Society*, New Delhi: Munshiram Manoharlal, rpt., 1975, p. 2.
22. J.S. Grewal, *The Sikhs of the Punjab*, New Delhi: Cambridge University Press, 1990, p. 9.
23. Ibid.
24. Zahir-ud-din Muhammad Babur, *Baburnama*, vol. II, Eng. tr. A.S. Beveridge, New Delhi: Munshiram Manoharlal, rpt., 1970, p. 380.
25. R.P. Tripathi, *Rise and Fall of the Mughal Empire*, Allahabad: Central Book Depot, 1957, p. 76.
26. For a detailed discussion see L.F. Rushbrook Williams, *An Empire Builder of the Sixteenth Century*, London: Longmans, Green & Company, 1918; Bakhshish Singh Nijjar, *Punjab Under the Sultans AD 1000-1526*, Delhi: Sterling Publishers, 1968; Muni Lal, *Babur, Life and Times*, Delhi: Vikas Publishing House, 1977.
27. Zahir-ud-din Muhammad Babur, *Baburnama*, pp. 167, 178.
28. Ibid., pp. 380-2.
29. Ibid., p. 10.
30. W.H. McLeod, *Guru Nanak and the Sikh Religion*, Delhi: Oxford University Press, 1996, p. 15. Also see *The Evolution of the Sikh Community: Five Essays*, New Delhi: Oxford University Press, rpt., 1996.
31. J.S. Grewal, *Guru Nanak in History*, Chandigarh: Punjab University, rpt., 1979, p. 27. Also see *The Sikhs of the Punjab*, Cambridge: Cambridge University Press, 1990.
32. Indubhushan Banerjee, *Evolution of the Khalsa*, vol. I, Calcutta: A Mukherjee & Co, rpt., 1979, p. 9.

33. J.S. Grewal, *The Sikhs of the Punjab*, p. 28.
34. These verses occur in the compositions of Guru Nanak referred to as *Babur-bani* or 'the utterances concerning Babur'; G.S. Talib, *Sri Guru Granth Sahib*, Eng. tr., 4 vols., Patiala: Punjabi University, 1990 (hereafter referred to as *AG*), pp. 360, 417-18, 722-3, *Tilang*, pp. 3-5; 1, *Asa Ashtpadian*, 1, pp. 3-5; 1 *Asa, Ghar*, vi, p. 39. Also see Ganda Singh, 'History and Culture of Punjab through the Ages', in *History and Culture of Punjab*, ed. Mohinder Singh, Delhi: Atlantic Publishers and Distributors, 1988, pp. 1-24, J.S. Grewal, op. cit., p. 9.
35. *AG*, Raga Majha, M.1, pp. 145, 1288.
36. *AG*, 63.
37. *AG*, 350.
38. Sant Kirpal Singh, *Asa di Var Steek*, Amritsar: Singh Brothers, 2011, pp. 112-13. Also see Sahib Singh, *Asa di Var Steek*, Sahib Singh (available online).
39. *AG*, 1342.
40. *AG*, 142.
41. *AG*, 1288.
42. Khaliq Ahmad Nizami, 'India's Contact with the Outer World', in *Studies in Medieval Indian History and Culture*, Allahabad: Kitab Mahal, 1966, p. 11-12.
43. Khaliq Ahmad Nizami, ed., *Politics and Society during the Early Medieval Period: Collected Works of Professor Mohammad Habib*, vol. I, Aligarh: Centre of Advanced Study, Department of History and New Delhi: People's Publishing House, 1974, p. 152.
44. For detailed information see Savitri Chandra Sobha, *Medieval India and Hindi Bhakti Poetry: A Socio-Cultural Study*, Delhi: Har Anand Publications, 1996.
45. J.S. Grewal, *The Sikhs of the Punjab*, p. 27.
46. Ibid., p. 4.
47. Yahya Ahmad Sirhindi, *Tarikh-i-Mubarak Shahi*, Eng. tr. H.M. Elliot and John Dowson, entitled *History of Indian as Told by its Own Historians*, vol. IV, Allahabad: Kitab Mahal, rpt., n.d., p. 32.
48. *AG*, p. 145.
49. *Asa di Var Steek*, op. cit., pp. 105-6.
50. J.S. Grewal, *Guru Nanak in History*, p. 181, n. 72.
51. Ibid., p. 229. *AG*, Sri Rag, p. 53.
52. J.S. Grewal, *Guru Nanak in History*, p. 231, *AG*, Var Majh, pp. 140-1.

53. *AG*, Var Malar, p. 1286.
54. Edward C. Sachau, *Alberuni's India*, London: Kegan Paul, Trench, Trubner & Co., 1914, p. 100.
55. Ibid., p. 102.
56. Sujan Rai Bhandari, *Khulasat-ut-Tawarikh*, ed. M. Zafar Hasan, Delhi: J. & Sons Press, 1918, p. 95.
57. Kanwar Muhammad Ashraf, *Life and Conditions of the People of Hindustan, 1200-1550*, New Delhi: Munshiram Manoharlal, rpt., 1970, pp. 192-3.
58. Ishtiaq Husain Qureshi, *The Administration of the Sultanate of Delhi*, New Delhi: Oriental Books Reprint Corporation, rpt., 1971, p. 97.
59. Niharranjan Ray, op. cit., p. 4.
60. The professions of agriculture and trade have been noted among the Rajputs even before AD 1200. Vasudeva Upadhyay, *Socio-Religious Condition of North India*, Varanasi: Chaukhamba Sanskrit Series Office, 1964, p. 65.
61. Ibid., p. 50; for a detailed discussion on the social conditions, Kanwar Muhammad Ashraf, op. cit., pp. 108-9; also refer to S.M. Ikram, *Muslim Civilization in India*, ed. Anslie T. Embree, New York & London: Columbia University Press, 1965; Aziz Ahmed, *Studies in Islamic Culture in the Indian Environment*, Oxford: Oxford University Press, 1964.
62. Ganesh Das Vadera, *Char Bagh-i-Punjab*, ed. Kirpal Singh, Amritsar: Sikh History Research Department, Khalsa College, 1965, p. 240.
63. Ibid., p. 291.
64. Sujan Rai Bhandari, *Khulasat-ut-Tawarikh*, ed. M. Zafar Hasan, Delhi: G. and Sons, 1918, pp. 24-5.
65. Kanwar Muhammad Ashraf, op. cit., p. 175; Ishtiaq Husain Qureshi, op. cit., p. 193.
66. Romila Thapar, *The Penguin History of Early India*, New Delhi: Penguin Books, 2002, p. 253.
67. Irfan Habib, 'Jats of Punjab and Sind', in *Essays in Honour of Dr. Ganda Singh*, ed. Harbans Singh and N. Gerald Barrier, Patiala: Punjabi University, 1976, pp. 95-9.
68. Richard M. Eaton, 'The Political and Religious Authority of the Shrine of Baba Farid', in *Essays on Islam and Indian History*, New Delhi: Oxford University Press, 2000, pp. 203-24.
69. Kanwar Muhammad Ashraf, op. cit., p. 193.

70. Zahir-ud-din Muhammad Babur, *Baburnama*, pp. 427-8, Kanwar Muhammad Ashraf, op. cit., pp. 202-3.
71. Aziz Ahmad, op. cit., p. 73.
72. For the diversity among Muslims, see Murray Titus, *Islam in India and Pakistan*, Calcutta: YMCA Publishing House, 1959, pp. 87-115.
73. J.S. Grewal, *Guru Nanak in History*, p. 36.
74. Kanwar Muhammad Ashraf, op. cit., p. 170.
75. J.S. Grewal, op. cit., p. 32.
76. Ganesh Das Vadera, *Char Bagh-i-Punjab*, p. 279.
77. Abdul Qadir Badauni, *Muntakhab-ut-Tawarikh*, vol. III, Eng. tr. Wolseley Haig and B.P. Ambashthya, Patna: Academica Asiatica, 1973, pp. 28-39. It may be added here that Sayyid Bahawal Qadiri founded his hospice in the 1540s at a place later included in the district of Montgomery. Mufti Ghulam Sarwar, *Tarikh-i-Makhzan-i-Punjab*, Lucknow: Nawal Kishor Press, 1877, p. 238; both Shergarh and Hujre Shah Muqim were situated in the Bar region amidst the Dogar and Gujjar tribes. Ganesh Das Vadera, *Char Bagh-i Punjab*, p. 302.
78. For a detailed understanding of the process of conversion, with reference to the tribes of western Punjab such as Gakkhar, Jud, Janjuha, Gujjars, Jats, and Rajputs, see Zahir-ud-din Muhammad Babur, *Baburnama*, vol. I, pp. 380, 388, 441, Sujan Rai Bhandari, *Khulasat ut-Tawarikh*, pp. 293, 350; Ahsan Raza Khan, 'The Problem of the North Western Frontier of Hindustan in the First Quarter of the Sixteenth Century', *Proceedings of the India History Congress*, vol. 28, Mysore, 1966, pp. 152-3.
79. *Gazetteer of the Lahore District, 1883-4*, pp. 52-3.
80. J.S. Grewal, *Guru Nanak in History*, p. 52.
81. Abdul Qadir Badauni, *Muntakhab-ut-Tawarikh*, vol. III, p. 323-4.
82. Khwaja Nizamuddin Ahmad, *Tabaqat-i Akbari*, vol. II, Eng. tr. Brajendranath De, Calcutta: The Asiatic Society, rpt., 1996, pp. 686-99; Abdul Qadir Badauni, *Muntakhab-ut-Tawarikh*, vol. III, pp. 51-5; Abul Fazl, *Ain-i Akbari*, vol. I, Eng. tr. H. Blochmann and D.C. Phillot, Kolkata: The Asiatic Society, rpt., 2010, pp. 606-17.
83. J.S. Grewal, *Guru Nanak in History*, p. 42.
84. J.S. Grewal, *The Sikh Ideology, Institutions and Identity*, p. 195.
85. J.S. Grewal, op. cit., p. 14-15. For a detailed presentation of Islam in India based on contemporary evidence, Peter Hardy, 'Islam

in Medieval India', in *Sources of Indian Tradition*, ed. W.M. Theodore de Barry, New York: Columbia University Press, 1958, pp. 371-435.
86. Khaliq Ahmad Nizami, *Religion and Politics in India during the Thirteenth Century*, New Delhi: Oxford University Press, 2002, pp. 190-245.
87. Surinder Singh, *The Making of Medieval Panjab: Politics, Society and Culture, c.1000–c.1500*, New Delhi: Manohar, 2020, pp. 597-601.
88. J.S. Grewal, *Guru Nanak in History*, p. 62.
89. Fauja Singh, *History of the Punjab, (AD 1000-1526)*, vol. III, Patiala: Punjabi University, 1972, p. 294.
90. P.V. Kane, *History of Dharamshastras*, vol. V, part II, Poona: Bhandarkar Oriental Research Institute, 1962, p. 1921.
91. J.S. Grewal, *The Sikhs of the Punjab*, p. 23.
92. Niharranjan Ray, op. cit., p. 8.
93. J.S. Grewal, *The Sikhs of the Punjab*, p. 24.
94. *AG*, p. 15.
95. Ibid., pp. 56, 221, 355, 358, 413, 432, 470-2, 635, 1171, 1256, 1290.
96. Ibid., p. 21.
97. Ibid., pp. 662, 951.
98. Zahir-ud-din Muhammad Babur, *Baburnama*, p. 440.
99. J.S. Grewal, *Guru Nanak in History*, pp. 9-10.
100. Ibid., p. 9.

CHAPTER 2

Guru Nanak and *Bhakti Sants* on Women

> The traditional view, of women, which was voiced by Ravana, was that women had eight negative qualities – foolhardiness, falsehood, way wardness, lustfulness, cowardice, lack of discrimination, suspicion and cruelty.
> —Tulsi Das[1]

> It is in the context of Bhakti that the women's private and public religion intersected.... Popularity of Bhakti resulted in no small measure from its inclusion of such marginal groups as women and Sudras.... Being female was generally no bar to Bhakti.
> — Katherine K. Young[2]

The above quotations indicate the conventional view about women and the contribution of the Bhakti movement to the betterment of their position in society. It is generally believed that the Bhakti movement contributed immensely in empowering the worldview of the disempowered. The movement emphasized an egalitarian and humanitarian social structure, criticizing social evils such as the caste system and idol-worship, which had an implicit impact on gender relations.[3] Savitri Chandra Sobha, in her seminal work on medieval Indian Hindi Bhakti poetry, puts it succinctly when she says,

While women continued to be regarded as inferior to men, and dependent on them, the Bhakti movement tended to diminish the strong prejudice against women by those who emphasized *jnan* and

Guru Nanak and Bhakti Sants on Women

yoga-sadhana in various forms. The essential humanism of the Bhakti poets is very often credited with having raised the stature of women and giving them a more honoured position in society.[4]

Though the Bhakti *sant*s (saints) might differ in their nuanced presentation of a 'better' social order, women were, after all, accorded a subordinate and inferior status and were always expected to serve their 'lord', the husband, which was the only way for them to achieve salvation. It is in the backdrop of this framework that the present chapter has been conceived.

The opening section of this chapter briefly talks about the role of ideology and the relationship between religion and society. It also touches upon the condition of women so that the ideological formulations of the Bhakti *sant*s can be contextualized. The second section recapitulates the perceptions of important *nirgun* and *sagun sant*s on women. The third section discusses the nuances in the usage of the term *sant* and the connotations attached to its usage, specifically in context of the Punjab. It also deals with the question of whether it is appropriate to use the term *sant* for Kabir and Guru Nanak? The fourth section discusses the similarities and differences between Guru Nanak and Kabir and attempts to find an explanation for the difference in their ideological formulations.

SOCIAL BACKGROUND: A REALITY

No ideology can be properly understood without analytically locating it in its specific historical, sociocultural, economic and political context. One of the basic functions of the dominant religious traditions of any society is to articulate a social ideology intended to serve as a sort of psychological glue that helps preserve both harmony and privilege within the religious community and the society as a whole (including its subordinate classes).[5] Certainly, there is a complex interplay between religion and social change. While religious traditions have been important players in the transformation of societies, religion can also be understood as being

> among the foremost institutions which conserve society, encoding stabilizing worldviews and values and transmitting these from generation to generation. . . . Religion has been an instrument of liberation for women. But religion has just as often become an instrument of women's social oppression.[6]

The influence of Guru Nanak and Kabir becomes still more relevant in the light of Clifford Geertz's assertion that religion is experienced as 'a system of symbols which acts to establish powerful, pervasive, and long-lasting moods and motivations in men'.[7] Regarding the social process, it has been observed that many religious beliefs and practices are employed, not only to define a given community's identity, but also to provide a utopian vision for the future of the community, and the society of which it forms a part.[8] It is acknowledged that these religious beliefs and practices which are translated, or rather advocated, as the ideal social norm do constitute both the identity and the ideology of the community. It might be, at great variance, that the tenor and thrust of the message of these religious communities is 'liberating' for women or a further legitimization of the subversion of women. Yet, the close connection between religion and social discourse, and the overarching influence of religion is beyond doubt. In fact, one may further argue, as did Antonio Gramsci, that the ideology of the privileged classes – in this context, the religious protagonist – tends to have a 'hegemony' over that of the underprivileged, women of all castes and classes being a significant part of the underprivileged section.

A brief reference to the social inequalities of that period, especially with respect to women, helps to contextualize the perceptions of Guru Nanak, Kabir or, for that matter, other important religious figures of the medieval period. First and foremost, we have to remind ourselves that what we are saying about the general condition of women should be viewed as the overlapping of religious categories in the subcontinent and, to use Raj Kumari Shankar's term, the analysis becomes an even more complex task in case of 'fusion of traditions'.[9] For centuries, the status of women in India was systematically downgraded. Centuries ago, Manu, the Hindu lawgiver, went to the extent of declaring that the service of the husband by the woman is considered to be equal to the service of God. It has been further asserted,

> Though he be a destitute of virtue, or seeking pleasure elsewhere or devoid of good qualities, yet a husband must be constantly worshipped as God by the faithful wife. No sacrifice, no vows, no fast must be performed by women apart from for their husband's; if a wife obeys her husband, she will for that reason alone be exalted in heaven.[10]

According to K.M. Ashraf and A.B. Pandey, a woman in medieval Indian society was regarded as inferior to a man; her position, at any rate, was subordinate to his. In sharp contrast, in the eleventh century, Alberuni noticed what he regarded as a strange custom – Indians consulted their women on all matters of importance. The practice of polygamy and child marriage, according to Vasudeva Upadhyaya, was prevalent in India before AD 1200. *Sati* in the early centuries, according to Romila Thapar, was synonymous with 'virtuous woman'. Alberuni also states that he was familiar with the practice of *sati*. The widow, who refused to become *sati* was ill-treated as long as she lived. Old women and mothers were not expected to become *sati*. More attention was given to the male child than to the female child. With reference to *sati*, Amir Khusrau expressed great appreciation for the supreme sacrifice of the Indian woman for her husband. Ibn Battuta noticed an example of *sati* near Pakpattan and several other places, elsewhere in India. He recorded that the act was regarded as honourable and meritorious.

As scholars widely deliberated, the deterioration in the position of women was attributed to the caste system, economic oppression, denial of the right to property and inheritance, a false sense of impurity attached to menstruation and childbirth, and deliberate deprivation of education. A woman was never fit for independence in any stage of life. This was justified by religious sanctions as cited earlier. According to another quote,

> By a girl, by a young woman, or even by an aged one, nothing, must be done independently, even in her own house. In childhood a female must be subject to her father, in youth to her husband, when her lord (husband) is dead to her sons; a woman must never be independent. She must not seek to separate herself from her father, husband, or sons; by leaving them she would make both her own and her husband's families contemptible.[11]

Marriage is one of the most important social institutions in all communities. Perhaps in ancient times, when the institution of marriage was consolidating, women were married only when mature (after puberty). Gradually, in the succeeding centuries, especially during the period under review, they were married before puberty. This was done to establish a more effective control over the sexuality of women.[12] Whereas once both daughters and sons were viewed as important, even though there was some preference for sons on account of patrilineal/patrilocal social organizations, now sons were not only highly preferred (a man could attain heaven only if his son performed his cremation), but daughters came to be viewed as major liabilities. This occurred largely because marriage in elite circles was the gift of a daughter (*kanyadan*) accompanied by dowry. The fact that brides accompanied by gifts were transferred to their husbands meant that they were a poor investment.[13]

The segregation of sexes became more severe after the twelfth century, especially in the areas of the subcontinent that were under Muslim rule. Hindu women, already carefully controlled by, or segregated from men, imitated the practice of *purdah* (veil) by Muslim women. The consequence was that many upper-caste Hindu women, already bound to the home, were further restricted so that they rarely left their residence.[14] In the late fifteenth century, when Guru Nanak started preaching his message, both Hindus and Muslims considered women to be inferior to men, an impediment in the way of spiritual progress and the cause of man's moral degradation. Polygamy was common, at least in some sections of society. Widows were denied remarriage and social recognition. *Sati* was practised, though it was not widespread as a general practice. Child marriage and female infanticide were widespread. Women were economically, socially, and psychologically dependent on men.

In sum, during the late fifteenth and early sixteenth century, the social situation in Punjab in particular, and northern India in general, was marked by the continuous process of change due to circumstances brought about by the Turko-Afghan rule in the sphere of politics and administration. Significant changes were noticed in the urban and rural economy, besides the sociocultural life with extensive impact on the social milieu. The continuities, however, remained as important as the changes. Sensitive individuals responded to the changed situation according to their intellectual inclinations and moral fervour. Their social background and context were equally relevant to the nature and character of their response. Social change was accompanied by social tension of various kinds. These tensions were probably the strongest in the Punjab.[15] This might explain, at least partly, the distinctive response of Guru Nanak to the social situation in which he lived and moved. Niharranjan Ray also credits Guru Nanak for achieving the tedious task of giving the adherents a system of ideas, images, and symbols and a set of discipline, all in precise and clear terms and in a coherent and consistent manner. His social purpose was clear, and he worked out that purpose efficiently and well.[16] Ray further elaborates that neither the leaders of the Bhakti movement nor of the Nath Panth and the Sant tradition attempted to do what Guru Nanak did, not in any systematic manner at any rate.[17]

*BHAKTI SANT*S ON WOMEN

While discussing a comparative trajectory between the perceptions of Guru Nanak and Kabir on women, we will view their perceptions in the larger framework of a major societal development known as the Bhakti movement (800-1700).

'Bhakti' in Sanskrit is to serve, honour, revere, love and adore. In the religious idiom, it is defined as 'that particular affection which is generated by the knowledge of the attributes of the Adorable One'. What was common to various regional articulations of this phenomenon was the idea of devotion to a personal God, so that it became an emancipation from the cycle of death and rebirth. The Bhakti movement spawned into several different offshoots all across north and south India. In north India, this movement is not differentiable from the Sufi movement of Chishti fame. Within the Hindu framework, a further distinction is made between *nirgun* and *sagun bhakti*, and also between Vaishnava *bhakti* and the *sant* tradition. Today, it is possible to see a greater affinity between the articulation known as the *sant* tradition on the one hand and Vaishnava *bhakti* on the other. The attributes of the Sant tradition will be discussed later, but it must be mentioned here that within the *sant* tradition too, it is possible to notice important differences. It is in this context that a comparative analysis of the perceptions of Guru Nanak with those of Kabir acquires added importance. Although they share much of the vehement opposition to the caste system, idol-worship, and other social evils, yet, they differ, quite apparently and significantly, in their attitude towards women.

Before drawing a comparative trajectory between Guru Nanak and Kabir, it would be appropriate to briefly discuss the perceptions of other Bhakti *sant*s on women as it forms the sociocultural background of their ideological formulations.[18] First and foremost, we have to remember that these *sant*s were neither social revolutionaries nor even consistent social reformers. However, their writings do, to some extent, reflect the sentiments of the common people. The Bhakti poets as a whole tried to identify themselves with the sufferings of the common man. Further, their voice of dissent and protest was not confined to the religious domain, but it extended to the existing social, economic and political spheres, and to the cultural ideas and institutions as well. In this way, they continued and even broadened the traditions of dissent and protest against the prevailing ideas and institutions. This had been a persistent feature of Indian thought and culture and it repeatedly manifested itself even when traditionalist ideas and beliefs appeared to dominate the scene.

As has been pointed out above, the political, sociocultural, and economic realities of the time played a crucial role in the formulation, modification, and manifestation of the ideology of an individual. The life and works of Kabir are generally aligned to the fifteenth century. During that period, Kashi, Jaunpur and the larger eastern part of Uttar Pradesh were active not only in the field of traditional sciences but also in the liberal school of Sufism and Bhakti. In brief, Kashi and Jaunpur were the axis around which a new cultural tradition of liberalism, dissent, and protest against the existing system was being developed. The life and social philosophy of Kabir must be seen against this background. Looking at the society of his times, Kabir found it to be overflowing with strife, sorrow, poverty, ignorance, avarice, and hypocrisy.[19]

Kabir classified women into two broad categories – first, those who were devoted to their husbands and were prepared to sacrifice everything, even their lives for the welfare of their husbands, and, second, the prostitutes. Kabir did not consider that a wife and family were obstacles in the path of self-knowledge. He constantly used the imagery of love between husband and wife as the relationship that should subsist between the individual soul (*atma*) and God (*parmatma*).[20] Kabir contrasts the devoted wife with the prostitute who sells her wares at the marketplace and tries to entice the innocent and unwary. Even the sight of such women was dangerous, let alone their touch.[21] Kabir expressed his sentiments in strong words, meaning that an attraction for gold and woman both lead to extinguishment (*ek kanak aur kamini, dou agni ki jhal, dekhe hi tan prajale, parsyeh vepaimaal*). Kabir warns against running after other people's wives. He says that love for someone else's wife was like eating garlic; adultery was like theft, which was found to lead to a miserable end ultimately. Kabir considered lust to be a major factor behind the troubles and sorrows in society and, thus, an obstacle in the path of the true devotee. He sadly concluded that there were few true devotees and that the bulk of men fell prey to temptations of various kinds. Of these, sexual urge (*kama*) was the most powerful from which few, not even the Bairagis, who had forsaken household ties, could escape.[22] While making the woman a symbol of sex, and, calling her sinful (*papini*), a destroyer (*dakini*) or enticer (*mohini*), Kabir upheld family ties. He was strongly opposed to the idea that a devotee should break his family ties and live in a jungle, like a recluse. He showed, by his own example that a true devotee was one who fulfilled his duty to his chosen profession and to his family. However, such a person should not be misguided by illusion (*maya*) or afflicted by the senses.[23] To bring forth the thrust of his perceptions about women, it would not be out of place to cite:

naari sawal purushhi khaii, taitee rahii akela.[24]

Kabir also adds:

Naari kund narak kaa, jooru joothen jagat kii.[25]

Kabir does not condemn child marriage or advocate widow-remarriage. Nor does he denounce polygamy by the upper classes. He speaks of the practice of purdah by women as a normal feature.[26] He even refers to the practice of *sati* in laudatory terms,[27] possibly because he considers it symbolic of the human soul (*atma*) annihilating itself for the sake of union with the Supreme. His entire perception reflects that he viewed women in a negative and derogatory fervour. With his narrow outlook about womenfolk, he was not even expected to speak against the social evils that afflicted the lives of the women.

Malik Muhammad Jaisi is considered one of the greatest Sufi poets. Though he was not a contemporary of Guru Nanak and Kabir, the reason for including him in this discussion is his attitude towards women. He does not place the entire onus of sex–lust on women and, thus, comes very close to a rationalist and logical stand. Though he does not criticize the caste system or social inequality, Jaisi's portrait of women's position is based on traditional ideas and beliefs, modified to some extent by the Sufi concepts, which had been established in the country by the time of his writings, that is the early part of the sixteenth century. In his most reputed work, *Padmavat*,[28] he divides women on the basis of caste and professions. He upholds the idea that a woman should be completely loyal to her husband. He, very effectively, brings out the acute insecurity of the upper-class women, who had to reconcile themselves to the ruler having a large number of wives and mistresses. The poet concludes, 'There is no difference between a rani and a servant, what matters is the master's favour.'[29] Unlike Kabir, Jaisi does not identify lust (*kama*) exclusively with women or denounce women as eternal temptresses. For Jaisi, lust is associated with youth, which afflicts both men and women. Youth, according to Jaisi, leads both to the pangs of separation and the pleasures of union. Despite this, he does say that women who control their sexual urges protect the family honour.[30] Likewise, the man, who can control this fire (desire) is praised.[31] While the sexual urge has to be kept under control, Jaisi does not distrust this urge as such. Human love is compared to divine love. Unlike Kabir, Jaisi does not condemn public women. They were a fact of life and displayed their wares and enticed men for money.[32]

When we talk about Dadu Dayal, the poet-*sant* from Gujarat, in relation to other Bhakti *sant*s, particularly Kabir, we have to remind ourselves that the differences in their perception of the social reality may perhaps be explained by the different situations in which the two were placed. Kabir's period was one of social unrest, while Dadu's period was one of growing stability and political unification under the aegis of Mughal emperor, Akbar. Dadu was not opposed to the caste system. He puts forward the view that caste is not based on birth, but on the deeds and noble ideas of individuals.[33] Unlike most *sant*s of the time, Dadu emphasizes that men and women are equal.[34] However, he shares with Kabir his many prejudices against women, as he upholds and reaffirms her dependent role in society. Thus, service to the husband is upheld as an essential part of her duty.[35]

Pativrata greh aapan kare khasam ki sev,
Jyoo raakhe tyohi rehe aghayakaari tev.[36]

As a symbol of both the phenomenal world (*maya*) and sexual urge (*kama*), a woman is considered a deadly danger not only to the sant, but to all those who sought unity with God.[37] In *Dadu Dayal ki Bani*, the poet says:

Naari varni purush ki, purisha vari naari.
Atti kaali tuunu muua, kathu naa aaya haath.[38]

Dadu advocates those sants should rise above illusion (*maya*) in order to overcome the sense of duality.[39] To fight the illusion of duality, it was necessary to conquer the sensibilities, above all, the sexual urge. Hence, the sant is advised to shun contact with women in every possible way. Both women and gold, that is, worldly possessions, are equally bad. A woman is considered the natural enemy of a man, just as a man was the natural enemy of a woman.[40] Dadu, in making these extreme remarks, made a distinction between women representing illusion (*maya*) and women in society who are divided into two categories – the unchaste women and the devoted wife who sustained the householder and is upheld as an ideal.[41] *Dadu Dayal ki Bani* contains as many as eighty verses where a true *sant* is compared with the wife who burns herself on the funeral pyre of her dead husband. However, this should not be viewed as a direct valorization of *sati*, as Dadu advocates those women should burn themselves (read sacrifice) in the service of Lord Rama, who is the real husband. Yet, this needs to be perceived in a larger context where service and loyalty to the husband is a social norm. In practice, however, the negative attitude about women as a symbol of sex was bound to get manifested in social dealings on a daily basis. It is also reflected in some of the prevailing prejudices against women.

To sum up, the three leading Bhakti poets – Kabir, Dadu, and Jaisi – have a more or less similar opinion about the dependent position of a woman and her obligation to serve her husband loyally and faithfully without questioning. However, there were differences in their perceptions regarding the position accorded to women in the religious and social fields. For Kabir, women were the eternal temptress, a representative of lust (*kama*), and a devotee was advised to keep away from her as far as possible. Jaisi, however, does not associate women alone with sexual urge, but blames it on youth, which needs to be kept under control by both men and women, especially by women, for the sake of the family. For Dadu, a woman is a distraction because of her lust (*kama*). He does not give any option to women except domestic servitude. Now, we would consider the perceptions of *sagun bhakti* sants on women. The two most important of them, Surdas and Tulsidas, were male. The third, Mirabai, was a woman.

Surdas lived during a period of rapid change. The fall of the Afghans and the rise of Mughal power culminated in the establishment of a stable empire under Akbar. The close connection between the political milieu and social change has already been highlighted in the context where variables, such as one's religious orientation, class, caste, and socio-economic-cultural backgrounds, play a pivotal role in the 'making' of an individual. The ongoing political situation does alter the equation of patriarchy. Surdas does not present a picture of the society as a whole, or the nature of relationship, actual or ideal, between the different constituents of society. Thus, he neither philosophizes on the nature of the caste system nor offers his observation on its working. However, Surdas does give a detailed description of rural society in the context of Braj – description of *gopi*s, their attire, daily schedules, level of freedom – shedding significant light on the actual position of women. His writings also reflect some values and prejudices of the society which is well represented by one of his often quoted sayings:

Bhamini aur bhujangini kari, inke vish hi darayo.
Rach aaho virchay sukh naahi, bhulit kabhhu paryaaye,
Inke vas man parey manohar, bahut jatan kari paaye,
Kaam ihoyi kaam aatur, tiihi kaise kee samujhaia![42]

At the same time, it should be noted that Surdas' attitude towards sex and carnal love was not based on distrust and suspicion. For him, a woman was neither a sex object nor a symbol of lust. Although she had human frailties, she was essentially the symbol of gentleness, love, devotion and compassion. Surdas was thus a non-conformist humanist. Even the stupid and cruel Ahirs,[43] nay, the entire mankind, could be won over by love, devotion, and compassion.

Tulsidas (d. 1623) lived in an age in which society and politics had acquired a certain degree of stability, after a long period of flux and uncertainty. He adopts a dual approach to society. On the one hand, he classifies society on the basis of the essential qualities of individuals, and on the other, he appears to conform to the traditional concept of *varnashram*. He divides society into three categories – *uttam*, *madhyam*, and *adham* (or *neech*). In his attitude towards women, Tulsidas combined at least two elements. On the one hand, he was influenced by the traditional views about women and, on the other, his views on the nature of the society and his overriding concerns for social stability considerably affected his attitude towards women. In his eyes, the majority of human beings consisted of the mean (*adham*) and wicked (*khal*), and needed to be controlled by social, religious, and political means, which implied that the large majority of the women fell into the same category. Tulsidas divides women into two broad categories – the women of high qualities (*uttam*), and the women of low quality (*neech*). He implies that it is the latter who ought to be kept under tight control. Expressing the prejudices of the upper class of the period, Tulsi includes villagers in this category and likens all of them to animals which need chastisement:

Dhol gawar shudra pashu naari, teeno tharan ke adhikari.[44]

Elsewhere, Tulsidas says that wherever women were made independent, they became wayward and broke boundaries, just like a water channel in flood.[45] In a different context, however, he says that although one might keep them in one's heart, but according to the legal texts (*shastra*s) a young woman and a ruler could not be kept under control.

Raakhiye naari jadpee urr maahi, jubti saastra nripati bas naahi.[46]

There has been an attempt to steer Tulsidas clear of 'popular misconception', to borrow Savitri Chandra's phrase,[47] that he was a strong critic of women and that he implied that only women need to be kept under tight control or discipline. It has been pointed out that for him, the dominant social concept was propriety (*maryada*), implying that the social and religious norms should not be transgressed. The observance of propriety was incumbent on men and women alike. Since the roles of men and women in society were not the same, their norms of behaviour and conduct also had to be different. Tulsidas draws up a series of ideal prototypes of women. They were devoted to their husbands and their prime role should have been the act of safeguarding and protecting the honour of their family. Their best roles were those of wife, mother, sister and daughter. The role of the wife was placed on a still higher pedestal and a woman's *dharma* was to serve her husband with absolute dedication of body and soul. Of women as a class, Tulsidas offers no positive 'impressions', because she desires every handsome man whether he be her brother, father, or son. A woman's sexuality was the greatest hindrance to a man's liberation. She represented the most dangerous form of illusion (*maya*). To him, the way to salvation for women was open only through marriage and devotion to Rama as householders.[48] They were to be honoured, as such women were endowed with *niti* and *vivek* which could be crucial in some situations.[49]

Mirabai, an important *sagun* poet, was a devotee of Lord Krishna.[50] This devotional fervour not only led to the production of poetry of a highly emotive, lyrical, and sensual nature, it also challenged many existing social values and traditions. There are a number of aspects in Mirabai's life and writings which help us understand the dichotomy in contemporary attitudes in relation to women. First, although

Mirabai was a widow, she was by no means mistreated in the Rana's house before she came into conflict with him about her devotion to Krishna and her association with *sadhu*s and *sant*s. Second, although Mirabai left the Rana's household as a mark of protest, she did not advocate a similar path, that is, renunciation of worldly duties for women devotees, married, or otherwise. While Mirabai herself acted as a rebel, her basic attitude towards women's role in society was traditional. It shows how tradition impinged on women's roles and behaviour patterns in family and society. Yet Mirabai represents a voice of protest against it and suggests that these values need to be modified or applied in a more humane and liberal manner. Thus, there is a dichotomy between Mirabai's behaviour pattern and the ideas and values which she upheld. Though her basic attitude towards women's role in society was conventional, she represented a voice of protest.[51]

Our discussion would be incomplete without a reference to Chaitanya's Bhakti movement in Bengal. The cardinal message is that Hari has mercifully descended as Chaitanya to protect humankind from evil, especially women, Shudras, and sinners. Much stress was laid in Bengal Vaishnavism on sweetness, humility and loving service by males as well as females. In the theology of the movement, all humans were ultimately females in relation to God. The prominence of Radha as Krishna's loving consort could further reinforce the value of being female. However, it is not very appropriate to equate religious poetic symbolism with the existing empirical social situations. In the sixteenth century, both the offering of hospitality and alms within the community and the enhancing of personal esteem of the women devotees could become points of departure for more radical efforts at altering economic and social structures. However, there is no evidence of any radical departure in Chaitanya's movement.[52] In sum, it can be safely deduced that the protagonists of *bhakti* were more liberal in their perceptions of women vis-à-vis the religious sphere, albeit with many caveats, than the social sphere. The patriarchal family was generally accepted as the norm and the urge to serve her 'lord', the husband, was the prime goal of a woman's life. Many protagonists of *bhakti* advocated her unflinching loyalty and service to her husband, in varying degrees, as the only gateway to a woman's salvation.

The above discussion on the perceptions of the important *bhakti sant*s about women gives us a foundation to focus on a comparative analysis of Guru Nanak's and Kabir's attitudes towards women. Here it would also be relevant to discuss the nuances in the usage of the term *sant*, and whether both Kabir and Guru Nanak could be categorized as *sant*s in the eyes of modern scholarship.

USAGE OF THE TERM *SANT* AND GURU NANAK: HISTORIOGRAPHICAL UNDERSTANDING

While it is customary to discuss the Bhakti movement from an overall perspective, stressing its underlying unity and the role of the saint-poets as spokespersons of the ongoing religious and cultural formulation, one is tempted to conceive it as a cluster of individual Bhakti groups, each with its particular emphasis.[53] Moreover, most modern academic studies on the lives of Hindu *sant*s have not attempted to make a systematic comparison between the lives and ideological formulations of the different *sant*s.

The term *sant* itself ignites a lively debate as it has several overlapping usages. Derived from the Sanskrit word *sat* (truth, reality), its root meaning is 'one who knows the truth' or 'one who has experienced ultimate reality', that is a person who has achieved a state of spiritual enlightenment or mystical self-realization. By extension, it is also used to refer to all those who sincerely seek enlightenment. Thus, conceptually as well as etymologically, it differs considerably from the cognate 'saint' – which has also taken on the more general ethical meaning of a 'good person' whose life is a spiritual and moral exemplar.[54] What binds the north Indian *sant*s together is neither a historical connection nor an institutional focus, but the similarity in their teachings. It is worth reiterating that the *sant*s expressed their beliefs and opinions, sort of a social commentary, in the language and idiom of the common masses, as evident in the case of Namdev, Ravidas and Kabir, who themselves belonged to the lower echelons of the caste hierarchy.

An examination of the early Punjabi usage of the term *sant* will inevitably carry us back to the works of Guru Nanak. The Guru is conventionally ranked as a distinguished representative of the saintly tradition (*sant parampara*) of northern India.[55] In so doing, we immediately encounter the first hint that the Punjabi usage of the term *sant* may perhaps bear connotations distinguishing it from the meaning attached to it elsewhere in north India. Although Guru Nanak may be acknowledged as a representative of the *sant parampara*, he will never be called 'Sant Nanak'. W.H. McLeod equates Kabir and Guru Nanak because both offer a synthesis. However, in each case, the nature of the synthesis reflects the personality of the author.[56]

McLeod placed Guru Nanak squarely in the *sant* tradition as a synthesis of elements drawn from Vaishnava *bhakti* and the *hatha-yoga* of Nathyogis, with a marginal contribution from Sufism. Among the *sant*s, McLeod mentions Namdev, Ravidas and Kabir. For him, the pattern evolved by Guru Nanak is 'a reworking of the "*sant* synthesis"'; it does not depart far from the *sant* sources 'as far as its fundamental components are concerned'.[57] Guru Nanak uses *sant* categories and *sant* terminology and affirms *sant* doctrines. However, Guru Nanak amplified, clarified, and integrated the *sant* synthesis in considerable measure, particularly through his concepts of *shabad*, *nam*, *guru* and *hukam*. What we find in his works is an 'expanded' and 're-interpreted' *sant* thought. Within the pattern of *Sant* belief, Guru Nanak's synthesis possesses 'a significant originality' and 'a unique clarity', as well as the quality of survival.[58]

Grewal has summed up the position of McLeod, for further elaboration.[59] McLeod has been criticized for his hypothesis about Guru Nanak's relationship with the *sant* tradition.

However, he has not discarded his hypothesis, arguing that, whereas for a believer it may be natural to believe his religion is a revealed religion, it is legitimate for a historian 'to explore the surrounding religious landscape and the society in which a particular religion was born'.[60] In his article 'Sant in Sikh Usage', McLeod states that along with the transformation of the Sikh Panth, there was a considerable shift in the popular understanding of piety. Changes in notions of piety are naturally accompanied by corresponding changes in the meanings of associated terminology and the term *sant* has thus travelled a considerable distance since the days of Guru Nanak. McLeod underlines the 'unqualified emphases of the *sant*s on the interior nature of spiritual understanding' and the 'the discipline' required for *moksh* as 'an eternal equipoise'. The ideas of incarnation, idol-worship, sacred scriptures, and pilgrimages are discarded in favour of the world.[61] The essence of *sant* belief remains loving devotion to a personal deity.[62] McLeod examines the teachings of Guru Nanak and comes to the conclusion, 'In Guru Nanak, as in Kabir, there is the same rejection of exterior forms, the same insistence on the need for inward devotion and its sufficiency as the sole means of Liberation.'[63]

Furthermore, the question of whether or not Guru Nanak was a *sant* is strictly a question of antecedents and influences. As Grewal rightly points out, there is much that is 'profoundly original' in Guru Nanak's verses and there is an integrated and coherent system no other *sant* has produced, there is a clarity no other *sant* has matched. Add to this the appointment of a successor by Guru Nanak, 'Nothing in the *sant* experience can remotely compare to the Panth which was eventually to emerge from that decision of Guru Nanak.'[64]

Grewal further states that McLeod dwells on shared terminology and categories of thought and tends to think in terms of influences and borrowings, but his approach leaves out the creative response of both Kabir and Guru Nanak to their historical situation.[65] Moreover, McLeod does not take into account what Kabir and Guru Nanak did, quite apart from what they said. McLeod himself says that Guru Nanak's concepts of *shabad* and *guru*, as much as the concept of *hukam* and *nam*, carry us beyond anything that the works of earlier *sant*s offer in any explicit form.[66] Grewal concludes that only the entire range of ideas can enable us to see the differences as well as similarities between Kabir and Guru Nanak.[67] The result is a new synthesis, one which is cast within the pattern of *sant* beliefs but which nevertheless possesses significant originality and, in contrast with its *sant* background, a unique clarity. Moreover, it possesses the quality of survival, for it remains today the substance of a living faith.[68]

In his relatively recent work, McLeod reiterates that while being the founder of the Sikh Panth, Guru Nanak's position is intact within the *sant* tradition. He states,

If, however, the question implies a lack of originality on the part of Nanak, the answer must be emphatic negative. Plainly there is much that is profoundly original in hymns which we find recorded under his distinctive symbol in the *Adi Granth*. There is in them an integrated and coherent system which no other *sant* has produced; there is a clarity that no other *sant* has equalled; and there is a beauty which no other *sant* has matched. There is, moreover, the question of permanence. The fact that Nanak appointed a successor to follow him is scarcely unique, but nothing in the *sant* experience can compare to the Panth which was eventually to emerge from that decision.[69]

Thus, McLeod does not seem to have altered his position, but in a profound manner reiterated his perspective. He concludes, on the basis of his nuanced study of the *sakhi*s, that Guru Nanak gave a 'practical expression to his own ideals' during the last three decades of his life. Highlighting the aspects of *satsang* and *kirtan*, McLeod emphasizes the act of balancing the endeavours of piety and regular everyday affairs of human life. In Grewal's words, 'At best it is a piety devoid of superstition and a practical activity compounded with determination and an immense generosity.'[70] This kind of balanced view of the everyday affairs of the common man and the religious arena was in sharp contradiction to the theories and practices of Nathyogis. The growing popularity of Guru Nanak must have had a formidable adverse impact on their popularity in the Punjab. McLeod also writes,

If we place Guru Nanak within his own historical context, if we compare his teachings with those of other contemporary or earlier religious figures, we shall at once see that he stands firmly within a well-defined tradition. What Guru Nanak offers us is the clearest and most highly articulated expression of the *nirguna sampradaya*, the so-called *sant* tradition of northern India.[71]

There have been a few scholars whose works are essential to understand if Guru Nanak owed his ideological crystallization only to the *sant* tradition, primarily to Kabir, and if he had an unprecedented originality in his messages. Gurdev Singh views Guru Nanak's messages as revelatory, emphasizing the amazing universality of his message and the originality of his thought. Singh points out the elements of egalitarian social order in Guru Nanak's injunctions about social relations.[72] Daljeet Singh concludes that far from being connected, Sikhism was in 'complete contrast' to Nathism and Vaishnavism in their 'fundamental ideologies, goals, methodologies and world views'. He also argues that McLeod's views about Sikhism, Nathism and Vaishnavism are 'not only without basis, but also betray an ignorance of the history and the essentials of the three systems'.[73] He views McLeod as placing Guru Nanak within the *sant* tradition and projecting that his teachings were a synthesis of the elements of Vaishnava *bhakti*, *hath-yoga*, and Sufism. He is not able to appreciate the 'originality', the rationality, and the social relevance of Guru Nanak's teachings. Daljeet Singh views McLeod as being of the opinion, by implication, that Guru Nanak should not be regarded as the 'founder' of Sikhism.

COMPARATIVE TRAJECTORY BETWEEN KABIR AND GURU NANAK

In recent scholarship, Guru Nanak's affinity with *nirgun bhakti* or the *sant* tradition is underlined, while Kabir is regarded as the most important exponent of this tradition. To understand Guru Nanak's attitude towards women and gender, it would be useful to compare his theological underpinnings with those of Kabir.[74] At the same time, we have scholars like Nikky-Guninder Kaur Singh, the primary objective of whose study is to 'analyse the feminine dimensions in the Sikh vision of the Transcendent One in both sacred and secular literature'. She clarifies,

> My study, I hope will accomplish a second, albeit ancillary, objective – modern scholarship has posited Kabir, the medieval Indian devotional poet as a precursor of the Sikh faith, and many have averred that Guru Nanak was a follower of Kabir. . . . Do not such constructs – Kabir as master, Nanak as follower – undermine the divine revelation that Guru Nanak received independently. . . . The scriptures and the Sikh Gurus, my study claims, have a *raison d'être* all their own.[75]

However, Kabir's influence has spread throughout the northern part of India, his sayings so widespread that they are a part of proverbial lore and his name virtually a household name.

It is Kabir that all later traditions look back as the fountainhead of the *sant* movement.[76] Though he never intended to found a Panth, and there is no direct historical connection between him and later *sant*s, all of them consider him their spiritual ancestor. Kabir lived 150 years before Guru Nanak, the similarity of their teachings is striking, and as Karine Schomer points out, it is precisely this aspect as opposed to historical connection or institutional foci that closely bind Guru Nanak and Kabir. The latter's compositions figure prominently in the sacred scriptures of the Sikhs.[77] About Kabir's sayings being included in the *Adi Granth*, she states that 'the selection must have been made and made on the basis of conformity to the "moods and motivations" of the Sikh religious community at that particular stage in its development'.[78]

However, most significantly, there appears to be a major break in the similarities between Guru Nanak and Kabir with regard to their attitude towards women. It becomes imperative to compare the perceptions of Guru Nanak with Kabir on women and her social position. There are important differences in their perceptions, for instance, in their understanding and presentation of concepts such as *nam, shabad,* and *hukam*. Grewal puts it appropriately when he says,

> The works of Kabir and Guru Nanak present systems of interrelated ideas which are independent of all other systems of religious ideas. Their positions are similar not because they belong to the same tradition but because each had a new path to show to his contemporaries. The paths were new but not the same precisely because they were differently conceived from the very beginning.[79]

Elaborating further, Grewal states that, among other things, Kabir's ideology was less comprehensive than Guru Nanak's and it remained unrelated to institutionalization which, by contrast, was the fundamental concern of Guru Nanak.[80]

Kabir denounced much of the religious beliefs and practices of his times. The *mullah* and the *pandit*, the guardians of Muslim and the Hindu orthodoxy, were 'pots of the same clay'. The paths that they advocated only led astray. The Hindu and Muslim revelatory scriptures, the Vedas and the Quran, were discarded along with their custodians. Kabir does not believe in Vishnu. All his ten incarnations (*avatar*s), including Rama and Krishna, are part of the *maya* which is constantly subject to annihilation. In unambiguous and uncompromizing terms, Kabir denounced the worship of images in temples, pacificator bathing, ritual feasts, and pilgrimage to sacred places. His God, neither Hari nor Allah [but one may prefer to call him Hari or Allah] does not reside in the east or the west; He resides in the heart of man. This and some other ideas reveal an affinity with the Sufis. 'When I was, Hari was not; now Hari is, and I am no more.' What led to God was the 'path of love cutting as the edge of the sword'. Separation (*virah*) involves torment in which the lover bleeds silently in the depths of his soul. He suffers many deaths everyday. This torment is nevertheless a divine favour, a mark of God's grace. Love involves the sacrifice of self and, metaphorically, of life itself. Kabir's *bhakti* is an ardent quest in which he is completely involved at the peril of his life.

Kabir's familiarity with the tenets and practices of the *yogi*s is equally evident in his compositions. The ideas of *jivan-mukt* (liberated in life), *sahaj-samadhi* (the state of unison with the divinity) and *shabad* (the word) are given great prominence in his verses. Kabir uses the terminology of the *yogi*s to convey his message to them. Otherwise, their practices are ridiculed and their claim to be on the right path is treated as self-conceit. They too are in need of the name of Rama. Kabir denounces the Shaktas, who indulge in meat, liquor, and sexual intercourse as a religious ritual. Kabir does not approve of any existing religious system. He denounces caste distinctions. Occasionally, he refers to God as the 'true guide' (*satguru*). Kabir integrated ideas from three major sources into a system which came to possess the originality of a new whole.[81] His ineffable God is both immanent and transcendent, and to Him alone Kabir offers his love and devotion.

It is true that Kabir uses the terms such as *nam*, *shabad*, *guru*, and *hukam* in his compositions, but not with the kind of emphasis that we find in the compositions of Guru Nanak. For instance, the concept of *hukam*, as McLeod elaborated, asks, 'How is Truth to be attained, How the veil of falsehood torn asunder? Submit to the *hukam*; walk in its way. Nanak thus it is written.'[82] The idea of walking in the way of *hukam* to attain the Truth is nowhere to be found in Kabir as it is in Guru Nanak. McLeod writes,

The *hukam* is beyond describing. All forms were created by the *hukam*; life was created through the *hukam*; greatness is imparted in accordance with the *hukam*. Distinctions between what is exalted and what is lowly are the result of the *hukam* and in accordance with it suffering comes to some and joy to others. Through the *hukam* one receives blessings and another is condemned to everlasting transmigration. All are within the *hukam*; none are beyond its authority. Nanak, if anyone comprehends the *hukam*, his ego (*haumai*) is purged.

McLeod further states that the *hukam* is 'an all-embracing principle, the sum total of all divinely instituted laws; and it is a revelation of the nature of God'.[83] Indeed, Guru Nanak's use of the *hukam* carries his thought most obviously beyond the thought of Kabir.[84] Incidentally, Guru Nanak's emphasis on divine grace (*nadar*) also carries him beyond Kabir.[85]

Similarly, Guru Nanak's emphasis on the *nam*(name) is much more than Kabir's, and the concept is more comprehensive, as Grewal elaborated in his work *Guru Nanak in History*,

> Through the Name one can cross the ocean of existence. Through the Name one can obtain the secret of true worship and honour. The Name is one's best ornament, intellect, and objective. Through the Name one gets recognition from others; without the Name there can be no honour. All other wisdom is mere pretence; there is no fulfilment without the Name. Through the Name come true honour of greatness and the mark of God's merciful grace. The state of eternal bliss is found in the Name, the proper way of adoration. The Name is nectar that purges the poison (of *maya*). Through the Name descends all happiness upon one's heart.[86]

McLeod puts it in perspective when he writes, 'Whatever God has made is an expression of the Name. There is no part of creation which is not an expression of God.[87]

For Kabir, too, there is no emancipation without Rama-*nam*. However, we do not get the impression that for Kabir, the Name holds strictly the same significance as for Guru Nanak. Indeed, it has been suggested that the Name in Guru Nanak's compositions is the creative and dynamic immanence of God. McLeod puts it more convincingly when he says that Guru Nanak's concept of the *shabad* and *guru*, as much as the concept of *hukam* and the *nam*, carry us beyond anything that the works of earlier *sant*s offer in any explicit form.[88] This variation in emphasis determines the entire tenor of his teachings and their impact. However, there are some important differences between Guru Nanak and Kabir. Guru Nanak rejects both asceticism and renunciation. In Kabir's opinion, a householder should either practice dharma as a householder or adopt *bairag*; if a Bairagi adopts the life of a householder, it is a misfortune.[89] Kabir's tolerance of mendicancy and renunciation go together; the renunciant has to depend on others for subsistence. This is something that Guru Nanak ridiculed in his contest with the yogis. Guru Nanak has no objection to meat-eating, but Kabir is strongly in favour of non-violence (*ahimsa*).

In sum, Guru Nanak's comment on the contemporary social order, polity, religious beliefs, and the dominance of Brahmins, *mullah*s, and Sufi *shaikh*s is extremely comprehensive and profound. His social critique comes very close to modern and rational perceptions. He not only offers a criticism of the three contemporary religious traditions – the Brahmanical, ascetic, and Islamic – but also pays due attention to their different manifestations, like the Vaishnavas, Shaivas and the Shaktas. He also refers to different categories of ascetics, specifically the Jain monks, as well as from orthodox Islam and popular Sufism. He also advances a categorical viewpoint on the administration, government and contemporary political events, as evident in the *Babur-bani*, four hymns by Guru Nanak alluding to the invasions by Babur. We do not get any other outpourings, so profound and comprehensive, so rational and egalitarian, so practical yet so ethical, in the writings of any other *nirguni sant*. Only Guru Nanak had such a holistic vision, of a balanced, comprehensive view of worldly and religious lives.

Kabir's attitude towards women has already been discussed. It is apparent that his stance is ambivalent. He rejects the idea of impurity associated with the woman, who has given birth to a child. However, he does not contest the idea of a woman's subordination. Outside her home, she can probably become a recluse (*bairagan*), the counterpart of the male renunciant. On the whole, Kabir's compositions contain a set of ideas which appear to suggest a system outside the traditional Hindu and Muslim practices. For our present purpose, Kabir figures rather largely in Kumkum Sangari's comparative perspective on Mirabai.[90] The author seeks to place Mirabai in what is called 'the spiritual economy of Bhakti' and to relate her to both the *sagun* and *nirgun* articulations. Here, we may notice some of her basic propositions about Kabir.

In Kabir, the egalitarian concepts – regarding body, soul, knowledge, *maya*, creation, and a *nirgun* God – contest caste and sectarian differences in religious denomination and orthodox ritual, but not patriarchal value structures. The concept of an attributeless *nirgun* God allows Kabir to be a social reformer; however, the moment his God becomes *sagun*, he acquires male attributes. It is possible to enter into a relationship of love with a personal God, and Kabir dwells in all emotions related to love-longing, intoxication, pain of separation, delirium, and suffering. At the same time, he constructs a patriarchal typology of women for ascetic transcendence. The woman is an obstacle to salvation; her sexuality should be subjected to usual regulation. Kabir appears to postulate three sorts of femaleness: the *stri svabhav*, the *stri dharma*, and the 'higher femaleness' of *bhakti*. The three become interdependent; *strisvabhav* must be opposed both to *stri dharma* and the higher femaleness of *bhakti*. The first is to be totally subdued, while the commendable traits of the second are to be etherealized into spirituality for transmutation into the femaleness of *bhakti*.

Kabir works with two notions of *maya*. At one level, it is a pervasive cosmic illusion; it is everything that is false. Therefore, it is a levelling, democratizing, and egalitarian concept which can be used to attack caste, sectarian differences, and Brahmanical institutions. This *maya* is ungendered; it is neither male nor female. At another level, woman and *maya* become indistinguishable, if not virtually interchangeable. The idea is elaborated further; women are represented as impediments to male salvation. Woman is equated with *maya* and becomes the conceptual basis for differentiating between various kinds of woman. The woman of the *stri svabhav* becomes the mistress of the senses and the use of patriarchal metaphors evokes the typology of *dohagin*. By contrast, the *sohagin* is the model of *stri dharma*, a model in which sexual desires are well channelled. She is all fidelity, without the slightest trace of promiscuity. She surrenders her heart, body and mind to her husband; her *shringara* is to please him alone. In Kabir's perception, patriarchal values centre on the family as an institution which guarantees licit righteous progeny, restrains female sexuality, and reproduces a normative notion of marriage. Women and *maya* are identical obstacles to *bhakti* and salvation. So, Kabir advises:

> *Kabir naari parayi aapni, bhugtya nark hi jaai*
> *Aagi aagi sab ekhai, taame haath na baahi*[91]

Whether the woman is your wife or another, to have alliances with her is to go to hell. One fire is the same as another; do not put your hand in it all.[92]

> *Kabir naari kund narak ka, birla thaame baagi*[93]

Women are the pit of hell: few can stop themselves from falling.

Not only is woman the offscouring of the world; she separates the good from bad:

> *Kabira joru joothini jagat ki,*[94]

But,

> *Kabira naari nasai teeni such, jo nar paasai hoi*
> *Bhakti mukuti mil gyan mei, paisi na sakai koi*[95]

Falling in love with a woman is all evil; the man loses his access to *bhakti*, salvation, and knowledge.[96]

The *maya*, as women personified, is an obstacle to *bhakti* and thus must be defeated. Kabir poses an active opposition between sexual desire (*kam*) and spiritual desire (*prem*). Sangari finds in Kabir a sustained and complex adjustment with patriarchal values in uneasy companionship with an egalitarian *bhakti* which offers direct access to God and claims a single origin for all human beings. It describes the body, heart, soul and true knowledge as ungendered. Patriarchal values are not incidental to Kabir's *bhakti*; they actively compose it.

Focusing our discussion on Guru Nanak, Grewal aptly observes that the Guru's explicit statements leave no doubt about his goal of emancipation being open to women as much to men.[97] His God is both *nirgun* and *sagun* at the same time. In the state of attributelessness (*sunn mandal*), he is ungendered, that is neither male nor female. God has revealed himself in his creation, the *nirgun* becoming *sagun*, as the creation of vessels (*bhandey*) placed the same light (*jot*) in all of them like in every heart (*ghat*). It is His light, the same light that shines in all. He is the only giver (*data*) for all living beings. More explicitly, he created both 'man and woman'. His light is in both 'man and woman'. He has female as well as male devotees (*sevak*s). Thus, in the arena of life that was all-important to Guru Nanak, he upholds women's equality with men. At a more abstract level, Guru Nanak introduced the concept of *sangat* (holy congregation), where both men and women sit together and equally participate in reciting the praises of the Divine, and the *pangat* (sitting together), when irrespective of caste or social status differences, the congregation sits down to eat a common meal in the *langar* (common kitchen). Women were never excluded from any specific task (*seva*). Guru Nanak says,

Come my sisters and dear comrades! Clasp me in twine embrace. Meeting together, let us tell the tales of our Omnipotent Spouse (God). In the True Lord are all merits, in us all demerits.[98]

It is often repeated that Guru Nanak did not advocate asceticism and renunciation. It has been asserted that Guru Nanak's writings and those of the subsequent Gurus contain a range of views on women – positive, negative, and ambivalent – suggesting a tension between an inward psychological struggle and outward social decorum. According to an oft-quoted verse,[99]

We are born of woman, we are conceived in the woman's womb and we grow in it. We are engaged to women and we wed them. Through the women's cooperation, new generations are born. If one woman dies, we seek another, without women there can be no bond. Why call her bad who gives birth to rajas? The woman herself is born of the woman, and none comes into this world without women; Nanak, the True One (Lord) alone is independent of the woman.[100]

Scholars like Doris Jakobsh and Raj Kumari Shankar feel that this oft-quoted verse, supposedly indicative of Guru

Nanak's positive evaluation of womanhood, points to an appreciation of woman only vis-à-vis the procreative process. However, procreation, specifically of sons, was central to Nanak's vision of the ideal women.[101] Jakobsh draws a parallel between Guru Nanak's verse and the *Brihaspatisutras*, written in the fourth century CE. Jakobsh further writes,

While Guru Nanak's words have been lauded as the slogan of emancipation for women in the Sikh tradition, they had more to do with the rejection of prevailing notions of ritual purity and support of the social hierarchy of the time. For women gave birth to sons, especially those of noble birth; how then could they be considered ritually impure? The birthing of sons was the most elevated of aspirations; sons were avenues to fulfilment and the fervent wish of any woman during Indo-Islamic times. Thus, Guru Nanak's challenge, in referring to the contemporary hierarchical order, one which placed the rajahs at the top of that order also indicated his support of the dominant social and political order of his time.

However, it seems anachronistic to fathom Guru Nanak's perceptions against modern perceptions of gender equality. In times when a woman was considered inferior in all respects because of her sex, Guru Nanak openly chides those who attribute pollution to women because of menstruation and asserts that pollution lies in the heart and mind of the person and not in the cosmic process of birth. This declaration definitely requires women to be placed in esteem. Guru Nanak is clearly and emphatically on the woman's side when he relates to the pain of observing *sutak*[102] which is denounced in rather strong terms when he says:

If pollution attaches to birth, then pollution is everywhere [for birth is universal]. Cowdung [used for purifying the kitchen floor by Hindus] and firewood breed maggots. Not one grain of corn is without life. Water itself is a living substance, imparting life to all vegetations. How can we then believe in pollution inheres within staples? Says Nanak, pollution is not washed away by purificatory rituals. Pollution is removed by true knowledge alone.[103]

However, there is another dimension to God's creation. It is impermanent and 'false' in contrast with the 'truth' of God.

This intoxicating *maya* is poison (*bikh*)[104] and, because of his affiliation to *maya*, man remains attached to falsehood against truth and he remains chained to the cycle of death and birth.[105] Man and woman belong to the realm of falsehood, but there are things in this realm which keep them attached to it. There are several verses of Guru Nanak, wherein the objects of attachment are specified. They relate to political, economic, social, and moral aspects of life. For example,

There is pleasure in gold, pleasure in silver, pleasure in women, pleasure in scents, pleasure in horses, pleasure in the conjugal bed, pleasure in sweets, pleasure in flesh – there are so many pleasures of the body that there is no room in it for the Name.[106] Among the things which induce man to forget God are pearls, gems, diamonds, thrones, armies, political power, supernatural power, and beautiful women.[107] What has deceived the world is thirst for *maya*: sons, relations, house-wife, wealth and youth; avarice, greed and pride keep man attached to *maya* which serves as the herb with which the thugs make their victims unconscious.[108]

Elsewhere Guru Nanak brackets woman with 'sons, gold, horses and elephants as the objects of attachment'.[109] The more popular pair of folklore, gold, and woman, too finds mention.[110] At another place, the wife was mentioned with son, daughter, mother, and father. The five potent thugs are power (*raj*), riches (*maal*), beauty (*roop*), caste (*jat*), and youth (*joban*).

Thus, it becomes evident that Guru Nanak does not denounce women as a part of *maya* in the way Kabir has done. In the compositions of the Guru, a substantial number of metaphors relating to woman refer to conjugal relationships. In these metaphors, God is the true Husband and man, as his wife, seeks union with Him. Possibly, Guru Nanak's conception of a good wife (*suchaji*, *gunvanti*, or *sohagan*) or the bad wife (*kuchajji*, *nirgun*, *dohagan*, *rand*, or *pir-choddi*) can be inferred from these verses. The image of the ideal wife that emerges from these metaphors is not unconventional. Even if she is beautiful, accomplished, and well-connected, she is humble and modest before her lord. She is completely devoted to him and obeys his commands with pleasure. She pines for him in separation and adorns herself with ornaments only to please her lord. She is faithful to him and expects him to be faithful to her. In contrast, the life of a bad wife (*dohagun*) is pointless, because of her inclination towards the 'other'. For countless lives, such a woman suffers the misery of 'separation'. When a woman abandons deceit and falsehood, and she awakens to the *shabad*, she becomes acceptable to her lover-God. The abandoned woman is totally indifferent to the lover-God. She has the demerit of lust, anger, and pride. She remains deprived of the 'True Name'. Without the love of God, she remains chained to duality (*dubidha*) due to her attachment to *maya*, family and relations. The boon of the truth, the name, and the *shabad* is obtained only through God's grace.

The ultimate objective for woman, as for man, is *sahaj*, the state of eternal bliss in union with God and the mingling of light with light. Guru Nanak advocates the regulation of sex. However, this principle applies to both men and women. To covet the wife of another person, or an unwedded woman, is immoral in his system of values. This does not necessarily ensure monogamy, but the whole tone and tenor of Guru Nanak's compositions appear to be monogamous.

The use of female voice is often taken as a yardstick to fathom the perceptions of Guru Nanak, Kabir, and other sants about women. However, to use the female voice in the verses (*bani*) to gauge the respective *sant*'s attitude towards women is not only inappropriate but rather misleading. Scholars like Nikky-Guninder Kaur Singh have extensively relied on the use of female devotional voice in the *Adi Granth* as evidence to emphasize the 'principles' of femininity in the *Adi Granth*. She advocates the belief that the Gurus, though male, understood their words and message to be female, in congruence with the feminine *bani*.[111] Here, the question arises: is it appropriate to assume that the male Gurus intended, perceived and understood their poetic utterances to be feminine,[112] or whether their notation of sacred speech in the feminine gender is simply indicative of the surrounding religious milieu?[113] To leap from the grammatically feminine form of a word to an understanding of the Guru's inclusivity is perhaps more a reading into the term as opposed to the actual intent of the Gurus. Alternatively, it could be just adding variety by using a female voice to their sayings to break the monotony of didactic presentation. After all, women account for more or less half of the population. Thus, to derive the metaphors of a 'bad' or 'good' woman must have made the message more comprehensible and appealing to the common masses. We cannot ignore the fact that if we study Guru Nanak or Kabir or any other religious figure, then it clearly attests to their level of popularity, and this level of popularity could have been possible only if they would have touched the hearts of the masses, and their messages both in content and presentation would have appealed them. It is significant to note that Guru Nanak is seldom so immersed in femaleness as to lose his discrete identity for long. Possibly, for this reason, it is easier to paraphrase his metaphors in terms of the human soul than in some verses of Kabir.[114]

Guru Nanak's concern was not exclusively with men, as there are at least a few verses where the woman does figure prominently. One of these is the well-known *Babur-bani* verse in which the luxury of the women of the ruling class is incidentally depicted. They suffered punishment because they had forgotten God due to their indulgence in the luxuries of this world, including the enjoyment of their conjugal bed.[115] They are the counterpart of men, who had suffered a similar fate for the same reason, including their enjoyment of beautiful women 'whose sight banished sleep'.[116] The rape and brutalities committed against women by the Mughal army of Babur is condemned as a mark of social degradation of values. Guru Nanak says,

Modesty and righteousness both have vanished and falsehood move about as the leader, O Lalo. The function of the qazis is over and the Satan now reads the marriage rites (rape). The Muslim women read the Quran and in suffering call upon God, O Lalo. The Hindu women of high caste and others of low caste may also be put in the same account, O Lalo.[117]

Grewal, on examination of these verses, aptly maintains,

> It appears that Guru Nanak has very little to say about what today are called 'social evils'. The Guru disapproves of the custom of becoming *sati*, but almost incidentally, he appears to be familiar with the institution of slavery, while having little to say about it. He has little to say about child marriage or about the disabilities of the widow. . . . Guru Nanak is most articulate in his social criticism when customs and institutions appear to touch upon religion.[118]

As evident from the above discussion, there appears to be a huge difference in the attitudes of Kabir and Guru Nanak towards women. How can this difference be explained? Grewal explains this in terms of their relative standings in the *sant* tradition of northern India, which is looked upon as a synthesis of three constituents: *Bhakti*, *hath-yoga*, and Sufism, in that order of importance. It appears to us that *hath-yoga* was much less important to Guru Nanak than to Kabir. The woman in *hath-yoga* is the tigress of the night, the great temptress in the path of the *yogi*, who aims at subduing all sexual desires. She is the greatest obstacle in his path. His denunciation of women is in direct proportion to the perceived threat. As noted, Kabir's attitude towards women was similar to that of the *yogis*, as he too viewed women as seductive and tempting men away from their true calling. Guru Nanak, by contrast, denounces the *yogis* for their strict renunciation, including their ideal of subduing sexual desire. He has a great appreciation for the householder.[119] It may be significant that the femaleness attributed to the *stri svabhav* is not all prominent in Guru Nanak. In fact, there is hardly anything comparable with Kabir on the point.

In summing up, one is inclined to agree with J.S. Grewal that Guru Nanak, within the traditional patriarchal framework of his time, created a large space for women, much larger than what we find in Kabir or perhaps in the whole range of Indian literature springing from devotional theism. Total equality of the woman with man in the spiritual realm was a radical idea in Indian history, especially because it was not confined to female renouncers (*bikhu*s) or devotees (*bhakta*s).

Guru Nanak's symbolic attack on discrimination against women due to physiological differences carried the idea of equality a long step forward. If he does not carry it into the home, giving an equal share to the daughter in inheritance, nor does he say anything which can be used in support of inequality of any kind. The principle of equality upheld in one area of life carries important implications for other areas as well.

While scholars like Doris Jakobsh are not able to appreciate the contributions of Guru Nanak and his spiritual successors, she nonetheless writes,

It is important to expand on both the positive and the negative within the scriptural canon. To know only the negative message is disempowering; to uphold only the positive images is a naïve and superficial empowerment. To proffer both leads to a more accurate and genuine discussion of feminine dimension within the Sikh tradition.[120]

Although theoretically, her position is appreciable, in practice it seems painful to observe that her perception is anachronistic. For a society struggling for a respectable position of women as a wife, as a daughter, to consider women as equal and worthy of spiritual enlightenment as Guru Nanak preached was undoubtedly an idea much ahead of its times. We must acknowledge that Guru Nanak is articulate in his social criticism when customs and institutions touch upon religion. In the spiritual field, his injunctions of equality between men and women are commendable. As religion is an important aspect of life, it influences its many aspects, directly as well as indirectly. To say that Guru Nanak appreciates women only for procreative qualities is clearly to undermine the spirit of his sayings. To view his views in this narrow perspective would be oversimplification or rather concluding out of context. When a whole gamut of restrictions and superstitions (*sutak*) were being attached to childbirth, Guru Nanak, on the contrary, highlighted this physiological trait of hers as a quality. He emphasized that without women the world cannot exist. This thought process extended further in respecting women as a 'mother' and went a step further by advocating conjugal relationships in marriage. One is inclined to remind ourselves that gender, according to J.W. Scott,[121] is an ongoing fluid process whereby sexual differences acquire a socially or culturally constructed meaning. Scott appropriately advocates an understanding that gender, as constructed for both women and men has significant consequences. In her words,

The term 'gender' suggests that relations between the sexes are a primary aspect of social organization (rather than following from, say, economic or demographic pressures), that the terms of male and female identities are in large part culturally determined (not produced by individuals or collectivities entirely on their own) and that differences between sexes constitute and are constituted by hierarchical social structures.[122]

The perception of some scholars, including Jakobsh, is guided by the 'principle of negation', in their own words, for which they accuse the Sikh historiography at large. This exercise of 'negation' or undermining the contribution of Guru Nanak became still more evident when we compare his sayings about women with other important *bhakti sant*s like Kabir, Surdas, and Tulsidas and further contextualize Guru Nanak's verses in the ethos of the time. Grewal, summing up the contribution of Guru Nanak, states that the principle of equality upheld in one area of life, that too an important area as religion, all-encompassing and influential, carries important implications for other areas as well. Guru Nanak's compositions do not prove a radical departure from the existing order, but a radical departure can be justified on the basis of his compositions.[123]

NOTES

1. Tulsi Das, *Ram Charitmanas*, 8th edition, Gorakhpur: Gita Press, n.d., No. 6/16/2.
2. Katherine K. Young, 'Hinduism', in *Women in World Religions*, ed. Arvind Sharma, Albany: N.Y. Suny Press, 1987, pp. 76-7.

3. See, for example, Joseph T. O'Connell, *Religious Movements and Social Structure: The Case of Chaitanya's Vaishnavas of Bengal*, Simla: Indian Institute of Advanced Studies, 1993, pp. 4-5.
4. Savitri Chandra Sobha, *Medieval India and Hindi Bhakti Poetry: A Socio-Cultural Study*, Delhi: Har-Anand Publications, 1996, p. 141.
5. David N. Lorenzen, Introduction, 'The Historical Vicissitudes of Bhakti Religion', in *Bhakti Religion in North India: Community, Identity and Political Action*, ed. David Lorenzen, Delhi: Manohar, 1996, p. 13.
6. Nancy Falk and Rita M. Gross, eds., *Unspoken Worlds: Women's Religious Lives in Non-Western Cultures*, San Francisco: Harper and Row, 1980, pp. xv, xxi.
7. Clifford Geertz, 'Religion as a Cultural System', in *Anthropological Approaches to the Study of Religion*, ed. Michael Banton, London: Tavistock Publications, 1966, p. 4.
8. David N. Lorenzen, op. cit., p. 3.
9. Raj Kumari Shankar, 'Women in Sikhism', in *Women in Indian Religions*, Arvind Sharma, New Delhi: Oxford University Press, 2002, p. 115.
10. *Manava Dharma Shastra*, Eng. tr. G.C. Haughton, ed. Rev. William Jones, Delhi: Asian Educational Services, rpt., 1982, pp. 151 (henceforth cited as *MDS*).
11. *MDS*, 5, pp. 147-9.
12. Katherine K. Young, op. cit., p. 9.
13. Ibid.
14. Ibid., p. 79.
15. J.S. Grewal, *The Sikhs of the Punjab*, New Delhi: Cambridge University Press, 1990, p. 27.
16. Niharranjan Ray, *The Sikh Gurus and the Sikh Society*, New Delhi: Munshiram Manoharlal, rpt., 1975, p. 40.
17. Ibid.
18. For detailed discussion, see, Savitri Chandra Shobha, op. cit.
19. Kabir, *Sakhi*, 12/47; Kabir, *Pada* 323; for a detailed study see *Kabir*, ed. Prabhakar Machwe, Delhi: Sahitya Akademi, 1968; Parasnath Tewari, *Kabir*, New Delhi: National Book Trust, rpt., 1981.
20. Kabir, *Pada*, 1-3.
21. Kabir, *Sakhi*, 20/21: *Ek kanak aur kamini, douagni ki jhal.*
22. Kabir, *Sakhi*, 16/3, 4, 6-10.
23. Kabir, *Sakhi*, 16/1: *Jag hatwara svad thag, maya baisan lai.*

24. Kabir, *Bijak*, p. 189.
25. Kabir, *Vachnamrita*, pp. 71-3.
26. Kabir, *Pada*, p. 217.
27. Kabir, *Sakhi*, 45/34-6.
28. Malik Muhammad Jaisi, *Padmavat*, ed. V.S. Aggarwal, Chiragaon, Jhansi: Pitambar Books, 2nd edn., n.d.
29. Ibid., Nos. 84, 90-1.
30. Ibid., Nos. 170, 174.
31. Ibid., No. 205.
32. Ibid., No. 38.
33. *Sri Dadu Vani*, ed. Narayan Das, Jaipur, vs 2026, 2nd edn., p. 25.
34. Dadu, 29/6, see App. I (iii).
35. Dadu 8/35.
36. *Dadu Dayal ki Bani*, p. 95.
37. Dadu, 12/68, App. i(iv).
38. *Dadu Dayal ki Bani*, pp. 131-2.
39. Dadu, 12/113.
40. Ibid., 12/68.
41. Ibid., 12/103.
42. Surdas, *Sur Sagar*, ed. Nand Dulare Vajpai, Kashi: Kashi Nagari Pracharini Sabha, 4th edn., 2 vols, 1916, *pada* 1187. Also see Savitri Chandra Sobha, 'Social Life As Reflected in the Works of Surdas', in *Surdas: A Revaluation*, Nagendra, New Delhi, National Publishing House, 1979, pp. 235-51.
43. Ibid., pada no. 1507, 1525, 1541.
44. Tulsidas, *Ramcharitmanas*, p. 778.
45. Ibid., 4/15/4.
46. Ibid., 3/37/5.
47. Savitri Chandra Shobha, op. cit., p. 134.
48. Ibid., pp. 134-41, 190.
49. Tulsidas, *Ramcharitmanas*, No. 6/14/4; for detailed discussion on the point, see, Savitri Chandra Shobha, op. cit., pp. 130-41.
50. For songs of Mirabai, see, *Mirabai ki Padavali*, ed. Krishna Deva Sharma, New Delhi: Regal Book Depot, 1992.
51. Savitri Chandra Shobha, op. cit., pp. 131, 133.
52. Joseph T. O'Connell, op. cit., pp. 17-19.
53. Karine Schomer, 'Introduction, The Sant Tradition in Perspective', in *The Sants: Studies in a Devotional Tradition in India*, eds. Karine Schomer and W.H. McLeod, Delhi: Motilal Banarsidass, Delhi: 1987, p. 1.

54. Ibid., p. 3.
55. Parshuram Chaturvedi, *Kabir-Sahitya Ki Parakh*, Allahabad: Bharti Bhandar, 1955, p. 15; and *Uttar Bharat Ki Sant Parampara*, 2nd edn., Allahabad: Bharti Bhandar, 1965, p. 421; Ramkumar Verma, *Hindi Sahitya Ka Alochanatmak Itihas*, 4th edn., Allahabad: Ramnarayan Benimadhav, 1958, p. 57.
56. J.S. Grewal, *Recent Debates in Sikh Studies: An Assessment*, New Delhi: Manohar, 2011, p. 57.
57. Ibid.
58. J.S. Grewal, 'Foundation of the Sikh Faith', in *Five Centuries of Sikh Tradition, Ideology, Society, Politics and Culture*, ed. Reeta Grewal and Sheena Pall, Delhi: Manohar, 2005, pp. 43-4.
59. W.H. McLeod, *Guru Nanak and the Sikh Religion*, New Delhi: Oxford University Press, 1996.
60. W.H. McLeod, *Sikhism*, New Delhi: Penguin Books, 1997, p. 88.
61. Ibid., pp. 91-2.
62. Ibid., p. 94.
63. Ibid., p. 101.
64. J.S. Grewal, 'Foundation of the Sikh Faith', p. 102.
65. Ibid., p. 44.
66. W.H. McLeod, *Guru Nanak and the Sikh Religion*, p. 161.
67. Ibid., p. 45
68. Ibid., pp. 163-77; J.S. Grewal, *Recent Debates in Sikh Studies: An Assessment*, p. 58.
69. W.H. McLeod, *The Sikhs: History, Religion and Society*, New York: Columbia University Press, 1989, pp. 18-19; 22-31.
70. J.S. Grewal, *Recent Debates in Sikh Studies*, p. 59.
71. W.H. McLeod, *The Evolution of the Sikh Community: Five Essays*, New Delhi: Oxford University Press, rpt., 1996, p. 5.
72. Gurdev Singh, ed., *Perspectives on the Sikh Tradition*, Chandigarh: Siddharth Publishers, 1986, pp. 15-21.
73. Daljeet Singh, 'Nathism, Vaishnavism and Sikhism: A Comparative Study', in *Perspectives on the Sikh Tradition*, ed. Gurdev Singh, pp. 135-6.
74. For a comparative trajectory, see Doris R. Jakobsh, *Relocating Gender in Sikh History, Transformation, Meaning and Identity*, New Delhi: Oxford University Press, 2003, pp. 23-7; Kumkum Sangari, 'Mirabai and the Spiritual Economy of Bhakti', *Occasional Papers on History and Society*, (Second Series, Number XXVIII), New Delhi: Nehru Memorial Museumand Library, 2001, pp. 73-89; J.S. Grewal, 'A

Gender Perspective on Guru Nanak', in *Women in Indian History: Social, Economic, Political and Cultural Perspectives*, ed. Kiran Pawar, Patiala and Delhi: Vision & Venture, 1996, pp. 141-57.
75. Nikky-Guninder Kaur Singh, *The Feminine Principle in the Sikh Vision of the Transcendent*, Cambridge [England]; New York, NY, USA: Cambridge University Press, 1993, pp. 6-7.
76. Karine Schomer and W.H. McLeod, ed., 'Introduction: The Sant Tradition in Perspective', in *The Sants: Studies in a Devotional Tradition in India*, p. 5.
77. Ibid.
78. Karine Schomer, 'Kabir in the Guru Granth Sahib: An Exploratory Essay', *Sikh Studies: Comparative Perspective on a Changing Tradition*, ed. Mark Jurgensmeyer and N. Gerald Barrier, Berkeley: Berkeley Theological Union, 1979, p. 77.
79. J.S. Grewal, 'Foundation of the Sikh Faith', p. 50.
80. J.S. Grewal, 'Guru Nanak and his Panth,' in *The Sikhs: Ideology, Institutions and Identity*, New Delhi: Oxford University Press, 2009, pp. 3-21.
81. Ibid., p. 27.
82. W.H. McLeod, *Guru Nanak and the Sikh Religion*, New Delhi: Oxford University Press, 1996, p. 200.
83. Ibid., p. 203.
84. Ibid., p. 191.
85. Ibid., p.10.
86. J.S. Grewal, *Guru Nanak in History*, p. 237.
87. W.H. McLeod, *Guru Nanak and the Sikh Religion*, p. 196.
88. Ibid., p.161.
89. Bhai Jodh Singh, ed., *Bani Bhagat Kabir Ji Steek*, Patiala: Punjabi University, rpt., 2016, p. 212.
90. Kumkum Sangari, 'Mirabai and the Spiritual Economy of Bhakti', pp. 73-89.
91. Shyamsunderdas, ed., *Kabir Granthavali*, Varanasi: Kashi Nagari Pracharini Sabha, vs 2034, G: 68. (Henceforth cited as *KG*).
92. The English translations are from William J. Dwyer, *Bhakti in Kabir*, Patna: Associated Book Agency, 1981, *BK*: 168.
93. *KG*, G: 68.
94. *KG*, G: 68, *BK*: 168.
95. *KG*, G: 67.
96. *KG*, *BK*: 168.

97. J.S. Grewal, 'A Gender Perspective on Guru Nanak', p. 147.
98. G.S. Talib, *Sri Guru Granth Sahib*, Eng. tr., 4 vols., Patiala: Punjabi University, 1990 (Hereafter referred to as *AG*), Sri Rag, p. 17.
99. Raj Kumari Shankar, 'Women in Sikhism', in *Women in Indian Religions*, ed. Arvind Sharma, New Delhi: Oxford University Press, 2002, p. 115.
100. *AG*, Var Asa, p. 473.
101. Raj Kumari Shankar, op. cit., p. 116; Doris R. Jakobsh, op. cit., p. 24.
102. The custom of *sutak* is associated with the concept of ritual impurities. A woman who has given birth needs time to heal. Also, the physiological act of procreation and its effects is considered 'unclean'. According to prevalent traditions and norms, she was supposed to stay in a separate room, was served food in breakable utensils and many such restrictions were followed. At the completion of the *sutak* she was given a bath by the *dai* (maid), her nails were clipped, and only then was she allowed to enter the main premises of the home.
103. *AG*, Salok, M.I. p. 472.
104. *AG*, Rag Suhi' [Chaupadai], Ghar I, p. 728 and Rag Majh [Ashtapadian], Ghar I, p. 109.
105. *AG*, Rag Majh [Ashtapadian] Ghar I, p. 109.
106. *AG*, Sri Rag, p. 15.
107. *AG*, Sri Rag, p. 15.
108. *AG*, Sri Rag. P. 61.
109. *AG*, Gauri, (Guareri), p. 222.
110. *AG*, Asa, p. 416.
111. Nicky-Guninder Kaur Singh, *The Feminine Principle in the Sikh Vision of the Transcendent*, p. 43.
112. Ibid.
113. Doris R. Jakobsh, 'Gender Issues in Sikh Studies: Hermeneutics of Affirmation or Hermeneutics of Suspicion', *The Transmission of Sikh Heritage in the Diaspora*, ed. Pashaura Singh and N. Gerald Barrier, New Delhi: Manohar, 1996, p. 49.
114. J.S. Grewal, 'A Gender Perspective of Guru Nanak', p. 152.
115. *AG*, Rag Asa (Astapadian), p. 417.
116. Ibid.
117. *AG*, Tilang, p. 722.
118. J.S. Grewal, *Guru Nanak in History*, pp. 195-6.
119. AG, Suhi, p. 730; Prabhati, pp. 1329-32.

120. Doris R. Jakobsh, 'Gender Issues in Sikh Studies: Hermeneutics of Affirmation or Hermeneutics of Suspicion', p. 55.
121. Joan Wallach Scott, *Gender and the Politics of History*, New York: Columbia University Press, 1988, pp. 20-3.
122. Ibid., p. 25.
123. J.S. Grewal, 'A Gender Perspective on Guru Nanak', p. 156.

PART II

CONTEXTUALIZING WOMEN IN MEDIEVAL PUNJAB

CHAPTER 3

Stri Svabhav, *Stri Dharam* and Prevailing Realities

A woman performs several roles in the family, community, and wider society. Her status is determined based on her various positions and roles. To an extent, it also depends upon her consciousness of her social status. In India, the religious factor has been of utmost importance in determining the status of women, since it exerts a powerful influence on the thought, culture and behaviour of the people. Religion permeates their personal and family lives like nothing else and regulates interpersonal and intergroup relations. There is hardly any aspect of social conduct that is not affected by the sanction of religion. It is inextricably interwoven with social, cultural, and political concerns. Religion is often a vehicle for expressing social relations. The complex interplay between religion and society has been very well captured in the study of Nancy Falk and Rita Gross.[1] While religious traditions, movements and upheavals have been important players in the transformation of societies, religion can also be understood as being

> among the foremost of the institutions which conserve society, encoding stabilizing world views and values and transmitting these from generation to generation. . . . Religion has been an instrument of liberation for women. *But religion has just as often become an instrument of women's oppression.*[2]

In other words, religion has simultaneously, or alternately been a source of power for women as well as one of subordination. Religious authorities have often functioned as powerful political figures exercising immense social presence and influence. Religious beliefs may point to the equality of women as sacred beings or the importance of female life, while at the same time, religious beliefs may both reflect and reinforce the subordination of women.

It is religion that emerges as the most powerful vehicle, if not the sole contributor, in the 'engendering' of the varied roles played by women. The protagonists of almost all religions have succeeded in laying down the framework of *stri dharam*; it is they who desire legitimacy from this kind of social arrangement. Their message might vary in its tenor, but the thrust remains the same and its androcentrism is constantly and continuously accentuated by its practitioners. We do not come across, even remotely, any reference to *purush svabhav* or *purush dharam*. It is only the woman whose *svabhav* is something to be tamed, as she is reckoned foolish enough to get enticed by all the vices in the world. It is the woman who has to be constantly reminded of her *stri dharam* to keep the social edifice operating. And the best is that she is never acknowledged. As far as the references to the *dharam* of the *purush* are concerned, the solitary reference on a cursory glance is to Maryada Purushottam Ram. Here also, Ram is projected as the 'ideal' son. In the context of Ram, a great deal of value is attached to the chastity of Sita. Chastity has been projected as the pillar of *stri dharam* and as a corollary extension, this has been the social norm.

Many scholars, cutting across chronological zones, have elaborated upon the emphasis on chastity of women. Uma Chakravarty emphasizes that the strongly felt need for effective control over women was not only to maintain the purity of the patriarchal succession, a requirement of all patriarchal societies, but also caste purity, something that was unique to the Brahmanical Hindu social set-up.[3] One may concede that this kind of mentality might not be limited to Brahmanical patriarchy alone. It was a much wider, rather omnipresent, reality. Veena Das' analysis[4] reinforces quite the same view.

She argues that women were seen as 'gateways' to the caste system and that any sexual contact with a male outside caste (and, of course, outside the husband in specific) would contaminate that particular caste. Thus, the sexuality of women, particularly that of higher caste women, became an important tool to control them. In case of any aberration, not only the purity of women but that of the entire caste group would be endangered.[5] This connection is evident when women's bodies become a site of heinous crimes at the time of wars, designed to hit the dignity of a particular caste, class, or nationality. The enemy indulges in these crimes to contaminate the ethnic purity of a particular group.

As often stated, the repression of women had to be sanctified by religion. It was done so powerfully that a man, however lowly placed in the social hierarchy, was made to be much superior to the women in his family and social space. Religion was used along the same lines for legitimizing patriarchy as it was powerfully utilized for justifying the caste system and consequent class divisions. The role of prevalent ideology is so deeply entrenched into the psyche of the people, that is the mentalities that, in the words of the Annales School,[6] the women, though suppressed and curtailed, also accepted their state as God-given.

Women's secondary, rather subordinate, status is the cornerstone of both Islamic and Hindu social order. Unfortunately, women are often projected as licentious, dishonest, distrustful, immoral and thus a 'danger' to the men and the society at large. According to Manu (II.213-14), it is ingrained in her to seduce men and lead them astray. To her, while being created, were allotted 'impure desires, wrath, dishonesty and bad conduct' (IX.17); all her good qualities can come only from her husband (IX.22-3). The woman's intrinsically defective nature justifies her absolute subordination to man, day and night women must be kept in dependence by the males (of) their families (IX.2; cf. also V.147-8).[7]

It is in this background of the overarching influence of religion that the Punjab, for a micro-study of the societal status and position of women, captures great academic curiosity and opportunity. As has often been pointed out, Punjab in the sixteenth century was home to Hindu and Muslim populations, while experiencing the emergence of Sikhism. As a new religious and ideological formulation, Sikhism advocated a better position for women. Could it succeed in influencing all sections of society or would it be able to modify the existing dominant patriarchal social structures? Apart from being home to the three religious communities, the Punjab also provided an ideal social milieu, wherein the caste system and class distinctions played their part in social relations, particularly with regard to the position of women. Marital alliances emerged using women as symbolic 'indicators' of high caste and class, based on the values of seclusion and chastity. The pervasive influence of caste as a marker of status and as an organizing principle of daily life persisted. How does caste intersect with gender in rituals, normative, and prescriptive contexts? Here, one must underline that vast differences distinguished the lives of women not only in different parts of the country but within different castes and classes, besides religious and ethnic groups. It is, therefore, difficult to make generalizations and put together a comprehensive description of the life and struggle of women even in a particular region at a given point of time.

Although challenging yet encouraging, there are limitations which fetter the scope of any investigation on the status of women in sixteenth- and seventeenth-century Punjab. There is a severe lack of evidential literature on the subject. The main focus of the contemporary sources is political, administrative, and economic. The few references these sources make to the society of the times are usually in the context of only the upper echelons. It must also be stressed that women have not generally written their own histories and historical accounts are written through the lens of the male gender. What was and is important to man thus becomes the focus of historical analysis. The general impression one formulates is of women remaining inconsequential to any social reality in traditional historical accounts. Women are mentioned in the annals of history only when they deviate from the norm, that is the exceptional woman who plays a role projected as exemplary conduct to be imitated by other women. In this way, these constructs of 'ideal women' play a part in what is considered to be 'normative history'. Thus, only upon an unmasking of the androcentric presumptions of writers and their writings, including sacred scriptures, and only upon a suspicious reading and entailing a thorough evaluation of the inherent sexist attitudes and practices within religious and historical works, is one to understand the sources and symbols within the tradition that has sustained the subordination of women throughout history.

It must be emphasized that while perusing through the sources, we are bound to avoid making an anachronistic reading. We should be wary of ideas that flatter and homogenize experiences. Experiences are multiple and the multiplicity of reality coexists. Stephanie Jamison explores myths, prescriptive texts, and narrative traditions. While recognizing that arriving at a 'real' or even a single ideal representation of women's status is highly impossible, she suggests that juxtaposing multiple perspectives permits us to break through the simplistic monolithic formulations.[8] It must also be underlined that one of the principal innovations of the Bhakti movement was the central role given to telling stories about the lives of deities (*avatar*s) and saints. Such sources emerged as a major repository of information on the history of the Punjab in the sixteenth and seventeenth centuries. However, here a distinction needs to be made between stories that are myths, that is, have little or no historical foundation and those that are legends, that is, which involve a mixture of myth and history. However, the dividing line between these two categories is sometimes rather blurred.

The inadequacy of sources makes it necessary for scholars to employ the difficult and somewhat dangerous technique of working backwards, that is studying the earliest definite data available and then proceeding to examine to what extent it can be used to study and evaluate the earlier period. Although this methodology has its limitations, yet, for a subject like the position of women, customs, and rituals, it can be effectively employed as any social change, because the change in values, attitudes, and behavioural patterns do not take place over a short period. The respectable position of women is one issue that human society or, at least, specifically the Indian social structure, is still grappling with. Along with this, we have the task of constructing sociological and anthropological field investigations as well as the collection of oral traditions and folklore before the blurred memories are completely obliterated. It must be kept in mind that the written texts assembled from oral traditions are part of a collective oeuvre. Certain parts must have been re-accentuated and certain potentials in the images actualized, while others were allowed to fade away over time.

Mute evidence from the past is of great importance to the historian, but literary evidence is qualitatively superior. This is true more or less of all forms of literature. However, no form of literature has a one-to-one equation with society. Literature as the 'mirror of life' is a good metaphor. That is precisely the reason why it should not be taken literally. Each literary form can have its own peculiar merits and limitations. Though the character of a literary form in itself becomes relevant to historians, it has to be carefully investigated before it becomes a source.

Another social reality, quite significant during the period under review, is the fusion of traditions. In sixteenth- and seventeenth-century Punjab, Sikhs had not emerged, or displayed any collective concern in distinguishing themselves from the predominantly Hindu culture and religion. In fact, Muslims outnumbered the Hindus and Sikhs put together. At this point, Sikhism had not emerged as a distinct religion, though the adherents were continuously increasing. All three communities, as a rule, lived peacefully, and in social and religious matters, they often followed the practices of co-operation. The British administrators, during their earliest studies, had observed that, generally, cultural differences on the ground of religion were comparatively minor.

The Gazetteer of Punjab, Provincial, 1888-9[9] notes,

In the borderlands where the great faiths meet and especially among the ignorant peasantry the various observances and beliefs that distinguish the followers of the several faiths in their purity are so strongly blended and intermingled that it is often almost impossible to say that one prevails rather than the other. Thus, the Musalman peasantry of Delhi territory is still in many ways almost as much a Hindu as their un-perverted brethren; the Sikh of Sirsa is often a Sikh only in speech and habit.

In a similar spirit D.C. Ibbetson notes,

The various observances and beliefs which distinguish the followers of the several faiths in their purity are so strongly blended and intermingled that it is often impossible to say that one prevails rather than the other, or to decide in what category the people shall be classed.[10]

As the religions of India grew from a variety of cults and beliefs, the citizenry did not perceive themselves as belonging to any 'one' religion; the categories of religions extended, intermingled and coexisted in the region and the common masses carried on with their daily chores of life without considering their association with particular religious beliefs. Harjot Oberoi, though speaking of a later period, aptly observed,

People did not conceive of themselves as 'Hindus' or 'Sikhs'. These categories overlapped and it is historically more precise to speak in terms of the continuum or simultaneity of religious identities rather than of the distinct religious collectivities. An 'either-or' dichotomy is often of very little value in conceptualizing Indian religious traditions.[11]

In spite of an intensely intermingled and blended culture, one cannot presume homogeneity in patterns of social behaviour. One needs to be sensitive to the nuances, the role played by caste and class, and acknowledge the multiplicity of realities, particularly regarding the position of women and their social status holding true. It must be emphasized that while studying the nuances and complexities of the social fabric in relation to the position of women, one cannot presume that the normative teachings of the Gurus had a universal and uniform impact. To use Clarence McMullen's[12] views once again, the gap between normative and operative beliefs has to be clearly acknowledged. It is here that the need of reading the 'fissures' and the 'fracture lines' has to be carefully observed in the secular literature or the folk songs or the nuanced study of popular rituals and customs. Only then can we be hopeful of assessing whether the Sikh Gurus were able to influence the dominant patriarchal ideology or modify its formulations in the relevant period. Considering the religious injunctions of the Sikh Gurus on the one hand and the operative value system on the other, one observes innumerable deviations. The picture that emerges is rather that of defiance and deviance, a wide divergence between the precept and the practice.

Family is not only an important primary institution in all civilized human societies, it is the basic social unit where women have a formidable role to play. It is this role and her status in the family that emerges as the most important yardstick to assess her position in the larger social fabric. Family needs to be studied in its relationship to caste, class, gender, and religion. Joan Wallach Scott observes that the category of gender not only illuminates the unequal relations of power between males and females, but it also helps one understand how unequal relations are extended via metaphors to varied areas of social life, thereby signifying unequal relations of power.[13] In other words, the position of women should not be studied in isolation, but in relation to men. It needs to be underlined that there is a need to place social and economic institutions in their ecological and physical settings while accepting the multiplicity of cultural practices which exist in the region without treating it as a homogenized space. If we decide to put aside, for a moment, the contemporary critics of patriarchal religion – whether Hinduism and Islam at large, or Sikhism in its nascent stage – the varied expressions of subordination are striking. Sometimes, for instance, we find that male authority and power are not always found together. While the male might represent authority in the household, it is the female who exercises the real power in the domestic domain. Sometimes, the same religious concept may be appropriated differently by men and women. While the male version may appear oppressive to the female, it is not always the male version which is foremost in women's minds. Second, there may be a difference between precept and practice. What may appear as a male exclusion of women from a certain aspect of the religious or sociocultural life, it may actually be a consequence of something other than misogyny or may have a parallel articulation in the female exclusion of men from certain religious activities or some sociocultural customs and festivals.

Indeed, it is not difficult to demonstrate how religious traditions, ideological formulations, perceptions of 'patriarchy', 'equality' or 'position' (desirable social norm and value system) of women may vary over time. What may be true of one period is not necessarily true of another. The variety within the existing social milieu of a specific region comes to the foreground when we examine the evidence with care. The adverse effects of patriarchy varied in severity. Despite realizing the reality and assessing the power to represent particular forms of marriage, family, and social hierarchy as normative and others as deviant, contemporary sources have themselves attempted to flatten out the diversity. Alternatively, such sources have created a system of gradations, a hierarchy of the types of family, an 'ideal' form of marriage and different variations as compromises. Despite acknowledging that women were only physically included, if at all, within recorded history, and were often emotionally and intellectually excluded, we can and must nevertheless recover some of the complexity of the past. For this, we must be aware of how the social domain and its multiple levels must be approached on its own terms, rather than passing sweeping generalizations. Even within a single region, notions of sexuality, purity, and their implications for caste or social identities are not uniform, monolithic, or static. While it may not be easy for us to retrieve the dynamism of such notions in the sixteenth and seventeenth centuries, and the historical context in its entirety, an awareness of the possibility of variation may provide for a more nuanced, historical understanding.

In other words, a focus on an overarching ideology limits the possibility of looking at inner modifications and the particular ways in which ideology is transformed. We can try to query some of these issues by looking at folk literature and folk songs. Recognizing that the power ideology does not fully domesticate women within the rigid mode, the 'ideal' women, her attributes, and behavioural patterns are subject to negotiation and change. The existence of a few customs, which clearly attack male dominance, suggests that women pushed the boundaries of a particular social system (read patriarchy), still trying to create a space for their selves, within it. Yet, it is not as if they are continuously resisting structures of control. Transgression of boundaries can go along with acts of conformity, adaptation, acquiescence, and renegotiation. Every idea has a variety of meanings. Notions attached to a particular idea, for instance, 'women's position', not only change over time but, at a given point in time, it may have a variety of meanings. To gain from Ginzburg's work *Cheese and Worms*,[14] the 'reality' is what and how we filter our knowledge, and it has different connotations and meanings to different people at different points in time.

A renowned Hindi-Punjabi poet, Sharad Kokash, poignantly alludes to *stri dharam*, the innumerable expectations from a woman. It is equally disheartening to know that the core tenets of this *stri dharam* have not changed much over time. It may have changed appearances, maybe become more blatant and naked, or may be more sugar-coated, yet the reality remains the same.

Wah kehta tha
Wah sunti thi

Jaari tha ek khel
Kehne sunne ka

Stri Svabhav, Stri Dharam *and Prevailing Realities*

*Khel me thi do
parchiyan
Ek me likha tha
'kaho'
Ek me likha tha
'suno'*

*Ab yeh niyati thi
Ya mahaz sanyog?*

*Uske haath lagti rahi
Wahi parchi
Jis par likha tha
'suno'*

*Wah sunti rahi
Usne sune aadesh
Usne sune updesh*

*Bandishe uske liye
Thi
Uske liye thi
Varjanaayen*

*Wah jaanti thi
'kehna-sunna'
Nahi hai kewal kriyaaye*

*Raja ne kaha,
'zehar piyo'
Wah Meera ho gayi.*

*Rishi ne kaha
'patthar bano'
Wah Ahilya ho gayi*

*Prabhu ne kaha
'nikal jao'
Wah Sita ho gayi.*

*Chita se nikali
Cheekh
Kinhi kaano ne nahi
Suni
Wah sati ho gayi*

Ghutati rahi uski
Fariyaad,
Atke rahe shabd
Sile rahe honth
Rundha raha gala

Us ke haath kabhi nahi lagi wah
Parchi,
Jis par likha tha,
'kaho'

[He was saying
She was listening
A game was going on.
to hear what to say

There were two slips in the game.
In one of them it was written 'Say'
One of them said 'Listen'

Now it was destiny
or mere coincidence
Her hand seemed to pick
the same slip
On which it was written 'Listen'
She listened

She heard the order.
She heard the sermon
The restrictions were for her.
There were taboos for her.
She knew
She had to listen to
abominations.

The king said, 'Drink poison'.
She became Meera
The sage said, 'Be a stone'.
She became Ahilya
The Lord said,
'Get out of the house'.
She became Sita
Screams from the pyre

No one listened to her screams.
She became Sati.

Choking her plea
Her words stuck.
Her lips are sewn
Her throat was slitting

Her hand never picked.
that slip
On which it was written – 'Say'

(Published in 'Navbharat' in 1995 and in 'Vagarth' in 1998).

NOTES

1. Nancy Falk and Rita M. Gross, eds., *Unspoken Worlds: Women's Religious Lives in Non-Western Cultures*, San Francisco: Harper and Row, 1980, pp. xv, xxi.
2. Ibid.
3. Uma Chakarvarty, 'Conceptualizing Brahmanical Patriarchy in Early India: Gender, Caste, Class and State', *The Economic and Political Weekly*, 3 April 1993, p. 589.
4. Veena Das, 'Indian Women: Work, Power and Status', in *Indian Women: From Purdah to Modernity*, B.R. Nanda, New Delhi: Vikas, 1976.
5. It has been emphasized that the lives of women exist at the interface, thus suffering from extreme vulnerability of caste and class inequality. Thus, the management of gender and female sexuality is a cardinal feature in the entire *modus operandi* of the maintenance and accentuation of social inequality. Kumkum Sangari and Sudesh Vaid, eds., *Recasting Women: Essays in Colonial History*, New Jersey: Rutgers University Press, 1990, Introduction, pp. 1-34.
6. The Annales School of history was established by French historians Lucien Febvre (1878-1944) and Mark Bloch (1886-1944). After Second World War Fernand Braudel (1902-85) emerged as Febvre's intellectual protege and heir. Under Braudel's influence the Annales School advocated an interdisciplinary approach to history. The emphasis was on a 'total history'. Inquiries into the hallowed trio of politics, diplomacy, and wars were replaced with inquiries

into climate, demography, agriculture, commerce, technology, transportation and communication, as well as social groups and mentalities.
7. George Buhler, *The Laws of Manu*, rpt., Charleston, South Carolina: BiblioLife, April 2009.
8. Stephanie W. Jamison, *Sacrificed Wife/Sacrificer's Wife: Women, Ritual, and Hospitality in Ancient India*, New York: Oxford University Press, 1996, pp. 21.
9. *The Gazetteer of Punjab*, Provincial, 1888-9, p. 122.
10. D.C. Ibbetson, *The Religion of the Punjab*, Calcutta: Government Printing Press, 1883, p.101.
11. Harjot Oberoi, 'From Ritual to Counter Ritual: Rethinking the Hindu and Muslim Question', in *Sikh History and Religion in the Twentieth Century*, ed. Joseph T. O'Connell et al., Toronto: Center for South Asian Studies, University of Toronto, 1988, p. 140.
12. Clarence O. McMullen, *Religious Belief and Practices in the Rural Punjab*, New Delhi: Manohar, 1989.
13. Joan W. Scott, 'Gender: A Useful Category of Historical Analysis', *The American Historical Review*, vol. 91, No. 5, December 1986, pp. 1053-75. This position has been revised and elaborated further in 'Gender: Still a Useful Category of Analysis?', *Diogenes*, vol. 57, Issue 1, October 2010, pp. 7-14.
14. Carlo Ginzburg, *The Cheese and the Worms: The Cosmos of a Sixteenth-Century Miller*, Baltimore, MD: Johns Hopkins University Press, 1992.

CHAPTER 4

Aspects of the Marital Bond

> The girl is regarded as a valuable piece of property, betrothal is a contract to transfer it, and marriage is the transfer of ownership and *muklawa* is the transfer of possession.
>
> – CHARLES LEWIS TUPPER[1]

THE INSTITUTION OF MARRIAGE: AN OVERVIEW

The centrality of marriage in structuring gender relations is universally accepted. Marital status constitutes by far the most important element of women's identity in most societies. Yet, marriage is by no means a unitary institution. Certain forms of marriage are fairly known from a range of texts (prescriptive and otherwise), while others are relatively unexplored and are often perceived as problematic. The power of ideology becomes apparent when certain sources project a few particular forms of marriage as 'ideal' and 'normal'. Diversity is either levelled out or at best projected as 'deviant' or 'rare' practices. Alternatively, such sources have created a system of gradations, a hierarchy of the types of marriage with *kanyadaan* at the top, being regarded as the ideal form of marriage and then marriage with a 'bride price' or *wattasatta* seen as inferior alternatives. Whether it is the 'family' or 'marriage' or any other social and economic institution, these concepts need to be contextualized in their ecological and physical setting. Further, the multiplicity of cultural practices that exist in the region needs to be accepted, rather than treating it as a homogenized space. In other words, different marital practices often coexisted in societies, being considered typical of distinct socio-economic strata. Moreover, as often stated, 'gender is an ongoing fluid process', while polyandry and most other forms of marriage are as much about the relationship amongst men as they are about women and men.

This brings us to an important aspect of ideological basis of marriage. The dominant discourse of women in Indian society has its roots in the ideology of patriarchy, that is a strong social urge to control the sexuality of women. Marriage is the mechanism through which her sexuality can be controlled, and her procreative capabilities can be channellized. It becomes still more apparent in the discussion on widow remarriage.

Women's nature or *stri svabhav*, was perceived as deceitful and driven by uncontrolled sexual desire and, thus, problematic and, hence, had to be controlled through an insistence on women's duty or *stri dharam*. It is seen as sinful for women to have desires and these are explicitly opposed to their *dharam*.[2] At the same time, women are cast as the eternal temptress, that is the object and the very form of sexual desire, which can ensnare the wisest and most ascetic of men.[3] Methods of containment and of extracting obedience and virtue from the wife are coded as *stri dharam*, while the essentially disruptive nature of female desire, a part of their essential wickedness, is coded as *stri svabhav*. The *stri dharam* or the *pativrata dharam* was a rhetorical device to ensure social control over women, especially over their chastity, and was well accepted.[4]

It would not be out of place to mention the oft-quoted sayings of the Gurus about marriage. Against the backdrop of the general social perception about the position of women in marriage, this endeavour would not only enable us to appreciate the positivity in their messages, advocating a position of respect and dignity for women's role as a wife, urging men to be loyal to their spouses. It would also help us assess whether their ideological position could actually influence, alter, or even modify the dominant patriarchal ideological current, or whether there was an immense gap between the normative and operative realities.

Aspects of the Marital Bond 161

The first important reality is that all Sikh Gurus were married men, except the eighth who died very young. They also led a normal life as a householder and regarded sexual desire as a normal phenomenon. The Sikh religion does not make any virtue of sexual abstinence, in contrast to the Nath-panthis, Yogis, and Bairagis, who vowed celibacy. In fact, Sikhism upheld the householder's life as an important adjunct to the spiritual life. According to Sikh teachings, true abstinence or renunciation is in the practice of ascetic virtues without having to renounce family and society. What is stressed is self-restraint and self-control in sexual desires. Guru Nanak observed, in this context, 'The pepper and salt if treated in ghee dissolve not in water, so do the Lord's devotees abide in the midst of maya and yet remain detached.'[5] The Guru reiterates the importance of the institution of marriage when he says:

Living with in family life,
One obtains salvation.[6]

The Gurus not only strongly denounced asceticism but also castigated *yogis*, who left their homes and lived on the generosity of the common people. The *yogis* took pride in being celibate, but inwardly craved sexual indulgence. Expressing the same sentiments Guru Nanak said, 'In his hands is the begging bowl and he cast like a mendicant's but within him is immense raving. And, though he abandons his own wife, he's attached to another's, lured by sex desire.'[7] Bhai Gurdas[8] notes the discussion of Guru Nanak with the Siddhas, which highlights the importance that the Guru attached to the life of the householder as follows:

Khadhi khunasi jugisard gosati karani sabhe uthi ai,
Puche jogi bhangar nathu tuhi dadhu vichi kiu kanji pai,
Phitia chata dudh da rirakia makhanu hathi na ai,
Bhekh u uteri udasi da vati kius andari riti charai,
Nanak ache bhangar nath teri mau kuchaji ahi,
Bhanda dhoi na jationi bhai kuchaje phulu sarai,
Hoi atitu grihasati ta ji phiri unahu ke ghari mangani jai,
Binu dite kachu hathi na ai[9]

The above passage indicates that all the *yogis*, annoyed that the Guru was advocating against renunciation, came forward to have a debate. Yogi Bhangar Nath[10] asked, 'Why have you put vinegar in milk. The spoiled (split) milk cannot be churned into butter. How have you put off yogic garb and attired yourself in a household way.' Said Nanak,

O Bhangar Nath, your mother-teacher is unmannerly. She has not cleansed the inner-self of your body-pot and your clumsy thoughts have burnt your flower (of knowledge which was to become fruit). You, while distancing and repudiating household life, go again to those householders for begging. Except their offerings you do not get anything.

In Var 1, Pauri 38 of *Varan*, Bhai Gurdas describes Guru Nanak in the attire of householders. In Pauri 48, the Guru criticized Bhangar Nath and his like for their superficial knowledge and pointed out that they have to beg from the family of a householder only for their sustenance. Var 6, Pauri 18 also upholds the life of a householder. It emphasizes the importance of the act of balancing all the pleasures of life. It concludes that the life of a householder can lead to the path to salvation; a householder rises above the level of pleasures and sorrows.[11]

Pjhiri bab aia kartarpuri bhekh udasi sagal utara;
Pahiri sansari kapare manjit baithia kia avatara.[12]

The above verse meant that Baba (Nanak) returned to Kartarpur where he put aside his attire of a recluse. Now putting on a householder's dress, he sat splendidly on a cot (and executed his mission). In a similar ideological spirit, Guru Gobind Singh supposedly tried to convince the son of a Sikh family, who had almost renounced all worldly pleasures and, thus, was unwilling to marry. Here, the Guru tried to make him appreciate the relevance of the householder through the story of a pigeon couple.[13]

It is remarkable that in a social milieu where a woman has been considered the 'property' of her husband, the men are constantly reminded of chastity and loyalty to their spouses as well. In the Ram Kali Raga, Namdev refers to the practice of offering women in charity at the places of pilgrimage. He says, 'If man makes gifts of horses, gifts of elephants, gifts of women with their couches and land – even then all these equal not the Lord's name.'[14] In sharp contrast, we have Guru Amar Das emphasizing, 'Bride and groom are not they who pose as one whole. Bride and groom are they who are two bodies with one soul.'[15] Here, the Guru advocates marriage between two equal partners and emphasizes that the sacred institution of marriage aims at the fusion of two souls into one. Guru Hargobind, called woman 'the conscience of man' without whom normal living was impossible.

The Gurus redefined celibacy in the framework of chastity. A man is celibate who is married to one wife. They taught the disciples, men and women alike, the value of conjugal fidelity. Bhai Gurdas opines that the nose and ears of a man who roams with women other than his wife should be chopped off (*naku kanu fari vadiya ravey par nari*).[16] The Gurus recommended the monogamous ideal of marriage. In Sri Raga, Guru Amar Das refers to it:

> If we enjoy myriad of women
> And rule over nine divisions of world,
> We receive not God's grace without true Guru and are cast
> Into wombs again over again.

> Should man lust with females a million,
> And rule over the entire earth (*nav-khand*),
> Without guidance of the holy Preceptor no joy shall find,
> And again and again into transmigration be thrown.[17]

There is repeated emphasis on chastity in Sikh sources. In *Gurbilas Padshahi Chhevin*, there is an instance where Guru Hargobind met the begums of Jahangir, and they tried to seduce him, probably to gauge his piety. However, the Guru explained to them the importance of chastity in life. The Guru instructed that their prime objective should be to 'serve' their husbands. He further stated that in a family every woman should view, except her husband, every other male as father, brother, or son. Similarly, every man should view all other women as mother, sister, or daughter.[18] In a similar spirit, *Sri Guru Panth Parkash* narrates the episode of Anup Kaur. A rich prostitute (*randi*) of Lahore named Anup Kaur tried to seduce Guru Gobind Singh. To her inviting gestures, the Guru responded in a firm manner, explaining to her the value of chastity:

> *Nij nari ke saath nehu tun nitbathjo,*
> *Par nari so nehu chhuri paini kar janhu.*[19]

According to the above lines, one was advised to consider the other woman as forbidden company and never have any sexual contact with any other woman, even by mistake. Such women had to be considered as a sharp knife who would bring about one's end. In *Hukum Namah* 15, Guru Gobind Singh states:

> *Par stri ma-bhain dhi bhain kar janan,*
> *Vilas layi par stri da sang nahi karna – Par triya rakhi na hoth anand*

In *hukum namah* 16, the Guru states:

> *Stri da muhn nahin phit karna*
> *Putri da dhan vikh janna*[20]

The thrust of both *Hukum Namahs* is to consider all women, other than a wife as mother, sister, and daughter. These forbid the seeking of another woman's company for (sexual) pleasures. Grewal, in a nuanced analysis of Guru Nanak's verses,[21] concludes,

Guru Nanak supposes the regulation of sex. This principle applies to both men and women. To covet the wife of another person, or an unwedded woman, is immoral in his system of values, but the whole tone and tenor of Guru Nanak's compositions appears to be monogamous.

Guru Gobind Singh, advancing his views on chastity, said,

As I grew up, my Guru instructed me this: O son, as long as you live, keep up thy vow (of chastity). Let no thought of other women cross even thy dreams. And let the wedded spouse be the exclusive objective of the ever-increasing love.[22]

Aspects of the Marital Bond

Loyalty to their spouses has been repeatedly emphasized as a trait of an ideal Sikh. Bhai Gurdas defines it in the framework of celibacy. According to him, 'A celibate is one who is married to one wife only and treats all other women as if they were his mothers, sisters, and daughters.'[23] The Sikh ought to treat beautiful women other than from their own family as his mothers, sisters, and daughters. For him, the wealth of others is proscribed, as beef is for a Hindu and pork for a Muslim. Out of infatuation for his son, wife or family, he should not betray and deceive anyone. While listening to praises and slander of others, he should not talk ill of anybody. Neither should he count himself as great and glorious nor should he (out of his ego) snub anybody. A *gurmukh*[24] of such a nature practises *raj yog* (highest *yog*), lives peacefully and goes to sacrifice his self unto the holy congregation.[25] In another Var, Bhai Gurdas says that *Eka nari jati hoi par nari dhi bhain vakhanai*,[26] meaning having one woman as wife, he (the Sikh) is a celibate and considers any other's wife as his daughter or a sister (*Dekhi parayeean changiya mavan, bhaina, dhiyan jaaney*). In yet another Var, he states, *Hau tisu gholi ghumaia par nari de neri na javai*, meaning, I love him deeply, who does not go near another's wife.[27] In fact, the symbol of drawers (*kachh*) is important among the five symbols of baptized Sikh. The other four, *kesh*, *kangha*, *kirpan* and *karha* signify continence and are indicative of the Sikh's manly control over his appetite even as he commits himself to the procreative world. The same principle is applicable in the case of women. Guru Nanak's ideological position recognizes the useful role played by women. She is not evil or a seductress, but the mother of mankind. This is the spirit that emerges from an oft-quoted verse of Guru Nanak.

> We are conceived in women,
> We are born to women,
> It is to the women to which we get engaged,
> And then get married. Women is our lifelong companion,
> And pillar of our survival.
> It is through women,

That we establish social relationships.
Why should we denounce her,
When even kings and great men are born from her?[28]

The thrust of the message is that a married woman performs a very useful role in society through maintaining sexual discipline and establishing a morally healthy society. She is an embodiment of virtue and fortitude. The element of lifelong companionship between man and woman is emphasized and that both are incomplete without each other. There has been substantial criticism from scholars like Doris Jakobsh on the basis of this quote. They opine that women are being acknowledged primarily for their procreative capabilities. In a similar vein, Rajkumari Shankar argues,

Analogous to other religions, Sikh religious tradition has been dominated by a patriarchal power structure, the Sikh Gurus authenticated a normative *modus vivendi* for women by formulating ideas of feminity and by including them in the *Adi Granth*. There is a range of views – positive, negative, and ambivalent – suggesting a tension between an inward psychological struggle and an external social decorum.[29]

It would not be out of place to mention that Guru Arjan described an ideal woman as having thirty-two qualities (*batisulakhni*). Gopal Singh, in his translation of *Sri Guru Granth Sahib*, has listed these virtues as beauty, cleanliness, modesty, humility, cheerfulness, concord, observance of religion, cleverness, knowledge, service, compassion, truth, dedicated love for the husband, purity of mind, patience, frugality, beneficence, sobriety, chivalry, active habits, house decoration, respect of elders, proficiency in music, poetry, painting, domestic science and embroidery, respect and attention to guests and upbringing of children.[30] Guru Arjan also mentions sixteen embellishments of women (*solah kiya singar ki anjan payai*).[31]

The same virtues were valued in women in the perception of all other communities as well. Abul Fazl's elaboration of the following virtues can be viewed as a representation of Muslim perception. In the *Ain-i Akbari*, he describes the sixteen embellishments as bathing, anointing with oil, braiding hair, decking her crown head with jewels, anointing with sandalwood, wearing dresses of various kinds, sectarian marks of caste and often decked with pearl and golden ornaments, tinting with lamp-black like collyrium, wearing earrings, adorning with nose rings of pearls and gold, wearing ornaments around the neck, decking up with garlands of flowers or pearls, staining the hands, wearing a belt hung with small bells, decorating the feet with gold ornaments, eating *paan* (betel leaf) and finally, blandishment and artfulness.[32]

According to Irfan Habib, a mystic theologian like Shaikh Ahmad Sirhindi (d. 1624), taking his cue from the Quran, acclaimed the benevolence shown by God to man by allowing him to marry as many as four wives, take any number of concubines and change wives through the instrument of divorce. All decoration of women is provided by Him simply for the enjoyment of men.[33] Habib further writes,

As for women, says the same divine, their nature is so wicked that in every adultery the women must be regarded as the main culprit, since the act would not, for example, be possible without 'her consent'.[34]

Paradoxically, 'this illuminating discovery is conveyed in a letter to an unnamed "pious woman"'.[35] On expected lines, Sirhindi views women as the main culprit when he says that the Quran, in its condemnation, puts the 'adulteress' first and the 'adulterer' second.

The picture that emerges from the oft-quoted verses is of the Gurus' focus on marriage as a site for the dignity and honour attributed to women. Her social role as a wife and a procreator of mankind is acknowledged. The ideal of loyalty towards the spouse and chastity is advocated equally and unequivocally for both men and women. Husband and wife are seen as two equal partners, complementary to each other and sharing a bond of love, affection and mutual trust. This perception of marriage was the basic foundation of medieval society. It was a major component that defined the identity, position, and status of women and appears to be flawless, specifically in the medieval Indian context. Sounding a note of caution, we need to refrain from our anachronistic yardstick. If most of these adjuncts of the Gurus had been put into practice, then the entire construct of the social fabric would have been dramatically and drastically different. Why was there such a startling gap between normative ideas and operative realities? The value system in operation appears to be sharply at variance with the code of conduct advocated by the Gurus and which was later inscribed in the *Adi Granth*, with the consequence that the favourable impact which these ideas should have made was largely thwarted.

As this study shows, there existed a wide gap between the normative and operative beliefs. What were the reasons for this wide divergence between the precept and the practice? First and foremost, it is very difficult to influence or modify the value system of a society at any point in time. It is not reasonable to expect any kind of dramatic change in the patriarchal mindset. In fact, it is very often the women who are the vehicles of this overarching patriarchal tenor of social relations. Moreover, the attitude of the Gurus towards women were by no means simple. For instance, Guru Nanak refers to the wife as a snare and yet places the householder above renunciation. He has no appreciation for a widow becoming *sati*. Yet neither the widow nor the divorced woman appears in any commendable light in his verses. Though the Gurus are in favour of monogamy, there seem to be a few aberrations. Sikhism presents monogamy as an ideal form of marriage. It is in line with the principle of equality of men and women, which the Sikh Gurus advocated. How is it then that the sixth and the tenth Gurus had more than one wife? In the later phase Banda Bahadur, Ranjit Singh, and many other Sikh rulers had many wives. Why was polygamy not rejected and discouraged by the Sikh Gurus and their followers in a categorical manner? Is it not the negation of equality of status between man and woman?

It has also been pointed out that women have been appreciated for their procreative capabilities. In the *Sri Guru Granth Sahib*, the relationship between God and the human soul is depicted in terms of the relationship between man and woman, as in a feudal society. The relationship is not of equality but of inequality, where the husband is treated as a lord and the wife exists merely to serve him and yearns for his grace. Here one is not oblivious of the contribution of the Sikh Gurus in acknowledging the respect, dignity, and honour of women as wives and mothers. Even when we are not making an anachronistic reading of the then social milieu, we have to admit that the ideological formulations of the Sikh Gurus strongly sanctify the patriarchal social structure in which marriage, motherhood, and service to the husband become the most valuable attributes of women. They were respected for the above-mentioned roles, but they were generally placed in a secondary position to men.

The bulk of Guru Nanak's verses refer to conjugal relationships where God is the only true husband and human beings are His wives. The metaphors further relate to the good and the bad wife. The ideal wife is humble and modest before her lord, even if she is beautiful and accomplished. Indeed, she adorns herself only to please her master. She is totally devoted to him and obeys his commands with pleasure. She pines for him in separation. She is faithful to him and she expects fidelity from him. The bad wife, by contrast, has no moral or physical trait to make herself pleasing to her husband. She adorns herself but not to please her lord. She is heedless, slothful, and not even faithful.

> *Gunvanti guna vitharaia gunvanti jhuri*
>
> The woman of good qualities increases her merits.
> One without merit pines away.
> Beauteous female! Should thou seek the bridegroom.
> Not by ill-doing is he attainted,
> Far off is the lord's abode;
> To reach him hast thou neither boat nor raft.[36]

The women of merit (*gunvanti*) spreads merit and the one without merit (*agunvanti*) constantly her deprivation. She who seeks her 'husband' (*var*) should know that he cannot be met through falsehood.[37] The ego-directed man (*manmukh*) after another's woman goes restless. The ego-directed are like a widow to a stranger surrendering her body. For lust and money, under another's sway, she places herself. Without her spouse, no fulfilment will she find.[38]

Further, 'If I apply scent to my body and dress in silken robes but do not appropriate Harnam, I cannot attain peace (*sukh*)'. The women may be beautiful and her eyes even more, and she may adorn herself with all the sixteen items of *shringar*, she will still suffer the daily insult of being rejected.[39] The *Adi Granth* elaborates on how to win over the love of her husband (*shauh*); go inquire of the happily wedded wives by what devices have they attained the love of their spouses:

> All his doings should one gladly accept,
> And discard cleverness and self will.
> He by whose love is attained the boom,
> At his feet should devotion be offered,

Whatever be the spouse's will, obey, let this be the women's applying scent to herself,

> Thus, states the happily wedded wife,
> Sister! This wise is the love of spouse attained.
> By discarding egoism is the spouse's attained
> No other device avails.
> Blessed is the day when the spouse casts his glance of grace:
> Then has the woman the Nine Treasures' attained,
> The woman winning the spouse's love is alone happily wedded,
> And blessed with brothers.
> One that in such love is absorbed and by poise intoxicated,
> Day and night in love involved:
> Is truly beauteous of lovely aspect.[40]

In the same Raag, it is further emphasized,

Go and ask the *suhagan*s how to get to the Lord. Whatsoever he does should be welcome and his command should be obeyed. Only he whose love enables her to receive the gift should be the object of her devotion. Do what he says and dedicate your body and mind to him – this is the 'scent' that attracts him. This is what the *suhagan*s say should be done.[41]

On similar lines, Guru Amar Das says,

Kamini tau singaru kari jan pahilan kantu manae

Women, before decking thyself,
Make thyself acceptable to the Lord,
Lest He should visit not thy couch,
Not thy make-up be gone waste,
In the women finding acceptance with her Lord,
Lies the beauty of her make-up.
Should her make-up be acceptable,
Shall she have Love (acceptability) of her Lord,
To her couch came not her Lord –
All her preparation wasted.[42]

In Sakhi 34, Guru Gobind Singh appreciated the urge of a woman to serve the faith. He also approved the cultural values that her parents and parents-in-law inculcated and which she practised. Yet, the conclusive message is that all her actions should be in compliance with the wishes of her husband (*bharta*). For a woman, the obedience of her husband is most important.[43]

When we speak in terms of this kind of ambivalent attitude of the Gurus, one is cautious of not taking their injunctions literally which, in the face of precepts of Sikhism, strongly advocated a respectable position for women. Otherwise, it is not possible to realize the gap between the normative injunctions and the then existing operative reality. A dispassionate reading makes us estimate the tenacity of the patriarchal frameworks but also compels us to see them as providing conducive context, where the gap between normative and operative beliefs emerged and thrived.

CASTE AND MARRIAGE

This brings us to an important aspect of social institutions in the Indian subcontinent, i.e. the caste system. The term 'caste' refers to what is popularly called *zat* or *jati*, which is an endogamous group. Each *zat* has a name usually associated with the traditional occupation. Most social anthropologists concerned with the Indian caste system accept Srinivas' definition of a traditional caste as 'a hereditary, endogamous, usually localized group having traditional association with an occupation and a particular position in the local hierarchy of the caste'.[44] The caste system has imposed its imperatives on family systems. Caste as a system of graded inequality, inequality with the most 'revered' placed on top and the most 'contemptible' placed at the bottom, is not merely significant at the level of establishing ritual and social hierarchy. This elaborate structure of gradation in occupations, labour, and property relations is reproduced through a tightly controlled marriage system, also entailing a tight control of the sexuality of all women but particularly of upper-caste women. These markers of high caste – their rituals and customs, professions and occupations or their attitudes towards women, including wives, widows, and daughters – are manifested in many forms.

The caste system is inextricably linked to gender relations. An insightful essay by Nur Yalmen (1962)[45] on the castes of Ceylon and Malabar shows that the sexuality of women, more than that of men, is the subject of social concern. In fact, the complex relationship between caste and gender becomes apparent by the effective sexual control over the women of upper castes. The central factor for the subordination of women is to maintain not only patrilineal succession (a prerequisite of all patriarchal societies) but also caste purity, an important identity marker in the Indian social structure. The fundamental principle of an Indian social organization is to construct a close structure to preserve land, women, and ritual purity within it. The three are structurally linked and it is difficult, rather impossible, to maintain all three without stringently guarding and controlling female sexuality and her procreative abilities. Indeed, neither land nor ritual quality, that is, the purity of caste can be ensured without closely guarding women who form the pivot of the entire structure. The honour and respectability of men are protected and preserved through their women. The appearance of puberty, thus, marks a profoundly 'dangerous' situation and is the context for major rituals, which indicates the important relationship between female purity and purity of caste. As already discussed, to guard the purity of castes and not allow young women to go astray, pre-puberty marriages were recommended. The safeguarding of the caste structure is further ensured through the highly restricted movement of women or even through female seclusion. Women are regarded as gateways, that is literally, the points of entry into the caste system. It must be noted that caste identities have different meanings and implications for men and women. While a man and a woman may share a certain commensality in external relations when it comes to other castes, relationships of men and women within their own caste are structured along the lines of difference, with the man exercising dominance. However, here we will focus only on the relation of caste and marriage and not on the variation in the position of women, their rights and status in relation to caste, high or low, which will be discussed in the subsequent chapter.

It may also be pointed out that Sikhs had a tradition that unequivocally criticized the caste system, which finally found its beautiful expression in the usage of the epithets of 'Singh' and 'Kaur' at the time of the establishment of the Khalsa Panth. Guru Nanak rejected the fourfold division of society as it was prevalent in the *varna* system. The *Puratan Janam Saakhis* strongly suggest that in the marriage procession of Guru Nanak, people from all castes and classes had accompanied the *barat* (marriage procession). It further indicated that people of different castes had their food sitting in one place. This is in sharp contrast to the description of the marriage party of Sri Ram as Tulsidas described in the *Ramcharitmanas*. In this account, while people from different castes and classes had accompanied the marriage procession of Sri Ram, they were accorded a treatment according to their status in the hierarchy of the caste system. Their arrangement of stay as well as serving of food was along the lines prescribed by the caste system. Even if we accept this piece of information as a later construct, a kind of *de facto* presentation of knowledge, one cannot deny the fact that the latter adherents wanted to perceive Guru Nanak as the one who had strongly denounced the caste system and practised the idea of a casteless society in his own life. This certainly had the desired effect on the perceptions of the adherents of the faith.[46] Moreover, it is noted in the *Adi Granth* that according to him, the real criterion to judge a man was his conduct (*karma*) and not birth. The Sikh theologian Bhai Gurdas stated that Guru Nanak had coalesced the four castes into one. An oft-quoted saying in the *Adi Granth* states this viewpoint even more categorically,

> *Jaat janam naa puchiya sach ghar lohe batiyen*
> *Ma jaati ma pati hai johe karam kamayee*[47]

The *Adi Granth* contains many hymns which question the practice of caste distinctions and differences. Guru Nanak declared his attitude in a widely quoted *shabad*:

> Worthless is caste and worthless is an exulted name. For all mankind, there is but a single refuge (*Phakar jati phakar nausa bhana jia ika chhau*).[48]

This is one of the most prominent of his pronouncements on this subject, though many more can be added.

> Observe the divine light in the man and ask not his caste,
> for there is no caste in hereafter.[49]
> Sacrifice, oblation, the reading of sacred text – all are futile.
> Only that which pleased Thee is acceptable in Thy sight.
> Kingship, possessions, beauty and riches, all are but transient clouds,
> and when the Sun's chariot ascends, the true landscape comes into view.
> In the hereafter, name and caste count for nothing.[50]

Guru Amar Das repeats the same message both by precept and the institution of distinctive customs of *langar* and *pangat*. He declared:

> When you die you do not carry your caste with you.
> It is your deeds (not your caste) which will determine your fate.[51]

The cardinal institutions of the Sikh faith, the community kitchen (*langar*) and the holy congregation (*pangat*), not only intended to erase the caste divisions but also bring about a compulsory commonality. Guru Ram Das tried to instil the same message when he said, 'There are four castes and four traditional stages in the holy life, but he who mediates on God, he who is supreme.'[52] Guru Arjan expressed his agreement by including in the *Adi Granth*, the works of two earlier poets, Kabir, a low caste weaver (*julaha*) and Ravidas, an outcaste leather worker (*chamar*). Both had made the same point with even greater force; for instance, one of Kabir's hymns directly questions the authority of Brahmins over Sudras. Kabir argued:

> There is no clan or caste while dwelling in the womb,
> Everything is created from the seed of Brahman (God). Say, O Pandit! When were the Brahmans created?
> Do not waste thy life by proclaiming thy Brahmanhood.

If thou art a Brahman, born of a Brahman woman, why hast thou not come through another way? How art thou a Brahman? How am I a shudra? How am I blood? How art thou milk? Whosoever reflects a Brahman (God), Saith Kabir. He is called a Brahman.[53]

Thus, Guru Arjan indicated his agreement by retaining his pronouncements in *Adi Granth*, besides including the works attributed to Namdev, a low caste calico printer (*chimba*).

The egalitarian ideas of the Sikh Gurus were complimented and further accentuated by concrete actions, which were impressive and rather revolutionary. These actions, along with the injunctions, clearly reinforced the message that the Sikh Gurus were not only strongly opposed to the caste system but were also practical denunciators of its inhibiting practices. As noted, Guru Amar Das introduced the practice of compulsory commensality' or eating together, which was a formidable attack on the practice of maintaining ritual purity by not eating anything touched by the lower castes. Practices of *langar* (common kitchen) along with *pangat* (enjoying the food sitting in a line without any distinction of caste, class, creed and religion) were undoubtedly a powerful beginning and succeeded in giving a powerful message to the adherents of the new faith. A reference in the works of Bhai Gurdas suggests that consecrated dessert (*karha prasad*) was deposited by one and all, not only the low castes but even the outcaste Sikh as an offering. Subsequently, it was consumed by every devotee, including the high caste Sikhs.

As a logical extension, Guru Gobind Singh brought the ideological perceptions of the Sikh Gurus into practical reality. At the time of the institution of Khalsa during the ceremony of initiation, it required all the candidates to drink from the common bowl, striking once again at the roots of caste purity. In the Sikh tradition, the anti-caste cardinal principle of Khalsa initiation is further strengthened by the belief that the first five to become 'Khalsa' included a representative ranging from high caste Khatri to a middle caste Jat to low caste barber and a washerman. While there was no ambiguity in the Sikh Gurus' strong rejection of the caste system, the pertinent question to be asked is in what ways and to what extent this egalitarian ideal was practised by the Panth. Did it remain more of a normative prescription or was it able to penetrate, even partially, to the operative realities? It appears that the idea of caste, both as a marker of social and ritual status and as an organizing principle of the important aspects of life persisted, as is to be seen in the marital alliances of all the Sikh Gurus. Yet, the use of epithets of 'Singh' and 'Kaur' instead of surnames certainly would have at least saved the reminder of caste identities in everyday social interactions; admittedly the ideological influence was not powerful enough to not consider the caste affiliations when it came to the question of the marital alliances.

Coming to the specific question of the influence of the caste system in the Punjab, many scholars are of the opinion that it is not of much relevance. As a region which bore the brunt of multiple foreign invasions, it was not conducive for Brahminism to survive. The Punjabis had to adjust to the presence of different ethnic people, their creeds, and social practices. The influence of Sikhism, with its egalitarian ideological formulations, must have checked the growth of stringent Brahmanical customs. Yet, to believe that the caste system did not have any role to play in social relations is a fallacy. If that had been the case, then we would not have had the recurrent and powerful injunctions against the caste system from almost all the Gurus. The situation in the then Punjab clearly reflected the social fluidity, where boundaries of both caste and religion were not rigid. The fusion of traditions and plurality of sociocultural customs have already been discussed in detail. A major aspect of the ritual purity and social relations within the framework of the caste system is the diversity of cultural practices that prevailed among different castes. This diversity is most visible in terms of family forms and marriage practices, including divorce and widow remarriage.

Admittedly, caste and kinship played the most important role in marital alliances. The traditional classical hierarchy of all four *varna*s in the context of marriage provides a misleading starting point for any discussion of the relationship between caste and marital alliances. Instead, we shall begin with the two components of the 'system' most meaningful to those within it, namely the *zat* (Hindi *jati*) and the *got* (Hindi *gotra*). The *zat* is the larger grouping, distinguished above else by the fact that it is endogamous. In the Punjab, the important *zat*s included Brahmins, Khatris, Rajputs, Jats, Aroras, Tarkhans (carpenters) and many more. Each *zat* is divided into several smaller groups. These are the *got*s and the *got* (in contradistinction to the wider *zat*s) is exogamous. This meant that the marital alliances were to be arranged outside a particular *got* (to whom the bride/bridegroom) belonged but had to be within an approved range of *got*s in the same *zat*.

In other words, in Punjab (both among Hindus and Sikhs) patrilineal and patri-virilocal systems seem to have been followed. Marriage takes place within one's *zat* (caste/sub-caste) but outside of one's *got* (exogamous clan*)*. While the rule of endogamy, by and large, ensures that one does not go outside one's identifiable group for marriage, the rule of exogamy takes care that one does not marry within one's close agnatic kin group. Lewis (1958) and Mayer (1960),[54] among other social anthropologists, have reported that a caste group at the village level in most parts of north India is essentially an agnatic kin group. Within a village usually all the members of the caste belong to a single *got*, but in the case of some large castes, such as Jat Sikhs, they may belong to several exogamous groups. Even in the latter case, it would be most unusual for members of a *zat* in a village to intermarry. This exogamy ensures that marriage takes place, not only outside the *got* but also outside the village. Overall, for a male member of a *zat* in a village, the most important agnatic ties are within his village, while affinity ties are outside it. What repercussions this custom of marrying outside the village had on women will be discussed in subsequent sections.

In the caste system, in the context of the Punjab, what emerges as the startling reality is the evidence of a gap between normative beliefs and operative realities. Sikh Gurus, beyond all doubts, appear to be vigorous and practical denunciators of the caste system. In fact, acknowledging the 'fusion of traditions' between Hindus and Sikhs, Muslims were not treated, culturally at least, as a great distinct social group; the influence of Gurus should have extended much more beyond the 'Sikhs per se'. Yet, the caste restrictions were the most important, if not the sole criterion of marital alliances. Even in present times, the Sikhs of Punjab state are divided into a number of named endogamous castes and sub-castes.

Writing on the inconsistency between the Sikh ideological thrust of equality and the presence of caste distinctions among the Sikhs, McLeod says, 'A reasonable conclusion appears to be that where as they (Sikh Gurus) were vigorously opposed to vertical distinctions of caste they were content to accept it in terms of its horizontal linkages.'[55] Although McLeod does not define these terms, it would appear that he is using the term 'vertical' to refer to the hierarchical status aspect of the caste system, while the term 'horizontal linkages' refers to the features of endogamy and separate cultural identities of the caste groups. To put it differently, McLeod seems to be arguing that while the Sikh Gurus rejected status distinctions between castes and their relevance to salvation, they did not object to the practice of endogamy and other cultural differences between caste groups in relation to marital alliances. Although the distinction is useful in understanding the caste system (among the Sikhs), these two aspects are closely connected. Status differences that are articulated in the vertical aspect between castes cannot be fully maintained if endogamy and other inter and intra-caste differences are obliterated. The latter provides identity to groups that are required for any rank-order system.

In sum, McLeod acknowledges 'the significant degree to which the Panth has succeeded in eliminating many of the discriminatory aspects of caste'. Yet, the persistent existence of 'the caste diversity' in the Sikh Panth and the notions of status on the basis of caste was actually a reality. The insistence on the egalitarian social construct was not just a normative injunction, though it might not have been a complete success. McLeod further writes,

Freedom within the Panth may not be a total freedom, but it represents an impressive achievement nevertheless and an endeavour which is still proceeding. Sikhs are above all loyal to the Guru. The question of equality within the Panth offers no exception to this inflexible rule.[56]

There has been significant academic discussion on the system of caste and its formidable impact on the larger social relations. Jagjit Singh, in his essay on the caste system and the Sikhs, articulates how the Sikh Gurus criticized the inhibiting effects of the caste system and its 'constitutive elements' and worked towards creating a new society.[57]

The second point that emerges is that on the one hand there are numerous pronouncements by almost all the Gurus denouncing caste and advocating an egalitarian social structure. In contrast, the marital alliances of all the Gurus, without an exception, presented a wholly contrasting picture. All the ten Gurus were Khatris by caste, that is belonging to a mercantile caste. Khatris, as indicated by the similarity in the names, claimed their allegiance to the elevated rank of Kshatriya, commanding a high status in Punjabi society. All the Gurus, themselves Khatris, married Khatri wives, except for two Gurus Guru Harkrishan who died before the age of marriage. Apart from their own marriages, all the Gurus arranged marriages for their children in strict accordance with traditional caste prescriptions. There is no instance of a Guru having contracted, on behalf of his children, marriages with boys or girls from lower castes. For instance, Guru Nanak, a Khatri by *zat* belonged to the Bedi *got*. This meant that his parents were required to arrange for him a marriage outside the Bedi *got*, but within the approved range of other Khatri *got*s. *Got*s into which Bedis may marry include that of the Chonas and it was to a Chona girl that his parents duly betrothed him to. The second Guru Angad was a Khatri of a Trehan *got* and his successor Amar Das was a Bhalla. Since the Bhalla *got* may intermarry with the Sodhi *got*, it was to a young Sodhi that Amar Das married his daughter. This young man, Ram Das, became the fourth Guru and thereafter the office was hereditary in the line of his male descendants.

A list of marital alliances in the families of Gurus can be prepared substantiating the practice of marrying in accordance with caste norms. One thing that emerges clearly is that all the sons and daughters of the Gurus' families were married according to the correct *got* prescription. This kind of picture inclines one to agree with McLeod's opinion of their (the Gurus) apparent acceptance of the horizontal relationship, an acceptance unmistakably demonstrated by their willingness to observe customary marriage conventions. Though the Gurus were not addressing the ills of the caste system per se, they categorically and repeatedly emphasized that the way to salvation was open to all, irrespective of caste. Even if the clutches of the caste system were loosened only to the extent of reducing the discriminatory aspects of the vertical relationships, it was undoubtedly an achievement which needs to be acknowledged.

There is hardly any doubt that Sikh ideology strongly advocated equalities in the religious, social, and political spheres of the Sikh Panth, which was much ahead of the prevailing traditional social order. If we do not judge the impact of the Sikh Gurus' powerful social message of egalitarianism by a modern yardstick, we realize that they did not support any notion of hierarchy based on birth and occupation. To comprehend why the caste system did not lose its relevance in social relations, particularly marital alliances, it is necessary to make an obvious but critical point. To understand the working of the caste system, the link between caste and kinship, the long history of tenuous ideological control of the caste system, the role of Sikh ideology and the economic and political power of the different sections (region) of Punjab must be examined.

To sum up the existing state of affairs, one can safely infer that the need to maintain a group's status governs the rule of endogamy. As is indicated by the works of Waris Shah, Muqbal, Agra Sethi, Lakh Shah and Ahmed Yaar, different castes – the Khatris, Rajputs, Jats, Qazis, Brahmins, Dhobis, and Ghumiars – adhered to the rules of caste pertaining to endogamy.[58] Within the endogamous group, the status of an individual was the primary concern. For example, the size of the land holding – an indicator of the economic position – determined the social status among the well-off Jats. It figured as an important criterion at the time of marital alliances.[59] Even among the artisan castes, people preferred nuptials at least with those equal in status.[60] As already noted, the system of exogamy was followed with respect to one's sub-caste, village, town, or locality.[61]

VARIED FORMS OF MARRIAGE

In Punjab, different types of marriages were prevalent. Rituals constituted a key element in the construction of religious identity, particularly those that fall under the rubric of the rites of passage. As has been pointed out, the cultural practices, even of an extremely important social institution like marriage, were not categorized into a set of rituals and practices followed exclusively by either Hindus and Muslims or even Sikhs. In the sixteenth and seventeenth centuries, the Sikhs had not emerged as a distinct religious identity. Prior to the Khalsa transformation, Sikhs do not seem to have possessed a distinct set of life cycle rituals. Given the fluid nature of the Sikh identity, in all probability, no need for such exclusive rituals as distinct identity markers was remotely felt by the adherents of this new faith. Caste played a major role in marital alliances, and it was, more importantly, the cumulative social positioning of caste and class, which had an overarching influence on marital alliances, marriage practices, and allied rituals. It, in fact, was the most important determinant in shaping marital alliances and associated social relations.

To attempt to construct the complex and intermingled marriage practices, three related points need to be highlighted at the outset. *Qissa*s like Heer-Ranjha, Sohini-Mahiwal and Mirza-Sahiban, have evoked the indigenous aspect of the Punjabi countryside. An elaborate picture of some social institutions and rituals is seen in the *qissa*s of Waris Shah, Muqbal, Ahmed Yaar, Fazal Shah and Mohamad Bakhsh. Marriage as an institution not only figures in the works of these poets but also emerges as a direct theme of folk songs furnishing meaningful and live evidence of some contemporary marriage customs. Yet, the evidence on marriage customs and rituals available in literature does not provide any comprehensive and compact view in this regard, as some of the rituals can differ from caste to caste and from region to region. In other words, it is important to see the marriage practices as a continuum of cultural practices within the larger Punjabi society rather than as points of sharp distinctions dividing the Hindus, Sikhs and Muslims. Second, it is significant to note that the notions of 'ideality' of marriage customs were not new. In real life, a variety of marriage customs existed among the Punjabis as there were different forms of secondary marriages. Was there any attempt towards recognizing one form as honourable and, therefore, suitable for those cautious of maintaining or enhancing their prestige and social status? Third, we need to speculate upon what these different forms of marriages and practices meant for women. Since the girl child was seen as a great economic and social burden, what did the different forms of marriage mean for women of some sections of the populace that practised 'selling' a daughter in marriage, or a marriage with dowry or, in some agricultural communities, where a girl child was considered another working hand in the family. How could a society, which had a fetish for the vigilance needed to manage the sexuality of females, whether as daughters or wives, solve its dilemma of widow remarriage? What mechanism did it evolve to control the sexuality of widows in a social scenario, where there must have been a huge proportion of young widows as child marriage was the norm. How did society try to absolve the property rights of the widows, if they had any at all?

Hindu scriptures record eight forms of marriage, though we come across mainly three of them among the Hindus in Punjab:

- Class I *Dharamnata* (*Pun*)
- Class II *Wattasatta* (Marriage by exchange)
- Class III *Takka* (On payment of money)

To put it more clearly, the marriage form *pun* indicated 'without price'; *takka* for bride price; and *wattasatta* by exchange involving a reciprocal betrothal. There was also a fourth form of marriage for widows known by different names such as *chaadar andazi* or *chaadar dalna* or *karewa*. The marriage by *chaadar andazi* was practised for remarriage of widows in specific. It will be discussed in detail in the section on widow remarriage and its logistics.

Evidence from ancient scriptures shows that only in one out of the eight forms, a girl was given in marriage along with gifts. The 'tradition' of marriage, the idea of an honourable, meritorious, and expensive marriage of a daughter was present among the upper castes of the Punjabis. Though the marriage of *pun* was the ideal, other forms of marriage like *wattasatta* were more popular. These forms of marriages later came to be criticized vehemently by a section of society, who styled themselves as high castes. In the nineteenth century, one sees the clear attempt to project the *pun* as an 'ideal' type of marriage. The marriages of exchange seemed to be especially shameful because they often involved taking money for the hand of the daughter or a sister. It was also stressed that the *wattasatta* marriages led to mismatched couples and an element of disgust was aroused as the spouses of such marriages were equated with the tabooed relationships in Punjabi society. This kind of social reaction is well represented in a monograph, although of a much later period, by Mohan Lal Shampotra, written with an intention to cure such 'social evils' as clearly reflected by the title *Kuriti Nivaran* (meaning 'cure of social evils'). He writes, 'When you get women by giving a sister, not your wife, she will be called your sister' (*Bhain diya jab aurat aai, aurat nahi goya veh bhain kahai*).[62]

Wattasatta or marriage by exchange was popular among large sections of the society. Ibbetson, commenting on this widespread practice, noted that exchange betrothals were found among all sections of society in western Punjab,

> In the west of the country among all classes in the hill and sub-montane districts apparently among all but the highest classes, and among Jats almost everywhere except in the Jamuna districts, the betrothal by exchange is the commonest form.[63]

Among the Muslims too, in certain cases, matrimonial alliances were settled on a mutual basis. Herein a boy of one family married a girl of the other family and one from the latter's family married into the former. This type of marriage was called *golat* or *golavat* and such type of marriage was found in the imperial households as well. Aurangzeb's daughter, Zeb-un-Nisa and his son Mohammad Azam were given in marriage to Dara Shukoh's son Sipihar Shukoh and daughter Jahan Zeb Banu.[64] For the common masses, we do not come across any recorded information on the subject.

The custom of *watta*, that is exchange, was quite prevalent in all the communities, as it gave a mechanism for the not so well-to-do families to get both their daughter and son married without incurring much financial cost. However, this type of marriage added another dimension of adjustment – either as a sister or a wife – because both the families had a member of the 'other' family easily available who could be humiliated. As has always been noted, it is the woman who is victimized, at least verbally abused in case of any problems in the relationships of the two families. At times, there was the involvement of the bride price too. The repercussions of such marriages, and their availability as a means to 'settle scores' between two families will be discussed later.

In the case of *takka* marriages, the practice of accepting money from the boy's parents by the bride's parents was quite a prevalent feature of the age. So much so that young daughters were an asset and 'according to the customary law of the Shah Pur district, a girl is looked upon as a valuable piece of property and betrothal is a contract, by which the girl's family binds itself, often for money considerations or an exchange for another betrothal'. About the Customary Law of Moga, Zira, and Ferozepur, it is stated,

The parents on both sides have already made their enquiries and arrangements and have settled the considerations which is accepted among those tribes and families who pretend to superior dignity. As generally paid for the girl by the boy's side.[65]

Among the large Jat population of Punjab, marriages involving bride wealth were common and openly acknowledged.[66] The bride price was prevalent among higher castes in exceptional circumstances. When the groom was older, disabled, or a widower, he could get married only through the (custom) payment of the bride price. The practice was prevalent to an extent that the young daughters were married to old persons for material considerations, as Waris Shah has indicated.[67]

The custom of selling girls was largely on the increase among all castes, especially Khatris. In fact, in the secular literature such as the *Puran Bhagat*, it is reflected that the parents with inferior economic status had difficulty in finding spouses for their sons.[68] Where the boy's side, being poor, could not pay for the bride price, he could go and live with his parents-in-law and serve them in the fields and forests, grazing flocks. After some years, he could claim the hand of the girl. This practice was known as 'Marriage by Service'. As Ahmed Yaar noted, the practice of working for a bride existed among the artisan class. To earn a bride, the boy could do labour for her father.[69] In later times, the census authorities noted this custom even among the Khatris of Lahore, where the mother of the relatively poor boy would go and serve the elderly lady of the household and after some time would request the girl in marriage. This custom was known as *chaakri*.

CHILD MARRIAGE

Marriage was considered to be the ultimate, sole goal for a girl. It was considered improper, rather disgraceful, for a girl to remain unmarried. By way of conjugal union, women formed the basis of human existence.[70] Marriage, says Waris Shah, constituted a large link between the domain of caste and kinship.[71] Fathers, failing to perform the marriage of daughters at the proper time, faced severe social criticism. The traditional Hindu marriage had two components. The wedding ceremony, considered binding, was performed before the girl had reached puberty. The girl bride continued to live with her parents. The second component was the *garbhadhaan* or *muklawa* when the bride finally moved to the bridegroom's home. As early as the second century AD, Manu had recommended eight years of age as the ideal age for marriage of girls.[72] The girls were already the sexual property of their husbands at the time of their puberty. All sexual activity would then be exclusively concentrated upon the husband and there would be less possibility of the woman going 'astray'. Immediately on the onset of puberty, referred to locally as inauspicious (*shanee*), she became 'dangerous'[73] and needed to be safeguarded. Thereafter, the ritual consummation of the marriage was performed through the *garbhadhaan* ceremony. After this, the bride went to her husband's house, thus, harnessing female sexuality for the sole purpose of ensuring legitimate reproduction. In case a girl began to menstruate before she was married, her marriage could be performed only (if anyone was willing to marry her) after the prescribed ceremony of penance.[74]

Similar concerns were evinced by the secular literature of the Punjab. Parents were required to make the earliest provision for their daughter's marriage.[75] A premature liaison for a girl was a social norm, somewhat of a compulsion.[76] A grown-up, unmarried girl was a source of pain for the parents.[77] Sikh history is replete with innumerable examples of child marriage. The marital alliance of Gurditta, the son of Guru Hargobind, was fixed with a girl of seven years (daughter of a Khatri named Rama, belonging to Batala).[78] Bibi Veeron was also married at the age of seven.[79] The *Bansawalinamah* reports the marriage of Lakhmi Das, the son of Guru Nanak, at the age of eight.[80] As far as Sikh Gurus are concerned, we do not come across any direct or indirect injunction criticizing child marriage. Probably, it did not even enter as something inappropriate or objectionable in their entire discourse. That is why the family histories of the Gurus are replete with innumerable such examples. The Gurus appear to have accepted it as the norm. Among the Muslims too, young girls were regarded as unmanageable and parents remained anxious to get their daughters married as early as possible.[81] For the Muslims, early marriage was the norm, with girls generally being married at the age of seven, eight, or nine years of age.[82]

Akbar, befitting his liberal and rational outlook, was against the practice of child marriage because of the adverse effects it posed to the health of the child brides. There were clear injunctions prohibiting the marriage of girls below the age of puberty, defined as 12 or 14 years. Hindu marriages were also covered under this injunction, as manifested in Akbar's comment on the inequity of marrying off a minor girl, especially under a law where a woman, being so much younger than her husband, could not marry again.[83] This kind of psyche must have contributed to the practice of child marriage. The Khatris were more cautious of their upward mobility. As a marker of high caste, they wanted to manage the sexuality of their females and thus married them young. From various indications, we find that the approximate marriageable age was about ten years.[84]

The rationale for the dual ceremony was strongly patriarchal. In the larger social perception, it was rooted in the innate nature of women, *stri svabhav*, as already discussed above. Women were declared to be deceitful, evil, and prone to immoral behaviour and therefore in need of severe disciplining from the closely related male at each stage in their life. This pervasive view of female sexuality was constituted on the basis of four closely interrelated but conceptually separable dimensions. First, a woman's supposedly uncontrollable sexual desire was assumed to be awakened at puberty and had to be harnessed in advance through marriage to legitimate sexual activity. Second, the woman's consent in the choice of spouse was immaterial. With marriages being arranged by families, this choice was denied to both spouses. However, the husband's polygamous options and extramarital sexual freedom remained firmly closed to the wife. From whatever little and indirect evidence is available, it can be deduced that adulterous women of the middle and the upper castes must have been regarded as serious offenders. Adultery was regarded as offensive not merely because of the need for legitimate reproduction but also because it was thought to represent 'excessive' sexual energy and was considered deeply reprehensible in the case of women. Third, women were the object of sexual gratification for their husbands. Fourth, women were an instrument of procreation. Obviously, these reasons must have at least ensured the continuance of the system of child marriage.

POLYGAMY

Polygamy was prevalent both among the Hindus and Muslims, as often noted, especially among the ruling elite. It was quite common among kings and nobles, who often found it a useful instrument in strengthening their political power by contracting numerous but judicious matrimonial alliances.[85] Akbar was the classic example of polygamy due to marital alliances guided by political reasons as evinced by his policy towards the Rajputs. According to Abul Fazl, Akbar had a seraglio of 5,000 women supervised by a separate staff of female officers.[86] Generally, common men preferred to have one wife only.[87] A large harem was a privilege of the aristocracy, the prerogative of chieftains, and was common among the Hindus and Muslims. Guru Amar Das refers to it in the Sri Raag.

> If we enjoy myriad of women
> And rule over nine divisions of world,
> We receive not God's Grace
> Without true Guru and are cast
> Into womb again over again.[88]

The existence of harems points to the practice of polygamy in society. Guru Nanak refers to the harems when he says, 'Those who possess horse fast as wind and harems colourfully decked; have chambers, halls and bowers and in shows of these are absorbed; indulge in pleasures after heart's desire.'[89] According to another hymn, 'Where the betel purveyors, the chamber maids? All vanished as shadows.'[90]

Bhai Gurdas also hints at the existence of harems of the kings. He observes,

> The king keeps hundreds of queens and, turn by turn, visits their beds. For him. All are the principal queens and he loved all of them more and more. Decorating the chamber and the bed, they all enjoy coition with him. (*Rajai de sau rania sejai avai varo vari, sabhai hi patarania raje ikdu ik piari.*)[91]

According to Muslim tradition, the Sunnis and Shias could have four wives.[92] However, it was prevalent only among the rich Muslims, as they could afford to keep three or four wives at a time. This practice was common among aristocratic families in the Punjab.[93] The Hindus, by and large, restricted themselves to monogamy. Edward Terry states that they (Hindus) married one wife and were not afraid or jealous of her. They married at a very early age, the choice being made by the parents.[94] They married a second time only if their wives were unable to bear a male child or were barren or the first wife had died. Remarriage was common after the death of one's first wife. Hindus married but had only one wife and never divorced her till death except for the cause of adultery.[95] Though it was a later reference as already mentioned, such social practices do not emerge all of a sudden nor dissipate.

The Census of 1901[96] clearly notes that the religious character of the regular form of marriage was responsible among the higher castes, like Khatris of the Chopra section and the Mohammedan Khojas of Bhera (in Shahpur), for a strong prejudice against a man's taking a second wife during the lifetime of the first. However, polygamy was quite prevalent amongst the lower castes such as the Chamars, Chuhras, Dagis, Nais, and several other menial and artisan castes. It was also common among the lower agricultural tribes especially those of the hills. Groups like the Kanets, Ghirths, Gujars, and Jats all practised it somewhat extensively.[97] Among all these castes, polygamy could have been practised largely due to the practice of widow remarriage. Marrying by *chaadar pauna* was often a way to maintain a brother's widow. Among the Kulu Kanets, at least, polygamy was a form of investment, as women did most of the work in the fields. This also applied to Kangra Ghirths, but to a lesser degree.

In sum, it emerges that polygamy was, if not very widespread, prevalent among the high-class aristocracy among both Hindus and Muslims as well as the lower classes. If not popular, it was still substantially present in society at large. Akbar favoured and commended monogamy. Almost all the contemporary chroniclers claim that a decree was issued to enforce monogamy.[98] Badauni says that in 1587 Akbar issued a decree

Aspects of the Marital Bond

that no one should marry more than one wife, unless she was barren, on the principle of 'one God, one wife'.[99] Abul Fazl tells us of no such order, but he records a saying of Akbar: 'To seek more than one wife is to hurt oneself; one may do so only if the first wife proves barren or her offspring does not survive.'[100] In all probability, the royal family was exempted from this injunction. When Abul Fazl in the official history mentions Prince Salim's marriages in 1593, he seems to have felt called upon to explain this departure from monogamy: 'Just as it is not suitable for others to have more than one wife,' he says, 'it is indispensable for the great ones of the Court to have more numerous (consorts); so that the prosperity of the house gains more splendour and there is refuge provided for a large number.'[101] In fact, during Akbar's reign, matrimonial alliances were a cardinal tenet of the Mughal Rajput policy. Akbar had issued definite order that a man of ordinary means should not possess more than one wife unless the first proved to be barren.[102] It indicates the prevalence of the system. The common mundane social wisdom considered it injurious to a man's health if he kept more than one wife.

The implications of polygamy for women must have been, quite understandably, a severe sense of insecurity, as their entire social-economic status depended on their husbands. In the case of many wives, it would have been directly affected by the position the specific woman held in the eyes of her husband. Her social esteem would have been commensurate to the love and favours bestowed by her husband. As often noted, the prime goal of a wife (*suhagan*) should be to serve her lord (husband) and win his favours. In a situation where there was a constant race for such favours among a group as wives, it must have inevitably generated a sense of rivalry and jealousy among them. We do not get any clear evidence from the Punjab of such situations, the manifestation of human emotions would have led to a sense of insecurity in other socio-religious strata as well, given that they also had to bear the agony of 'sharing' a husband with another woman or women.

It must be noted that the sixth Sikh Guru had three wives: Damodari, Nanaki, and Marvahi. Mata Ganga played a pivotal role in keeping their relations smooth and pleasant. The latter two visited the elder sister of Mata Damodari along with Mata Ganga to Daroli.[103] Kesar Singh Chibber's *Bansawalinamah*, as well as Bhai Sheetal Singh's *Rahit Namah* reports that Guru Arjan's first marriage took place in Mongra district in a Suri Khatri family with a girl named Ramdevi. When she could not conceive for a long time, he was wedded to Ganga Devi. This piece of information is not corroborated by any other source. The cordial relationship, mutual respect and trust, evinced by the wives of Guru Hargobind (this nature of relationship between the co-wives) was carried forward as it marked the relations of Mata Sundari and Mata Sahib Deva, too, the wives of Guru Gobind Singh. Admittedly, we do get some inkling of the mutual rivalry among the wives of Guru Hargobind. That's where Mata Ganga, his mother, is accredited with keeping the family together and nurturing a bond of mutual respect and cordiality among the wives. It is true that we do not get any reference for daily occurrences. Yet at the time of accession to the *gurugaddi* (Guru's seat), there are very clear references to it. When the *gurugaddi* was bestowed upon Guru Har Rai, Mata Marwahi was annoyed that her son Suraj Mal was not considered worthy of accession and shifted to her parent's place along with her son. Similarly, Mata Nanaki also enquired about the fate of her son, Teg Bahadur. To her credit, she did not manifest her concerns as a mother in the form of tantrums or utter annoyance.[104]

Another interesting evidence comes in the form of a *hukamnamah* issued by Mata Sahib Deva, the second wife of Guru Gobind Singh.[105] In it, she almost scolds Bhai Duna, Bhai Sabha, Bhai Kabida and others for showing favouritism towards Mata Sundari and not sending money (*karbheteyan*) for the common kitchen (*langar*) to her. She rhetorically questioned them if they were closer to her (*tusi mata sundari de vakhrey* [special] *aayehon?*) and instructed them that the Guru's households should receive equal treatment. Probably

Aspects of the Marital Bond

Mata Sundari and Mata Sahib Deva maintained separate kitchens. In nine *hukamnamah*s, Mata Sundari and in seven *hukamnamah*s, Mata Sahib Deva, instructed the *sangat*s either to send the money or acknowledge the receipt of the same. One does not infer that the number or the language of the *hukamnamah*s indicate the proportionate power exercised by them, but certainly, it indicates a power tussle over their respective shares.

In Var 10, Pauri 1, Bhai Gurdas too captures the emotional state of child Dhruv and the sense of rivalry and jealousies prevalent among the co-wives. He writes,

Boy Dhruv came smiling to his house (palace) and his father full of love put him into his lap. Seeing this, the stepmother got angry and catching hold of his arm, pushed him out of lap of the father (the king). Tearful, with fear, he asked his mother whether she was a queen or a maidservant.[106]

EXOGAMOUS MARRIAGES: IMPACT ON WOMEN

As noted in the context of marriage, there is a well-observed tradition of marrying off daughters into families who live far away. This custom had significant implications for women in their daily lives. Women were effectively prevented from keeping day-to-day contact with their natal families. As evident in contemporary literature, among the Jats and the lower castes, the sacramental aspect of marriage was only limited to the extent of retaining and securing their wives by all means. In some cases, wives were not even allowed to visit their parental homes (*meke*).[107] Daughters were seldom married to men living in their parental villages. There are a few exceptions like Bibi Bhani and Bibi Dani, daughters of Guru Amar Das. They not only stayed in the same village but with their parental family. The structure of this type of patriarchal family must have made it more difficult for women to resist maltreatments, since they were suddenly transferred to a completely strange environment and were expected to please a family of strangers who, the brides are told, will gradually 'accept' them if they persevere in their efforts to please. This transfer is viewed in folklore and folk songs as the beginning of a new life for women.

Many folk songs bear witness to the anguish experienced by women in leaving their natal families on marriage. This anguish is expressive of the fact that the desired needs of a woman are not fulfilled in her conjugal family. One hears many kinds of voices in the folk songs that the women sang. A large number of them expressed the anguish of the daughter, who has to leave her childhood home and the pathos of the father destined to bid farewell to his daughter. Many others give poetic descriptions of the mystery of the new relationship and make lyrical allusions to the bride who symbolized an ecstatic union. It is beyond doubt that the position of a new bride in her conjugal family was indeed a difficult one.

In *sikhiya*, a kind of moral teaching given to the newly-wed at the time of departure from her natal family, great emphasis was laid on the advice, that the newly-wedded woman should treat her mother-in-law at par with her own mother, her *devar* (younger brother of the husband) as her own brother, and her *nanad* (sister of the husband) as her own sister. Serving the needs of each member of the family is the ultimate goal of your life. This kind of displacement went to the extent that even the first name of the woman was still changed by her in-laws to complete the idea of 'newness'. *Gurbilas Padshahi Chhevin* informs us that Guru Hargobind's mother renamed his second wife Nanaki.[108] A daughter is commonly thought of in terms of alien wealth (*paraya dhan*), who is only a temporary guest in her natal home and who really belongs to her husband's house, where she often remained like an outsider to the family for most of her life. She had to strive constantly and continuously hard to carve out a niche for herself in the 'new family'. The reality that the bride has to win over the love of her in-laws by her virtues and by serving them is acknowledged by Bhai Gurdas when he says that an unmarried daughter is loved by everyone in the parental house and enjoys respect in the in-laws' house primarily because of her virtues and good deeds.

Naihar kuar(i) kannia ladili kai maniat,
Biaha sasurar jae gunan kai maniat.[109]

In his Kabit No. 119, Bhai Gurdas asserts similar sentiments when he briefly recaptures all the traits of a 'good wife', worthy of being called a 'Kulwadhu' *sati*:

Naihar kutanb taj(i) biahe sasurar jae,
Gunan kai kuta-badhu birad kahavai.
Puran patibrat(i) au gur jan seva bhae,
Grib mai gribesur(i) sujas(u) pragtavai.
Ant kal(i) jae pria sang(i) sab-gamani hue,
Lok parlok bikhai uch pad pavai.
Gurmukh(i) marag(i) bhai bhae nirbah(u) karai,
Dhann gursikh ad(i) ant(i) thaibravai[110]

The above passage meant that as a girl leaves her parental house after getting married and earns a respectable name for herself and her husband's family by virtue of her good traits, she earns the honourable title of 'all in all' and 'revered one' by devotedly serving her elders and remaining loyal and faithful to her partner. She departs from this world as an honourable companion of her husband and earns a name for herself here and in the world thereafter. In the *Kabit Swayye*, Bhai Gurdas voiced the general social expectation from a newly wedded daughter-in-law. It is to be noted here that similar sentiments and emotional gestures form the thrust of the *sikhiya* by the parents.

Jaise kula badhu budhivant(i) sasurar bikhai,
Savdhan chetan rahai achar char kai.
Sasur devar jeth sakal ki seva karai,
Khan pan gian jan(i) pat(i) parvar kai.[111]

According to the above verse, an intelligent daughter-in-law of a good family deals with everybody attentively and respectfully; decently with elders and affectionately with youngsters in the house of her parents-in-law. Realizing that this is her husband's family, she takes care of food and all other needs of her father-in-law, brother-in-law, and other members of the family diligently and respectfully. She speaks with all elders of the family respectfully, politely, and abashedly.

Laja-kul ankas(u) au gur-jan sil dil,
Kula-badhu brat(i) kai pati bratkahavaii.[112]

There was a continuous pressure to behave in a manner that honour of the family is enhanced; besides displaying calm and tranquil behaviour before the elders of the house and following the right ethos expected of a married woman, a daughter-in-law of a good family is called faithful and virtuous.

From the centrality of this transfer in a woman's life, there springs the whole culture of adjusting to her husband's family. Even today, women are discouraged from seeking the intervention of their parental families when they are maltreated in their in-laws' home. The knowledge that their parents might be available for help might deter maltreatment and thus lead to a breakdown of the marriage. Even at present, the woman could be sent back to her parents. This has always been considered such a disaster and disgrace that she was always pressurized to keep on 'adjusting'. This formula entailed a package of 'adjustments' only from the woman's side without minimal reciprocity from any of the relations at her in-laws house. The parting message to a daughter at the time of her marriage is meant to be adhered to, 'Daughter! Today we are sending your *doli* from this house to your in-law's house. May only your *arthi* (dead body) come out of that house!'

Through the reading of the primary sources, the general impression is that the strict restrictions on women's freedom of movement and their forming independent associations had become integral features of the patriarchal household in the then Punjab. As Bhai Gurdas put it, 'A faithful wife lives amongst the close relatives of her house and goes nowhere else.' (*sujan kutanh grih(i) gaun karai patibrata, an dev sathan jaise jal bin(u) min hai.*)[113] This quotation underlines the social behaviour of a faithful wife. Yet, one must note that the basic goal of a woman's life in such a conception was to serve the 'lord', that is her husband, and be faithful to him in all circumstances. We get similar statements, *andar baithi lakh di; bahar nikli kakh di.* It meant that within the safe confines of home, she is a treasure; but once she steps out of the confines of home, she became valueless. For a high-caste woman, stepping outside the boundary of the household compound for any purpose not approved by the head of the family amounted to endangering whatever tenuous status and security she was able to acquire. These restrictions were almost non-existent for the women belonging to peasant, artisan, and service classes. The participation of women in the labourious process of agricultural and artisanal production was an accepted norm. Female labour is recognized as a wage earner, that is someone who contributes to the upkeep of the family by her earnings. These women earn a vital portion of the family income.

Since these restrictions became a mark of high social status and respectability, women themselves are made to feel that they have a stake in secluding themselves from the outside world as far as possible. Many forms of segregation – veiling the face, not going out alone, not moving freely in those sections of the house considered the terrain of men, and not speaking in front of men or elders – were the normal practice among both the high caste Hindus and Muslims. All these customs and traditions cumulatively isolated the woman and kept her completely dependent on men for information and access to the outside world. As is well known, she had no interaction with other male members of the family. With her husband too, it was minimum. To compound the problems, women were never considered intelligent, as common sayings in almost all languages exhibit. Compatibility or sharing was not a desirable virtue of marital life. In fact, the prevailing social ethos perceived women as footwear (*pair ki jooti*), saw her as foolish, licentious, untrustworthy, and devoid of intelligence and wisdom. It was legitimized and propagated that this kind of treatment should be meted out to her. Such exclusion from the community, even in a present-day scenario, ensures a woman's isolation from and ignorance of possible sources of support in her struggle to make a viable, less subordinate place for herself in her husband's family and village. For men, marriage means an extended alliance derived from the alliance between male members of the immediate and extended kin group. In contrast, for women, it means losing whatever little foothold they had in the natal family. The pressures to loosen ties with the parental house have the effect of denying these women crucial emotional and other support in their day-to-day lives and make them increasingly vulnerable.

WIDOW REMARRIAGE: PATRIARCHAL GUARDIANSHIP

According to a definition,

Widowhood was read in Brahmanical traditions derived from the *smritis* pre-destined, Karmic product of transgression in past lives, which justified the customary treatment of the widow and helped to create hierarchy of dependence within the family. Widowhood was both a punishable crime and atonement through personal austerity, piety, or domestic drudgery.[114]

The caste system, guiding the social relations and ritual purity among the Hindus, pronounced marriage as the sacrament and the 'twice born' zealously guarded it. This, in practice, translated as women in these castes being allowed to marry only once in a lifetime. Neither abandonment nor the death of the husband dissolved the marriage. Widows were subjected to enforced widowhood and were expected to observe ascetic practices. A widow was debarred from the use of cosmetics to beautify herself.

> *Na sugandh lagayi, na daahi banai.*
> *Naa phoolan haar su payi galanoo.*[115]

The general expectation that a widow should lead the life of an ascetic becomes apparent from *Udasi Bodh* of Sant Rein, an Udasi mendicant who lived in Sangrur between the late eighteenth and early nineteenth centuries. Widows were expected to enter a state of social death. High castes perceived compulsory widowhood as a marker of elevated status. Denzil Ibbetson, serving as Officiating Director of Public Instruction in Punjab during the colonial period, observed, 'It is commonly used as test and spoken of as the mark of their superiority.'[116] Writing in the early fourteenth century, Ibn Battuta states that the widow who did not burn herself 'dresses in coarse garments and lives with her own people in misery, despised for her lack of fidelity'.[117]

The only clear reference we get of widow remarriage in the families of the Sikh Gurus is that of Tara Bai, the widow of Sahibzada Ajit Singh, at the initiative of Guru Gobind Singh. The Guru, father of the deceased, viewing the mourning of Mata Sundri and Tara Bai, adopted a young Sikh from the *Sangat* and got him married to Tara Bai with the consent of Mata Sundri.[118] The silence on the question of widow remarriage in all the contemporary sources is probably an indication of non-existence or rarity at large. The response to widow remarriage must have been a corollary to the general social attitude towards female fidelity and chastity. Alberuni states that becoming a *sati* was considered preferable because the widow otherwise was ill-treated as long as she lived.[119] A question arises about the wide prevalence of the practice in nineteenth-century Haryana, which formed a significant component of the then Punjab. Ganesh Das Vadehra corroborates the general social attitude towards widow remarriage. He observed that no respectable Khatri could ever marry a widow or even a divorced woman, and remain respectable.[120] What is perplexing is if it was non-existent, then why these reactionary statements? In the later period, lower down the caste system, women could be forced to remarry and, thus, required to observe enforced cohabitation, especially during the years when they were capable of reproduction. The agrarian needs sanctified widow remarriage. It was a feature that the agriculturist castes shared with the lower strata.

For a better conceptualization of the system of *karewa*, social scientist and historian Prem Chowdhry's understanding is invaluable. Here, it is said that Jats led the practice of *karewa* and other agriculturist castes (except the Rajputs) followed suit. Even among the Brahmins, the reports indicate that *karewa* was being followed (Karnal gazetteer). Even in a far-flung district such as Muzaffargarh, the Brahmins had declared their adherence to the Jat custom. According to Rattigan,[121] the Settlement Officer of this district pointed out that there was scarcely a Brahmin there who had even the slightest knowledge of Hindu law books. The Brahmins of the province who were not a priestly class but were mostly landowners, consequently followed the dominant social custom of this region in preference to the Sanskrit model. Among other Hindu castes, the 'low-grade Khatris' also followed this practice. Others like the Banias and Kayasthas, did not do so and, among the Muslims, the Sayyids did not.[122]

The question of widow remarriage is closely linked to the general perception of *stri svabhav* and the need to control the sexuality of women. Closely interlinked are the property rights of the widow. If these are acknowledged, then to avoid the circumstantial need to divide the agricultural land, a form of widow remarriage is evolved. In other words, in the name of widow remarriage and female guardianship, patriarchy exercised its power in yet another form. This was through the custom of *karewa*, *chadar dalna*, or *chadar andazi*. It was primarily exercised among the Jats, who married their deceased brother's widow to uphold the name of the family. In *karewa*, the ceremony was not accompanied by any religious ritual. *Karewa*, a white sheet coloured at the corners, was thrown by the man over the widow's head, signifying his acceptance of her as his wife. There could be certain variations.[123] In some regions, it could be placing glass bangles (*churies*), a popular symbol of being a wife (*suhagin*), on the widow's wrist in full assembly. Sometimes, it was a gold nose ring (*nath*) in the nose and a red sheet over her head with a rupee tied in one of the corners. This could be followed by the distribution of jaggery (*gur*) or sweets. This ceremony was not accompanied by any religious rituals. It fitted well with the religious instruction that no woman could be customarily married twice, that is, could go through the custom of a religious wedding (*biah*). The marriage through *karewa* had a social acceptance and the children of such marriages were regarded as legal heirs. After *karewa*, the widow merely resumed wearing her jewels and coloured clothes that she had abandoned after her husband's death. Sometimes, mere cohabitation was considered sufficient to legitimize the relationship and it conferred all the rights of a valid marriage. However, the patriarchal social psychology reiterated itself. For instance, cohabitation was socially accepted as a remarriage if it took place in the man's house. In contrast, a visit to a woman was considered adulterous.

The practice of widow remarriage among the Jats, followed by other agricultural castes, should be understood as closely linked with the idea that the landed property should remain within the family. In addition, women's productive and reproductive potential was not allowed to go to waste, especially when there was an adverse female/male sex ratio. In other words, the prevalence of *karewa* among the landowning classes became popular when land became a prized possession. It emanated from the need for retaining landed property within the family. The main reason for making the marriage arrangements inside the family was to transfer the control of the deceased husband's land from the widow to his brother or a patrilineal family member. If a widow remarried, she lost all her rights to property even if she married her deceased husband's brother. Remarriage, therefore, deprived her even of the limited right to the land which she came to possess after her husband's death. This practice successfully managed to pass on the property rights to her husband's male line.

Within the framework of *karewa* too, the widow's right as to whom she could marry was not only severely restricted, but it could also only be settled by her late husband's family. Though the widow could not be compelled to remarry, she was not free to marry without their consent. So complete was the control over the woman on the question of her remarriage that it was freely admitted that the widow was often practically forced and made to yield to the wishes of her late husband's family and society at large. The basic intention behind the system of widow remarriage, in fact, poses a big question mark regarding the extent this system was beneficial for widows and whether it was really in the spirit of social reform. A British barrister-at-law, F. Cunningham, who compiled the draft *Gazetteer of Rohtak District* between 1870 and 1874, made an apt observation, '*Karewa* under these conditions may be called remarriage with reference to reasons affecting the women; but such unions often take place for causes which have regard to men only.'[124]

When we try to construct a picture of the Muslim widows, it emerges as better than their Hindu sisters. Unlike Hindus, a Muslim widow was allowed to attend and enjoy the festivities of the betrothal, *nikah*, and birth ceremonies. The only ban on her, after her husband's death, was to strictly observe the period of *iddat*, which was four months and ten days. During this period, she had to give up all physical adornments and make-up. She could not attire herself in new, or gaudy silk garments.[125] She was forbidden to wear ornaments made of flowers or metals. The use of perfume, antimony (*surma*) and *missi* were also not allowed. During the period of *iddat*, she could not use scented oil for her hair and was forbidden to comb it smoothly. She had to be secluded in the house and was not permitted to move about except under unavoidable circumstances, that too, during the day and after covering herself with the veil.[126] In case of pregnancy, she had to follow the Islamic rules of *iddat* only up to the birth of the child.[127] Generally, the Muslim widow strictly observed these rules. In her *iddat* she was regarded with more respect and the people had a more sympathetic attitude towards her.

After the completion of the period of *iddat* a widow was free to remarry if she so desired. All foreign travellers of the Mughal period recorded the system of remarriage prevalent among the Muslims and it was not looked down upon till the reign of Aurangzeb. However, the attitude of Muslim society too underwent a change. It started viewing widow remarriage as an undesirable social practice. During the reign of Mohammad Shah (r. 1719-48), widow remarriage was considered unacceptable, especially among the higher and respectable families.[128] This changing social attitude was in contradiction to the Islamic faith, which considered widow remarriage as desirable as fresh marriage. It is worth noting that all the wives of Prophet Mohammad, except the youngest, Aishah, were previously wedded. Due to religious sanctions and, thus, the wider social acceptability, widow remarriage was widely practised by the rich and the poor alike.

Among the Muslims, we find a form of widow remarriage equivalent to *karewa*. The widow was married to the younger brother of the deceased, with the origins of this practice traced back to a Turkish custom. Manucci refers to this custom thus, 'Since the law thus directed that the wives of the dead elder brother belonged to the living younger brother.'[129] It must also be highlighted that in Muslim society, the woman also had some say on whether she wanted to remarry or preferred to live in solitude with the memories of the deceased husband. Commendably, such widows did not have to bear social ostracism or even criticism. They were highly respected not only in the family but also in society. Analysing the then social milieu, this seems to be the behavioural norm among the families of very high status like those of rulers. Otherwise, the reality for a common Muslim widow would not have been much different from her Hindu sisters, where social pressure and acceptability would have been the main guiding force of her widowed life and she must have bowed down to the wishes of her family (read her deceased husband's family). Within the family too, the opinions of the male members would have been the most assertive.

In Muslim society, the larger picture is that the position of the Muslim widow was better than her Hindu counterparts, at least in theory. A Muslim widow could enjoy property rights and had a share in the property of her late husband, howsoever small.[130] After the observation of *iddat*, the Muslim widow was not forbidden from putting on jewellery, fine dresses, or shoes. She was not deprived of social privileges and her appearance on festive occasions was not considered inauspicious as among the Hindus. A Hindu widow was constantly reminded of her misfortune when she was not allowed to participate in birth, marriage, or any other auspicious ceremony. She was made a stranger in her own family. She could not be present even when a child was born to her own son or during the naming of the child (*namkaran*). It must have been an emotional soother for Muslim women that she was not debarred from social festivities; yet, in general, they were either busy fulfilling the needs of the family or led a life of solitude and prayer.[131] Among Muslims, widows generally dressed themselves in white clothes.

NOTES

1. Charles Lewis Tupper, *Punjab Customary Law*, Calcutta: Superintendent of Government Printing, 1881, vol. I, pp. 5-6.
2. *Manava Dharma Shastra*, Eng. tr. G.C. Haughton, ed. William Jones, Delhi: Asian Educational Services, rpt., 1982, pp. 231, 234.
3. Ibid., p. 42.
4. For a typical description of *stri svabhav* see *Manava Dharma Shastra*, pp. 232-3, for a suggestive discussion of *dharma* vs *stri svabhav*, see Julia Leslie, *The Perfect Wife*, New Delhi: Oxford University Press, 1989, pp. 262-6.
5. G.S. Talib, *Sri Guru Granth Sahib*, Eng. tr., 4 vols., Patiala: Punjabi University, 1990 (hereafter referred to as *AG*), p. 877.
6. Ibid., p. 661.
7. Ibid., p. 1030.
8. Bhai Gurdas (1551-1637) is a revered figure in Sikh history. He inscribed the first copy of the *Adi Granth* under the supervision

of Guru Arjan Dev. He was one of the three prominent people who supervised the establishment of the Akal Takht along with Guru Hargobind and Baba Buddha Ji. His poetry, *Varan* in Punjabi and *Kabit Sawaiyye* in Braj Bhasha, is often sung with Gurbani in *sangat*s. Bhai Gurdas devoted his life to the growth of Sikhism and died at Goindwal in August 1636.

9. Bhai Gurdas, *Varan*, Text, Transliteration and Translation, Jodh Singh, Patiala: Vision & Venture, 1998, Var 1, Pauri 40, p. 70.
10. Bhangarnath was a Gorakhpanthi *yogi*. According to the *Bala Janamsakhi*, Guru Nanak met him in the mountains. In the discourse that followed, Bhangarnath reprimanded Guru Nanak for re-entering the life of the householder in clear terms. Guru Nanak's reply is documented in *Varan* of Bhai Gurdas.
11. Bhai Gurdas, *Varan*, Var 1, Pauri 38 and 40, p. 68 and 70; Var 6 Pauri 18, p. 179.
12. Ibid., Var 1, Pauri 21, p. 38.
13. *GurRattan Mal: Sau Sakhi*, ed. Gurbachan Singh Nayyar, Patiala: Punjabi University, rpt., 1995, Sakhi No. 4 & 6, p. 8.
14. *AG*, p. 973.
15. *AG*, p. 788.
16. Bhai Gurdas, *Varan*, Var 36, Pauri 3, p. 337.
17. *AG*, p. 26.
18. Sohan Kavi, *Gurbilas Padshahi Chhevin*, ed. Giani Inder Singh, Amritsar: Jiwan Mandir Pustkalya, 1968, pp. 317-18.
19. Gyani Gyan Singh, *Sri Guru Panth Parkash*, Patiala: Bhasha Vibhag, 1970, p. 204.
20. Ganda Singh, ed., *Hukum Nameh*, Patiala: Punjabi University, rpt., 1993, Hukum Namah 15 & 16, pp. 93-4.
21. J.S. Grewal, 'A Gender Perspective on Guru Nanak', in *Women in Indian History: Social, Economic, Political and Cultural Perspectives*, ed. Kiran Pawar, Patiala & Delhi: Vision & Venture, 1996, pp. 156-7.
22. Gopal Singh, *Thus Spake The Tenth Master*, Patiala: Punjabi University, 1978, p. 142.
23. Bhai Gurdas, *Varan*, Var 29, Pauri 11, p. 271.
24. *Gurmukh* literally means 'from the (auspicious) mouth of Guru'. That is why Punjabi script is referred to as Gurmukhi. As an extension, *gurmukh* refers to one who is leading his life on the path shown by the Guru. This is juxtaposed against *manmukh*, the one who is led by his own will and fancies.

25. Ibid., Var 29, Pauri 11, p. 198.
26. Ibid., Var 6, Pauri 8, p. 169.
27. Ibid., Var 12, Pauri 12, p. 305.
28. *AG*, p. 473.
29. Rajkumari Shankar, 'Women in Sikhism', in *Religion and Women*, ed. Arvind Sharma, Albany: SUNY Press, 1994, p. 191.
30. *Sri Guru Granth Sahib*, Eng. tr. Gopal Singh, Delhi: Gur Das Kapoor and Sons, 1964, vol. II, p. 362.
31. *AG*, p. 1361.
32. Abul Fazl, *Ain-i-Akbari*, vol. III, Eng. tr. H.S. Jarrett, Corrected and Annotated by Jadunath Sarkar, Calcutta: The Asiatic Society, 1949, p. 343.
33. Shaikh Ahmad Sirhindi, *Maktubat-i-Imam-i-Rabbani*, vol. I, Letter No. 192, Lucknow: Munshi Nawal Kishore, quoted in Irfan Habib, *Exploring Medieval Gender History*, Symposia Paper No. 23, Indian History Congress, 2000, p. 266.
34. Ibid.
35. Ibid., p. 273.
36. *AG*, Sri Raag, p. 17.
37. Ibid.
38. Ibid., Raag Gauri, 225.
39. Ibid.,
40. Ibid., Tilang, p. 722.
41. Ibid., Tilang, p. 772.
42. Ibid., p. 788.
43. *Gur Rattan Mal* or *Sau Saakhi*, Sakhi 34, p. 46.
44. M.N. Srinivas, *Caste in Modern India and Other Essays*, Bombay: Asia Publishing House, 1962, p. 3.
45. Nur Yalmen, 'On the Purity of Women in the Castes of Ceylon and Malabar', *Journal of the Royal Anthropological Institute of Great Britain and Ireland*, vol. 93, 1962, pp. 25-8.
46. Meharban, *Janam Sakhi Shri Guru Nanak Dev Ji*, ed. Kirpal Singh and Shamsher Singh Ashok, Amritsar: Sikh History Research Department, Khalsa College, 1962, p. 31.
47. *AG*, p. 1330.
48. Ibid., Var Siri Raag, 3:1, p. 83.
49. Ibid., Asa 3, p. 349.
50. Ibid., Malar 8, p. 1257; for all other pronouncements of Guru Nanak, see Var Majh 10, *AG*, p. 42; Var Asa 11:3, *AG*, p. 469; Saarang 3, *AG*, p. 198; Prabhati 10, *AG*, p. 1330.

51. Ibid., Asa, p. 363.
52. Ibid., p. 861.
53. *AG*, Bhagat Kabir, Ashtapadi, p.330.
54. Oscar Lewis, *Village Life in Northern India*, New York: Vintage Books, 1958; A.C. Mayer, *Caste and Kinship in Central India*, London: Routledge and Kegan Paul, 1960.
55. W.H. McLeod, *Evolution of the Sikh Community*, Delhi; Oxford University Press, 1975, pp. 83-104.
56. Ibid.
57. Discussing on a larger time frame, Jagjit Singh views the empirical inequalities in the Sikh Panth as a remnant from the pre-Sikh past and Sikh ideology as advocating an egalitarian social structure. Jagjit Singh, 'Caste System and the Sikhs', in *Perspectives on the Sikh Tradition*, ed. Gurdev Singh, Chandigarh: Siddharth Publications and Patiala: Academy of Sikh Religion and Culture, 1986, p. 231.
58. Waris Shah, *Hir*, Agra: Chetna Prakashan, rpt. 2010, pp. 55, 206; Muqbal, *Kissa Hir Ranjha*, ed. Dilbara Singh Bajwa, Chandigarh: Unistar Books, 2013, p. 19; Agra Sethi, *Var Haqiqat Rai*, ed. Ganda Rai, Amritsar: Kitab Trinjan, n.d., p. 52; Ahmed Yaar, *Qissa-i-Kamrup*, Lahore: Qadiri Press, 1881, p. 333; Lakh Shah, *Kissa Sassi Punnu*, ed. Hazura Singh, Amritsar: Kitab Trinjan, n.d., p. 32; Fazal Shah, *Sohni Fazal Shah*, ed. Diwan Singh and Roshan Lal Ahuja, Jalandhar, 1979, p. 145; Ahmed Yaar, *Qissa Sassi Punnu*, ed. Nihal Singh Ras, Amritsar: Kitab Trinjan,1963, pp. 19, 21.
59. Waris Shah, *Hir*, p. 56; Muqbal, *Kissa Hir Ranjha*, pp. 19, 21.
60. Ahmed Yaar, *Kissa Sassi Punnu*, pp. 50-72, 75, 79.
61. Muqbal, *Kissa Hir Ranjha*, p. 19; Hashim Shah, *Kissa Sohini Mahiwal*, ed. Gurdev Singh, Ludhiana, 1969, p. 114.
62. Mohan Lal Shampotra, *Kuriti Nivaran*, Lahore, 1890, p. 7.
63. D.C. Ibbetson, *Census of the Punjab: 1881* (henceforth *COP* 1881), Calcutta: Superintendent of Government Printing Press, 1883, p. 356.
64. Saqi Mustad Khan, *Maasir-i-Alamgiri*, Eng. tr. Jadunath Sarkar, New Delhi: Oriental Reprint Corporation, rpt., 1986, p. 77; Kalika Ranjan Qanungo, *Dara Shukoh*, vol. I, Calcutta: S.C. Sarkar, 1952, pp. 18-19 and 330-1.
65. *Gazetteer of the Ferozepur District: 1915*. Printed by the Superintendent, Government Printing Press, Punjab, 1916, Relied Sale Agents: Rama Krishna & Sons (Lahore, 1916), Tracker Spine & Company, Calcutta & Shimla p. 56.

66. Ibid., p. 65.
67. Waris Shah, *Hir*, pp. 72-3.
68. Qadir Yar, 'Puran Bhagat', in *Punjab Dian Lok Gathawan*, ed. Richard Temple, Patiala: Languages Department Punjab, 1970, vol. II, p. 220.
69. Ahmed Yaar, *Qissa Sassi Punnu*, p. 51.
70. Waris Shah, *Hir*, pp. 168-9; Muqbal, *Kissa Hir Ranjha*, p. 14.
71. Waris Shah, *Hir*, pp. 177, 168. Bulleh Shah, *Kalaam Bulleh Shah*, ed. Shah Chaman, Agra: Chetna Prakashan, 2010, p. 97.
72. *Manusmriti*, op. cit., vol. IX, p. 88.
73. Nur Yalmen, op. cit., pp. 25-8.
74. P.V. Kane, *History of Dharma Shastra* (8 vols.), Poona: Bhandarkar Oriental Research Institute, 1962, vol. III, pp. 444-5.
75. Hashim Shah, *Kissa Sohini Mahiwal*, pp. 114-15; Waris Shah, *Hir*, op. cit., pp. 31-2; Bulleh Shah, *Kalaam Bulleh Shah*, op. cit., p. 97; Fazal Shah, *Sohni*, op.cit., pp. 136, 141.
76. Muqbal, *Kissa Hir Ranjha*, p. 27; Waris Shah, *Hir*, pp. 31-3, 46, 206; Fazal Shah, *Sohni*, pp. 132, 138.
77. Waris Shah, *Hir*, p. 181.
78. Sohan Kavi, *Gurbilas Padshashi Chhevin*, op. cit., p. 375.
79. Ibid., p. 386.
80. Kesar Singh Chhibbar, *Banaswalinamah*, ed. Piara Singh Padam, Amritsar: Singh Brothers, 1997, 1 (127), p. 47.
81. Babur, on his death bed, commanded to arrange the marriages of his daughters, Gulrang Begum and Gulchehra Begum. Gulbadan Begum, *Humayun Namah*, Eng. tr. Annette S. Beveridge, New Delhi: Atlantic Publishers & Distributors, rpt., 2018, pp. 106-7.
82. M.S. Commissariat, ed., *Mandelso's Travels in Western India*, London: Oxford University Press, 1931, pp. 51, 115; Jan Huyghen van Linschoten, *The Voyage of Jan Huyghen van Linschoten to the East Indies 1874-75*, New Delhi: Asian Educational Services, rpt., 2004, p. 197.
83. For a detailed study of Akbar's attitude towards women, see Irfan Habib, 'Akbar and Social Inequities: A Study of the Evolution of His Ideas', Proceedings of the Indian History Congress, vol. 53 (1992), pp. 303-6. (Published by Indian History Congress).
84. Waris Shah, *Hir*, p. 81; Tulsa Singh, *Jhagra Jatti Te Khatrian Da*, Ms 800, A.C. Joshi Library, Panjab University, Chandigarh, p. 8, Agra Sethi, *Var Haqiqat Rai*, p. 34; Lakh Shah, *Kissa Sassi Punnu*, p. 32.

Aspects of the Marital Bond 209

85. Abu Raihan Alberuni, *Alberuni's India (Tahqiq-ul-Hind)*, Eng. tr. E.C. Sachau, New Delhi: S. Chand and Co., rpt., 1964, p. 155; A.S. Altekar, *The Position of Women in Hindu Civilization*, Delhi: Motilal Banarsidas, 16th edn., 2016, p. 104.
86. Abul Fazl, *Ain-i Akbari*, vol. I, Eng. tr. H. Blochmann and D.C. Phillot, Calcutta: The Asiatic Society, 1977, pp. 45-6.
87. Abdul Qadir Badauni, *Muntakhab-ut-Tawarikh*, vol. II, Eng tr. W.H. Lowe, ed. B.P. Ambashthya, Patna: Academica Asiatica, rpt., 1973, p. 212.
88. *AG*, p. 26.
89. Ibid., Raag Asa, p. 472.
90. Ibid., Raag Asa, p. 417.
91. Bhai Gurdas, *Varan*, Var 17, Pauri 10, p. 418.
92. Pran Nath Chopra, *Some Aspects of Society and Culture during the Mughal Age (1526-1707)*, Agra: Shiva Lal Agarwala, 1963, pp. 113-14.
93. Ibid. p. 117; S.A. Ali, *Islamic History and Culture*, Delhi: Idarah-i-Adabiyat-i-Delli, 1978, p. 8; Joannes de Laet, *The Empire of the Great Mogol*, ed. J.S. Hoyland and S.N. Banerjee, Delhi: Idarah-i-Adabiyat-i-Delli, 1975, pp. 90-1.
94. William Foster, ed., *Early Travels in India, 1583-1619*, London: Oxford University Press, 1921 (Rpt., Delhi: Low Price Publications, 2012).
95. Pietro Della Valle, *The Travels of a Noble Roman into East Indies and Arabian Deserta*, vol. I, ed. Edward Grey, London: The Hakluyt Society, 1892, pp. 82-3.
96. Census of 1901, H.H. Risley and E.A. Gait; Calcutta: Office of the Superintendent of Printing, India, 1903. vol. I (For a better understanding refer to pp. 421-3, 449-50 focusing on 'endogamous marriages', 'exogamous marriages', and 'marriage by caste').
97. Ibid., pp. 218-20.
98. Abdul Qadir Badauni, *Muntakhab-ut-Tawarikh*, vol. II, p. 356.
99. For a detailed discussion also see Irfan Habib, 'Akbar and Social Inequities: A Study of the Evolution of His Ideas', pp. 300-310.
100. Ibid, p. 303 citing *Ain-i-Akbari*, vol. II, p. 243.
101. Abul Fazl, *Akbarnama*, 3 vols., Eng. tr. H. Beveridge, New Delhi: Atlantic Publishers & Distributors, rpt., 2019, p. 632.
102. Abdul Qadir Badauni, *Muntakhab ut-Tawarikh*, vol. II, p. 357.

103. Sohan Kavi, *Gurbilas Padshani Chhevin*, p. 353.
104. Ibid., pp. 555-6; Gyani Gyan Singh, *Tawarikh-i Guru Khalsa*, ed. K.S. Raju, Patiala: BhashaVibhag, 1993, pp. 602-3.
105. Ganda Singh, ed., *Hukumnamah*, No. 74, p. 209.
106. Bhai Gurdas, *Varan*, Var 10, Pauri 1, p. 248.
107. Waris Shah, *Hir*, p. 77.
108. Sohan Kavi, *Gurbilas Padshahi Chhevin*, p. 345.
109. Bhai Gurdas, *Kabit Sawaiyye*, Hindi tr. Shamsher Singh Puri, Amritsar: Singh Brothers, 2007, Kabit No. 118, p. 146.
110. Ibid., Kabit No. 119, p. 147.
111. Ibid., Kabit No. 395, p. 423.
112. Ibid., Kabit No. 164, p. 192.
113. Ibid., Kabit No. 449, p. 477.
114. G.N. Sharma, *Social Life in Medieval Rajasthan*, Agra: Lakshmi Narayan Aggarwal, 1968, p. 118. For a detailed discussion also see. Kumkum Sangari, 'Mirabai and the Spiritual Economy of Bhakti', *Occasional Papers on History and Society* (Second Series, Number XXVIII), New Delhi: Nehru Memorial Museum and Library, 2001, pp. 73-89.
115. The *Udasi Bodh* composed by Sant Rein (1741-1871), an Udasi saint, contains detailed information on the Udasi views regarding the nature of God and their theological ideas A photocopy of the text, found in a famous Udasi *dera* in the Malwa Region – the Sant Rein *ashram* at village Budannear Malerkotla – Is Available in the library of the Department of History, Guru Nanak Dev University, Amritsar; also see Balwinder Jeet, 'Social Evils During the Reign of Maharaja Ranjit Singh: A Contemporary Perspective', *Proceedings of the Punjab History Conference*, 37th session, March 2005, pp. 216-19; Sulakhan Singh, 'Some Problems of Udasi History Upto 1849', *Punjab History Conference Proceedings*, Patiala: Punjabi University, 1979, pp. 138-43; Sulakhan Singh, 'Literary Evidence on the Udasis: Sant Rein's Udasi Bodh', *Proceedings of Indian History Congress*, vol. 44 (1983), pp. 292-7, published by the Indian History Congress.
116. Selections from the Records of the Government of India, *Papers Relating to Infant Marriage and Enforced Widowhood in India*, India, Home Department, January 1886, Superintendent of Government Print, India, p. 135.
117. Ibn Battuta, *Travels in Asia and Africa, 1325-54*, Eng. tr. H.A.R. Gibb, London: Routledge & Kegan Paul, 1929, p. 191.

118. Bhai Swaroop Singh Kaushish, *Guru Kian Saakhian*, ed. Piara Singh Padam, Amritsar: Singh Brothers, 1995, Saakhi No. 108, pp. 194-5.
119. Abu Raihan Alberuni, *Alberuni's India (Tahqiq-ul-Hind)*, Eng. tr. E.C. Sachau, New Delhi: S. Chand and Co., rpt., 1964, p. 155.
120. Ganesh Das Vadera, *Char Bagh-i Punjab*, ed. Kirpal Singh, Amritsar: Sikh History Research Department, Khalsa College, 1965, p. 292; also see Vasudeva Upadhyay, *Socio-Religious Conditions of North India*, AD *700-1200*, Varanasi: Chowkhamba Sanskrit Series Office, 1964, p. 152.
121. W.H. Rattigan, *A Digest of Civil Law for the Punjab* (First published in Lahore; *Civil and Military Gazette*, 1880), ed. Om Prakash Aggarwal, 13th edn, Allahabad: University Book Agency, 1953, p. XVII.
122. Census of India, Punjab and Delhi, 1911, vol. 17 pt 1 p. 219, Karnal District Gazetteer, 1976, p. 85
123. For details, although for a later period, see Charles Lewis Tupper, *The Punjab Customary Law*, vol. II, pp. 93, 123; See also E. Joseph, *Customary Law of the Rohtak District, 1910*, Lahore, Superintendent of Government Printing, 1911, p. 45.
124. Cited in *Rohtak District Gazetteer, 1883-84*, compiled and published under the authority of the Punjab Government, Calcutta, n.d., p. 51.
125. Ibid., p. 53.
126. Ashraf Ali Thanvi, *Behishti Zewar*, Eng. tr. Mohammad Masroor Khan, Delhi: Urdu Bazaar, 1979, vol. IV, p. 34.
127. Ibid., p. 36.
128. Maulana Syeed Abul Hassan Ali Nadvi, *Hindustani Musalman Ek Nazar Mein*, Lucknow: Majlis-e-Tahqiqat o-Nashriyat-e-Islam, 2nd edn., 1974, p. 63, cited in *Status of Women in Islam*, Lucknow: Academy of Islamic Research & Publication, 1996, p. 15.
129. Niccolao Manucci, *Storia Do Mogor*, Eng. tr. William Irvine, Calcutta: Indian Text Series, rpt., Calcutta: Indian Text Series, 1965, vol. I, p. 361.
130. If she had a child or son's child, her right over this property was one-eighth; if she was childless, then it was one-fourth, according to the Islamic rule, as interpreted in the *The Holy Quran*, Chapter IV, Surah 4: Verse 12.
131. H.G. Keene, *A Sketch of the History of Hindustan*, Delhi: Idarah-i-Adabiyat-i-Delli, rpt., 1972, p. 182.

CHAPTER 5

Women in the Social Sphere

> She is defined and differentiated with reference to man and not he with reference to her: she is incidental, inessential as opposed to the essential. He is the subject; he is the Absolute – she is the other.
>
> – SIMONE de BEAUVOIR[1]

The above statement rightly signifies the position of women not only in medieval Punjab, our area of study, but it is also reflective of women's position in the larger world, even today.

RITUALS AND CEREMONIES

Regarding the ceremonial aspect of marriage,[2] we come across a long process of ceremonies and rituals beginning with the betrothal, the bridegroom's marriage procession (*baraat* or *janj*) going to the bride's house after sunset, the performance of numerous wedding rituals under the supervision of *nai*s and Brahmins until the co-habitation of the couple. With the exception of *nikah* and Vedic eremonies, which were essentially religious in character, most of the other ceremonies and rituals had much in common among the Hindus and Muslims. As already noted, the Sikhs, had not emerged as a distinct social entity and people, who had been influenced by the ideology of the Sikh Gurus followed the same practices as Hindus. Even the families of the Gurus followed the same rituals and customs as any other Hindu family. As stated above, society in the Punjab during the sixteenth and seventeenth centuries had a common culture in which people (including Hindus,

Muslims and people under the influence of Sikh Gurus) followed more or less the same rituals. The marriage rituals have often proven useful to express a sense of collective identity in the evolution of different religious communities. Rituals constitute a key element in the construction of religious identity, particularly those that fall under the rubric of rites of passage. In all pre-industrial societies, such rites tend to express the relationship between individuals and the society in which they live. Ritual enactments are a condensed statement of the most deeply held values of a society.[3]

A marriage proposal, among Hindus, emanated from the girl's family. Among Muslims, it was generally initiated by the boy's side.[4] However, there is no injunction in Islam regarding which party should initiate the proposal. It was the choice of the guardian of the girl to accept or reject the proposal. Among Muslims, in general, a marriage proposal from the girl's side was considered to be humiliating or indecent and, with few exceptions, it was always avoided.

Among Hindus, the girl's parents sent their representatives (*lagi*s) with certain gifts and sweets called *shagun* or *roqna* for the chosen bridegroom. A little oil was poured at the door (*tel chona*) upon the entry of the *lagi*s in the house. In the presence of all the family members and relatives, the boy was seated in front of the *lagi*s, who put some sweets (*shakar*), dried dates (*chhavara*s), sugar puffs (*patasha*s) and some cash into the lap (*jholi* or *palla*) of the boy. This was followed by the distribution of sweets among all those present on the occasion to greet the boy and his family. The host family served meals to the *lagi*s.[5] The parents of the boy, according to their status, could send gifts like sweets, dried dates, coconuts, ornaments, cash and dresses through the *lagi*s to convey their agreement and the confirmation of the betrothal (*kurmai*) to the latter.[6] Since the *lagi*s played an extremely important role, it was customary among the parents to satisfy them with gifts. At times, the *lagi*s were rewarded with rich ornaments.[7] Among the Muslims, at least for the royal households, we get clear evidence that the betrothal ceremony, known by different names such as *imam zamin, nisbat, sherbat khori* and *lahri bel*, was performed by the mother of the boy. The mother, accompanied by relatives and friends, paid a visit to the house of the girl on the appointed day.[8] They took with them several trays (*khwan*s) full of gifts for the bride and her parents. These consisted of costly dresses, ornaments, cosmetics, perfumes, betel leaves, fruits, and sweets according to the status of the family. In the royal families, goods worth lakhs and thousands were presented to the would-be bride. However, this practice seems to have been limited only to the royal families as we do not get any clear reference for common Muslim masses following such practices. This kind of lavish lifestyle, both in terms of finances as well as social freedom and mobility enjoyed by womenfolk was not expected in the social milieu that existed during the period.

Among both families, nothing further was done until the girl's parents announced their readiness for marriage. The average time span between betrothal and marriage seems to have been two to three years. At times, it exceeded this limit.[9] Generally, the girl's parents opted for a suitable date, which was then communicated to the groom's family and after their consent, it was finalized.[10] Guru Hargobind received the *lagi*s with the proposed date for the marriage of Sri Gurditta.[11] The Guru directed the *lagi*s to Mata Ganga who received them with celebration. She served them food and gave them gifts.[12] The girl's parents sent this date of marriage only with due respect and modesty. For instance, a Sikh took the letter of date fixation (*saha*) to the parents-in-law of Bibi Veeron.[13] Similarly, Diwan Purohit appeared before Mata Bassi with the letter stating the date of marriage of Har Rai.[14] Among the Muslims, the date (*ukad*) of the actual marriage was fixed at another meeting, accompanied by ceremonies and courtesies, arranged at the instance of the boy's father. Among Hindus, it was equally important for both the parties to consult a Brahmin astrologer, who calculated a suitable date (*tithi*), propitious moment (*mahurat*) and day (*var*) for the marriage. This practice was called *saha sudharna*.[15] In selecting the dates (*saha*), the astrologers followed the Indian calendar. The lunar days in general and, the full moon days in particular, were considered auspicious for the marriage ceremony.[16] As indicated by Ahmad Yaar and Waris Shah, the most propitious day (that is, night) for a *nikah* ceremony was Thursday night (*jumme raat*).[17]

Fixation of the date of marriage (*saha*) was termed as *gand pauna*.[18] Among Muslims, it was called *gand nikah*.[19] Bulleh Shah makes its meaning explicit. In this observance, a piece of cloth or string was given as many knots as there were the days remaining till the wedding day. In the Rawalpindi district, coloured threads were presented for the same purpose and the knot was tied by the Brahmin or a Mulla. The parents untied a knot every day. Particularly, the bride's parents did it in view of their preparatory measures.[20] After fixing the date, the parents of both sides dispatched a similar knot, which was circulated among the relatives with the presents of jaggery (*gur*) through the hands of the *nai*s, who received small gifts at each house in the form of money or grain. It was called *gand pherna*, which was an invitation as well as an intimation of the date of marriage. *Gurbilas Padshahi Chhevin* indicates the invitation being sent to all the relatives at the time of the marriage of Sri Gurditta.[21] *Sri Guru Panth Parkash* contains references to the marriage of Suraj Mal,[22] besides the invitations to the relatives at Guru Gobind Singh's marriage through *gand pherna*.[23]

> *It guru ghar mein tyaari bhaari saari bhai udari*
> *Chaar vansh ke hans-ans gursaaksam bandha paari*[24]

Girls (that is, brides) were carefully prevented from going outside after this *gand* ceremony.[25] With a few days, generally, a week, remaining for the wedding ceremony, the perfumed paste (*maian* or *vatna*)[26] was anointed on the bodies of the bride and the bridegroom respectively.[27] Gyani Gyan Singh gives a graphic description of *vatna* on the occasion of Guru Gobind Singh's marriage:

Batna malat dalat rati rambha manas kasi urvashi,
Kalangi dhare sapras koran miss batne rahe sahiroo bas![28]

The ceremony was called *maian pauna* or *tel charhauna*. At times, this ceremony was performed on the morning of the day of marriage with the bathing ceremony of the bride and the groom.[29] The groom was seated on the basket-stool (*khara*). The womenfolk of the house held a piece of cloth stretched over him. Then he was bathed by the *lagis*.[30] Connected with this was the ritual of *chappan bhannana* as the groom was required to break the cover (*chappan*) of an earthen vessel by jumping from the *khara*.[31] The same graphic description of the marriage of Guru Nanak Dev is available in the hagiography of Meharbaan. At the time of giving a bath to Guru Nanak, he was made to sit on a stool (*chauk puraya par kharay par baithaya*). He was given a bath and a piece of red cloth was stretched over him. The women, while anointing the perfumed paste, sang auspicious songs. Then, the Brahmins bathed him. Wearing a fresh loincloth (*dhoti*), he got up from the *khara* and broke the earthen plate (*chappaniya*). He dressed in a new outfit. A mark (*tilak*) was applied on his forehead and a crown (*mukut*) was placed on his head. A veil of flowers (*sehra*) was arranged on the crown, while prayers were made to Lord Ganesh. The entire gathering gifted him money (*shagun*) on this auspicious occasion.[32]

In the bride's home, the girls brought water from the village well to perform the bathing ceremony (*gharigharoli*).[33] In contemporary Punjabi households, this ceremony is performed in the bridegroom's family as well. The only difference is that the water is fetched by the brothers' wives (*bhabis*). After this ceremony, the hands of the bride were anointed with henna (*mehndi*). She wore wedding bangles (*suhag chura*) and a wedding nose ring (*suhag nath*) that were supposed to be a gift from her maternal uncles (*mamas*). These ornaments were considered auspicious for the longevity of a husband's life. Immediately after the bathing ceremony, multi-coloured threads (*ganas* or *kangaras*) were tied to the wrists of both the bride and bridegroom. After this ceremony, the bride is carefully watched and guarded for fear that *jinn*s may do her mischief. Following this, the womenfolk of both the families assembled and sang songs. These marriage songs are repositories of great information, particularly the expression of love and affection shared by the family members. For instance, a very popular folk song exhibits the bonding of a brother and sister in a very touching manner when she says:

Jarey rahan mera vir janj chadiya,
Una rahan da reta khand benayya.

The above lines translates to the paths from where the marriage procession of my brother passed, the sand of those roads tasted like sweets to me.

The songs impart practical knowledge to the would-be bride of her life ahead, such as her relationship with her mother-in-law, father-in-law and sisters-in-law (*saas, sasur, nanad*, and *jaithani*). In most of these songs, the bride's mother-in-law is not spoken of in a positive light. At a more tautological level, these assemblies provided the women with a forum to vent out their feelings against the families of their parents-in-law. The lyrics ranged from sarcasm to humour to pangs of separation from the biological family. It would be difficult for the bride to carve out a niche for herself in a new set up, where there was nobody to support her and safeguard her interests. We get repeated references that marriage, for girls at least, is perceived as a second birth.

On the morning of the day of the wedding procession, the bridegroom dressed up in a gaudy outfit with a crown (*mukut*) over his turban and a veil of golden lace (*sehra*) hanging from his forehead.[34] On the occasion of Guru Gobind Singh's marriage, he was given a bath and dressed in a nice outfit with a gemmed crown on his head (*kar snaan poshaak saji guru mukut puri manijartay*).[35]

At this moment, the assembled relatives bestowed blessings on him along with some gifts in cash (*tambol* or *neunda*).[36] After this, the bridegroom was mounted on a mare (*ghori*), while his younger brother or a relative (*sarbala*) sat behind him.[37] The patriarchal ideology was emphasized in the use of mare as well. The mare, in folk tradition, signified the woman and her physicality. Hence, it was not a horse that is the mount for the bridegroom. In the folk lyrical idiom of the Punjab, it was common to refer to a restless young woman as a young mare (*vachheri*). The wedding procession was called *janj charhni*.[38] At the start of the procession, the sister of the bridegroom held the reins of his mare for a short distance. By doing so, she received some money from the brother as a token for *vagpharai*.[39]

The arrival of the wedding party in the bride's village or town was popularly known as *janj dhukni*.[40] We get a detailed description of *janj* and *janj dhukni* in Sikh stories. In *Gurbilas Padshahi Chhevin*,[41] we find a graphic description of the rejoicing at the time of the marriage of Sri Gurditta.[42] The *lagis* of the bride's village welcomed the wedding party.[43] Muqbal informs that the close male relatives of the bride went out of the village to receive the wedding procession.[44] While the guests were still distant from the bride's home, some rituals were performed. Among the Hindus, some uncooked food items and sweets were sent by the brides' parents for the dinner of the bridal party. At the same time, some gifts including *dhoti* were sent for the bride's use by the father of the bridegroom. This rite was known as *kuar dhoti da suhagan*.[45] The wedding party approached the bride's residence quite late in the evening. The occasion was celebrated with dance, music, and fireworks.[46] The bride's father, brother, and kinsmen waited outside the house.[47] According to *Sri Guru Panth Parkash*, when the wedding procession of Guru Gobind Singh reached the village of the bride, the parents-in-law (*samdhi*) came and welcomed them.[48] It was followed by the introduction (*milni*) ceremony, where the relatives of the respective parties met their counterparts. For instance, the maternal uncles of the bride and groom embraced each other. The bride's maternal uncle presented gifts to his counterpart. Sohan Kavi offers a vivid description of this ceremony.[49] Their respective *nai*s assisted them in this exchange of gifts.[50] Genealogists (*bhat*s) and bards (*dum*s and *dhadhi*s) sang praises of the guest and host families. They received their usual dues at that time.[51]

Generally, after the *milni*, the bridegroom was brought to the women's gathering, where the prospective *sali*s (sisters or close friends of the bride) and other women played jokes with him.[52] As Waris Shah indicated, at such times embarrassing and suggestive remarks were made for the bridegroom. This hopefully made the bride and bridegroom somewhat familiar with each other.[53] At this point, some rituals were performed. Muqbal notes that the bride, escorted by her friends, was made to pass under the mare of the groom.[54] Perhaps, it was symbolic of her submission to the latter. In another ritual, an earthen lamp (*diya*) was placed in a sieve (*chhannin*) which was hung in the middle of the doorway.[55] In order to test his manly skill, the groom was required to remove the lamp out of the sieve with his sword. The girls obtained a finger ring (*challa*) from the groom, which was put onto the bride's finger.[56] One can trace the similarity between the old practice and the present-day ring ceremony.

The actual wedding, that is *nikah* among the Muslims and *lavan phere* according to Vedic rituals among the Hindus, was performed on the first night after the arrival of the wedding party. As regards the *nikah*, Muqbal and Waris Shah provide some relevant pieces of information. The Qazi or the learned Mulla was summoned and made to sit on the carpet in the gathering of the assembled males.[57] The bridegroom was brought to sit in front of the *qazi*, while the bride remained in the women's chambers.[58] Two responsible males commanding social respect were chosen as the witnesses (*gawah*) and one more was chosen as a representative (*vakil*) for the purpose of correspondence.[59] The *qazi* invoked the blessings of God (*niyatkhair*) and recited the prophecy of faith (*kalma*) five times along with the *Sifai-i-Imam*.[60] After defining the rules of the Shariat, he sought the formal consent of the bride and the groom through the *vakil* and *gawah*s. In theory, Islamic law attaches great importance to mutual consent to marriage. But, according to the existing social realities, it appeared to be more of a theoretical position, a mere formality which was nowhere close to the reality. In fact, the choice of the groom was in the purview of the elders of the family. The will and choice of the parents were final.[61] Solemnization of marriage included the joining of the gaze of the couple which was called *akad niqah*.[62]

Agra Sethi and Najabat offer information regarding the Vedic wedding ceremony. A wooden altar or pavilion called *vedi* was set up in the house by the Brahmin.[63] Two basket-stools (*khara*s) were placed beneath it. The bridegroom and the bride were seated on it.[64] The learned Brahmin prepared a square place on the ground with flour and marked them with the names of all the planets to obtain favourable omens. It was called *chauk pauna*.[65] Then, the Brahmin performed the ceremony by reading sacred verses from the Vedas. This was called *lavan pheran*. The ends of sheets worn by the bride and the groom were tied together in a knot. This was called *gand chitarna*.[66] They took the rounds together around the fire which was known as *phere lena*.[67]

The last important ceremony in the bride's house was the display of her dowry. Its content depended on the nature of the marriage, besides the social and financial status of the family. It served the purpose of bringing the dowry to the notice of the clan (*biradari*). From the references of Waris Shah and Muqbal, it becomes clear that the articles included in one's dowry (*khatt* or *daaj*) were publicly displayed and announced.[68] According to Muqbal, the gifts from the bridegroom's family (*var* or *vari*) were displayed among the kinsmen and announced.[69] Broadly speaking, a daughter's dowry included clothes, kitchen utensils, jewels, carpets, cash, bedsteads, cattle, and horses.[70] Generally, the clothes and other items were packed in huge wooden boxes (*sanduk*s). The dowry was a symbol of social and economic status. A rich Khatri might spend his life's earnings on his daughter's dowry.[71] The description of the marriage of Guru Teg Bahadur mentions the giving away of dowry (*daaj*),[72] *Sri Guru Panth Parkash* reports:

Ganak ganey ko vastu anekdha pahnay janj saari

This line indicates the scale of gifts given at the time of Guru Gobind Singh's marriage.[73] *Banswali Namah* reports that Mata Banarsi brought along huge dowries (*mata aayi banarsi le ke bahuta daaj*).[74] Bhai Gurdas revealed the stark reality of dowry and the consequent loss of girl's side in a crisp manner:

Biah samai jaise dubun or gaiat(i) git,
Ekai hue labbat ekai han(i) janiai.[75]

The above lines indicate that in a marriage it was the bridegrooms family which seemed to gain. Celebrations were arranged both in the bride and bridegroom's house, but the bride's family had to suffer the pangs of separation. So also materialistically, the bridegroom's side gained a dowry and the arrival of the bride, whereas the bride's family lost wealth and their daughter. Waris Shah, being a sensitized social observer, observed that the dowries of rich families must have caused a sense of deprivation among the poorer sections of society and an urge to follow the example of the rich.[76]

The last important ritual in the series of marriage rites was the departure (*doli*) of the bride for her parents-in-law's place, which meant separation from her biological family. Due to the custom of not marrying the daughters within the village, it practically meant the cessation of regular contact with her natal family. The parents always impressed upon their daughter that they were sending her *doli* and would like only her dead body (*arthi*) to come out of the marital home. It was like a declaration of the social limitations of the parental side in not providing her adequate support required to make adjustments in a new environment. The bride was seated in a palanquin (*doli*), while her relatives and friends came to bid farewell with tears.[77] In relatively more prosperous families, her family *nain* (a barber's wife) or a *dai* (the wet nurse) usually accompanied her.[78] The bearers (*kaharas*) lifted and carried her palanquin. The father of the bridegroom showered coins over the litter, which were picked up by the poor and the menials. Owing to the general social attitude towards women and the availability of cash in an agricultural economy, it would have existed either among the rich sections or just for token value. If the parents of the bride were rich, then their menials accompanied the palanquin. For example, a cattle caretaker could be asked to escort the buffaloes given in the dowry.[79]

The discussion on the departure of their dear daughter would not be complete without a reference to the sermon (*sikhiya*). It was a local colloquial word for teachings (*shiksha*). It was the last parental advice on the cultural values and lessons to lead a happy married life. Its thrust was that the service to her husband was the ultimate goal for a wife. A new bride must consider her mother-in-law as her mother. She must view her father-in-law in the same light as she would her father. She must see her brothers and sisters in all her *devar*s and *nanad*s. She must win over the trust of all the members of her new family through humility, modesty, courteousness, service, and love and affection. The parents put it in a touching manner when they said that her palanquin must enter the other house and only her corpse must depart from there. While instructing her, they almost begged that her conduct in her new family should bring a good name to her parents and not complaints (*ulahenay*) from anyone.

At the time of sending of Mata Gujri's *doli*, her mother Mata Bishen Kaur gave her the *sikhiya*, 'Serve your husband as your Lord! There is no match to serving the Lord in the world!' *Gurbilas Padshahi Chhevin* states it in these words:

> *Pati sam ish pachan ke, te putri kar seva!*
> *Pati parmeshwar janeeye, aur tuch lakh aiv!!*[80]

Mata Gujri's father also advised her that she should serve her husband all her life. At the time of seeing off Bibi Veeron's *doli*, Guru Hargobind is known to have said:

Dear daughter, I don't want to say anything else except that without a husband nothing looks good, it is only in the company of a husband that all the pleasures attract a woman. Respect all the elders and have genuine respect and care for your mother-in-law. Serving the husband is the greatest goal of a woman's life.

Sun bibi mein tujhe sunao,
Pati ki mahima kahi bhar gaon
Pati ki sewa karni safli,
Pati bin aur karey sabh nafli,
Guru jan ki ijjat bahukarni,
Sas sewa ridu mahin mudharni!

Mata Damodari also advised her daughter that being the daughter of Guru Hargobind and granddaughter of Guru Arjan Dev, she must never seek bad company. This was followed by mundane practical knowledge for daily life. Mata Ji explained to Bibi Veeron that under all circumstances she must take her bath early in the morning, before sunrise. She reminded that Guru Nanak Dev had declared that an imperfect woman (*kuchajji*) wasted the early hours sleeping (*kuchajji, oh hi hain jo sutiyaan hi suraj chaad dandiya hain*).[81] She must never drag the issues (small quarrels) in the family. She must be modest and sweet to everyone. She must finish the entire household chores without anyone reminding her. Her conduct should be such that her parents should not get any complaints. God is invoked to bless her.[82]

After the departure of the *doli*, the atmosphere at the bride's home was one of dullness, but that was combined with the satisfaction and relief of having conducted the wedding in the expected social manner. On the other hand, the family of the bridegroom, in a jubilant mood, performed another set of rituals. The bride, being a new entrant in the family, was given a special welcome by the mother, sister, and other female relatives of the bridegroom. The feet of the bride were anointed either in red colour or turmeric paste. She had to walk into her new home with these anointed feet. Considered auspicious, the practice was hoped to bring luck and prosperity to the family. At the entrance, a small container filled up to the brim with rice was kept. She had to spill the grain with her feet so that it fell into the house. This was considered favourable as grain was symbolic of prosperity, particularly in an agricultural economy. She was also welcomed with folk songs that were indicative of her arrival. At times, the new bride was welcomed by bursting crackers as at the time of arrival of the *doli* of Mata Nanki, second wife of Guru Hargobind.[83] The bride's mother-in-law came out of the house with a cup (*chhanna*) of water, which she drank after waving around the head of the couple. This was called *pani varna*.[84]

According to Waris Shah, the bride was then given seven bites of *churi* (sweetened bread crumbs) and *khichri* (a preparation of rice and lentils).[85] Upon first glance of the *nu* (daughter-in-law), the *saas* kissed her and gave her some money; it was popularly known as *muh dikhai*.[86] The womenfolk of the neighbourhood would be present at this auspicious moment and would congratulate them and wish for the long life of the couple.[87] Then the younger brother of the bridegroom (*devar*) or some other boy in relation was made to sit in the lap of the bride with a wish that may God bless her with sons only. After a day or two, the ceremony of untying *gana*s was conducted when the bride and the bridegroom joined hands in untying the *gana*s of each other. Another associated ceremony was the game of *lassi-mundari* in which a finger ring was dropped in curd milk and the couple was supposed to pick it out.[88] Whosoever won the game was supposed to be a more dominating partner in their marital life, which seems more like wishful thinking on the part of the womenfolk. Rationally, both untying of *gana*s and the *lassi-mundari* game seem to be indicating that there would be no secrets between them in future. Much attention has been focused in recent years on the ideological control upon women through the idealization of chastity and wifely fidelity as the highest duty of women reinforced through custom and ritual and through the construction of notions of womanhood, which epitomize wifely fidelity. In this context, it must be noted that in the *Adi Granth* as well as other Sikh sources, pleasing the husband is the prime duty of a wife. As evident from the above discussion, marriage not only formed a major social institution of society, but rather the mechanism, which defined and decided the pattern of life, especially for women.

OTHER LIFE CYCLE RITUALS

After marriage, the next important stage in the life of the householder was the birth of a child. Among the Hindus, when a woman was pregnant, a ceremony called *ritan* was performed in the fifth or seventh month. The pregnant woman received a new set of clothing for the occasion as well as sweets from her mother. The women of the *biradari* assembled to dress her up in the new clothes and be part of the celebrations. Folk songs blessing the would-be mother were sung. The main theme was about the wish for a son. Sweets were distributed among the assembled. On the birth of a son, there was much rejoicing and exchange of gifts. On the other hand, the birth of a daughter became a cause of sorrow and remorse for the family. Unfortunately, quite often, the parents resorted to the inhuman practice of female infanticide, which will be discussed in a separate section. On the birth of a son, the doors of the house were decorated with leaves of the *ashoka* tree. Among the Jat Sikhs, the image of an outspread hand was made with a red dye on the outside walls of the house and an iron ring tied over the lintel. Day and night, a lamp, or a cow dung cake was left to burn outside the mother's room, so that the newborn infant was protected from malevolent forces. Six days after the birth, the family priest (*purohit*) was called to cast a horoscope for the newborn and the occasion was known as *chatthi*.

In the post-natal phase, the mother was considered to be polluted. Therefore, she was kept in seclusion for a period varying from eleven to thirteen days, depending on the ritual purity of the caste to which she belonged. This period of impurity was commonly called *sutak*, but was also known as *chhut*, especially in the north-western Punjab. On the eve of the thirteenth day, the females of the household started the rites of purifications by smearing the walls and floors of the house with a mixture of mud and cow dung. The earthen vessels, which had been used during this period, were smashed and metal vessels thoroughly cleansed. On this day, the *purohit* lit a sacred fire in the house and sprinkled members of the household with holy water from the Ganga. In the case of certain castes, on the thirteenth day, the mother gave away her old clothes to the midwife, who sometimes shared them with the *nain*. The *nain* brought with her some cow urine, green grass and a nail parer (clipper). After sprinkling the cow urine with the grass, the *nain* clipped the lady's nails for the first time since her confinement. After these ceremonies, the mother and the child were allowed to come out of the room in which they had been confined for thirteen days. As on all auspicious occasions, oil (generally mustard oil) was sprinkled on the ground outside the threshold by the *nain*. After the ritual cleansing, the child was named by a Brahmin, who used his almanack to find a name. The mother was deemed to be fully purified only after forty days of confinement, after which she was allowed to enter the domestic kitchen and tend the hearth.

As noted in the context of other rituals and ceremonies, the Muslims had so largely incorporated the customs of Hindus that it was sometimes difficult to distinguish those rituals that were special characteristics of Islam. It holds still truer for the customs observed at the birth of children. A few specific variations, like the custom of reciting *azaan* and *iqamat*, were observed without fail. The naming of the newborn infant was a very important ceremony among Indian Muslims. Like the Hindus, the Muslims of India celebrated *chhatti* on the sixth day of the child's birth with great enthusiasm.[89] It was commonly observed on the sixth day, but sometimes also on the seventh or the ninth, or in case any death had occurred in the house, then *chhatti* was performed on the third day in order to change the infant's luck.

Now moving on to the unfortunate but inevitable end of a

human being and the rites and rituals associated with death. The *shraddh* ceremonies were often repeated on each anniersary of the death. The objective of such mortuary rituals was to earn merit for the deceased and reduce his/her suffering. The women were always deeply disturbed at any death in the family, partly due to their emotive being and sensitive nature and partly due to the fact that the family had always been the epicentre of their life. Yet, she realized the inevitability of death as evident in an anecdote. When the women of the area came to Mata Ganga to mourn Guru Arjan's demise, she consoled them and reiterated the ultimate reality that whoever was born had to meet the fateful end of death.[90]

The rituals connected the husband and wife, but in a clear hierarchical manner. The wife was relegated to a subordinate position while attempting to cloak the hidden conflicts and anxieties under the garb of ritual protocol. In many instances, during a given ceremony, women were traditionally excluded. In the Hindu death rituals, the son alone was permitted to light the funeral pyre. The salvation of the father or the mother solely depended on the son's intervention. The parent's soul could not proceed on the right route (that is, the path of light) if there was no male offspring to perform this rite. The funeral procession also consisted only of men. The wedding party again comprised solely of male friends and relatives, who were expected to carouse their way to the bride's home and bring the newly wedded wife to her parents-in-law's home. The conceptual implications of rituals signified that the ritual enactments were a condensed statement of the most deeply held values of the society. As metaphors of collective consciousness, they informed cultural boundaries and communicated notions of time, space, and sanctity. It establishes and reinforces the position of men and women, their roles, and the existing, largely accepted, gaps in the social order. On one hand, the rituals and ceremonies often reinforced the social order. On the other hand, from a purely systemic viewpoint, rituals were the ceremonies of a mediating institution that shaped the future of society. They were, in effect, the vehicles of hope for both individuals and the social order.[91] The symbols, gestures, formulae and emotions that made up ritual performance helped transform the chaos and vicissitudes of human existence into an ordered and meaningful sequence. More simply, to paraphrase Meyerhoff and Moore, rituals helped people overcome indeterminacy in life.[92] However, there was a tension between the ritual and the social order, and sociologists often insisted on the distance between rituals and everyday life.[93] This became blatantly obvious in the feeling of importance and welcome experienced by the new bride at her parents-in-law's house and her position in the household affairs for years to come. The meaning of the term *samskar*, widely used in lay parlance to denote the life cycle rituals, is to 'prepare', 'refine' and 'complete'.[94] In other words, these rituals (*samskars*) had the power to distil and complete what was undistilled and incomplete in human life.

FAMILY: A COMPLEX WEB OF LOVE AND CONFLICT

The family was the basic social institution. It was the primary unit of organizing reproduction and production as well as passing down the bloodline and the control of property to successive generations. It was a realm where its members were linked to each other through mutual duties and obligations. In medieval Punjab, it was more of a paternalistic dominance within the family, where members had unequal access to the family's material assets and the right to make decisions. Oppression and powerlessness of women coexisted with an ethos of social respect and honour in certain roles like that of a 'mother'.

Another important relationship in the family has always been the brother-sister bonding. It became apparent in the relationship of Guru Nanak with his sister Nanaki and her husband. She was the first person to recognize the spiritual inclinations of her brother. She helped him during his low phases. Guru Nanak, before his marriage, stayed at his sister and brother-in-law's place for quite some time, when he was employed at the government store (*modikhana*). In the eyes of Guru Nanak, the high and pure value attached to the brother-sister relationship became apparent in the parallel he drew between the soul and the body, where the soul was synonymous with the brother. During the pangs of separation, the body (sister/*behen*) meets the fatal end.

Veeran veeran kar rahi, veera veera bhaiy bai rai yey!
Veer chaley ghar apney behan virah jaljaye![95]

Similarly, Guru Teg Bahadur is told to visit his elder sister Bibi Veeron at Malla village and stay there for a month.[96] Although there was no conclusive evidence, one was wishfully inclined to believe that staying at one's sister's place was not a taboo. Maybe, it was a later development.

Sikh history was replete with instances where the norms of behaviour were spelt out through the exemplary conduct of the Gurus. The prominent episode of an unprecedented urge to serve the father on the part of a daughter involved Bibi Bhani. According to popular tradition, when Guru Amar Das was taking bath, the leg of his bathroom seat (*pidhi*) broke. When Bibi Bhani observed this, she placed her hand underneath, so that her father did not have to bear any inconvenience. When Guru Amar Das saw the water on the floor turning red, he realized that Bibi Bhani's palm was bleeding profusely. This episode exemplified the unparallel devotion and urge of a daughter to serve her father. The fatherly affection reciprocated in Guru Amar Das bestowing the seat of the guru (*gur gaddi*) to Bibi Bhani's husband Ramdas and then to be passed in their family among the male line. The popular tradition had different versions about the transfer of the position. The *Mahima Parkash* indicated that Guru Amar Das, touched by the great urge of Bibi Bhani to serve, bestowed these blessings willingly on his own.[97] However, few other sources project Bibi Bhani requesting such a blessing.

The most obvious thing that emerged in the family life for a woman was the ideology of seclusion and domesticity. As discussed, the social understanding of *stri svabhav* forced society to control the sexuality of women. The hegemonic influence of the economically upper and middle peasant classes had established their family structure and landholding pattern as a well-accepted norm, which most other groups lower down the village hierarchy seemed to have adopted.

The patriarchal structure of the families has come to be characterized by the ideology of hierarchical deference, with the greatest power resting in the male head of the family, who was the sole proprietor of the chief source of family income, the land, cattle, and other related economic assets. The hierarchical relations of dominance and submission within the family were a crucial starting point of his power. Its key part was keeping women of the family under strict control and at the bottom of the hierarchy. Admittedly, relations within the household would be shaped through a complex process involving material and ideological resources and, of course, people. Yet,[98] one is forced to agree when anthropologists tell us that within the patriarchal set up the ability of household men to control their women was one of the many indicators of their strength. Conversely, evidence of 'lack of control' indicated weakness and revealed men's vulnerability to other challenges in the public arena. The patriarchal social structure and the expected social ethos from a male became clear when Adi Granth states, 'Men obedient to their womenfolk are impure, filthy, stupid. Men, lustful, impure, follow their womenfolk.'[99] In sharp contrast, subservience and obedience were projected as virtuous qualities (*gun*) among women and made them better human beings.

This hierarchical structuring of relations generated another source of power in relations, which Pierre Bourdieu defines as 'symbolic relations of power' that 'tend to reproduce and to reinforce the power relations that constituted the structure of social space'.[100] For instance, when one analyses the relationship between a mother-in-law and daughter-in-law and the unquestionable authority associated with a mother-in-law, it becomes a tenable observation. After marriage, a woman lived in the joint family of her husband, where the mother-in-law exercised control over her, and her commands were to be carried out. If the bride failed to come up to her expectations, her life became miserable. The words of Guru Nanak reflected the social fate of a daughter-in-law at the hands of her mother-in-law. He states, 'My mother-in-law is vicious; she lets me not stay in peace at home or seek the joy of my spouse.'[101]

Quite probably, it would have been the daughter-in-law who would have been at the mercy of the mother-in-law. Bhai Gurdas offered a different perspective, which should not be ignored.

Mata pita anand vichi putai di kurmani hai,
Rahasi ang na mavai gavai sohilare such soi,
Vigasi put vishiai ghori lavan gav bhaloi,
Sukhan sukha mavari putu nunh dam el aloi,
Nuhu nit kant kumantu dei vihare hovah sasu vigoi,
Lakh upkaru visari kai put kuputi chaki uthi jhoi,
Hovai saravan virala koi.[102]

According to this passage, the parents were happy that the betrothal ceremony of their son had been solemnized. The mother became overjoyed and sang songs of happiness. Singing eulogies of the bridegroom and praying for the welfare of the couple, she felt very happy that the son got married. For the well-being and harmony of the bride and the bridegroom, the mother made vows of offerings (before the deities). Now, the bride started ill-advising the son, goading him to get separate from the parents and consequently the mother-in-law became sorrowful.

Bhai Gurdas further writes,

Forgetting lacs of benefactions (of mother), the son becomes disloyal and sets himself at loggerheads with his parents. Rare is any obedient son like Sravan of mythology, who was most obedient to his blind parents.

Kamani kamaniariari kito kamanu kant piare,
Jamme sain visaria vivehian man pia visare,
Sukhan sukhi vivehia saunu sanjogu vichari vichare,
Putu nuhain da melu vekhi ang na mathani man piu vare,
Nunh nit mant kamant dei man piu chhadi vade hatidare,
Vakh havai putu ranni lai man piu de upkaru visare,
Lakachari hoi vade kuchre.[103]

In the above passage narrated it is said that the enchantress wife with her charms made the husband dote on her. He forgot the parents who had given him birth and got him married. Having made vows of offerings and considered many good and bad omens and auspicious combinations, they arranged his marriage. Seeing the meeting of the son and the daughter-in-law, the parents had felt overjoyed. The bride then started continuously ill-advising the husband to desert his parents, instigating that they were tyrants. Forgetting the benefactions of the parents, the son along with his wife, got separated from them. Now, the way of the world has become grossly immoral. However, it must be admitted beyond doubt that there must have existed a gap between the expectations and the realities of the existing relationships between the two generations.

In the foregoing study of the power relations that are built into the family, the foremost aspect needing focus is the issue that what appears as 'oppression' to us might be a difference of perception in the context of the Punjab of the sixteenth and seventeenth centuries. The varied expressions of power relations in the households, whether Muslim or Hindu, could not always be attributed to a lack of love, care, or goodness in people. All of these have always existed in abundance in Indian family life. Even while the dominant family structure concentrated immense unchecked power in the hands of men, every man did not necessarily abuse that power. For example, the tradition of the benevolent patriarch who looked after the interest of every member of the family with care, concern, and fairness remained as prevalent and real as the tradition of the self-effacing and nurturing mother figures. Even dominant and authoritarian male family members might at the same time often be loving and caring fathers, brothers, and sons. While women's freedom and rights might have been severely restricted within the prevailing family structure, there was also a strong tradition of adhering to certain forms of respect and veneration for women, especially as mothers. Since the family has been the only source of social and emotional support available to most women in India, it occupied a central place in their world view and they poured all their energies into working for its well-being. While doing so, they sometimes attained considerable prestige and influence within the family. Dependence and restrictions were often found coexisting with an unusual kind of veneration and caring attitude for women.

The key problem of women within the family was that if they were badly treated, they were unable to offer effective resistance because of their total dependence in every respect and considerable vulnerability. Few effective sources of support were available to most Indian women outside their families. They had nowhere to go for help if they suffered abuse and neglect at the hands of the family.

In real life, it was not easy to draw a neat dividing line between the oppressors. It was not always men who beat or maltreated women. Very often women suffered cruel treatment at the hands of other women. For example, a daughter-in-law suffered at the hands of the mother-in-law or sister-in-law. When a woman mistreated another woman, she enhanced the total power of men as a group within the patriarchal family. Women could attain power only as agents of domination and oppression within the male-dominated family structure. The woman who came to gain the upper hand was usually the one who had the backing and approval of a powerful man. This tussle among women played a crucial role in most families.

Women's placement in society was unfavourable to the extent that it led to their exploitation, abuse, and subjugation. Societal conditions gave rise to women's suffering. The exploitative societal environment towards women can be attributed to both structural and behavioural aspects.

WOMEN AS MOTHERS: LIFELINE OF A SOCIETY

In almost all sections of Hindu and Muslim societies, the mothers and other elderly women were given utmost respect and honour and their commands were carried out by one and all. The image of a mother has always commanded respect and veneration from times immemorial. In all religions, she had been projected as the life-giver. We get innumerable references where mother figures exercised great influence. For instance, the Mughal kings or the Rajput rulers always paid great respect to their mothers and sought their blessings. In Punjab, the position of the mother was one of honour and command without any distinction of religion, caste, or class. With regard to the feminine images within Sikh sacred scripture, motherhood was indeed celebrated. In the Sikh perspective, she exists as a person upon whom depends the responsibility of creating and nurturing. The structure of her body is prized. She is accorded value as a woman, that is, as a giver of life without whom God's creation, the world cannot exist. Guru Nanak vehemently opposed the custom of impurity associated with childbirth, menstruation and related biological functions. Guru Nanak states,

We are conceived in the woman's womb, and we grow in it. We are engaged to women, and we wed them. Through the woman's cooperation, new generations are born. If one woman dies, we seek another; without the woman, there can be no bond. Why call her bad who gives birth to rajas? The woman herself is born of the woman, and none comes into this world without the woman; Nanak, the true one alone is independent of the woman.[104]

The Sikh scripture affirms the centrality of menstrual blood in the creative process. It asserted that the mother's blood and father's semen created the human form (*ma ki raktu pita bindu dhare*).[105] The same biological contribution of the mother is admitted in the statement that one was created from blood and semen (*raktu bindu kari nimia*).[106] She was respected as a paragon of womanhood through her procreative functions as the bearer of children. She was inextricably entwined within a world of children and attachment to them. However, within the 'mother' image too, unfortunately, the mother of sons was more valued. The woman who gave birth to daughters became a victim of social taunt and ridicule. She could well be deserted by her husband if she was unable to bear him sons.

In domestic affairs, the women were consulted on all matters of importance. The mother was a confidante of her children and, thus, was a friend who would offer them the best advice based on the experiences of her life. Guru Gobind Singh shared such a relationship with his mother. In Sakhi 17, he not only unwinds by discussing the events of the past with his mother but also shares the bestowal of blessings of the Devi and includes a prophecy of the extinction of the Turks. Even as the contents of this source cannot be accepted at their face value, as they were exaggerated like any hagiographical text, they are still a window into the rapport the children shared with their mother.[107]

gyan dhian pran sut rakhi jan-ni prat(i)!
avgun gun mata chit main a chethai![108]

The above lines indicate that just as a son leaves his understanding, perception, and protection of his life to the care of his mother, she too does not think of her son's merits and demerits. In fact, mothers played a very significant role in selecting their children's spouses. Guru Arjan summed up the mother's position in a household when he stated,

In all the family she is the noblest, she is the counsellor of her husband's younger brother and elder brother, Blessed is the house, where-in she has appeared, O Nanak she passes her time in perfect peace.[109]

Nikky Singh has explored the central themes of Guru Nanak's maternal images, the 'infinite matrix' of the mother as the initiator of wisdom, beauty, and chastity. A parallel is drawn between the role of the mother and the popular household chore of churning butter which stands for the possibility of having a spiritual journey, a closeness to god along with the worldly responsibilities of the householder. Once Guru Nanak gave up the life of a renunciant and accepted the life of a householder, his life was seen as 'soured' by the *yogi*s. Just as butter cannot be churned out of 'soured' milk, Guru Nanak's 'soured' life cannot produce knowledge or enlightenment. The churning of butter metaphorically stands for epistemological insights. In fact, it's an oft-used literary expression in north Indian households. Nikky Guninder says that 'Bhai Gurdas shows Guru Nanak rejecting the Yogic ideal . . . he disapproves of Bhangar Nath's intelligence, "*teri mao kuchaji hai*".' She appropriately concludes that the term *mao* is used for intelligence. Overall in the Sikh tradition, the equation between mother and intelligence is a prevalent one, *mata mati, pita santokh* (mother is intelligence, father is contentment), an equation that actually underscores the importance of the feminine in Sikh epistemology.[110] It is the central image of the mother which she projects as creating, preserving, and nurturing within the Sikh canon.[111]

Interestingly, all the successive Guru histories were replete with the anecdotes of Guru Matas where their image was projected as a figure of honour and veneration. As mothers, they were known to have exerted great influence on her sons. To quote a few instances that further testified to the point. When Guru Hargobind was busy garnering arms, armaments, and horses, a group of *masand*s approached Mata Ganga to exert influence over the Guru to keep away from confrontation with Mughal authorities, particularly Chandu Shah,[112] which they warned would prove fatal for the Sikh Panth. When Mata Ganga promised Bhai Mehra of Bakala that the family, along with Guru Hargobind, would visit his new home and bless him, the Guru obeyed his mother and fulfilled her wishes.[113] While such expressions of respect and veneration may not have applied to the common masses, the basic emotional spirit towards the mother figure was the same in content. Ironically, in the Indian context, brutal oppression and powerlessness of women coexisted with a prevailing ethos of awarding social respect and honour in some of her roles.

WIFE: AN *ARDHANGANI* OR BURDEN

Jaise bhartar(i) bhar(i) nar(i) ur har(i) mani,
Tan te lal(u) lalna ko man(u) man(i) let hai.[114]

Women in the Social Sphere

According to this verse, just as a wife, filled with love for her husband, shares his mental stress and bears all the load in her mind, the husband too makes a loving and respectful room in his heart. The verse emphasizes the mental compatibility and reciprocity in the relationship of a husband and his wife.

The ideal wife was supposed to be blessed with 32 virtues (*battigunni*):

> Possessor of thirty-two merits, holy truth is her progeny.
> Obedient to nobleman. To her husband's wishes.[115]

The major thrust of contemporary sources for the ideal and appropriate female role emphasized humility and submissiveness on the part of the woman. She was required to control her aggressive and sexual urges. Through a systemic formulation of the social norms, which defined the maternal role of a woman, she was accorded a place of dignity, respect, and honour.

As a wife, a woman's prime duty was to 'serve' her husband and all her activities were aimed at winning over the love of her husband. In the compositions of the *Adi Granth*, several metaphors relating to women referred to the conjugal relationship.[116] Though the language of the *Adi Granth* is considered to be allegorical, it reflected the social reality.[117] In Guru Nanak's verses, we can infer a conception of a good and bad wife from the usage of these value-loaded terms. Guru Nanak calls a bad wife *kuchaji*, *dohagan* and *kulakhanni*,[118] by which he means a bride without merit and a non-virtuous woman. On the other hand, *suchajji*[119] (doer of good deeds), *suhagan*[120] (wedded) and *sulakhani*[121] (virtuous or an ideal woman) indicated an opposite woman, who knew how to win over the love and affection of her husband. As stated earlier, unquestioned obedience was the hallmark of the husband–wife relationship. The husband was equated to the Lord, 'The Lord is my husband, I, his wife; The Lord is immensely great, I am so small.'[122]

The image of a wife that emerges from the *Adi Granth* complies with the social reality and, at times, appears to hammer the patriarchal psyche, that is, her intimate goal in life should be to please and serve her husband, her lord (*pati*). Even if she was beautiful, accomplished, and well mannered, she had to be humble and modest before her husband. She never felt proud of her beauty. In a humble and submissive manner, she pined for her desired subordinate position, feeling that she did not possess any charm or merit to please her husband:

I am shorn of all merit O Lord; then how shall I attain into Thee? Neither have I beauty nor lustrous eyes, neither family nor culture, nor sweet speech.[123]

I have neither intention nor intellect.

I am ignorant and unwise. Bless me Thou, O my Lord, that I lie in Thy feet.[124]

The centrality of love for the spouse in marital life is beyond question. It was held that 'true loving wives for their spouse are embellished. Day and night engaging in devotion, no impediment they reck'. (*Nari purakh piyaru premi singariyan.*)[125] In the eyes of Guru Nanak, it was the duty of a woman to be a devoted worshipper of the lord (husband), to be a seeker of a good name, to be virtuous and chaste, and a faithful companion of her husband. Guru Nanak believed that a woman was beautiful if she adorned her head with the jewel of love. This was the glory she cherished in her mind the love of the true lord.

'O' thou Bride, bedeck thy hair with truth;
Wear thou the robe of love.
Gather in the *chandan*-like (God) in thy conscious mind
and leave them in the temple of inner consciousness.[126]

Bhai Gurdas expressed the general social expectation for the wife to remain loyal even if her husband was adulterous. He held that if the husband enjoyed (immorally) at many houses, the wife should preserve her chastity. (*Je piru bahu gharu handhana satu rakhi nare.*)[127]

In sharp contrast, Guru Nanak, in Sri Raag, commands

that all make-up was in vain for a woman who was not blessed with the love of her lord. He stated,

If a woman uses the fragrant perfumes and with saffron fills the parting of the hair and chews the betel leaf mixed with camphor, if she is not accepted by her Lord, all her flavouring is of no avail.[128]

If a wife (or any woman) was to lead an adulterous life, she was inviting social wrath, not only ostracism. Bhai Gurdas effectively captures the fate of an adulterous woman:

Sahuru piharu palaria nhoi nilaj na laja dhovai,
Ravai jaru bhataru taji khinjotani khusi kiu hovai,
Samajhai na samajhai marane parane loku vigovai,
Dhiri dhiri milade mehane hui saramindi anjhu rovai,
Pap kamane pakariai hani kani dibani kharovai,
Marai na jivai dukh sahai rahai na ghari vichi par ghar jovai,
Dubidha augun haru parovai.[129]

The above lines indicate that by abandoning both the families of the father and father-in-law, the shameless woman cares not for modesty and does not wish to wash away her immoral reputation. Deserting her husband, if she enjoys the company of her paramour, how can she, moving in different lustful directions, be happy? No advice prevails upon her, and she is unwelcomed at all social gatherings of mourning and rejoicing. She weeps in contrition because she is disdainfully reproached at every door. For her sins, she is arrested and punished by the court, where she loses every iota of honour that she had. She is miserable because now she is neither dead nor alive; she still looks for another house to ruin because she does not like to live in her home. Similarly, doubt or double-mindedness (flickering loyalties) weaves for it the garland of vices.

Echoing the value attached to the sexual control of women, a deceitful woman is strongly criticized:

Aisi naika sai kuar patra bi supatra bhali,
As piasi mata pita ekai kah det hai.
Aisi naika sai dinta kai dubagan(i) bhali,

Patit pavan pria pae lae let bai.
Aisi naika sai bhalo birba siog sog,
Lagan sagan sodhe sardha sabet hai.
Aisi naika mat rabbh hi gali bhali,
Kapat saneh dubidha jio rahu ketu bai.[130]

The above lines indicate that a virgin maid, who is ever hopeful of achieving a place of superior authority in the house of a husband that her father will find for her one day, is far better than a deceitful woman. A woman, who has been disassociated with her husband and who regrets her actions by her humility and, as a consequence of which, is forgiven by her husband, is far better than a deceitful woman. That woman, separated from her husband, who bears the pangs of her separation, and is devotedly involved in finding an auspicious time and good omens for the reunion is better than a treacherous and deceitful woman. Such a woman of deceitful love should have perished in her mother's womb. Deceit-filled love is full of such duality as the two demons Rahu and Ketu, who cause a solar and lunar eclipse.

The wife's humble position in relation to her husband was expressed in the custom of the wife's eating her husband's leftover and polluted food. As many authors have pointed out, the sharing of pollution was also an index of love and bodily intimacy. Leaving the favourite food items of his wife uneaten on his plate, so that only she eats these, was a well-known means by which a man might publicly proclaim love and bodily intimacy with his wife. It is true that the family would have to share in a well-tuned system of non-verbal communication for such cues to be picked up. Yet, it demands a methodological commitment to explore such patterns of communication rather than to restrict oneself to adjurer prescriptions alone.

It would not be out of context to briefly recapitulate the conception of *pativrata*, and the ideal behaviour associated with it. Apart from the *Adi Granth*'s oft-quoted injunctions of *suhagin* and *suchhaji*, Bhai Gurdas recapitulates it in clear terms:

Log bed gian updes bai patibrata kau,
Mam bach kram svami seva adhikar hai.
Nam isnan dan sanjam na jap tap,
Tirath barat puja nem na nat akar hai.
Hom jag bhog naibed nabi devi dev sev,
Rag nad bad na sanbad an duar hai[131]

The above lines indicate that the teachings of folk traditions and the Vedas have laid down that a faithful and loyal wife was solely interested in serving her husband devotedly in words and actions. Such a loyal, devoted, and faithful wife did not even look at the futile rites and rituals, rites like meditations on various names, bathing at the places of pilgrimage on specific days, charity, self-imposed discipline, penances, and fasts. For her, the sacrificial fire (*yagya*), offerings, and other rituals connected with the worship of numerous deities were meaningless. She was not interested in any modes of singing and musical instruments. It did not seem logical to go to any other door (other than her lord's).

Jaise patibrata kau pavitra ghar(i) vas nbat,
Asan basan dhan dham lokachar hai.
Tat mat bhrat sut sujan kutanb sakha,
Seva gur jan sukh abharan shingar hai.
Kirat(i) birat(i) oarsut mal mutra-dhari,
Sakal pavitra joi bibidh (i) achar hai.[132]

According to the above lines, just as living in her house, bathing, eating, and sleeping and discharging worldly duties according to her husband's wishes were important, the social customs and traditions were sacred for a faithful wife. It was her natural duty to embellish herself with ornaments for the happiness of her husband, besides serving and respecting the parents, brothers, sisters, sons, friends, elders, and other social contacts. It was a sacred duty of a faithful wife to attend to the household chores, bear children, bring them up and keep them neat and clean.

Bhai Gurdas further states:

Man bach kram kai patibrat karai jau nar(i),
Tahe mam bach kram chahat bhatar hai.
Abharan singar char sibja sanjog bhog,
Sakal kutanb hi mai ta ko jai jaikar hai.
Sahaj anand such mangal suhag bhag,
Sundar mandar chhab(i) sobhat suchar hai.[133]

The above lines indicate that if a wife discharges her duties faithfully and loyally and is devoted to her husband, such a wife is loved dearly by her husband. Such a lady is blessed with the opportunity of adorning herself and bonding with her husband. Being virtuous she is praised and appreciated by the whole family. She acquires the comforts of married life gently and gradually. Because of the beauty of her high merits, she adores the beautiful mansions with her presence.

Jaise tau patibrata patibrat mai savdhan,
Tabi te gribesur hue naika kabavai.
Asan basan dhan dham kamna pujavai,
Sobbit singar char sibja samavai.[134]

According to the above lines, a loyal and faithful wife is ever conscious of fulfilling her wifely obligations, and that makes her the prime person of the family. Her husband fulfils all her needs of bedding, clothing, food, wealth, house, and other property and she in return embellishes herself to enjoy oneness with her husband on the nuptial bed.

Bhai Gurdas further observes:

Jaise patibrata patibrat sat(i) savdhan,
Sakal kutanb suprasann(i) dhann(i) soe hai.[135]

When a faithful, truthful, and virtuous wife remains attentive in the service of her husband, the whole family praises her and adores her very happily. Bhai Gurdas complements a faithful wife, who discards desires (for other men) and lives in the refuge of one husband (*patibrat ek tek dubidha nivari hai*).[136] Bhai Gurdas did not only speak of the adherents and newly emerging followers of the Sikh faith. Rather, his writings presented a larger social reality. His social observations were in no way confined to any particular religious community or caste or class. They provided us with a peep into an extensive social world, which appeared to be much closer to the one existing at that time.

Though discussed in the context of widow remarriage, it must be mentioned that in the light of the centrality of the lord (husband), every action of the wife and every emotion of hers revolved around the goal of pleasing the husband. Apart from this social and cultural dependence and emotional anchor, the survival of the husband was a prerequisite for the economic sustenance and affluence of the wife. In sum, the very life of a wedded woman not only revolved around her husband but was solely dependent on him for social, cultural, economic, and emotional well-being. In such a social scenario, it was not difficult to assess the situation of a woman, who lost the epicentre of her life, her husband. One can empathize with not only a sense of emotional loss and agony at the loss of her husband but, at worst, a state of emotional trauma imagining her life without her lord and thus opting to be a sati.

Another exclusive social role of a wife was her procreative abilities. Foreign travellers have noticed, with appreciation, the great respect for pregnant women, not only by their husbands and relations but all the inhabitants of the place belonging to her caste, praying for her health and safety.[137] Bhai Gurdas expressed the same sentiment:

Jaise priya bhetat adhan nirman hot,
Banchhat bidhan khan pan agrabhag(i) bai.[138]

According to the above lines, as a wife presents herself to her husband with humility and becomes pregnant, the husband brings her all the foods of her liking and taste. On the birth of a son, she abstains from eating all that may be harmful to the child.

The preference for a son was evident in the discussion on female infanticide. Sikh history is replete with instances of such a preference. There is repeated reference to Mai Desso Jatti, who was bestowed with a blessing for being a mother of seven sons;[139] Mata Damodari begged Guru Hargobind for his blessings for the birth of a son in the household of Sri Gurditta.[140] The *Adi Granth* held that as the mother cherished her progeny and pinned her hopes on her son, the son, on growing up, would give her the wherewithal, bringing joy and pleasure (*jiun janani garbhu palati sutki kari asa*).[141] Further, the scripture states that the mother reared the child after bearing him and ever kept him in her sight; every moment she fed him it with morsels and patted him both inside the home and outside (*jiun janani sutu jani palate rakhai nadari majhari*).[142]

It would suffice to say that the birth of a daughter has been usually regarded as an unwelcome event, often an occasion for sorrow and mourning. The woman who failed to produce a male heir was seen as accursed, as one who had failed in her essential duty. A wife's worth, therefore, came to be crucially determined by her ability to produce male heirs. The woman who gave birth to sons was considered worthy of high social esteem. She was honoured and looked after. She was taken proper care of in her post-natal phase.[143] The sentiments of the would-be mother wishing to give birth to a son were well represented in the following couplet in *Adi Granth*,

As does the mother cherish her pregnancy in her son pinning her hope; that grown up, would he give her wherewithal, and bring joy and pleasure. Even such is the love of god's devotee to the lord.[144]

While noticing this preferential longing for a boy and a special treatment awarded to him in the society, Guru Nanak observes, 'The father and mother like their son, the father-in-law their son-in-law.'[145] A son was considered to be the binding link between the parents because, 'if a piece of bronze or gold or iron breaks into bits, the smith welds them again in fire, if the husband breaks off from the wife, the sons unite them again'.[146] Bhai Gurdas highlights the importance of a queen, who is blessed with a son in the harem of the king:

Jaise nrip dham bham ek sai adhik ek,
Naik anek raje sabhan ladavai.
Janmat ja kai sut(u) vabi kai suhag(u) bhag(u),
Sakal rani mai patrani so kahavai.[147]

According to the above passage, as a king has many queens in his palace, each of remarkable beauty, he cajoles and pampers each one of them; the one who bears him a son enjoys a higher status in the palace and is declared as chief among the queens. In a social milieu, where the goal of the wife was to please her husband and to achieve the fulfilment of her female body with the birth of a child (read son), one could easily imagine the agony of the barren woman and the social stigma attached to her.

Sihja sanjog bhog nispal banjh badhu,
Boe na adhan, dukho dubidha durav kai.[148]

The above lines indicate that an infertile woman remains bereft of pregnancy, despite enjoying the nuptial bed with her husband and keeps hiding her distress.

It is further stated:

Santat(i) nimit nrip anik bivah karai,
Santat(i) bibun banita na grib(i) chhaj hai.[149]

The above lines indicate that a king marries many women for obtaining an heir to his kingdom, but the queen who does not bear him a child is not liked by anyone in the family. It may be added that a barren woman always suffered from the insecurity of sharing her husband with a co-wife. Very often, it must have been a crude reality that she would have been forced to live with all her life. It was believed,

Jaise tan manjh banjh rog sog sanso pram,
Saut ko sutah(i) pekh(i) mahan dukh pavai.[150]

The above lines indicate that a distressed and fatigued woman suffering from her inability to bear a child feels much distressed and seeing a son of her co-wife curses her own self.

The woman, as a wife, might have suffered innumerable restrictions. Yet, she emerged as a confidante and friend of her husband. She advised him in his best interest and that of the family at large. As noted in the context of choosing the marriage partners for their children, the wife played a significant role in the decision making. In the existing social scenario, she might not have been able to voice her opinion openly but would have exercised influence through her husband. For instance, Baba Langah bought a piece of land from the Muslim Ranghars at TaranTaran. When their womenfolk got to know that their husbands had accepted the money in return for land, they strongly disapproved of the financial transaction and the acceptance of money. They pointed out that the house of Gurus was going to use the land for religious purposes. On their insistence, the men were induced not only to return the money but also to beg for the Guru's pardon for having accepted it thoughtlessly.[151] This anecdote reflects the role of women in decision making in a Muslim household. This positive aspect of social reality, fortunately, cuts across all the communities. Sohan Kavi portrayed the wife of Chandu Diwan (a Mughal official, who had played an instrumental role in the death of Guru Arjan Dev) criticizing him. Consequently, Chandu Diwan paid heed to his wife's advice. On her insistence, he wrote a letter to Guru Hargobind, in which he claimed to be innocent of Guru Arjan's death. Chandu Diwan pointed out that the Guru had suffered from dysentery and claimed to have done his best to save the Guru's life, though his efforts proved to be in vain. In the same letter, on the advice of his wife, he requested Guru Hargobind that their daughter might be accepted as a 'servant' (wife).[152]

INHERITANCE LAWS AND WOMEN'S ECONOMIC CONTRIBUTION

At the outset of this section, one must avoid identifying (through our present-day wisdom) a set of criteria that were mechanically applied to historical situations. For instance, access to property might be regarded as an index of a woman's status. If this rests on a definition of property, which is treated as absolute and invariable without being qualified or contextualized, it could lead to faulty historical analysis.

The powerlessness of women and the devaluation of their labour on the family land and the household was in part a product of exclusive control of men over land. As land became more and more valuable as a commodity, its control became an increasingly important determinant of power and wealth within the family and in the larger society. The near-total disinheritance from property rights in land – the dominant form of income-generating property in medieval times – is perhaps the key factor in ensuring women's dependence and subordinate status in the family. Even when women were contributing substantially by way of labour, they rarely came to acquire any real power in the crucial day-to-day decisions made in the family. Several studies among peasant families of the present day have shown that, in most of them, a woman had little or no say in basic decisions regarding income allocation and expenditure of the family. In sum, the woman's lack of independent access to sources of income in a peasant household was a salient factor in reinforcing her powerlessness. The economic status of a woman as an individual was not only the deciding factor, the economic status of the family also had significant implications for the condition of women. The complex interconnection of economic status and condition of women as evident in widow remarriage and *sati*, though not universally practised, reflected the paradox that emerged in the condition of the peasant landowning class and the landless agricultural labour. Unlike the family structure among the peasant landowning castes, the family was relatively less restrictive for women among the landless poor. One of the main reasons for this was that the landless agriculture labour woman, however much she was exploited, was recognized as a wage earner, as someone who contributed to the upkeep of the family by her earnings, which formed a vital portion of the family income.

Customs, traditions, or conventions were unwritten laws governing social and economic relationships in myriad ways. It must be noted that there was no distinction between the Hindu and Muslim laws of inheritance on the basis of religion. The process of identification of the right of inheritance was complex and multifaceted. The present attempt is to take cognizance of the status of rural women in relation to their rights in succession and the alienation of landed property. Although the question of inheritance has been dealt with by Islamic law, most Muslims adhered to their tribal customs, which were generally those of the Hindu races from which they were originally converted. There was no distinction between the Muslims and the non-Muslims regarding the rules regulating the devolution and disposal of property. In theory, as well as in practice, property was recognized as involving a community of interests; because in the rural society of Punjab, the village communities (*bhaicharas*) consisted of groups of families bound together by the tie of common descent. The customs regarding succession to property as land were governed by the ties of kinship as well as by the local common interests. Only the agnates had the right to succeed to property.[153] Since sisters or daughters were to be married in another caste, there was no need to give them a part of the village patrimony. To give her a share in the property would have amounted to the encroachment of an outsider in the community. C.L. Tupper, aptly summing up the social psychology, wrote that a woman was considered the 'terminus of the family with whom the branch or the twig of the genealogy was closed'.[154]

In the event of the extinction of male lineage, there were specific customs for succession. The daughters and the widows of the deceased were excluded from the rights of succession. A daughter had a right to maintenance till her marriage. A widowed daughter or a daughter who had been deserted by her husband and had returned to her father's house to live had the right to maintenance for life provided she did not remarry and remained chaste. The customs did not take into consideration whether she had any children or not. The maintenance was provided for her life, and after her death, it reverted to her father's agnates.[155] It was generally recognized by almost every tribe that a daughter could not inherit landed property so long as there was any male relative on the father's side. There were local variations, but in the larger picture it was the daughters claim that suffered significantly. Among the Sandhu Jats, for instance, they were excluded generally up to the seventh degree of collaterals, whereas among other tribes this custom varied between the sixth and fifth degree.[156] The exclusion of a daughter was so prevalent a social norm that even in cases where there were no agnates at all, she was debarred of succession to her parental property by members of the village community, even if they had no relationship with the deceased. Not only daughters but their offspring were also excluded from succession by the near male collaterals.

In a situation where one wished to adopt a child, there were certain limits within which one could do so. In the absence of a male issue, the would-be father's first preference for adoption was his brother's son and, second, his daughter's or sister's child. If he failed to get one from either of these two, he was allowed to adopt a child from any one of his blood relations but not beyond that. Adoption was almost unknown among Muslims. It was only permissible on the failure of issue, and even then, must be proclaimed openly by the adopter during his lifetime and supported by a written deed.

In the absence of a male issue, a widow inherited the property of her deceased husband for life. However, she had no right to alienate any portion of the property for sale or by gift or mortgage without the consent of the next of kin. Although for a later period, C.L. Tupper reports that among the Gujjars and Arains of Gurdaspur, under certain circumstances like the marriage of a daughter or payment of land revenue or payment of her late husband's dues, she was allowed to sell land to collaterals first and only if they refused, then she was allowed to sell to outsiders.[157] Such provisions for raising money for necessary expenses were also allowed to a widow in some villages of Shahpur district.[158] Though this evidence was of a later period, it must have been tenable for the sixteenth and seventeenth centuries as well, because the customary laws and traditions did not change over a short span of time and that too in favour of women.

In many parts of Punjab, succession to landed property was regulated by two rules, *pagwand* and *chundawand*. *Pagwand* was a word derived from a turban (*pag*) and signified that an estate was being distributed in equal shares amongst the sons. *Chundawand* was derived from the hair braided on the top of the head (*chunda*). It signified equal division between the groups of sons by each wife, or in other words, each wife's family came in for an equal share. The former was generally a tribal custom, whereas the latter was just a family custom and was exceptionally prevalent in Punjab.[159]

Admittedly, the Shariat was a significant departure from women's legal and juridical rights of inheritance as compared to the Dharmashastras. Though the Shariat viewed women as worthy of a 'secondary' status, there were significant features that allowed the woman to inherit property. The Shariat provided for a male guardian (*wali*) for women. Remarkably, it did treat women as legal persons with their own rights of inheritance, howsoever limited. It was set at half that of the brother's share to a dower (*mahr*) from the husband and to the benefits from the terms of marriage as stipulated by the contract.[160] These elements of Islamic law, at least theoretically, acknowledged women as property owners. Irfan Habib observes that Muslim women in seventeenth-century India were in possession of land rights (*zamindari* or *satarahi*, which was partly received in inheritance and partly in the form of a *mahr*).[161] On the basis of a detailed study of the land revenue system of the Mughals, Irfan Habib concludes that the Hindu women too appeared as *zamindar*s. In one case, a woman *zamindar* seems to have inherited her right from her brother. In another case, two sons, selling a share of the *zamindari*, gave their mother's name, suggesting that they had inherited it from their mother.[162]

Habib further notes that 'Muslim women constitute a significant category among the recipients of revenue grants from the Mughal government'.[163] By Aurangzeb's order of 1690,

Women in the Social Sphere

they could also inherit revenue grants.[164] As far as the inheritance of the revenue-free grants was concerned, Habib observes that 'the rules of inheritance did not conform to the Shariat; the widow would hold the whole grant in her lifetime and married daughters were excluded'.[165] As noted in Akbar's 'Sayings' in Abul Fazl's *Ain-i-Akbari*, the Emperor was of the opinion that women did not get enough; being weak, he said, women were entitled to a 'larger share' than men.[166] Akbar also found it immoral that when there were only daughters, other male kinsmen should have claims on the inheritance.[167]

Interestingly, the social understanding of her lustful nature (*stri svabhav*), affects the widows' proprietary rights. A widow could continue to be in possession of ancestral or self-acquired property of her husband for life, with the condition that she remained chaste and did not re-marry. In case of her re-marriage or her infidelity being proved, her property reverted to the collaterals of the deceased husband. The ideal of female chastity has always been upheld in society as the prime virtue associated with a good wife, complete devotion, and dedication to her lord (husband) even after his death.[168]

Women contributed substantially to varied economic activities, over and above the household chores which were labour-intensive. In the division of labour, gender played a significant role. Spinning was done almost exclusively by women. In the earliest illustration of the spinning wheel, as early as *c.*1500, the women were depicted as working the wheel (Figure 15.1)[169] The tedious task of cotton-seed separation, as cotton was being picked from the fields, was also a woman's job. Women were pictured in Ajanta Cave frescos of the sixth century (Figure 15.2)[170] being engaged in almost all the stages of processing, including working with cotton-gin. As shown by scholars,[171] women's role in the textile industry was not limited only to helping the weaver set up the loom, warp and weft, but also included dyeing, printing, and embroidering cloth.

Women's labour was not limited to the domestic industry. According to Irfan Habib, India has been one of the few countries in the world, where so much of the hard labour in building construction has been assigned to women. Sixteenth-century Mughal miniatures showed women breaking stones or bricks, sieving lime, and carrying mortar on their heads at building sites (Figures 15.2 and 15.3).[172] It was the women who performed the labour-intensive and rigorous tasks of preparing raw materials. The final processes were performed by men, whether it was in the textile industry or the potter's wheel. Shireen Moosvi has dealt with the reconstruction of the economic past and women's contribution to almost all productive activities.[173] Ploughing was a man's operation, but women contributed immensely to the fields in operations such as sowing, transplanting, weeding, harvesting, husking, milling, fetching water, cooking food, and carrying it to the men. Managing the cattle and preparing milk products were also considered exclusively women's arena.

Apart from this, women were engaged in pastoral activities and processing. There were several references in Shah Hussain's mystical verses (*kaafiyan*) of women's groups engaged in weaving and spinning. Spinning was done invariably in the afternoon when the girls of the neighbourhood gathered, laughed and joked. This gathering was commonly called the spinning bee (*trinjan*). Bhai Gurdas has depicted these gatherings and then the ultimate fate of these girls leaving their maiden homes, friends and memories to lead new lives in a family of strangers, and the endless struggle to carve out a niche for themselves. He said, 'The girls spin in groups. But then spread and go away like birds from a tree.'[174] They also made pots, baskets and the traditional embroidery of *phulkari* as a part of a large preparation of dowry (*daj*). They were also engaged in extracting oil and salt, besides making *papad*s and *waddi*s for the day. It must also be noted that various occupational possibilities were open to and exercised by women within a single region. The geographical features and economic requirements were the guiding principles for this distinction in engagement in various parts of the province. In the hills of south-eastern districts, the Jat women, and those from a lower social position worked in the fields. In the remaining parts of the province the Ahir, Jat, Arain, *and* Mali women lent a hand in agricultural work. In other words, vast differences distinguished the lives and economic conditions of women, not based on their religion but economic conditions of their families and the social organization of labour.

Shireen Moosvi suggests a certain amount of independence among women from the lower echelons of society. She opines that women's independence 'was sharply curtailed, and seclusion and the veil enforced among both Hindus and Muslims in the case of higher-class women'. Though one has serious apprehensions regarding Moosvi's observations, it is heartening to note her opinion that even these women managed properties and conducted business, being mostly educated, and were depicted in paintings reading letters and books. Though the evidence mainly referred to the port city of Surat, it was interesting to note that the surviving marriage contracts (*nikaahnama*) revealed challenges faced by middle-class Muslim women. The prescient/futuristic conditions imposed upon potential bridegrooms included strict monogamy, prohibition, or at least restriction, on domestic violence and redress on desertion (we may equate it to some sort of alimony).[175] Irfan Habib has argued that caste and gender interjections had a great role to play in the inequitable social order. In his words,

Just as the caste system, by cheapening labour of the lower castes, proved beneficial for the ruling class as a whole by lowering the costs of goods and services for them, such a role was also played by the low remuneration of women. In so far as this helped to sustain the structure of class dominance, there was, in essence, an overlapping of the zones of gender oppression and class exploitation. Each supplemented the other.[176]

WEAPONS OF THE WEAK

This usage is borrowed from the title of James C. Scott's work *Weapons of the Weak: Everyday Forms of Peasant Resistance*.[177]

The title appropriately captures the weak position of women in medieval India and their modes of defiance. Talking in the context of women of Punjab, or for that matter the whole of India in the sixteenth and seventeenth centuries, one cannot expect any violent upheavals or any concrete act of defiance per se. In the then prevalent social milieu, women couldn't resist any act of domination. Her 'weak' position was reflected, at its worst, by the prevalence of social evils such as female infanticide, *sati* and widow remarriage (to safeguard the vested property interests of the patriarchy). Contrary to these highly polarized positions, if our object of study is the woman of the sixteenth and seventeenth centuries, it is futile to pose the problem by simply dichotomizing lived experiences into dramatic episodes of confrontation and quotidian modes of defiance. Any project that seeks to write a holistic social history of resistance by women will then have to incorporate both the dramatic and the mundane without idealizing either. Women in their day-to-day lives carved out their own apparatus, that is their collective behaviour and rituals that James Scott called 'everyday forms of resistance' in the very title of his work focusing on peasant resistance.[178] In other words, any sensitized study of varied forms of protest or mere defiance of a sixteenth- and seventeenth-century woman has to focus substantially on these small and gestural ways of venting out her accumulated unrest in the context of the prevailing milieu. To expect such everyday forms of protests to make even a slight dent in the patriarchal structure was not only too wishful but oblivious of the realities on the ground and the tenacious patriarchal hold on our social relations. Yet, its importance for women, as a mechanism to keep her sane, is to be highlighted and acknowledged.

Social scientists have two distinct methodologies to study any form of resistance or protest. The initial push was towards probing modes of resistance by working at proper uprisings, riots, rebellions, and other confrontational popular movements. More recently, influenced by the writings of Michel Foucault, some scholars strongly recommend that if our goal is to recover the history of resistance, it is imperative to look at everyday forms of struggle and humbler forms of defiance, rather than studying spectacular riots and short-lived violent upheavals.[179]

In the context of the sixteenth and seventeenth centuries, we need to re-think notions of domesticity and seclusion. An important lacuna underlining discussion on gender was that it presumed an 'inner domain' (a feature closely associated with the notion of domesticity and seclusion) as a space of compliance and subordination, a place where women played out feminine roles of mother, wife and homemaker. Within this framework, women can play transgressive roles only outside the domestic sphere. The innumerable negotiations and contestations which permeate the everyday life of women within the home need to be observed carefully. What is an 'ideal' behaviour of a woman, the virtues associated with a wife according to the social norms and the acts of defiance or, at minimum, mere expressions of defiance and disobedience? Though notions of seclusion and domesticity are important, we should be wary of an excessive valorization of ideas that flatter and homogenize experiences. Experiences are multiple. This suggests that women pushed to the boundaries of patriarchy still make spaces within it. Yet it is not as if they are continuously resisting structures of control. Everyday processes of negotiation, acquiescence, and contestation which, at least, attempt to somewhat reshape these structures of power, need to be noticed and appreciated. One must remember that transgression of boundaries can go along with acts of conformity, adaptations, acquiescence, and re-negotiation. Quite often, fortunately, the power of patriarchal ideology is not able to fully domesticate women within a rigid mould or even the patriarchal ideology is not homogeneous and, most of all, its application by different sections of society, by different families or individuals is extremely varied. This difference only provides women with the 'opportunity' of carving out a niche. Even within the framework of the dominant ideology of domesticity, women from lower castes (as noted earlier) create their own codes. Public affirmation of dominant codes can coexist with subversion. Nita Kumar has characterized this process as finding the fault lines in the larger patriarchal structures; the positioning of a spotlight on areas where there are inconsistencies or cleavages surface in general activity.[180]

It is in this framework that we need to perceive the latent forms of deviant behaviour or, to use a strong term, protest of the sixteenth- and seventeenth-centuries women of Punjab. As we know, the folksongs were replete with sarcasm for the mother-in-law (*saas*), sister-in-law (*nanad*) and almost all the members of the parents-in-law's family. In fact, this is the main content of folk songs and can be the subject of an exclusive study.

As repeatedly observed, the 'ideal' female role emphasized humility and submissiveness on the part of the woman. She was required to control her aggressive and sexual drives. Such control, as shown by many anthropological studies, might have often led to various psychological problems, including sexual frigidity, somatization of conflicts, a propensity to hysteria and masochist tendencies due to internalization of aggression. This excessive emphasis on the social norms of humility and submissiveness, and the way these norms were internalized and understood by women, must have caused a great toll on the psychological health of women. Another formidable form of deviant behaviour was the possession by spirits (*mata-aana*) or anecdotes about ghosts (*bhoot-pret*). Macauliffe witnessed the typical spirit-possession behaviour among women at the shrine of Sakhi Sarwar. These examples, in large part, represented an effort on the part of a powerless section of society to voice its dissent and articulate needs and feelings which were normally suppressed. It was akin to an empowering world view of the disempowered. By labelling dissociative behaviour or sometimes rebellious attitudes as spirit-possession, Punjabi society, like many other agrarian societies, overlooked the transgression of social conventions by a possessed person and transferred the aetiology of dissociative behaviour to supernatural forces, thus freeing itself of any role in an individual's psycho-social problems.[181]

There were varied expressions of venting out of accumulated frustration of womenfolk. There is a popular ritual of the sister-in-law (*bhabhi*) beating the younger brother of the husband (*devar*) at the time of his marriage with a stick. In the garb of beating the younger brother of the husband, a male member of the family, she must have retaliated against her oppression. The younger brother of the husband must have emerged as a replica image of her husband and other elderly menfolk of the family in whose case she was supposed to have had only unquestioned respect and veneration.

Interestingly, there were a few women's festivals, like Kanagats, Moh-Mahi, and Sada Talla, which degraded male society. These customs struck deeply at the family honour (read male authority in the family) and, yet more directly, at the power and privileges of the Hindu husband. Though we get the graphic descriptions only from a much later period, these social practices often had their roots in much earlier times. At most, some modifications and local variations could be expected. These customs were sharply criticized by the orthodox leader Pandit Shardha Ram, who described the custom with disgust and a degree of apprehension. The graphic description states that

... during the period of Kanagats, the women of one *mohalla*, or locality, after putting on their best clothes and jewellery, according to their position and status, collect as a group and take their stand at any road, crossing or other places of importance and start hurling insults and abuses on the women of other *mohalla* or nearby (neighbourhood) and start quarrelling.

The women did not abuse each other but taunted each other's husbands, parents, or relatives. This form of public abuse expanded, and one cannot deny the role of these customs as the platforms to vent out the accumulated resentment of women towards the male society at large. However, this form of public ridicule dishonoured the wives and daughters of such a family, and if by chance 'any women of one *mohalla* or locality happens to pass another *mohalla* . . . within fifteen days of Kanagats, her clothes are torn and she is badly treated. . .' Very often, Kanagats degenerated into fistfights and wrestling among the women.

There is another way to assess these rituals. The inherent patriarchal psyche of viewing women as objects was further exemplified by the fact that in the rituals when a woman is venting out her accumulated frustration, striking back at the male members of the world, the ostensible victim of her actions is another woman. It was an epitome of the complex gender relationships in the context of Indian society, where a woman was not only a victim of oppression but the mechanism to bring about the same oppression.

Another similar festival, Moh-Mahi, was celebrated during the mid-winter. On this day, little girls and even grown-up adults and young women, both rich and poor, put on costly dresses and ornaments as they moved about the various localities and marketplaces in groups. As soon as they came across any miserly person or stranger, they would tease and harass him to the extent of tearing off his clothes. Another festival, popularly known as Sada Talla, was a fertility rite performed by the Hindu women of Amritsar, where hundreds of women, both from rich and poor families, collected at big public places and bared their bodies up to the breast and start rolling on the ground with great zest and enthusiasm, shouting 'I have laid down on a wheat field, may my womb become fertile'. Women believed that by this action of theirs, they could become pregnant immediately. Ironically, Sada Talla did not specifically state the desire of women to be the mothers of sons alone, which is a preferred offspring even today. Inferring from other evidence and contextualizing the general system of social values, perhaps fertility was equated to being blessed with only a son.

Another widespread and popular form of social expression of women was the genre of folk songs, which the women of the whole community sang at the time of marriage and associated occasions, and different celebratory or commemorative moments of their lives. The subjects of folk songs revolved around their relationships at their parents-in-law's place, especially highlighting the constant tussle between the mother-in-law and daughter-in-law. These folk songs were replete with information about all the relationships around which the life of the women revolved and evolved. They formed a potent subject of study. Such folk songs typically represented the thrust of the woman's psyche. Their immense value as an effective community platform for women to vent out their anger and resentment could not be denied. They would have added to women's general understanding of all these relationships; they would have made her more socially wise. They must have soothed her, that her life was the same as other women of the society. To sum up, these rituals and festivals were opportunities for socializing and for emotional relief. They must have gone a long way in keeping them mentally fit and vibrant.

Our discussion on the 'weapons of the weak' would be incomplete without reference to the *jhagrra*s and *kissa*s as a 'popular' literary form. There was no clear reference to such sources from the sixteenth and seventeenth centuries. In all probability, this genre must have been in existence, maybe in milder, diluted forms. The folk songs and folk culture were primarily the collected oeuvres of the past. Some gained preeminence over time and some were allowed to fade away. The *jhagrra* was a genre, which was not only an important component of popular culture but also played an extremely significant role in spreading reformist ideas in the eighteenth and nineteenth centuries. Anshu Malhotra states that 'many *pracharak*s, *updeshak*s and other preachers of the Arya Samaj and the Singh Sabha readily used the *jhagrra* form to carry forth their message.[182] It is a reasonable proposition that a genre, which seemed to have succeeded to bridge the gap between the word and the oral tradition and which provided such a potent form of expression, would not have suddenly emerged and acquired importance.

The writers of these *jhaggra*s and *kissa*s must have been males. This became evident from the choice of the subject matter, which included the negotiations of everyday social relations, especially the conflicts in the hierarchies of age, gender, and social positions. *Jhagrra*s and *kissa*s focused on mismatched marriages, with the conflict between the necessity of maintaining social norms as represented in conjugality, and the desire to transgress them through extramarital union. Such a conflict became the central tension in the classical *kissa*.[183] It would be appropriate to remind ourselves that these acts of contestation, acquiescence, and transgression of the social norms would have coexisted, especially when the society was, and still is, obsessed with keeping vigilance over the chastity of women, ensuring and enforcing it as the marker of social status.

NOTES

1. Simone de Beauvoir, *The Second Sex*, Eng. tr. H.M. Parshley, New York: Vintage, 1974, p. XIX.
2. Apart from the specified references, the following accounts of the life-cycle rituals owes a great deal to the following works which are great repositories of information. R.W. Falcon, *Handbook on Sikhs for the Use of Regimental Officers*, Allahabad: Pioneer Press, 1896, pp. 48-54; H.A. Rose, *A Glossary of the Tribes and Castes of the Punjab and North-West Frontier Province*, 3 vols., Lahore: The Civil and Military Gazette Press, 1911; A.H. Bingley, *Sikhs*, Patiala: Department of Languages, rpt., 1970, pp. 93-107; *Punjab State Gazetteers: Phulkian States (Patiala, Jind and Nabha)*, Lahore: The Civil and Military Gazette Press, 1901, pp. 231-7.
3. Harjot Oberoi, 'The Making of a Religious Paradox: Sikh, Khalsa, Sehajdhari as Modes of Early Sikh Identity', in *Bhakti Religion in North India Community Identity and Political Action*, ed. David Lorenzen, Delhi: Manohar, 1996, pp. 47-8.
4. Gulbadan Begum, *Humayun Namah*, Eng. tr. Annette S. Beveridge, New Delhi: Atlantic Publishers & Distributors, rpt., 2018, p. 151; Abul Fazl, *Akbarnama*, Eng. tr. vol. I, H. Beveridge, New Delhi: Atlantic Publishers & Distributors, rpt. 2019, p. 575;

Abdul Qadir Badauni, *Muntakhab-ut-Tawarikh*, vol. II, Eng. tr. W.H. Lowe, edited by B.P. Ambashthya, Patna: Academica Asiatica, 1973, p. 59; Francisco Pelsaert, *Jahangir's India: The Remonstrantie of Francisco Pelsaert*, Eng. tr. W.H. Moreland and P. Geyl, Delhi: Idarah-i-Adabiyat-i-Delli, rpt., 1972, p. 81.
5. Muqbal, *Qissa Hir Ranjha*, ed. Shamsher Singh Ashok, Patiala, pp. 19-20; Agra Sethi, *Var Haqiqat Rai* (ed. Ganda Rai), Amritsar: Kitab Trinjan, n.d., p. 34.
6. Muqbal, *Qissa Hir Ranjha*, pp. 20-1.
7. Muqbal, *Qissa Hir Ranjha*, pp. 19, 20, 21, 34; Waris Shah, *Hir*, Agra: Chetna Prakashan, rpt. 2010, p. 206.
8. Francisco Pelsaert, *Jahangir's India*, p. 81; Abdul Halim Sharar, *Guzishta Lucknow*, Lucknow: Nasim Book Depot, 1974, p. 338.
9. Agra Sethi, *Var Haqiqat Rai*, p. 34.
10. Muqbal, *Qissa Hir Ranjha*, p. 22; Waris Shah, *Hir*, p. 59; Agra Sethi, *Var Haqiqat Rai*, p. 36.
11. Sohan Kavi, *Gurbilas Padshahi Chhevin*, ed. Giani Inder Singh, Amritsar: Jiwan Mandir Pustkala, 1968, p. 379.
12. Ibid.
13. Ibid., p. 386.
14. Swaroop Singh Koshish, *Guru Kian Saakhian*, ed. Piara Singh Padam, Amritsar: Singh Brothers, 1995, Sakhi 4, p. 42.
15. Waris Shah, *Hir*, p. 59
16. Waris Shah, *Hir*, p. 79; Ahmad Yaar, *Qissa Sassi Punnu*, ed. Nihal Singh Ras, Amritsar: Kitab Trinjan, 1963, pp. 80-2.
17. Ahmad Yaar, *Qissa Sassi Punnu*, p. 80; Waris Shah, *Hir*, p. 59; Nihala, 'Sakhi Sarwar Di Shaadi', in *Punjabi Lok Gathawan*, vol. II, p. 67.
18. Bulleh Shah, 'Gandhan', in *Qafian Bulleh Shah (Arthat Kulliyat Bulle Shah)*, ed. Faqir Muhammad Faqir, Amritsar, n.d., p. 78, 183; Fazal Shah, *Sohni Fazl Shah*, ed. Diwan Singh and Roshan Lal Ahuja, Jalandhar, 1979, p. 145.
19. Muqbal, *Qissa Hir Ranjha*, p. 19.
20. Bulleh Shah, 'Gandhan', pp. 183-4, 187-8, 190-1.
21. Sohan Kavi, *Gurbilas Padshahi Chhevin*, p. 397.
22. Ibid., p. 443.
23. Gyani Gyan Singh, *Sri Guru Panth Parkash*, Patiala: Bhasha Vibhag, 1970, pp. 182-3.
24. Ibid., p. 183.
25. Waris Shah, *Hir*, p. 37.

262   *The Silent Voices and the Creation*

26. *Vatna* was a compound of oil and some fragrant ingredients that were supposed to make the skin glow and soft.
27. Bulleh Shah, 'Gandhan', p. 190; Muqbal, *Qissa Hir Ranjha*, p. 28; Ahmed Yaar, *Qissa-i-Kamrup*, Lahore: Qadiri Press, 1881, p. 335.
28. Gyani Gyan Singh, *Sri Guru Panth Parkash*, p. 183.
29. Ibid., p. 184.
30. Agra Sethi, *Var Haqiqat Rai*, p. 36; Nihala, *Sakhi Sarwar Di Shaadi*, p. 65.
31. Agra Sethi, *Var Haqiqat Rai*, p. 36.
32. Meharban, *JanamSakhi Sri Guru Nanak Dev Ji*, ed. Kirpal Singh and Shamsher Singh Ashok, Amritsar: Sikh History Research Department, Khalsa College, 1962, pp. 299-300.
33. Waris Shah, *Hir*, p. 64.
34. Agra Sethi, *Var Haqiqat Rai*, p. 36; Waris Shah, *Hir*, p. 63; Nihala, *Sakhi Sarwar Di Shaadi*, p. 65.
35. Gyani Gyan Singh, *Sri Guru Panth Parkash*, p. 184.
36. Agra Sethi, *Var Haqiqat Rai*, p. 37; Nihala, *Sakhi Sarwar Di Shaadi*, p. 64.
37. Waris Shah, *Hir*, p. 63; Nihala, *Sakhi Sarwar Di Shaadi*, p. 65; Agra Sethi, *Var Haqiqat Rai*, p. 37.
38. Waris Shah, *Hir*, p. 63; Agra Sethi, *Var Haqiqat Rai*, p. 37.
39. Agra Sethi, *Var Haqiqat Rai*, p. 37
40. Ibid.
41. Sohan Kavi, *Gurbilas Padshahi Chhevin*, pp. 389-91.
42. Ibid., pp. 443, 511-12, these comprise the marriages of Suraj Mal and Guru Tegh Bahadur.
43. Muqbal, *Qissa Hir Ranjha*, p. 33; Waris Shah, *Hir*, p. 63.
44. Muqbal, *Qissa Hir Ranjha*, p. 33.
45. Agra Sethi, *Var Haqiqat Rai*, p. 38.
46. For a detailed description of music, dance, performers and fireworks, see the works of Waris Shah, Agra Sethi, and Muqbal.
47. Waris Shah, *Hir*, p. 62.
48. Gyani Gyan Singh, *Sri Guru Panth Parkash*, p. 184.
49. Sohan Kavi, *Gurbilas Padshahi Chhevin*, p. 379.
50. Waris Shah, *Hir*, p. 63.
51. Nihala, *Sakhi Sarwar Di Shaadi*, p. 68; Waris Shah, *Hir*, p. 63; Agra Sethi, *Var Haqiqat Rai*, p. 38.
52. Gyani Gyan Singh, *Sri Guru Panth Parkash*, p. 184.
53. Waris Shah, *Hir*, pp. 64-6.

54. Muqbal, *Qissa Hir Ranjha*, p. 33.
55. Ibid.
56. Waris Shah, *Hir*, p. 64; Muqbal, *Qissa Hir Ranjha*, p. 33.
57. Waris Shah, *Hir*, pp. 65, 69, 70, 199; Muqbal, *Qissa Hir Ranjha*; pp. 34-35; Nihala, *Sakhi Sarwar Di Shaadi*, p. 67; Ahmad Yaar, *Qissa Sassi Punnu*, p. 81.
58. Muqbal, *Qissa Hir Ranjha*, p. 35.
59. Muqbal, *Qissa Hir Ranjha*, p. 35; Waris Shah, *Hir*, p. 69; Nihala, *Sakhi Sarwar Di Shaadi*, p. 67.
60. Muqbal, *Qissa Hir Ranjha*, pp. 34-5.
61. Fazal Shah, *Sohni*, p. 138; Waris Shah, *Hir*, p. 68; Muqbal, *Qissa Hir Ranjha*, pp. 36-7.
62. Muqbal, *Qissa Hir Ranjha*, p. 37; Waris Shah, *Hir*, p. 69.
63. Qadir Yaar, 'Puran Bhagat', in *Punjab Dian Lok Gathawan*, ed. Richard Temple, Patiala: Languages Department Punjab, rpt., 1970, p. 203; Najabat, *Var Nadir Shah*, p. 87.
64. Agra Sethi, *Var Haqiqat Rai*, p. 38
65. Ibid.
66. Najabat, *Var Nadir Shah*, p. 87; Ahmad Yar, *Kamrup*, p. 335; Agra Sethi, *Var Haqiqat Rai*, p. 38.
67. Najabat, *Var Nadir Shah*, p. 87.
68. Waris Shah, *Hir*, pp. 61-2, 71; Muqbal, *Qissa Hir Ranjha*, p. 39.
69. Muqbal, *Qissa Hir Ranjha*, p. 33; Waris Shah, *Hir*, p. 63.
70. Waris Shah, *Hir*, pp. 60-2, 70-2; Muqbal, *Qissa Hir Ranjha*, pp. 19, 39; Agra Sethi, *Var Haqiqat Rai*, p. 39.
71. Agra Sethi, *Var Haqiqat Rai*, p. 39.
72. Sohan Kavi, *Gurbilas Padshahi Chhevin*, p. 512.
73. Gyani Gyan Singh, *Sri Guru Panth Parkash*, p. 185.
74. Kesar Singh Chhibbar, *Banaswalinamah*, ed. Piara Singh Padam, Amritsar: Singh Brothers, 1997, 1(14), p. 46.
75. Bhai Gurdas, *Kabit Sawaiyye*, S 382, Hindi tr. Shamsher Singh Puri, Amritsar: Singh Brothers, 2007, p. 410.
76. Waris Shah, *Hir*, p. 82
77. Bulleh Shah, 'Gandhan', pp. 39, 67; Qadir Yaar, 'Puran Bhagat', p. 225.
78. Muqbal, *Qissa Hir Ranjha*, p. 43; Bulleh Shah, 'Gandhan', p. 184.
79. Waris Shah, *Hir*, p. 71; Muqbal, *Qissa Hir Ranjha*, pp. 39-41.
80. Sohan Kavi, *Gurbilas Padshahi Chevvin*, p. 513.
81. G.S. Talib, *Sri Guru Granth Sahib*, Eng. tr., 4 vols., Patiala: Punjabi University, 1990 (hereafter referred to as *AG*), p. 762.

82. Simran Kaur, *Prasidh Sikh Bibiyan*, Amritsar: Singh Brothers, 1991, pp. 114, 117.
83. Sohan Kavi, *Gurbilas Padshahi Chhevin*, p. 345.
84. Muqbal, *Qissa Hir Ranjha*, p. 42; Agra Sethi, *Var Haqiqat Rai*, p. 39; Nihala, *SakhiSarwar Di Shaadi*, p. 68.
85. Waris Shah, *Hir*, p. 71.
86. Muqbal, *Qissa Hir Ranjha*, p. 42; Nihala, *Sakhi Sarwar Di Shaadi*, p. 68.
87. Gyani Gyan Singh, *Sri Guru Panth Parkash*, p. 185; Muqbal, *Qissa Hir Ranjha*, p. 42.
88. Gyani Gyan Singh, *Sri Guru Panth Parkash*, p. 185.
89. Abul Fazl, *Ain-i-Akbari*, vol. III, Eng. tr. H.S. Jarrett, Corrected and Annotated by Jadunath Sarkar, Calcutta: The Asiatic Society, 1949, p. 317.
90. Sohan Kavi, *Gurbilas Padshahi Chhevin*, p. 278.
91. Richard K. Fenn, 'The Sociology of Religion: A Critical Survey', in *Sociology: The State of the Art*, ed. Tom Bottomore et al., London: Sage, 1982, p. 117.
92. Barbara Meyerhoff and Sally Falk Moore, eds., *Secular Ritual*, Amsterdam: Van Gorcum, 1977, pp. 3-24.
93. Richard K. Fenn, 'The Sociology of Religion', p. 117.
94. R. Nicholas and R. Inden, *Kinship in Bengali Culture*, Chicago: University of Chicago Press, 1977, p. 37.
95. *AG*, p. 935.
96. Swaroop Singh Koshish, *Guru Kian Saakhian*, Sakhi No. 23, p. 76.
97. Saroop Das Bhalla, *Mahima Parkash*, ed. Gobind Singh Lamba and Khazan Singh, Patiala: Languages Department,1971, p. 155.
98. M.Z. Rosaldo and L.L. Lamphere, eds., *Women, Culture and Society*, Stanford: Stanford University Press, 1974, pp. 253-59.
99. *AG*, 304.
100. Pierre Bourdieu, 'Social Space and Symbolic Power', *Sociological Theory*, vol. 71, Spring 1989, pp. 14-25.
101. *AG*, p. 355.
102. Bhai Gurdas, *Varan*, Text, Transliteration and Translation, Jodh Singh, Patiala: Vision & Venture, 1998, Var 37, Pauri 11, p. 366.
103. Ibid., Var 37, Pauri 12, p. 367.
104. *AG*, p. 473.

105. *AG*, p. 1022.
106. *AG*, p. 706.
107. *Gur Rattan Mal: Sau Sakhi*, ed. Gurbachan Singh Nayyar, Patiala: Punjabi University, rpt., 1995, Sakhi No. 17, pp. 29-30.
108. Bhai Gurdas, *Kabit Sawaiyye*, Kabit No. 58, p. 386.
109. AG, p. 371.
110. Nikky-Guninder Kaur Singh, 'Poetic Rhythm and Historical Account: The Portrait of Guru Nanak Through Bhai Gurdas', *International Journal of Punjab Studies*, vol. 5, no, 2, New Delhi: Thousand Oaks, London: Sage Publications, 1998, pp. 142-3.
111. Nikky-Guninder Kaur Singh, *The Feminine Principle in the Sikh Vision of the Transcendent*, Cambridge: Cambridge University Press, 1993, p. 23.
112. Sohan Kavi, *Gurbilas Padshahi Chhevvin*, p. 279.
113. Ibid., p. 381; Gyani Gyan Singh, *Suraj Parkash*, ed. Churaman Bhai Santokh Singh, Amritsar: Bhai Chattar Singh Jeevan Singh, 1997, p. 244.
114. Bhai Gurdas, *Kabit Sawaiyye*, Kabit No. 358, p. 386.
115. *AG*, p. 371.
116. *AG*, pp. 17, 56, 225, 242, 355, 722, 762, 764, 1107, 1109-10, 1171 and 1232.
117. Rajkumari Shankar, 'Women in Sikhism', in *Religion and Women*, ed. Arvind Sharma, Albany: SUNY Press, 1994, p. 194.
118. *AG*, pp. 72, 762; also see pp. 363, 426, 428, 430, 559 and 1197.
119. *AG*, p. 558.
120. *AG*, pp. 363, 391, 400, 737, 933, 1108.
121. *AG*, p. 89.
122. *AG*, p. 483.
123. *AG*, p. 750.
124. *AG*, p. 1171.
125. *AG*, p. 147.
126. *AG*, p. 391.
127. Bhai Gurdas, *Varan*, Var 35, Pauri 20, p. 331.
128. *AG*, p. 19.
129. Bhai Gurdas, *Varan*, Var 33, Pauri 6, p. 274.
130. Bhai Gurdas, *Kabit Sawaiyye*, Kabit No. 450, p. 478.
131. Ibid., Kabit No. 482, p. 510.
132. Ibid., Kabit No. 483, p. 511.
133. Ibid., Kabit No. 480, p. 508.

134. Ibid., Kabit No. 481, p. 509.
135. Ibid., Kabit No. 468, p. 496.
136. Ibid., Kabit No. 448, p. 476.
137. P.N. Chopra, *Some Aspects of Society and Culture during the Mughal Age (1526-1707)*, Agra: Shiva Lal Agarwala, 1963, p. 114.
138. Bhai Gurdas, *Kabit Sawaiyye*, Kabit No. 179, p. 207.
139. Sohan Kavi, *Gurbilas Padshahi Chhevin*, p. 429.
140. Ibid., p. 433.
141. *AG*, p. 165.
142. *AG*, p. 168.
143. Kanwar Muhammad Ashraf, *Life and Conditions of the People of Hindustan, 1200-1550*, New Delhi: Munshiram Manoharlal, rpt., 1970, p. 167.
144. *AG*, p. 165.
145. *AG*, p. 596.
146. *AG*, p. 143.
147. Bhai Gurdas, *Kabit Sawaiyye*, Kabit No. 120, p. 148.
148. Ibid., Kabit No. 237, p. 265.
149. Ibid., Kabit No. 415, p. 443.
150. Ibid., Kabit No. 513, p. 541.
151. Kartar Singh and Gurdial Singh Dhillon, *Stories from Sikh History*, Book II, New Delhi, Hemkunt Press, 1975, p. 103.
152. Sohan Kavi, *Gurbilas Padshahi Chhevin*, p. 284.
153. F. Hugo, *A Dictionary of the Social Sciences*, Delhi: Ambica Publications, 1977, p. 14.
154. C.L. Tupper, *Punjab Customary Law*, vol. II, Calcutta: Superintendent of Government Printing, 1882, p. 71.
155. A. Charles Roe, *Tribal Law in the Punjab*, Lahore: Civil and Military Gazette Press, 1895, p. 61.
156. *Customary Law of the Main Tribes in the Gurdaspur District*, Lahore: Punjab Government Press, 1913, p. 3; *District Gazetteer of Rawalpindi, 1883-4*, p. 53.
157. C.L Tupper, *Punjab Customary Law*, vol. I, Calcutta: Superintendent of Government Printing, 1882, pp. 77-80.
158. Ibid., vol. II, p. 215.
159. Ibid., pp. 80, 195.
160. For a detailed discussion see Natana J. DeLong-Bas, *Oxford Encyclopedia of Islam and Women*, (2 vols.), USA: Oxford University Press, 1st edn., October 2013.

161. Irfan Habib, *The Agrarian System of Mughal India, 1556-1707*, 2nd edn., New Delhi: Oxford University Press, 1999, p. 192; also see, 'Exploring Medieval Gender History', Symposia Papers, no. 23, Indian History Congress, 2000, p. 270, in *Recording the Progress of Indian History: Symposia Papers of the Indian History Congress, 1992-2010*, ed. S.Z.H. Jafri, New Delhi: Primus Books, 2012.
162. Irfan Habib, *The Agrarian System of Mughal India, 1556-1707*, pp. 191-2.
163. Ibid., pp. 352-3.
164. Ibid., p. 353.
165. Irfan Habib, 'Exploring Medieval Gender History', p. 274.
166. Abul Fazl, *Ain-i-Akbari*, vol. II, pp. 235-40.
167. Ibid., p. 238.
168. *District Gazetteer of Rawalpindi, 1883-4*, p. 53.
169. Irfan Habib, 'Exploring Medieval Gender History', p. 264.
170. Ibid., p. 265.
171. D. Schlingloff, 'Cotton-Manufacture in Ancient India', *Journal of Economic and Social History of the Orient*, vol. 17, no. 1, March 1974, pp. 89-90; Ishrat Alam, 'Textile Tools as depicted in Ajanta and Mughal Paintings', in *Technology in Ancient and Medieval India*, ed. Aniruddha Ray and S.K. Bagchi, Delhi: Sundeep Prakashan, 1986, Plate No. 29, p. 130.
172. Irfan Habib, 'Exploring Medieval Gender History', p. 265.
173. Shireen Moosvi, 'The World of Labour in Mughal India (c.1500-1750)', *Proceedings of the Indian History Congress*, vol. 71 (2010-2011), pp. 343-57.
174. Bhai Gurdas, *Varan*, Var 33, Pauri 5.
175. Shireen Moosvi, *People, Taxation and Trade in Mughal India*, New Delhi: Oxford University Press, 2010, p. 127.
176. Irfan Habib, 'Exploring Medieval Gender History', p. 266. Also see, Irfan Habib, 'Caste in Indian History', in *Essays in Indian History: Towards a Marxist Perception*, New Delhi: Tulika Books, 1995, pp. 161-79.
177. James C. Scott, *Weapons of the Weak, Everyday Forms of Peasant Resistance*, New Haven: Yale University Press, 1985.
178. Ibid.
179. Rosalind O'Hanlon, 'Recovering the Subject Subaltern Studies and Histories of Resistance in Colonial South Asia', *Modern Asian Studies*, vol. 22, 1988, pp. 213-15.

180. Kumar, Nita,'Introduction', in *Women as Subjects: South Asian Histories*, ed. Nita Kumar, Charlottesville: University Press of Virginia, 1994, pp. 3-6.
181. Harjot Oberoi, *The Construction of Religious Boundaries: Culture, Identity and Diversity in the Sikh Tradition*, Delhi: Oxford University Press, 1994, p. 159.
182. Anshu Malhotra, *Gender, Caste, and Religious Identities: Restructuring Class in Colonial Punjab*, New Delhi: Oxford University Press, 2002, p. 74.
183. Niladri Bhattacharya, 'Pastoralists in a Colonial World', in *Nature, Culture and Imperialism: Essays on the Environmental History of South Asia*, ed. David Arnold and Ramachandra Guha, New Delhi: Oxford University Press, 1995, p. 81.

CHAPTER 6

Discrimination and Social Evils

In the urgent effort at erasing Punjab's darkest gender blot, SGPC will soon ask important *gurdwara*s in Punjab to place cradles at their entrances and exhort unhappy parents obsessed with boys to leave 'those innocent children at god's door, not death's.

– Balwant Garg[1]

GIRL CHILD AND FEMALE INFANTICIDE

The evident gender crisis as expressed above in a prominent Indian daily highlights the fact that in modern-day India, the birth of a daughter is often regarded as an unwelcome event. We note the appeal to the sensitivity and humanity of society to protect female infants, by the representatives of God, and in the name of God. Indeed, it is tragic that the birth of a daughter, honoured in the *Sri Guru Granth Sahib* as a 'would-be mother' becomes a source of sorrow. Not much, one would say has changed from the Punjab of the sixteenth and seventeenth centuries.

As another example of the stark gap between the normative and operative beliefs, even in the Gurus' households, the sense of joy and the scale of celebration varied at the time of the birth of a son or a daughter. Sikh sources are replete with such instances. When Baba Gurditta was born to Mata Damodari, lots of charities were given to the poor and a continuous *langar* was started.[2] When Mata Ganga blessed Guru Hargobind that *jodi-ralein* (meaning, may God bless this son with a sister), the Guru replied:

Sil khan kanya ek hove
Nahin ta ma putrid vingrihasta vigavey[3]

The Guru's reply indicates that there should be at least one virtuous daughter, otherwise the family is like a chaotic household. Here, the Guru's wish for a daughter is quite apparent. However, this is the only source projecting such sentiments from a father. We get further information about the same scale of rituals and ceremonies being followed at the births of Gurditta, Suraj Mal, Anni Rai, and Atal Rai. However, such scale of festivities was noticeably absent in the case of Bibi Veeron. The same rituals of charities and donations were followed at the time of birth of Guru Teg Bahadur. The difference in the scale of celebration was evident from Bhai Gurdas' description of the joyous mood at the birth of a son. We do not get any such description even in the Guru families on birth of any of the daughters.

Duhu mili jammai janiai pita jati paravar sadhara,
Jammadian ranajhunana vansi vadhai run jhunakara,
Nanak dadak sohile viratisar bahu dan datara.[4]

According to the above passage, the son born of the union of mother and father gives happiness to the parents, because the lineage and family of the father multiplies and gets maintained. Clarinets are played upon the birth of a child and celebrations are arranged on the further development of the family. In the homes of the mother and father, songs of joy are sung, and the servants are given many gifts. The sense of rejoicing on the birth of a son is further attested in *Kabit Sawaiyye*.

Bhetat bhatar nari(i) sobhit singar char(u),
Puran anand sut udit bachitra kai[5]

According to the above lines, when the conjugal union of a well-adorned and embellished woman with her husband gives birth to a son, the wife is highly placed.

Janmat sut sab kutanb anand-mai,
Bal budh(i) ganat bitit nis(i) prat bai[6]

With the birth of a son, the whole family rejoices. The days of fun and frolic of his childhood and infancy just pass with everyone enjoying his pranks.

We come across evidence of female infanticide being quite prevalent among many sections of society in sixteenth- and seventeenth-century Punjab. It was part of the social hierarchy, often an important symbol of social status. Guru Amar Das was the first Sikh Guru who spoke against the prevalence of female infanticide. At the time of the establishment of the Khalsa on Baisakhi (1699), along with the clear injunction to wear the five symbols (articles) – *kesh, kangha, kirpan, kachha,* and *kara* – and use the appellation of Singh and Kaur, Guru Gobind Singh firmly prohibited a few customs, which included any social interactions with the killers of the female child (*kurri maar*). Yet, despite his strong criticism and prohibition of female infanticide, in one of the Sakhis, Guru Gobind Singh was projected to have approved of the popular perception of a male child as a superior being. Even if we do not take the Sakhi as authentic evidence of the Guru's perception, it certainly speaks a great deal about the general social preference for a male child. In this Sakhi, a Sikh woman narrates that her deceased father was Diwan of Agra and, when he died, he had seven daughters and her mother was expecting at that time. The Padshah ordered that if the child to be born was a male, then the family should be left alone, and their assets should not be touched. Otherwise, the family's entire property was to be confiscated. The Sikh woman went on to say that she realized the power of the male then (*mard ki daari aur keshaon ki sifat*). The Guru corroborated her sentiments.[7] The same anecdote has a different ending in *Tawarikh-i Guru Khalsa*, where the Guru said:

Guru ghar vich aiye farman hain dhiya poot sab harke kiya[8]

We get further evidence in the famous Punjabi saga of *Hir-Ranjha*, where Waris Shah described the various methods employed in the killing of infant daughters which included the heinous acts of strangulation, poisoning, drowning, and suffocation. We also get few references of leaving the female infant without warm clothes in the cold or pouring chilled water on the head of the newborn in the extreme winters of the Punjab.[9] We get the corroborative information from later works too; for instance, John Cave Brown, in a book on female infanticide in India brought out in 1857, also referred to various means deployed to kill the girl child by *dai*s (midwives) who asphyxiated the infant by covering her nose and mouth, by exposing her to extreme cold or heat but also by neglect.[10]

Other widely practised methods included a midwife choking the baby or stuffing the mouth of the girl child with cow dung or the infant's head being immersed in cow's milk. At times, the female infant was buried with a little jaggery (*gur*) in her mouth and a bit of cotton skein in her hands, referred to in the oft-quoted proverb:

Gur khaien, pownee katten
Aap na aieen, bhaiya ghalleen.[11]

In other words, eat your jaggery and spin your thread, but go and send a boy instead. This horrific practice of female infanticide and the methods adopted seem to generate a feeling of helplessness and disgust. Narrating a chilling example of female infanticide, F.A. Steel notes that the Hindu women, when losing a female child during infancy, or while it suckled milk, would take the baby into the jungle and put it in a sitting position under a tree. The following day, they returned to the place. If the dogs and jackals had dragged the child's body towards the home of the mother, it was taken as a bad omen, signalling the birth of another girl. If the body had been dragged away from home, it was taken to mean that the next born would be a boy.[12]

Among the Sikhs, the practice of female infanticide was most widely practised among the Bedis, the descendants of the first Sikh Guru. The Sodhis, the descendants of the fourth Guru onwards, who belonged to the subdivision of Sarin Khatris, a ranking lower in the internal Khatri hierarchy, were also closely aligned with the practice of female infanticide.

Sikh Jats, accounting for a major component of the Sikh populace, would have adopted the same means of upward mobility. The evidence furnished by *Hir-Ranjha*, as already discussed, primarily focuses on the Jats. The association of Jats with the practice of female infanticide can be inferred from the injunction of Guru Ram Singh, the head of the Namdhari sect. He resolutely censored the widely prevalent practice of female infanticide. It was relevant to note that a large number of his followers belonged to lower castes as well as the Jat Sikhs. Ram Singh, aware of the wide prevalence of the practice, issued circulars to his devotees vehemently attacking the custom.

The practice of female infanticide may well have stemmed directly from the esteemed Guru lineage. According to Punjabi lore, Dharam Chand, a grandson of Guru Nanak was humiliated at his daughter's marriage by the groom's family in many ways. This included the insult to her brother who went to drop her off to some distance at the time of her departure (*rukhsat*) and was taken much farther than the etiquette required. Dharam Chand viewed it as the last bit in the series of unwarranted humiliations and came up with a horrific injunction, that henceforth all Bedis kill their daughters as soon as they were born, rather than bear such humiliation. Dharam Chand, the story continues, took on the burden of the crime of female infanticide. From that day onwards, he walked stooped, as though bearing a heavy weight upon his shoulders.[13] The most generous rational explanation for legitimizing such a heinous crime was that the Bedis occupied prominent positions within the Guru lineages. By the logic of being descendants of the Sikh Gurus, they had a high social and ritual standing. Due to their extraordinary high status, they found it difficult to find castes/subcastes of equal status for their daughters. It was considered shameful to marry among those of a lower ranking. Being exogamous, they could not marry among themselves. In other words, the main ambition of the upper castes was that of hypergamy, with which were linked notions of marrying a daughter in the upward direction, as well as what was needed to be spent on such occasions. Thus, daughters were viewed as a 'burden'.

The birth of a girl child was perceived as an important point, where the father should be humbled in all his social interactions and demeanour. Hari Kishan Kaul, Superintendent of Census operations, in his 1914 note on female infanticide, observed that Raja Todar Mal, the protagonist of the land revenue system in Akbar's administration, ceased to adorn an aigrette (*kalghi*) on his turban at the birth of his daughter. The aigrette was indicative of an exalted position at the court. The act of avoiding its adornment indicated that his pride had been humbled by the birth of a female child.[14] The *Pandnama-i Jahangiri*, a text of moral counsels attributed to Emperor Jahangir (r. 1605-27) advises, 'Do not grieve over the death of daughters. Do not follow the advice of women. Never be complacent and neglectful of their deception and artifice.'[15] Irfan Habib states, 'It is fair to say that such statements or sentiments do not occur in Jahangir's own memoirs.'[16] Whether it was Jahangir's perception or not, the fact of projecting it as Jahangir's opinion implied a larger acceptance of such a mindset and, thus, appeal to a larger audience.

At a general social level, the dislike for a girl child had greater implications for women at large. The woman who failed to produce a male heir was seen as accursed, that is one who had failed in her essential duty. Among many communities, the husband of such a woman could marry again and he would have not only the full approval of the community but even encouragement. At times, his wife might be the one who encouraged the husband to a second marriage, perhaps due to social pressure or her individual perception or a combination of both. One could easily gauge the insecurity and sense of loss for such a woman, who was forced to accept the co-wife (*saut*). In other words, a wife's worth came to be crucially determined by her ability to produce male heirs. Sons were the only way to carry on the lineage and the genealogy. Sons were needed not only to work on the land (in case of an agricultural set-up) but, more importantly, to keep the land within the patriarchal family and to provide support to parents in their old age.

PURDAH

Women were made to observe the veil (*purdah*). They had to cover their face or body from outsiders, particularly from the gaze of males. The advent of Muslims has been viewed by a few historians as being the reason for the introduction of the purdah in Indian society. R.C. Majumdar says that the Hindus adopted *purdah* as a protective measure to save the honour of their womenfolk and to maintain the purity of their social order. According to the social reality, the cultural values of the higher classes percolated down to the lower classes. This probably influenced the viewing of purdah as a symbol of high social status and contributed substantially to its wide acceptance in an elaborate and institutionalized form. However, this does not seem correct. There are scholars like Ashraf, who are of the opinion that even in ancient India women observed a certain veil, which even now goes under the name of *ghunghat*. Ashraf admits that 'the present elaborate and institutionalized form of *purdah* dates from the time of the Muslim rule'.[17]

It can be safely suggested that purdah and child marriage were considered safeguards for women and an effective mechanism to control their sexuality. *Purdah* was a measure of respectability among higher classes, so that higher the rank, the more secluded the women. It might have existed in the varied form of *ghunghat*, a custom that was common among the Hindus,[18] particularly the high caste Hindu women. Among the Muslims, the system of *purdah* was more strictly observed. The popular proverbs of the time indicate the general social perception and its wide acceptability. It was believed that if the woman was safe in the four walls of her home, she was worth a treasure; the moment she steps out of protected boundaries she is worth ashes (*andar baithi lakh di, bahar gai khakh di*).[19] The system, though prevalent among the higher classes, could not have been widely prevalent among the lower classes such as peasants, artisans, and manual labourers. In case of any laxity, the woman became a target of social ridicule. If she roamed about with uncovered face, her mother-in-law and sister-in-law passed sarcastic remarks (*saas, ninayane daandi taaney phirdiai ghunghat khulli*).[20]

Among the Muslims, the importance accorded to *purdah* as a marker of social respect of women was quite strict. If, for any reason, a Muslim woman of rank, discarded *purdah* even for a temporary period, the consequences for her were disastrous.[21] In 1595, Akbar promulgated,

> If a young woman was found running about the lanes and bazaars of the town and while so doing if she did not veil herself or allow herself to be unveiled, she was to go to the quarters of the prostitutes and take up the profession.[22]

Manucci also reports that the purdah was more strictly observed among the Muslims than among the Hindus.[23]

It was a great dishonour for a family when a wife was compelled to uncover herself.[24] In this regard, there was such an 'extraordinarily distrustful'[25] approach that many Muslims did not even permit their wives to see their brothers and fathers except in their own presence.[26] However, this seems to be an exaggerated situation. Certainly, the *purdah* system did not permit women to mix freely with other members of the clan. Her education was also restricted. To top it all, her minimal social interaction not only deprived her of learning through social exposure but made her immensely vulnerable in a social system where she was married off in a different village. Being confined to the four walls of the home, it restricted her interaction among women too. In brief, the *purdah* system was a manifestation of the general social attitudes towards women. It emerged as a social mechanism, which not only restricted, but also led to the social, political, and intellectual stagnation of women.

As a pleasant social aberration, the peasants and working women did not wear any veil and were not expected to be confined to their houses. They were free from the bondage of *purdah*.[27]

They were just expected to bring down the end (*pallu*) of their *sari* or any other head dress to cover their face when they passed a stranger. This 'freedom' had genesis in the fact that they were expected to help their husbands in all 'external pursuits and internal economy'.[28] They took their bath publicly at the riverside. They visited the shrines travelling on foot without any restrictions. We get evidence from the Sikh Gurus' verses where a woman carrying pitchers of water was mentioned without any *purdah*.[29] The Sikh Gurus and Bhagats referred to the watercarrier as *panihari*. In sum, the common women moved far more freely than the women of the upper strata of both the communities.[30]

Apart from Guru Amar Das, we do not find any criticism of the *purdah* system from any of the Sikh Gurus. It was only Guru Amar Das, who strongly censured the covering of the face by women. According to a Sikh tradition, the wife of the ruler of Haripur visited the Guru in *purdah* despite the instruction that his followers would not observe *purdah*. The Guru was said to have spontaneously uttered, 'Why has this mad woman come here?' This shows the Guru's strong dislike for the *purdah* system. Quite probably, the *langar* and *pangat* system along with the active involvement of women in the *manji* and *peerah* systems must have contributed to breaking the shackles of the *purdah* system. The practice was closely linked to the ideology of seclusion, which was considered a marker of high social status. The following hymn of Bhakta Kabir shows his opposition for the system of *purdah*. He asserted that people had attached false pride to it.

> This only is the merit of veiling the face,
> That for a few days the people say, how noble is the bride.[31]

Guru Nanak also applauds a woman who had cast off her veil, though the context was her striving for spiritual attainment. In his words,

> I have cast off my veil: the values of the world haunt no more my ignorance; the mother-in-law has lost her moorings and no more is her sway over my head.[32]

PROSTITUTION

Admittedly, by and large, academia has tended to treat prostitutes as either a scandalous or frivolous topic of research. Treating the subject academically, prostitution can be defined as a phenomenon in which a socially identified group of women earn their living principally or exclusively from the commerce of their bodies. The profession had been in vogue in India and was considered a necessary social evil. Ashraf observes that, like marriage, prostitution was a recognized social institution and was known in India from ancient times. The tradition of offering girls to sacred places also continued in medieval times.[33] There were courtesans or dancing girls whose number was considerable. There were numerous references to them in the contemporary sources. Guru Amar Das, for instance, has confirmed their existence in ancient times when he writes, 'Ajmal who mates with prostitutes, he too was saved, uttering the name of God'.[34] In the *Adi Granth* there were about a dozen references to prostitutes.[35] Quite obviously, all these references were clothed in derogatory terms. The most blatant comment was that the father of a son of a prostitute cannot be identified.

> *Jiu bahu miti vesua chhadai khasamu nikhasami hoi.*
> *Putu jane je vesua nanaki dadaki naun koi.*
> *Naraki savari sigaria rag rang chhali chhalai chhaloi.*
> *Ghandaheru aherian manas mirage vinahu sathoi.*
> *Ethai marai haram hoi agai daragah milai na dhoi.*[36]

According to the above passage, a prostitute having many lovers leaves her husband and thus becomes unclaimed, masterless. If she gives birth to a son, he carries no maternal or paternal name with him. She is a decorated and ornamental hell that deceives people by loving apparent charm and grace. As the hunter's pipe attracts the deer, so do the songs of a prostitute allure men to their destruction. Here in this world, she dies an evil death and hereafter obtains no entrance into God's court.

The social attitude towards prostitutes has always been strongly negative. In the near-contemporary literature, she was viewed as a disgrace to society. Bhai Gurdas, in his verses and *Kabit Sawaiyye*, makes frequent comparative references to prostitutes and the Manmukh Sikhs, who did not follow the right path. However, all his writing demonstrated the general social attitude towards prostitutes. He blamed the prostitutes for bringing disgrace upon themselves, their maternal and paternal families, besides their parents-in-law. He goes to the extent of blaming them for spreading poison in society.

Jiu bahu miti vesua sabhi kulakhan pap kamavai.
Lokahi desahu bahari tihu pakhan no aulang lavai.
Dubi dobai horana mahura mitha hoi pachavai.
Ghanda hera mirage jiu dipak hoi patang jalavai.
Duhi sarai jaradaru pathar beri pur dubavai.[37]

The above passage indicates that a prostitute having many lovers commits every type of sin. An outcast from her people and her country, she brings disgrace to the families of her father, mother, and of her father-in-law. Ruined herself, she ruins others and still goes on gulping and digesting poison. She is like the musical pipe which lures the deer, or lamp which burns the moth. Due to her sinful activities, her face in the earthly and the other worlds remains pale; she behaves like a boat of stone which drowns its passengers.

Owing to the economic dependence and the wretched conditions of widows, they must have at times been forced to resort to prostitution. Those who were in the habit of visiting the prostitutes did not care to realize the feelings of their spouses. Bhai Gurdas states:

Besvarat(i) britha bhae, man main a sanka mania
Juari na sarbas (u) hare sai thakat hai.[38]

In effect, knowing that his visit to the house of a whore can cause him a serious disease, a licentious person still does not feel hesitant to go there. A gambler never feels tired of gambling even after losing all his assets and family. Bhai Gurdas warns that the prostitute looks beautiful, but ensnares the mind, and the man is ultimately finished (*khari swalio vesua jia bajha itaia*).[39] The general social attitude towards prosti-tutes placed the onus of their existence on them and not on her patrons. This was reflected in many contemporary injunctions. For instance, Bhai Gurdas says:

Pragat (i) sansar bibichar karai ganika pai,
Tahe log bed ar(u) gian kin a kan(i) hai.[40]

A whore openly commits vice with other men. She has no regard and respect for morality and a code of conduct, as laid down in the social and religious books. Guru Nanak has portrayed the feeling of a young woman whose husband visits prostitutes.

Break thy cosy bed and thy ivory bracelets, O woman,
And thy arms, and the arms of thy bed,
Even though the bedeckest thyself so.
The spouse enjoyed with others.[41]

Quite expectedly, the people who visited the prostitutes had to bear social disapproval. In a hymn, Guru Nanak states:

Thieves, illicit lovers, prostitutes and touts keep company together,
As do men of irreligion, who eat out of the same bow
They know not the Lord's praise, for within them abides evil.[42]

Akbar viewed prostitution as a social evil and tried to curtail its prevalence. A separate quarter was constructed outside the city and all public women were asked to reside there. Special officers were appointed to look after them.[43] Guru Arjan, a contemporary of Akbar, noted that the people had no shame in visiting prostitutes. He lamented, 'Man in con-templating evil no sloth feels. In enjoying harlot no shame he has.'[44]

Apart from widowhood and its associated problems, women might have been drawn into prostitution in a variety of situa-tions. There could have been marital problems, especially in a polygamous situation. Women could be victims of sexual violence. Instances of elopements of women were available in the literature.[45] The genesis of these problems lay in the general social attitude, which treated women as objects, who were part of a range of gift exchanges. It was ironic that women whose social status was legitimate (along with social acceptability) did not have equivalent legitimate access to independent economic status, whereas women whose socio-sexual status was ambivalent at best, were more easily recognized as economically independent individuals.

The entire discussion reflects the general social attitude towards prostitution. A social evil, which sustained and thrived because of the facilitator (prostitute) as well as her patron, was viewed only as a 'social crime' of the prostitutes. A social evil, which has survived from times immemorial in different forms, was due substantially, if not solely, to the perversion of men, who took advantage of the economic compulsion of widowed or deserted women. Yet, the society at large retained the right to transfer the entire blame and the entire onus of a perverted sexual desire to prostitutes. Is it not ironic that a society, which had such a clear understanding of *stri svabhav* had evolved mechanisms – child marriage, the veil (*purdah*) and varied forms of widow remarriage (*karewa*) – to control the 'uncontrolled' sexual desire of women, did not even attempt to curtail the practice of prostitution and yet blamed them alone?

SATI

In a larger context, both in terms of time and region, one may admit that the custom of *sati* was primarily confined to the upper classes among the Hindus. It was especially valorized among the Rajputs. From primary sources, we learn that the women of the common masses, the lower classes, were not even permitted to follow the biers of their deceased husbands to the cremation ground. *Sahmarana* or *sahagamana* referred to dying with the corpse, it was indicated by the word *sah* meaning 'together' and the word *anumarana* or *anugamana*, which meant dying in the absence of the corpse. Keeping in mind the relations between affluent economic status and polygamous reality, one can understand that in the case of more than one wife, the chief wife had the privilege of being burnt with the corpse, the other being burnt in separate fires. It was easy to imagine that the Brahmins must have played a pivotal role in this entire macabre process, from alluring the woman to joining her husband for all eternity to the actual burning. Ashraf aptly comments that the act of *sati* was viewed by society as 'the last proof of perfect unity in body and soul between a Hindu wife and her husband'. The resistance of a wife to be *sati* was interpreted as 'a sure index of want of fidelity and truthfulness on her part'. Abul Fazl observed that some women were compelled by their relatives to burn themselves; some accepted the ordeal deliberately and with a cheerful countenance since they were devoted to their dead husbands; some surrendered out of regard for public opinion; others were swayed by considerations of family traditions and customs; and some were dragged into the fire against their will, as manifest later in the case of Maharaja Ranjit Singh's queens.

The general social attitude towards *sati* was reflected in the opinions of contemporary writers. Abdul Qadir Badauni, a prominent theologian of Akbar's reign, views it favourably:

> In the path of love, how can one be behind a Hindu woman
> Who burns herself alive over a dead (beloved)[46]

Amir Khusrau, speaking of *sati*, says, 'There is no more manly a lover in the world than a Hindu woman. To burn oneself on a burnt-out candle is not what every flying insect does.'[47] Akbar had a diametrically opposite opinion on *sati*. It appeared to be coming very close to the modern rational perception, where he questioned the 'manliness' of men, saying,

> In India, there is an ancient custom that after her husband's death the wife, however ill she might have been treated, throws herself

into the fire, and, with all bravery, sacrifices her valuable life and considers it a source of her husband's salvation. Strange is the conduct of men that through such help from women, they seek to secure their own salvation.[48]

In the *Dabistan-i-Mazahib* (1615-70), the author observes,

The enlightened doctors say that by a woman's becoming suttee is meant that on her husband's decease she should consume in the fire along with him all her desires, and thus die before the period assigned by nature; as in metaphysical language woman signifies 'passion' or, in other words, she is to cast all her passions into the fire; but not throw herself into it along with the deceased, which is far from being praiseworthy.[49]

The word *sati* has been used in the *Adi Granth* in a different connotation. It implies truthful, moral, disciplined, virtuous, and generous. It also refers to the custom of *sati* by which a widow used to burn herself on the pyre of her dead husband. It was considered virtuous according to the general social ethos. The practice of *sati* was closely linked to widow re-marriage. Both seem to be a mechanism to deprive the women of their property, howsoever small property rights she had got after the death of her husband. Both the social institutions seem to be prevalent. Both had social acceptability as they ensured the transfer of the interests of widows in the landed property back to the male line of the family of her deceased husband. The *Adi Granth* testifies that the custom of *sati* was quite common in medieval Punjab. Bhai Gurdas, approving of *sati*, states,

If a woman reflects strong-will and bears through the pain in last few moments of her life, sits on the pyre of her dead husband, then the whole world praises her and calls her *sati*.

Ant kale k bhari nigrah kai sati hoe,
Dhann(i) dhann(i) kahat hai sakai sansar ji.[50]

The above lines indicate that when a woman, controlling her mind and with utmost determination, jumps into the pyre of her husband and self immolates herself, the whole world applauds her effort of being a loving and devoted wife.

Even at the cost of repeating, one must admit that the practice of *sati* was a common practice among the Hindus. Originally, it was restricted to high castes like Brahmins and Kshatriyas. It was quite popular with the Rajputs. Ibn Battuta, who visited India during the heydays of the Delhi Sultanate, and Niccolao Manucci, the Venetian traveller who visited India during the Mughal period, have described this custom in detail. Ibn Battuta observes that in the Sultan's dominions, the Hindus had to get the state's permission, which was easily granted to them.[51] Manucci writes,

> When the ceremonies are finished . . . (widows) mounts to the top of the pyre and lying down on her side closely embraces her husband and the relations bind her feet strongly by two ropes to two posts driven into the ground for this purpose. Next, they throw some more wood and cow dung on the two bodies . . . they apply light.[52]

Isami refers to the tradition of *jauhar*, whereby the Rajput rulers, after losing hope of holding out against a besieging army, burnt their women and children. In his account of the conquest of Ranthambore by Sultan Ala-ud-din Khalji, Isami writes that Rai Hamir Deo burnt alive the ladies along with the precious things and then came out to fight to the last.[53]

While looking for the earliest references to this custom, we cannot ignore the classical writers like Strabo and Diodorus Siculus, who provide the instances of *sati* in India as early as the fourth century BCE. Strabo refers to the practice of *sati* at Taxila and among the Kathians (Madra) in ancient Punjab of their time.[54] Diodorus Siculus cites the story of the younger wife of a general named Keteus. She committed *sati* in 316 BCE when her husband died fighting against the Greeks.[55] Describing the 'cause' of widow-burning, Diodorus says that in the olden days, depraved women fell in love with other men and got rid of their husbands by poison. When this nefarious practice had become quite prevalent and many lives had been sacrificed and when it was found that the punishment of the guilty did not deter other wives, they passed a law ordaining that a wife, unless she was pregnant or had already borne children, should be burnt along with her deceased husband and that, if she did not choose to obey the law, she should be compelled to remain a widow to the end of her life and be forever excommunicated from the sacrifices and solemnities as an impious person.[56] Diodorus himself doubts the existence of such a law and, necessarily, of the reason assigned for the enactment.

In a treatise against suicide published in 1637, John Sym writes,

> Laws and customs in some places seeming to require and warrant people in some cases to kill themselves. As among the Heathens and Indians, where by custom or law, servants and wives, in testimony of love to their masters and husbands, were wont to cast themselves into the fire to bee burnt, with the corpse of their dead masters and husbands; but the true cause of that law was, to restrain the frequent paysoning of masters and husbands, by their servants and wives; and that law and custome was practised to avoide suspicion and ignominie that they lived in, if they did not so kill themselves.[57]

The element of coercion, which Diodorus underlines in his description of *sati*, makes it quite certain that if the practice existed, it was a violent imposition. The same picture was corroborated in the travelogue of Manucci.

It must be underlined that both Diodorus and Strabo wrote around the beginning of the Christian era, drawing their information from the writings of the two generals who had accompanied Alexander to India for the purpose of conquest more than three centuries earlier. In sharp contrast, Megasthenes, who spent many years in the Mauryan court and was a keen observer of Indian life, was silent on this issue. Thus, the description of Strabo and Diodorus, indicating the wide prevalence of *sati* should be viewed with suspicion. At best, they can be credited with noting a custom which was prevalent among certain tribes on the north-western frontiers of India.

It needs to be pondered over as to the factors that allowed the custom of *sati* to continue.[58] Apart from the somewhat absurd explanation of Diodorus for the prevalence of the practice of *sati*, many centrifugal and centripetal forces were responsible for deciding the fates of the thousands of unfortunate widows in society. Sir A.C. Lyall aptly explains the factors that probably helped to encourage and perpetuate this custom. He writes:

> Perhaps the best example of the selfish device obtaining vogue under the cloak of a necessary rite is afforded by the famous practice of a widow becoming *sati* or burning herself alive with her dead husband, which is undoubtedly, as Sir H. Maine has pointed out, connected with the desire to get rid of her right, if she is childless, to a tenancy for life upon her husband's lands. It is also connected, among the great families as may be easily observed still in certain parts of India, with the wish of the heir to free himself by this simple plan from many inconveniences and encumbrances entailed upon him by the bequest of a number of step-mothers who cannot marry again.[59]

It was an ironic situation. When there were no property rights for widows, there was neither an eagerness nor the mechanism of getting rid of them. However, with the gradual development of the idea of a widow's right to property, the emphasis on the custom of *sati* was also enhanced till it was given the status of the 'only *dharm*' for the widow. In fact, the figure of *Sati* came to be closely associated with the virtue of *pativrata*. The role of the male relatives of the widow, who were guided by their ulterior economic motives, was crucial. The ostensible justification of widows offering themselves for self-immolation does not seem to be plausible. It not only seems to be against the basic human instinct of survival, but we also have irrefutable evidence of use of force from Manucci. Niccolo Conti, Bernier, and others have also recorded similar instances of the use of force. Abul Fazl has recorded numerous instances where reluctant women were forced to perform *sati* due to the pressure from relatives or public opinion. Owing either to use of force or fear, if the widow ran away from the pyre, she became an outcaste and was not acceptable either to the society or to the family of her late husband. Adding to the agonies, the degradation of the widow, who chose to survive her husband, was the extreme social disapproval. Her survival under such adverse circumstances, which were extremely cruel, forced the helpless widow to choose *sati* as the lesser of the two evils. P.V. Kane, summing up the social scenario, rightly argues that the 'greed of property frequently induced the surviving members to get rid of the widow by appealing at the most distressing hour to her devotion and love for her husband'.[60]

It is significant to note that Bernier poses serious questions to the general opinion that *sati* was not the action of a devoted wife. It is commendable on part of Bernier that he perceived it as the result of female conditioning and this, in turn, was a device to ensure male control. To quote Bernier:

Many persons whom I then consulted about this custome of women burning themselves with the bodies of their husbands, would persuade me, that what they did was from an excess of affection they had for them; but I understood afterwards, that it was only an effect of opinion, prepossession and custom, and that the mothers, from their youth bespotted with this superstition, as of a most virtuous and most laudable action, such as was unavoidable to a woman of honour, did also infatuate the spirit of their daughters from their very infancy; Although, at the bottom, it was nothing else but an Art of Men, the move to enslave their wives, thereby to make them have the more care of their health, and to prevent poisoning them.[61]

Akbar prohibited forced *sati* in or before 1583. In the same year, he was known to have personally ensured its enforcement after the death of a Rajput officer.[62] There was some tumult when the emperor went personally to stop the ceremony. The widow was rescued, and he had 'the misguided ones' imprisoned.[63] Abul Fazl says that Akbar had appointed in every town and district truthful observers to ensure that while those, who of their own impulse wanted to commit *sati* might be allowed to do so, any forcible *sati* was prohibited and had to be prevented. An instruction to the *kotwal* to the same effect is recorded in the Ain-i-Akbari.[64] Akbar's increasing concern about sati made him revise and review his position on widows as well. In 1587, Akbar allowed the widows to remarry 'in the manner that the people of India do not prohibit'.[65] Irfan Habib observed, 'Its effects were surprisingly long-lasting, since throughout the seventeenth century Mughal officials appeared to be sincerely trying to prevent the rite by prohibiting compulsion and dissuading of the victim.' He further writes that the testimony of this comes from contemporary European observers not generally disposed to credit Mughal officials with such credit.[66]

It is an irony that when the woman had the right to live after the death of her husband, she was denied property rights, and when the latter was provided for, she was induced to die. Social pressure on the widow to burn herself was accentuated by the deplorable conditions a widow was subjected to. In seventeenth-century travel accounts, the active agents of this social coercion, projecting *sati* as the most virtuous act that would pave the way to heaven for the widow and her deceased husband, were the Brahmins. Bernier, describing their method of intimidation, writes,

I have seen some of them (widows), which at the sight of the Pile and Fire, appeared to have some apprehension and that perhaps would have gone back, but it's often too late; those Demons, the Brahmins, that are there with great sticks, astonish them, and heathen them up, or even thrust them in.[67]

Many accounts portrayed a *sati* as a helpless frightened victim. Tavernier accused the Brahmins of drugging widows owing to their greed for the jewellery they wore into the pyre:

Many of our Europeans are of opinion, that to take away the fears of death, which terrifies humanity, the Priests do give her a certain Beverage to stupefy and disorder the senses, which takes from her all apprehensions of her preparation for death. Tis for the Bramins interest that the poor miserable creatures should continue in their resolution; for all their Bracelets as well about their legs as their arms, the Pendants in their ears; their Rings sometimes of Gold, sometimes of Silver . . . all these belong to the Bramins, who rake for them among the ashes when the party is burn'd.[68]

Abraham Roger, a Dutch missionary, provides a tenable reason/explanation as to why the widows chose to be *sati* than living through the horrors of widowhood. The English translation reads,

The women who remain and are not burnt are despised and made as it were to bear the mark of their infamy publicly, their hair is cut off, they can never chew betel, they can neither wear any jewellery, nor remarry; in short they are subjected to all the affronts and annoyances imaginable.[69]

Mandakranta Bose puts it very succinctly, though in relation to the modern context and the macabre case of Roop Kanwar,

> The sheer inhumanity of *sati* is of such magnitude that we begin to wonder what kinds of validating pressures, drive human beings, apparently including the subjects of the custom themselves to accept and even extol *sati*.[70]

The fate of a widow in medieval times would not have been very different, maybe much worse, as indicated in a Maharashtra woman's diary, describing her life after the death of her husband,

> Once the husband dies, the torture of his wife begins, as if the messengers of the death God, Yama themselves have come to take away her soul. . . . It is the custom that a widow should eat only once a day for a year after her husband's death; apart from that, she also has to fast completely on several days. . . . A woman whose husband is dead is like a living corpse. She has no rights in the home. . . . Thousands of widows die after a husband's death. But far more have to suffer worse fates throughout their life if they stay alive.[71]

Now, in this background of the prevalence of the custom of sati among different sections of society, (which included followers of Sikh Gurus), it would be appropriate to note the Sikh injunction. Could it actually modify or reformulate the psyche of society at large? Guru Amar Das, the third Sikh Guru, condemned the custom of *sati* much before Akbar's promulgation prohibiting it. Employing strong allegorical terms, he said:

> *Sati* is nor she, who burns herself on pyre of the spouse.
> Nanak: A *sati* is she who dies with the sheer shock of separation.
> Yes the *sati* is one, who lives contended and embellishes herself with good conduct;
> and cherish her lord ever and call on him each morn.

> Women burn themselves on the pyres of their lords,
> But if they love their spouses well,
> They suffer the pangs of separation even otherwise.
> He further asserted:
> She who loves not her spouse,
> Why burn herself in the fire?
> For, be he alive or dead, she owns him not.[72]

Though Guru Amar Das clearly spoke against *sati*, the denigrating custom continued to be prevalent among the Sikhs. One such incident, which received a good deal of attention was the cremation of Maharaja Ranjit Singh. According to a description of the incident, at ten o'clock, nearly the time fixed by the Brahmins, Kunwar Kharak Singh set fire to the pyre and the ruler of the Punjab with four of his queens led by Rani Mehtab Devi, daughter of Raja Sansar Chand Katach of Kangraand seven attendants burnt themselves as *sati* on the pyre of the Maharaja.[73] It must be noted that *sati*, being performed at the cremation of such an iconic figure of Sikh history, not only legitimized but glorified the custom. Though we do not get references to it being prevalent in the common masses, this episode certainly emphasized the relation between the 'virtuous' (*pativrata*) wife and the act of *sati*. The disheartening reality is that all descriptions of the queens trying to escape their inevitable fate by bribing the officials fell on deaf ears. What emerges is the loud proclamation of a gap between the normative and operative realities. According to *Tawarikh-i Guru Khalsa*, Guru Gobind Singh declared that self-killing was the biggest crime (*atamghati mahapapi honda hai*). In the context of *sati*, Sahib Deva insisted that rather than being separated from him and staying in Delhi, she would prefer to commit *sati* in his presence. The Guru then reiterated the oft-quoted saying of Guru Amar Das (as quoted above).[74]

GURUS ON WOMEN'S CONDITION

It would not be out of context to recapitulate the perception of the Sikh Gurus on different facets of women's life. Admittedly, while there are many elements within the Sikh scriptural tradition which are emancipatory, there are many facets which legitimize various forms of patriarchy. At the outset, the Sikh Gurus emphasized that both men and women are equal before God, and both can enjoy spiritual attainments through the recollection of God's name (*nam simran*). Though Guru Nanak's attitude towards women was by no means simple, there are some ambiguous statements. For instance, the woman has been compared to a snare (*maya*) and designated as a symbol of lust. Yet, he advocates the life of a householder. Apart from the hymns relating to *suchajji, suhagan, sulakhni*, he is able to not only empathize but address the agony of a woman at the hands of Babur's army. Guru Nanak had no appreciation for the widow becoming *sati*. Yet, the divorced woman and the widow have not been dealt with sympathetically. He disapproves of the custom of becoming *sati* almost incidentally. He did not explicitly criticize child marriage or the disabilities a widow suffered.

Guru Nanak's emphasis on conjugal relationship, fidelity, and chastity, both for men and women has been repeatedly emphasized. This contribution cannot be undervalued because it is a remarkable, profound leap of faith in the perspective highlighting the importance of loyalty, trust, and honesty in the social loci of marriage. If marital life, a prime social institution, was advocated and practised in an ethical and moral way for both partners, it could have gone a long way in improving the position of women. Guru Nanak appreciated the woman for her procreative capabilities. He asserted that all of us were born of her, and the world could not exist without her. A woman was considered impure for a certain number of days after delivering a baby and even during the menstrual period. Guru Nanak categorically criticized the social ritual of *sutak*:

Jekari sutaku manniyai sabhtai sutaku hoe.[75]

To elaborate further, Guru Nanak asked if *sutak* (impurity, believed by orthodox Hindus, that stick to a home for a number of days after a birth has occurred) should be believed in. He held that this impurity, if any, could be washed away with enlightenment alone.

> Such impurity occurs everywhere.
> Inside cow dung and wood are found worms.
> No single grain of cereals is without life in it.
> The first of living things is water, whereby is each object sustained.
> How many *sutak* impurities be believed, when even in the kitchen it is occurring?[76]

The Sikh scripture does not debase the female body. It does not place taboos around menstruation, childbirth, or any other female physiological functions. There is nothing inferior or abhorrent about feminine sexuality. Female activities and accoutrements are assigned a high value, even a transcendental one. The Sikh affirmation of the feminine as a category of being, with essential values and strength, is expressed through the symbol of the bride. There are clear injunctions against the most heinous social crimes. Guru Amar Das and Guru Gobind Singh prohibited the practice of female infanticide. The Sikh code of conduct at the time of initiation of Khalsa prohibited any social contact with the killers of daughters (*kurri maar*). Guru Amar Das denounced the practice of wearing the veil (*purdah*). In fact, he even assigned five positions of religious emissaries (*manji*s) to women, which indicated his trust in the intellect of women and their merit as propagators of the faith. Guru Amar Das spoke against the practice of *sati* and empathized with the disabilities that the widows suffered. All the Gurus emphatically emphasized the need for chastity and fidelity, both for men and women, advocating monogamy. Guru Hargobind termed women the 'conscience of men'.

It must be acknowledged that the Gurus contributed positively to the status of women. In the then social ethos, to view the role of women as a mother, as a wife endowed with varied virtues, being able to hold the family together was a great social contribution. The equality of men and women in the spiritual arena acknowledged the intellect of women in

Discrimination and Social Evils 293

contrast to the popular perception that women were stupid and worthy of beating with shoes (*khaley*). Bhai Gurdas describes the life of love and affection of an unmarried girl and then the blissfully happy life of a wife (*suhagin*). This projection might not be a reality. Yet, one must applaud the positivity of the message in the life of a woman.

> *Pevakarai ghari iaduli mau piu khari pidri,*
> *Vichi bhirawan bhainari nanak dadak saparavari,*
> *Lakh kharach viahiai gahanw daju saju ati ati bhari,*
> *Sahurarai ghari manniai sanakhati paravar sadhari,*
> *Sukh manai piru sejari chhatih bhojan sada sigari,*
> *Lok ved gunu gian vichi aradh sariri mokh duari*
> *Gurmukhi such phal nihachau nari.*[77]

This passage traces the different roles of a woman across the successive stages in her life. In her parents' home, the girl was fondled and dearly loved by her parents. Among the brothers, she was a sister and lived (joyfully) in the full-fledged families of the maternal and paternal grandfathers. Then offering ornaments and dowry, besides spending lakhs of rupees, she was married. In her father-in-law's house, she was accepted as the married wife. She enjoyed with her husband, ate a variety of foods and always remained bedecked. From a temporal and spiritual point of view, a woman was half the man's body and assisted him till the door of deliverance. She assuredly brought happiness to the virtuous.

However, negative attitudes towards women have been the norm as opposed to the exception. While the Gurus frowned upon certain practices, many denigrating customs regarding women continued, the most prominent being sati and female infanticide. In order to comprehend this paradoxical aspect of religion – the gap between the injunctions and utterances of the Gurus and the actual impact they had on the social ethos – it was important to deliberate on both the positive and negative aspects within the scriptural canon. To know only the negative message was disempowering and to uphold only the positive images was naive and superficial empowerment. To analyse both promised a genuine discussion on the feminine dimension of the Sikh tradition and appreciated the contribution of the Sikh Gurus. Driven by an urge to be rational, one would not like to agree with scholars like Rita Gross when they claimed that patriarchy had always valued the feminine traits of women and as values regulating private life.[78] They asserted that it was important to valorize these images, especially that of motherhood, it was equally important to be aware of the problem in invoking these images as well. It is precisely these images that led to essentialist notions of womanhood and women's role in society. They can be viewed as tools of control for what the ideal woman is to be and to do. Essentialist understandings of 'ideal womanhood' or what has been labelled as doing 'gender'[79] was viewed as having inherent problems.

Understandably then, the images utilized in the scriptures generally focus on important functions within the household. The *Adi Granth* is replete with images of the mother, of the bride and of 'feminine roles'. To this writer, it is anachronistic to blame, or not to appreciate, the Gurus, who are distant by just 400-odd years. It appears that if human civilization has not changed its perceptions with the changing times, then the onus of our failure is passed on to them. If these scholars had reflected the same level of concern for the widening gap between the normative beliefs and operative realities (for instance, the still prevalent practice of female infanticide), then it would have certainly been an academic contribution and might have led to some self-introspection as a society. Keeping the social milieu in mind, the Sikh tradition at least acknowledged the significance of the feminine component within human existence.[80] One cannot ignore or undermine the importance of the Sikh Gurus' perception. They accorded respect and value to the woman as wife and mother, especially for her procreative capabilities. In the then social milieu, pollution (*sutak*) was attached to the process of childbirth and many such restrictions were imposed on the woman due to her physiology. In such a situation, to award respect to a woman in her roles of wife and mother, applaud her contribution in the smooth functioning of society and family life, and to advocate the ideal of chastity for both men and women in their marital life, was a remarkable understanding.

NOTES

1. Balwant Garg, 'It's God and Gurudwara now for Punjab's Unwanted Girl Child', *The Times of India*, Bangalore edn, 18 November 2007.
2. Sohan Kavi, *Gurbilas Padshahi Chhevin*, ed. Giani Inder Singh, Amritsar: Jiwan Mandir Pustkala, 1968, p. 353.
3. Ibid.
4. Bhai Gurdas, *Varan*, Text, Transliteration and Translation, 2 vols., Jodh Singh, Patiala: Vision and Venture, 1998, Var 30, Pauri 3.
5. Bhai Gurdas, *Kabit Sawaiyye*, tr. Shamsher Singh Puri, Amritsar: Singh Brothers, 2007, Kabit No. 394, p. 422.
6. Ibid., Kabit No. 241, p. 269.
7. *Gur Rattan Mal: Sau Saakhi*, ed. Gurbachan Singh Nayyar, Patiala: Punjabi University, rpt., 1995, Sakhi No. 43, pp. 54–5.
8. Gyani Gyan Singh, *Tawarikh Guru Khalsa*, ed. K.S. Raju, Patiala: Bhasha Vibhag, 1993, p. 900.
9. Waris Shah, *Hir*, Agra: Chetna Prakashan, rpt. 2010, pp. 44-5.
10. John Cave Brown, *Indian Infanticide: Its Origins, Progress and Suppression*, London: W.H. Allen & Co., 1857, p. 117.
11. Ibid.
12. F.A. Steel, *The Garden of Fidelity: Being the Autobiography of Flora Annie Steel. 1847-1929*, London: MacMillan and Co. Limited, 1929, p. 38. Also cited in *Panjab Notes and Queries*, Berkeley: University of California, 1884, p. 51.
13. This story was repeated in many reports on infanticide in Punjab. For instance, see Brown's *Indian Infanticide*, op. cit., pp. 115-16.
14. Hari Kishan Kaul (Superintendent of Census Operations), 'Note on Female Infanticide, Home Police', in Stracey T.P. Russell, *History of the Muhiyals: The Militant Brahman Race of India*, Lahore: Civil and Military Gazette, 1911, p. 64-B; this statement might not be a representation of real feelings of Raja Todar Mal. Yet, it indicated the larger social reality of viewing a girl child as a 'burden' and her birth as the lifelong downslide in social standing.

15. *Pand-nama-i Jahangiri*, appended to Khwaja Niamatullah Harawi, *Tarikh-i Khan Jahani*, vol. II, ed. S.M. Imamuddin, Dacca: Asiatic Society of Pakistan, 1962, p. 703.
16. Irfan Habib, 'Exploring Medieval Gender History', Symposia Papers, No. 23, Indian History Congress, 2000, p. 273, in *Recording the Progress of Indian History: Symposia Papers of the Indian History Congress, 1992-2010*, ed. S.Z.H. Jafri, New Delhi: Primus Books, 2012.
17. Kanwar Muhammad Ashraf, *Life and Conditions of the People of Hindustan, 1200-1550*, New Delhi: Munshiram Manoharlal, rpt., 1970, p. 171.
18. Max Arthur Macauliffe, *The Sikh Religion: Its Gurus, Sacred Writings and Authors*, Delhi: Low Price Publications, rpt., 1990, vol. II, p. 347.
19. G.S. Chhabra, *Advanced Study of Punjab*, Jullundur: New Academic Publishing Company, 1968, p. 129.
20. Similar comments can be heard in rural areas of Punjab and Haryana in today's date too.
21. P.N. Chopra, *Some Aspects of Society and Culture During the Mughal Age, 1526-1707*, Agra: Shiva Lal Agarwala, 1963, p. 116.
22. Abdul Qadir Badauni, *Muntakhab-ut-Tawarikh*, vol. II, Eng. tr. W.H. Lowe and B.P. Ambashthya ed., Patna: Academica Asiatica, 1973, p. 405.
23. Niccolao Manucci, *Storia do Mogor*, vol. 1, Eng tr. William Irvine, Calcutta: Indian Text Series, 1965, p. 62.
24. Ibid., vol. II, p. 175.
25. Ibid., p. 352; Francois Bernier, *Travels in the Mogul Empire: 1656-1668*, Eng. tr. Archibald Constable and Vincent A. Smith, Delhi: Low Price Publications, 1994, p. 89.
26. Ibid., p. 60.
27. P.N. Ojha, *North Indian Social Life During Mughal Period*, Delhi: Oriental Publishers & Distributors, 1970, p. 120; James Tod, *Annals and Antiquities of Rajasthan*, vol. II, ed. William Crooke, Delhi: Motilal Banarsidass, rpt., 1971, pp. 710-11; Kanwar Muhammad Ashraf, op. cit., p. 172.
28. P.N. Ojha, op. cit., p. 120; Kanwar Muhammad Ashraf, op. cit., p. 172.
29. G.S. Talib, *Sri Guru Granth Sahib*, Eng. tr., 4 vols., Patiala: Punjabi University, 1990 (hereafter referred to as *AG*), pp. 325, 335, 347.

30. F.W. Thomas, *Mutual Influence of Mohammedans and Hindus in India*, Cambridge: Deighton, Bell & Co., 1892, p. 72.
31. *AG*, p. 484.
32. Ibid., p. 931.
33. Kanwar Muhammad Ashraf, op. cit., p. 166.
34. *AG*, p. 995.
35. *AG*, pp. 238, 528, 837, 1029, 1415.
36. Bhai Gurdas, *Varan*, Var 33, Pauri 9.
37. Ibid., Var 5, Pauri 17.
38. Bhai Gurdas, *Kabit Sawaiyye*, Kabit No. 323, p. 351.
39. Bhai Gurdas, *Varan*, Var 36, Pauri 5.
40. Bhai Gurdas, *Kabit Sawaiyye*, Kabit No. 490, p. 518.
41. *AG*, p. 557.
42. Ibid., p. 790.
43. Abdul Qadir Badauni, *Muntakhab-ut-Tawarikh*, vol. II, p. 311; P.N. Chopra, *Some Aspects of Society and Culture During the Mughal Age*, pp. 123, 170.
44. *AG*, p. 1143.
45. Ahmad Yaar, *Ahsan ul-Kasis*, ed. Piara Singh, Patiala: Languages Department Punjab, 1962, p. 134; Waris Shah, *Hir*, pp. 46-8, 56, 193, 198-9, 200, 204, Muqbal, *Qissa Hir Ranjha*, pp. 26, 69.
46. *Nijatuur-Rashid*, ed. S. Moinul Haq, Lahore, 1972, p. 412, as quoted by Irfan Habib, 'Exploring Medieval Gender History', p. 274.
47. Irfan Habib, 'Exploring Medieval Gender History', p. 270.
48. Abul Fazl, *Ain-i-Akbari*, vol. III, Eng. tr. H.S. Jarrett and Jadunath Sarkar, Calcutta: The Asiatic Society, rpt., 2010, p. 449.
49. David Shea and Anthony Troyer, *The Dabistan or School of Manners*, Paris: Oriental Translation Fund, 1843, p. 77.
50. Bhai Gurdas, *Kabit Swaiyye*, Kabit No. 70, p. 98.
51. Ibn Battuta, *Travels in Asia and Africa*, Eng. tr. H.A.R. Gibb, London: Routledge & Kegan Paul, 1929, vol. III, pp. 613-14.
52. Niccolao Manucci, *Storia do Mogor*, vol. III, p. 60.
53. Abdul Malik Isami, *Futuh us-Salatin*, vol. II, Eng. tr. Agha Mahdi Husain, Aligarh: CAS in History, Aligarh Muslim University and Bombay: Asia Publishing House, 1976, p. 450.
54. J.W. McCrindle, *The Invasion of India by Alexander the Great*, New Delhi: Cosmo Publications, rpt., 1983, pp. 69, 202.

55. R.C. Majumdar, *The Classical Accounts of India*, Calcutta: Firma K.L. Mukhopadhyay, 1960, pp. 240-1.
56. Strabo, Bk. XV, Chap. 30, cited in Women's UN Report Network, 8 September 2008, http://wunrn.wpengine.com (5.3, Ancient Travellers' Accounts).
57. John Sym, *Life's Preservatives Against Self-Killing*, London, 1637, pp. 192-3, as quoted by Kate Teltscher, *India Inscribed: European and British Writing on India, 1600-18*, New Delhi: Oxford University Press, 1995, p. 52.
58. For detailed understanding see John Stratton Hawley, *Sati, the Blessing and the Curse: the Burning of Wives in India*, New York: Oxford University Press, 10th edn. 1994.
59. Sir Alfred Lyall, *Asiatic Studies: Religious and Social*, London: John Murray, 1884, p. 56.
60. P.V. Kane, *History of Dharma Shastra*, vol. II, Part 1, Poona: Bhandarkar Oriental Research Institute, 1962, p. 365.
61. Francois Bernier, 'A Letter to M. de la Mothe le Voyer', 122-3, quoted by Kate Teltscher, op. cit., p. 54.
62. Abul Fazl, *Ain-i-Akbari*, vol. III, ed. Ahmad Ali and Abdur Rahim, Bib Ind., Calcutta, 1873-87, pp. 284, 402-3. Here a modification is stated to be made in 1591, permitting voluntary *Sati*.
63. Ibid., pp. 402-3.
64. Ibid., p. 403.
65. Abdul Qadir Badauni, *Muntakhab-ut-Tawarikh*, ed. Ali Ahmad and Lees, Bib, Ind., Calcutta, 1864-9, p. 355.
66. Irfan Habib, 'Exploring Medieval Gender History', op. cit., p. 270; also see, Francois Bernier, *Travels in the Moghul Empire, 1656-68*, pp. 306-7; Jean de Thevenot, *The Indian Travels of Thevenot and Careri*, Eng tr. S.N. Sen, New Delhi: National Archives of India, 1949, p. 120.
67. Francois Bernier, op. cit, 126, as quoted in Kate Teltscher, op. cit., p. 54.
68. Jean Baptiste Tavernier, *The Six Voyages of Jean Baptiste Tavernier*, London: Robert Littlebury and Moses Pitt, 1678, vol. II, p. 121; Thomas Coryat, *Early Travels in India, 1583-1619*, ed. William Foster, Delhi: Low Price Publications, 2012, pp. 278-9.
69. Quoted in Kate Teltscher, *India Inscribed: European and British Writing on India, 1600-1800*, pp. 133-4.
70. Mandakranta Bose (ed.), *Faces of the Feminine in Ancient, Medieval*

and Modern India, Oxford University Press, New Delhi, 2000, p. 22; for a modern perspective, see Ashis Nandy, 'The Sociology of Sati', *Indian Express*, 5 October 1987; Romila Thapar, 'In History', *Seminar*, vol. 342, February 1988; Rajeshwari S. Rajan, 'Subject of Sati: Pain and Death in the Contemporary Discourse on Sati', *Yale Journal of Criticism*, 3:2 (1990); Sharda Jain et al., 'Deorala Episode: Women's Protest in Rajasthan', *Economic and Political Weekly*, 22: 45, 7 November 1987, pp. 1891-4; Lata Mani, *Contentious Traditions: Debate on Sati in Colonial India*, Berkeley: University of California Press, December 1998.

71. Quoted in S. Tharu and K. Lalita, *Women Writing in India: 600 BC to the Present*, vol. 1, New York: Feminist Press, 1991, p. 358.
72. *AG*, p. 787.
73. Ganda Singh (ed.), *The Panjab in 1839-40: Selections from the Punjab Akhbars, Punjab Intelligence, etc. Preserved in the National Archives of India New Delhi*, Amritsar, Patiala: Sikh History Society, 1952.
74. Gyani Gyan Singh, *Tawarikh Guru Khalsa*, ed. K.S. Raju, Patiala: Bhasha Vibhag, 1993, p. 1135.
75. *AG*, p. 472.
76. Ibid.
77. Bhai Gurdas, *Varan*, Var 5, Pauri 16.
78. Rita Gross, 'Studying Women and Religion: Conclusions Twenty-Five years Later', in *Today's Woman in World Religions*, ed. Arvind Sharma, Albany: SUNY Press, 1994, p. 348.
79. Doris R. Jakobsh, 'Gender Issues in Sikh Studies: Hermeneutics of Affirmation or Hermeneutics of Suspicion', in *The Transmission of Sikh Heritage in the Diaspora*, ed. Pashaura Singh and N. Gerald Barrier, Delhi: Manohar, 1996, p. 48.
80. Nikky-Guninder Kaur Singh, *The Feminine Principle in the Sikh Vision of the Transcendent*, Cambridge [England]; New York, NY, USA: Cambridge University Press, 1993, p. 14.

CHAPTER 7

The Sikh Panth and Women's Identity

In light of the preceding chapters, it is logical to trace the evolution in the ideological position of the Sikh Gurus in response to the changing circumstances, changing nature of the community (*sangat*), and its evolving influence and popularity. To understand the nuances of the relation between the position of women in sixteenth- and seventeenth-century Punjab and the Sikh Gurus, one has to appreciate the perceptions of the latter, besides capturing the evolving thrusts, issues, and circumstances of the times and the reasons behind them. Over time, the ten Sikh Gurus either modified or drastically changed their position on issues related to the development of the Sikh Panth. The process of the evolution of the Panth was closely related to the changing circumstances and the vision of the respective Gurus. How did individual Gurus respond to their relationship with the Mughals? How did the composition of the Sikh Panth, at a particular point in time, influence the policies and agenda of the Gurus? The composition of the populace, the regional affiliations, and demographic profile, was closely related to the sociocultural understanding of the Sikh Gurus with regard to the sustenance and the development of the Panth. To aim for its ever-increasing adherents, the Sikh Gurus needed to change their issues of concern and fine-tune them. The focus of their activities also had to continuously evolve. Contextualizing the perceptions of the Sikh Gurus with the corresponding phases of the Panth enables one to appreciate their position and the underlying reasons. In the context of the Sikh Panth, a commendable feature was the successful institutionalization of the position of the Guru. The institution of the Guru, which lasted for nearly 200 years, gave the Sikh Panth a remarkable opportunity to grow, evolve, and consolidate over a long period of time. This gave Sikhism a continuing opportunity for over two centuries to respond to new situations and circumstances. In its long journey under the ten Gurus, the Sikh Panth inevitably witnessed gradual changes. Its social base too underwent transformation. J.S. Grewal, while discussing the changes in the focus of the Sikh community, notes that we have to identify and study the shift in the dominant concerns of the community with the passage of time, looking for historical and logical connections between the activity and ideas of the various phases.[1] In the following pages, an attempt is being made to correlate the phases in the evolution of the Panth, emphasis on militarization and the corresponding marginalization of women among the concerns and activities of the Panth or her more active participation when she was part of the *manji* and *peerah* systems.

The basic function of a dominant or newly emerging religious tradition of any given society is to articulate a social ideology that serves as a psychological glue to preserve harmony and privilege within that society. In the case of the Sikh Gurus, the messages and ideological perception advocated were meant to appeal to the masses. Many religious beliefs and practices were employed not only to define the community's identity but also to provide a utopian vision for the future of the community and of the society of which it formed a greater or lesser part. In other words, these beliefs and practices were definitional in an ideal and moral sense. Together they constituted both the identity and ideology of the community. At the same time, as already stated, with the evolution of a particular religious tradition, its ideological perceptions also evolved. In the context of Sikhism, the evolution from the socio-religious movement of the sixteenth century to the socio-political Sikh Panth of the seventeenth century was another important factor, while considering the incongruity between the affirming messages of the Gurus and the actual marginalized, peripheral role of women. At a tautological level, the attempt to trace the ideological perceptions and shifts in the focus and dominant concerns become more complex in the context of the immense gap between the normative positions of the Gurus and the operative realities in the then existing society. For instance, take the issue of female infanticide. Guru Amar Das, the third Guru, was the first to criticize the practice of female infanticide in categorical terms. Yet, at the time of the establishment of Khalsa in the last decade of the seventeenth century, we observe that Guru Gobind Singh prohibited a Khalsa from having any contact with a killer of the female child (*kurri maar*). This indicates that till then the practice of female infanticide had not stopped. These social realities, rather than answering the question of the degree of the Gurus' impact on the position of women, posed more questions than answers. This, even as the initial injunctions of the first few Gurus, particularly those of Guru Amardas, were quite positive in their perception. Yet, the desired impact on the position of women was lacking. It is a complex issue, which deserved a thorough and independent study. However, the main reason is that there was a clear change in the social concerns and priorities of the Gurus and, thus, the change in emphasis in their religious discourse. Therefore, the constant and continuous pressure, in the form of religious discourses, got deviated over a long period and, obviously, the impact too got adversely affected and diluted. As rightly understood, the relationship between religion and social change was significant. Moreover, the hold of the patriarchal psyche was quite tenacious and required a constant, continuous, and powerful intervention on part of the Sikh Gurus to actually effect a change in the position of women. Without intending to undermine their contribution, a clear message advocating a better position for women and equitable gender relations was equally important. To put it more succinctly, the egalitarian messages of the first three Gurus, especially Guru Nanak and Guru Amardas had to be replaced with more political thrust and engagement because of the changing nature of the relationship between the house of the Gurus and the Mughals; the rippling effect is clearly discernible from the times of Guru Arjan Dev, fifth Guru.

The distinctive features and the general outline of Sikhism are perhaps best expressed in the words of Niharranjan Ray. According to him,

To be able to achieve the integration of temporal and spiritual seems to me to have been the most significant contribution of Guru Nanak to the totality of the Indian way of life of medieval India . . . (where) one finds that, by and large, in thought as well as in practice, the temporal and the material were set in opposition to the eternal or perennial and the spiritual.[2]

Guru Nanak and his successors offered a new message and a new mission that was simple, direct, and straightforward. The message consisted of the recognition and acceptance of one and only one God in place of hundreds of deities. He argued that this God could be reached not through the intermediacy of priests but by honest efforts, through love, devotion, and God's grace and by following a disciplined life. The life of a householder was not only accepted but was also placed higher than the path of renunciation. It was viewed not as a hurdle but rather as a contributor to the path of spirituality. The mission comprised of rejecting all external forms of religious exercises, meaningless perfunctory rites, and degrading social abuses. The most important contribution of Guru Nanak to women was opening the gates to the path of spirituality for women. He proclaimed:

Come my sisters and dear comrades!
Clasp me in thine embrace.
Meeting together, let us tell the tales of our Omnipotent Spouse (God).
In the true Lord are all merits in us all demerits.[3]

This move to advocate that men and women are equal in the eyes of God and that the path of salvation was not prohibited for women was remarkable, especially looking at the existing sociocultural values. Till then, the religious arena was barred for women. She was not thought worthy of it because she was considered intellectually inferior, a creation of God just to serve men. By making emancipatory goals open to women, the woman was placed at par with man, just as the Sudra was placed at par with the Brahmin. However, the path of spirituality for women was accessible only by fulfilling her roles of a wife, a mother, and so on. Guru Nanak's attitude was not exactly revolutionary in its outlook. He could refer to his wife as a snare yet place the householder above the renunciant. In any case, the Sikh Guru advocated the life of a householder with discipline and restraint. In *Sri Raag*, Guru Nanak counted, among the things inducing man to forget God, pearls, gems, diamonds, thrones, armies, political power, and beautiful women. Elsewhere, Guru Nanak clubbed women with sons, gold, horses, and elephants as the objects of attachment.[4] The five 'potent thugs' were power (*raj*), riches (*mal*), beauty (*roop*), caste (*jat*) and youth (*joban*).[5] Guru Nanak sees a close link between (sexual) desire and beauty (*roop*).

Individual perceptions were the culmination of personal predilections, the social milieu, and value systems. To view Guru Nanak as unconnected to his times was academically flawed. Moreover, when Guru Nanak described the woman as one of the potential temptresses of worldly illusion (*maya*), there was no reason to suspect his position. Guru Nanak viewed women as temptresses and not as one of two partners having equal desires, equal to men. He was outspoken in his denunciation of caste and his successors followed him in its vehement rejection. Very often, scholars argue, the intention was a renunciation only of those aspects of caste, which accorded the privilege to some and imposed discriminatory penalties on others.[6] However, this does not dilute the fact that the Gurus were emphatic in their rejection of caste-based religious pretensions and that membership of the Panth was open for people of all castes and gender. This insistence on eradication of the caste system and gender division in the path of spirituality should be viewed as a characteristic feature of the Panthic development in its initial stages.

Even in the initial stages, there were distinctive features that deserve to be noted as factors contributing to the strength, appeal, and level of participation in the Panth. At least three such factors can be identified. The immediate impact of Guru Nanak's personality and the appeal it had to the common masses was the first factor in play. If we do not go by the *janamsakhi* tradition, which was more a post-de facto presentation of knowledge, we do not come across any conclusive documentary evidence. Yet, it is a reasonable assumption as, very often, the charismatic appeal of either the initiator or one of his early successors was a feature typical of successful religious movements and there was no reason to suppose that the Nanak Panth was in any sense an exception to this rule.[7]

Second, Guru Nanak succeeded in communicating his ideological perception and convictions in the form of religious songs and *shabad*s (hymns). In a social structure where literacy was limited, these musical compositions reached the masses and won their hearts. Music had a strong appeal. When combined with the issues affecting the daily lives of the masses, these songs turned out to be a great *modus operandi* to carry the message far and wide. It must have contributed significantly to the early strength and subsequent growth of the Nanak Panth. The role of *Nanakbani* becomes clear if we consider how Guru Amar Das got attracted to the Panth when he heard Bibi Amro singing the verses of Guru Nanak.

The third factor was its appeal to the Jats of rural Punjab. It would suffice to say that the Jat response owed much to the egalitarian emphasis of the Panth. During the period of Guru Nanak and his successors, the Jats had become economically prosperous. Yet, their social status due to the caste system did not match their economic position. Irfan Habib has suggested that the Jats were strongly attracted to a Panth, which rejected caste as a religious institution[8] and the caste system as a principle of social organization. This constituency of the Panth represented a great shift and major vitality in its sustenance, aspects of which would be discussed later. Niharranjan Ray adds a new dimension to the understanding of the early phase of the Panth. According to him, what held these countless people together was neither the message by itself nor the mission, not even by the two operating together. It was the institutionalization of both, and the organization that was built up stage by stage by the Gurus. The personal leadership and the charisma of the Gurus served only as incentives and gave the necessary inspiration and guidance.[9]

To sum up the discussion on Guru Nanak's perception of women, it would not be out of place to quote Doris R. Jakobsh, who was a good representation of the opinions of a set of serious scholars:

> He did not re-evaluate social institutions such as marriage and marriage practices to make them more equitable for women. Moreover, his silence regarding *sati* is rather surprising, given that it was primarily confined to the upper echelons of society, to which he belonged. There was also no critique of female infanticide, again, a practice closely aligned to the upper caste. In the final analysis, when it came to the social status of women, Nanak seemed content to leave the prevailing system in place. In the patriarchal world view, women were indeed assigned a position of inferiority in no way detracted from their ability to attain salvation; salvation, regardless of station on gender, was pronounced open to all who devoted themselves wholeheartedly to the ultimate.[10]

While evaluating Guru Nanak's perception of women, it must be appreciated that the establishment of the Panth was in its infancy and the ideological positions as well as their responses, reactions and expressions, in the form of religious injunctions, evolved with time. Second, we need to make an assessment of Guru Nanak only in relation to his social milieu when patriarchal values were the norm. Admittedly, he did not touch upon quite a few social evils related to women. Yet his contribution – such as questioning the validity of the caste system, opening the gateways of spiritual attainments to women, criticizing the pollution (*sutak*) related to childbirth and menstruation cycle, besides emphasizing women's role in procreation – must be appreciated. One must recognize that the validation of the intellect of the women by opening the gateways of spirituality to her was a very value-loaded social message. It needs to be viewed in the context of the prevailing socio-religious norms where only Brahmins could have a connection with God. To put it more sharply, one, the Brahmins owed their position in the caste system because of their access to knowledge and second, more importantly, women were considered the dumbest creation of God, lacking any intelligence and wisdom, and meant to serve their husband, even if the men were devoid of any virtue. One must admit that this ideological narrative and consequent sociocultural norms justified the control over women and the treatment meted out to them. In this backdrop, Guru Nanak's emphatic message of acknowledging a woman's individual calibre and endeavour for union with God (equated to knowledge in then socio-religious discourse) was laden with a powerful, rather 'empowering' message. Her self-esteem was upheld by acknowledging her contribution as a mother; her procreative abilities (nature's gift to her) and her worth as a wife for the well-being of the family would have certainly accentuated her social worth. In sum, there is a clear effort to draw her out from darkness and invisibility in the larger social construct. More significantly, Guru Nanak questioned the prevailing norms and raised his voice against well-entrenched practices. His tough stand provided a platform for the subsequent Gurus to further a change in the social ethos and norms, especially Guru Amar Das, who opposed the sociocultural practices stacked against women. Guru Nanak's egalitarian outlook became still more relevant when we notice that religious life and social life were intermingled, mutually influencing each other in medieval India. To conclude, we can safely infer that Guru Nanak was a visionary who, despite living squarely in a patriarchal social framework, contributed significantly by questioning the prevailing norms and his appeal lay in his assertion that salvation was open to all, regardless of gender or caste.

Guru Angad succeeded to Guruship (*gaddi*) following the

first Guru's death in 1539. He was already associated with Khadur, a village situated on the right bank of the Beas approximately 30 km above its confluence with Satluj. There was evidently no reason why he should remain in Kartarpur, Guru Nanak's base for eighteen years, and the focus of the Panth's devotion accordingly transferred to a location close to the point where the Majha, Malwa, and Doaba areas converged. His successor, Guru Amar Das remained within the same vicinity, a choice which presumably accounted for the spread of the Panth's influence in all three tracts.

Guru Angad seemed to faithfully follow the teachings of Guru Nanak. His tenure appears to have been a period of consolidation as indicated by *Ramkali Ki Var*.[11] According to *Mahima Parkas Vartak* and *Mahima Parkas*, Guru Angad stressed the need to strive for spiritual attainment, which can only be through regular meditation. To find and follow the path of salvation, one must depend on the grace of the Guru. For Guru Nanak, the Guru had been the inner voice of God. For Guru Angad the supreme guide was the first master, Guru Nanak.[12] McLeod rightly points out that the reference to Guru Nanak in these terms confirmed what we might legitimately have assumed, that, by the end of the second Guru's lifetime, the identity of the Nanak Panth was clearly established.[13] Moreover, the central position of the Guru in the ideology of the Panth was also emphasized, which culminated in the tenet of the same *jot* (divine light indicating God's grace and knowledge), being transferred from one Nanak to another Nanak (the ten Gurus). This, in fact, provided the strong ideological firmness to the Panth in its infant stage and implied a Panth with a clear identity, but an informal organization. It is under his successor that a more formalized structure began to appear. Guru Amar Das became the third Guru in 1552 and directed the affairs of the developing Panth until his death in 1574.

Guru Nanak initiated community dining centre (*langar*). Successive Gurus popularized, expanded, and strengthened it. The holy congregation (*pangat*) brought down the communal barriers of the rigid control of the caste system. The systems of *langar* and *pangat* encouraged and built up a community that was far more homogeneous, unified and integrated than the vertically graded and sharply stratified Hindu caste categories (*jatis*).[14] The system of *langar* allowed the women, particularly Mata Khiwi, to participate in the preparation of food in the common kitchen. Her contribution to the development of the Panth became crucial as the institutions of *langar* and *pangat* were closely connected with its developmental institutions. Mata Khiwi was known for her dedication to the discipline and organization of the community kitchen (*langar*). She gave a practical shape to the mission of Guru Nanak and dispelled all disparities. She believed that God had created all humans as equals. The status of Mata Khiwi is unique. Her contribution to the Panth was further attested by the fact that she was the only Guru Mahal mentioned in the *Sri Guru Granth Sahib*. In one of the references, it is projected that she was sitting graciously and regally with that person, who was balancing the whole universe. In the second reference, Balwand was seen telling the people that Mata Khiwi was like a leaf-laden tree under whose shade people came to rest. She distributed the dessert (*kheer*), which was prepared with milk, rice, and sugar.

Balwand khiwi nek-jan, jis bahuti chhav partaali,
Langar daulat wandiya, rav am rit kheer ghee wali![15]

The egalitarian values of *langar-pangat* system were further strengthened by the system of community singing and community prayer. These were supplemented with sharing of common objectives, low ebbs of adversity and suffering, besides success and failure.

Both scriptural and popular sources attribute to Guru Amar Das a shift towards the inclusion of women in the Sikh Panth. The Sikh tradition credits him with a definite criticism of society beyond that of religious ineptitude. Much of this criticism was directed toward the situation of women. Guru Amar Das forbade *sati*, saying, 'They are not Satis who burn themselves with their dead husbands. Rather, they are *sati*s, Nanak, who die with mere shock of separation from their husbands.'[16] He further clarified, 'They too are to be considered as *sati*s, who abide in modesty and contentment. Who wait upon their Lord and rising in the morn ever remember Him.'[17] The Guru expressed the same sentiment in *Suhi-Ki-Var*, stating,

Women are burnt in the fire with their husbands; if they appreciate their husbands, they undergo sufficient pain by their death. And if they appreciate not their husbands, Nanak, why should they be burnt at all?

Saroop Das Bhalla in his *Mahima Parkash*, which was written in 1776, chronicled that Amar Das became acquainted with the Sikh community through a woman. Up to the sixtieth year of his life, he had not yet become a Sikh. He was a contemporary of Guru Nanak and related to the Guru. However, even as the Guru was preaching, Amar Das did not know of his spiritual messages. Even during the pontificate of Guru Angad, he was not clued into the spiritual discourse of Guru Nanak. It was reserved for Bibi Amro to bring him to the Sikh fold. She was the daughter of Guru Angad and was married to the nephew of Amar Das, who lived in the adjoining house. One early morning, she was churning milk and, as usual, reciting the Japuji, a prayer which holds the core of Sikh thought. Tradition has it that Amar Das was so moved that he insisted that she immediately introduce him to the source of the composition, Guru Angad. Amar Das eventually succeeded Guru Angad as the third head of the Sikh community.

Later accounts present Guru Amar Das as having denounced the practice of veil (*purdah*). The later traditions also noted that when the queen of Haripur visited him with a veil, he spontaneously reacted, 'Who is this mad lady?' It has been added that Guru Amar Das condemned the practice of female infanticide. A few scholars, like Doris Jakobsh, have inferred that Guru Amar Das' condemnation of the practice may well have stemmed from a need to distance the Sikh Panth under his leadership from the Guru lineage that was at the forefront of the practice of female infanticide. This does not seem to be convincing, as it was an uncharitable argument. If we look at the perception of Guru Amar Das on the position of women, his stance appeared to be holistic, as he addressed social evils like *sati* and *purdah*, besides going to the extent of appointing women as religious missionaries. Even if the condemnation of female infanticide was intended to distance the Sikh Panth from the Guru lineage, the result was undeniably positive. The contribution of Guru Amar Das does become more significantly holistic, humane, and thus, appeals to modern scholars.

It was Guru Amar Das who appointed missionaries to spread the message of the Sikh Panth beyond the immediate surroundings of Goindwal. The community had obviously expanded and owing to the increasing number of new congregations (*sangat*s) with large followings, contact with the Guru became increasingly difficult. The expansion of the Panth took it to new geographical areas, which made it further difficult to get in direct and regular contact with the Guru. It was, undeniably, remarkable on the part of the Guru to acknowledge the need to evolve a system of propagation and to keep in touch with the adherents or people who were attracted to the message and were potential new devotees to the faith. Thus was created the *manji* system, a word literally meaning 'spring bed' and referred to the seat of authority. *Manji* were leaders of local gatherings, who were directly accountable to the Guru and, thus, an extension of his influence.[18] While sources differ regarding the actual number of *manji*s, there is evidence that women were also sent out to preach the Gurus' message of emancipation. Some scholars believe that twenty-two seats of religious preaching were established and, out of these, two seats were allotted to women, Matho Murari and Sachan Sach.[19]

In the same manner, seventy-two cradles were established. These women, while rocking their children in cradles, used to preach the ideals of the Gurus in their neighbourhood. In sum, the appointment of *manjis* indicated growth in institutionalization of the Sikh Panth as well as its ever-swelling adherents. Given the exalted place of these religious emissaries, the very possibility of being included speaks a great deal about the trust Guru Amar Das awarded to women. His contribution attained a still greater significance if we recollect that a mere thirty-forty years earlier, which is a short span to expect a social change of this magnitude, Guru Nanak had professed to open the path of spirituality for women. Guru Amar Das took over its logical extension. In a social milieu where women were regarded unworthy of any spiritual attainments, awarding them the respect and responsibility of religious emissaries speaks a great deal about Guru Amar Das's genuine concern about women and complete faith in their abilities. Presumably, the women missionaries might have been fairly effective in recruiting other women into the Sikh fold.

When we move to the writings of Guru Ram Das, what has generally been pointed out in Sikh historical writings was an increasingly institutionalized community of followers. This included the emergence of the pilgrimage site, Goindwal. Surjit Hans points out that there is also a noticeable increase of feminine imagery in the writings of the fourth Guru,

Lyricism in Guru Ram Das has a social counterpart. It points to the entry of women in appreciable numbers in the *sangat*, in particular, and in the community at large. It may be reasonable to suggest that a large-scale entry of women into Sikhism contributed to the lyricism of Guru Ram Das.[20]

Earlier Gurus had indeed addressed the divine element in the female voice as a symbol of their submission, projecting God as the Lord (husband) and the devotee as the wife. However, with Guru Ram Das, the symbolism had taken on a more concrete shape. In fact, the female perspective towards the body of the Guru was conspicuously emphasized. His corporeality was central in these writings, as it was asserted, 'Looking again and again at the body of the Guru has filled me with intense Joy'.[21] According to Surjit Hans, the increased presence of women in the *sangat* and their greater participation in Sikh Panth were very much evinced in the compositions of

Guru Ram Das. As Hans notes, the influx of women must have been a great possibility and obviously their increasing share in the composition of adherents must have had a corresponding, if only marginal, change in the ideology as well as the expression of Gurus on issues related to women. Ironically, the fourth Guru was highly critical of women in his writings. With their influx into the young Sikh tradition, besides the emphasis on egalitarianism and a lack of control over women in their marital lives, the Guru commented, 'Sinful men, licentious and stupid, act as their women command. Lust abounds; thus do impure men take orders from their women and act accordingly.'[22] Such perceptions about women in the prevailing social milieu might be related to the composition of the Sikh Panth at this point in time. The implications of the composition of the Sikh adherents will be discussed in detail later. Here, it would suffice to say that the Jats accounted for a substantial component of the Sikh following. Needless to add, this newly acquired presence of Jat constituents would have threatened the established order of the Sikh Panth. It became necessary to take action to stem the tide of an unwarranted egalitarian ethos. The Panth was being increasingly moulded to satisfy the needs of the growing numbers of followers.

During the pontificate of Guru Ram Das, the *manji* system was transformed into the order of *masand*s. The word *masand* was the corrupt form of the Persian word *masnad* or 'high seat'. The nobles were addressed as *Masnad-i-Ali* (or high dignitaries) during the Afghan rule. Zulfiqar Ardistani writes that the Guru's agents, who deputized for him, took the title of *masand*s because they considered the Guru as *Sacha Padshah*.[23] It brought about the appointment of a class of officials, who were entrusted with the responsibility of preaching the faith and looking after the members of the community. More importantly, they collected the obligatory contribution of a tenth of the income of all the members of the community, which was originally a voluntary one. As with the *manji*s, the *masand*s also had the authority to initiate the entrance to the Sikh Panth. The *masand*s, according to Gokul Chand Narang, were chosen for their piety, integrity, and devotion to the Sikh religious order and were probably honorary officials.[24] *Dabistan-i-Mazahib* noted that the *masand*s had a dual responsibility. They preached the message of the Gurus and collected voluntary tribute from the followers. Thus, the new order was tailored to suit both the missionary activity and the economic interests of the Gurus.[25]

It must be pointed out that the institution of *manjis* and *peeris*, initiated by Guru Amar Das, contributed significantly to the efficient organization of the expanding Sikh community. It was an important administrative step germane with significant political consequences. Its reformulation and re-modulation under the aegis of the *masand* system, along with making the Guruship hereditary under Guru Ram Das, had important political significance. The latter measure had important socio-psychological consequences for the prospective Gurus as well as the Sikh community at large. The accession to Guruship (*gaddi*) became a family-centric feature, as the succession moved along the male lines in the family of Guru Ram Das (Sodhis). One can see that the Panth was moving away from the interiority of the faith. While the emotive principle of faith was continually declining, the role, participation, and involvement of women was also becoming more compartmentalized and marginalized.

By the time Guru Arjan took over the Guruship, an elaborate paraphernalia was attached to the house of the Gurus. Contemporary works pointed to an augmented secularization and politicization of the Sikh Panth in the late sixteenth century. Guru Arjan was installed as the Guru in the full regalia of power and authority, besides impressive pomp and splendour. The Sikh community declared him *Sacha Padshah*, that is, their true or real ruler, spiritual, and temporal. Niharranjan Ray[26] highlights the usage of *Sacha Padshah* as evidently in contradistinction to the false *Padshah* who was sitting on the throne at Delhi and Agra. *Sacha Padshah*, the 'True King', led human souls to salvation as opposed to worldly kings who controlled mundane deeds. The *Dabistan* attested to a leader who was increasingly viewed as not only a religious but a political leader under whose tenure impressive buildings were built in Amritsar. In the words of its author, 'The Guru wore rich clothes, kept fine horses procured from Central Asia and some elephants and maintained retainers as bodyguards in attendance.'[27] Given Guru Arjan's elevated visibility as a regal leader, the Sikhs came to be perceived as a separate state within the Mughal dominion.

By the end of Guru Arjan's tenure, apart from the positive institutional developments for the construction of a distinct Sikh identity like the Panth, it also possessed a line of Gurus, a growing number of holy places, distinctive rituals, and a sacred scripture. During this phase, the Guru was entangled in a struggle for succession. This compulsive involvement in political affairs was the result of several factors. The first factor was the occasional challenge to Guruship from rival contestants. One of the most distinguished among them was Guru Arjan's elder brother, Prithi Chand. Another significant internal challenge to Guruship was posed by Dhir Mal, the elder son of Baba Gurditta and a grandson of the sixth Guru Hargobind. McLeod points out that although it is difficult to evaluate their influence on the Panth, it seemed reasonable to presume that successful resisting of these challenges involved a heightened loyalty on the part of those who adhered to the orthodox line.[28] During this phase, women were not entrusted with any additional responsibilities. Probably, at this point, they would have continued with the routine participation in the holy congregation and common kitchen.

The same effect resulted from the relations between the Sikh Gurus and the Mughals. As noted, Guru Arjan's title of *Sacha Padshah* and a regal lifestyle must have aroused a sense of threat among the contemporary rulers. Official concern on the part of the Mughal administration became evident during the period of Guru Arjan and eventually led to his death (1606) while in custody. Relations between the Panth and the Lahore administration deteriorated further during the time of Guru Hargobind (1606-44) with fighting taking place on three occasions. Guru Arjan's death came to be regarded as martyrdom and, according to tradition, it led directly to a deliberate arming of the Panth by his son Hargobind. Bhai Gurdas makes a significant comment on the situation in the days of the sixth Guru. According to him, the critics of Guru Hargobind asserted:

The former Gurus used to stay at their *dharmasal*s but he does not stay at any one place. Kings used to visit them, but he was imprisoned in a fort by the King. The Sikh cannot think of one resort now that he runs from place to place undaunted. The former Gurus used to gratify the Sikhs with discourses from their *manjis*, but he keeps dogs to hunt. They used to compose *bani* to recite and hear it recited, but he neither composes nor recites nor hears it recited. He does not keep the Sikh *sewak*s with him and he has befriended the enemies and the oppressors.[29]

However, Saroop Das Bhalla differs from the above observation. Describing the regular schedule of Guru Hargobind, he noted the Guru's faith in the daily recitation of prayers (*nit nam*) and listening to devotional hymns (*akhand kirtan*). He further states that after due completion of the *nit nam*, the Guru spent his time and energies in militaristic activities.[30] According to *Tawarikh-i-Guru Khalsa*, the major reason for unrest among a few Sikhs was the Guru's concern for the well-being of Kaula, the daughter of a *qazi*. However, it further states that since that was not the case, the Guru took care of her only because of her great devotion to the faith and as a mark of respect to Miyan Mir's request, who was held in high esteem by Guru Arjan.[31] Another episode further attests to the shifting thrust of the Panth on militarism. At the conferment of the turban (*pag di rasam*), a ritual where the son of the deceased person was bestowed with a turban, indicating that he was now responsible for upholding all the status, dignity, and responsibilities of his family, Guru Hargobind got the *seli* and *mala* deposited in the storehouse and commended that in lieu of garlands, aigrettes (*kalangi*s) would be used. He further elaborated that henceforth people would cite the bravery of the Guru's Sikhs when a large number of them would attain martyrdom for their faith. This social appeal at the time of an important life cycle rite became still more value-loaded.[32]

This emphasis on the militaristic ethos of the Panth made the women adherents almost invisible. With the kind of 'routinisation of the faith' in the form of pilgrimages, *sangat*, *pangat*, recitation of *bani* and so on, the practice of the faith suddenly suffered a jolt. One does not claim that the number of women adherents declined, but certainly, they had become invisible. Out of the few references we get of women followers, two are from the times of the seventh Guru, Guru Har Rai. The Guru visited an old devotee at Lakhmi Pur and an old mother appealed for the charismatic miraculous power of the Guru to cure her only son who was fatally sick.[33] At the time of Guru Hargobind, the *masand*s, in addition to collecting revenue meant for the organization and maintenance of Sikh places of worship and pilgrimage, were also directed to collect arms and horses for the standing army.[34] According to all accounts, women were excluded from this new practice. With the process of institutionalization, gender differences within the Sikh Panth became increasingly pronounced. The viability of a religion based on spiritual devotion for women suffered a setback. With increased institutionalization, the traditionally established roles for men and women became more socially and materially feasible and thus consolidated. As the *masand*s were missionaries as well as administrators, who travelled far and wide to collect the Guru's dues, the window of possibilities for women, which opened briefly during the early years of Panth, was thus effectively closed.[35]

Though women would still have been a part of the wider Sikh community, they were not part of the military retinue which formed an important constituent of Guru Hargobind's vision and understanding of his mission. More precisely, given the centrality of motherhood and other roles associated with a woman in the seventeenth century, she would not have been expected to accompany the Guru in the skirmishes with the Mughals on a routine basis. One is aware that the episode of

Mai Bhago,[36] which has been often quoted as an example of women's position in Sikhism, could not be equated with the norm. As some scholars like Simran Kaur point out, when Anandpur Sahib was surrounded by the enemy's army, it was only the women who fetched water from the Satluj at the time of scarcity. It was only the women who supplied food and water to the Sikh soldiers who were fighting in inhospitable lands.[37] *Gurbilas Padshahi Dasvin* narrates the sacrifice of Bhai Bhagat Singh and his wife, who lost their daughter while contributing to this task. At the time of discussing Bhai Taru Singh's contribution, one could not be oblivious of the support from the support of his mother and sister. The main complaint put before Zakariya Khan, the Mughal commander, was:

*Hain taru singh di ek bhain aur mai,
Pees kut we kare kamai.*[38]

This could not have been a routine affair. If one studies Mai Bhago's episode closely, her sarcastic idiom appealed to the sense of male dignity. The self-respect of a community was more in the nature of an appeal to their male ego. She declared, 'You sit at home, wear glass bangles and take care of the kids' (*tusi ghar baith ke chhuri paayon te bachey khidaon*). It was a clear reflection of the position of women in the seventeenth century. In other words, the Sikh male took on a new identity sanctioned by Guru Hargobind as a protector of the faith, armed and ready for battle. During the skirmishes with the Mughal forces, the Guru applauded the militaristic calibre of Tegh Bahadur when he said, 'You are not the master of sacrifice; rather, you are the master of the sword' (*tu tyag mal ta nahin, Tegh Bahadur hain*). This role was denied to women who, by a process of elimination, would have been relegated to a secondary position, possibly even viewed as impediments to the true calling of the Sikh community.

What happened to this sense of Panthic identity and its implications for women during the quarter century pertaining to the seventh and eighth Gurus, Guru Har Rai and Guru Har Kishan, was impossible to determine. The seventh Guru remained in the Shivalik Hills where his grandfather, the sixth Guru, had retired following the outbreak of hostilities with the Lahore administration. Though he held the Guruship for seventeen years, nothing of any striking importance marked the period. McLeod points out that we can do little more than fall back on assumptions, one of which might well be the supposition that a period of prolonged absence from the plains must have produced a measure of weakening in Panthic cohesion. Though this would be an unsubstantiated deduction, it was clear that nothing eventful could be noted. There was one exception to the trend. A group of women dressed up like Rani Pushpa Devi (queen of Raja Jai Singh), but the child Guru managed to identify the Rani and sat in her lap. In the traditional sources, this episode was presented as an indication of the piety of the Guru.[39] This entire quarter century was bereft of any significant utterances of the Guru on women or any other social practice per se. The Panth appeared to be moving on an auto-pilot mode. Here, one must recall the state of affairs just before the era of the seventh and eighth Gurus, that is at the time of Guru Hargobind. As already discussed, it was a male-dominated and militaristic ethos of the Panth that took precedence, wherein women did not have much to contribute to growth and development. For Guru Hargobind, improvement in the position of women or any other social reality per se was not high among the concerns and activities of the Panth. With regard to women, we do not get any evidence of charismatic leadership on the part of these two Gurus. There was no deductible inference on the position of women or even any perceptions of the Gurus. The basic reality of the women being marginalized must have continued as before.

During the tenure of the ninth Guru, we do not find any specific development or any injunctions related to women. In his *hukamnamah* to the Patna *sangat*, there was a reference to Bebe Per Bai, instructing her to take care of his family during his absence. The document was addressed to 38 (presumably) heads of the *sangat*, out of which one was a woman. It was indicative of the fact that women, though accounting for a majority of the adherents of the faith, were marginalized and rarely held a position of eminence. One wonders if the name of women appeared because the context of the order was to take care of the womenfolk of the Guru's family and not any military expedition. Presumably, a woman would have been able to understand their needs better.[40] *Hukamnamah* number 23 referred to another woman Bebe Jadoy Bai in the *sangat* of Patna.[41]

Guru Tegh Bahadur, on the advice of his mother, travelled far and wide. During this period, his mother Mata Nanaki came to exercise a dominant influence in the development of the Sikh community. Our attention is drawn to two *hukamnamah*s. There is a difference of opinion among the scholars whether these were issued by Guru Tegh Bahadur's mother or his wife Mata Gujri. Ganda Singh, the scholarly editor, claimed that probably Mata Gujri had authored them. At the time of Guru Tegh Bahadur's journey across eastern India, Mata Nanaki had achieved the age of seventy-five years and it was Mata Gujri, along with a few important Sikhs, who looked after different organizational matters during the Guru's absence.[42] Yet, Ganda Singh did not find himself equipped enough to conclude beyond doubt that Mata Gujri authored these two *hukam-namah*s, admitting that there was no other documentary evidence to corroborate the conclusion.[43]

While Guru Tegh Bahadur remained in the hills, relations between the Panth and the Mughal administration were largely uneventful. It was only when the Guru moved to the plains that serious tensions returned. Later, they resulted in the execution of the Guru. As discussed earlier, the impact of Guru Arjan's martyrdom culminated in his son and successor Guru Hargobind deciding on arming the Panth. A stronger impact was caused by the execution of Guru Tegh Bahadur on his son and successor Guru Gobind Singh. His main aim was to consolidate Sikh power and steel the entire community so that it offered the resistance that was called for.

The development of militancy among the Sikhs peaked with the ascendancy of Guru Gobind Singh. By the time of Guru

Gobind Singh, the Sikh community had been transformed from a purely religious group to a highly organized body of men and women within a given area, militant in spirit and oriented towards meeting any challenge to their faith and community. This challenge came from the Mughal emperors and their governors, besides chiefs of the hill principalities, perhaps more from the latter.

Before discussing the heightened militaristic concerns of Guru Gobind Singh, it would be appropriate to look at his compositions on Durga and Chandi. A set of scholars read them as the Guru's inclination toward Puranic-Brahmanical culture and as his perceptions of women. It can be argued that the Guru had no faith in the worship of Durga or Chandi or any other divinity of the Brahmanical pantheon. He used them and their myths as mere images and symbols, just as Guru Nanak employed tantric-yogic practices for his own purposes. Guru Gobind Singh's compositions of more than a couple of pieces on Chandi and Durga can be explained by the need of the community for power, which is adequately represented by these goddesses. He was literally trying to arouse that hidden energy (*shakti*) among the adherents of the faith.

The impact of militaristic ethos on the position, status, and role of women in the Panth has been discussed. Yet, the establishment of the Khalsa had immense implications for the women adherents of the Panth. During the Baisakhi festival of 1699, Guru Gobind Singh instituted the Khalsa. Some aspects of the Khalsa remain obscure. The actual word itself is an example of this obscurity, for its etymology and original purpose were still open to doubt. Though tradition implies that it was first introduced in 1699, the term had already been used well before this date as a designation of the Panth.[44] This change was made in order to consolidate the Guru's own position amidst the increasing rivalry of claimants. Some members of the Guru's lineage, by virtue of their ancestry, had established themselves as Sikh Gurus in their own right. The usage of the term Khalsa derived its relevance from the word *khalis*, meaning pure. Rather than going into the graphic description of the initiation ceremony, it would suffice here to say that *charan di pahul*, whereby the initiate would drink water touched by either the Guru's foot or the foot of a respected person, who was the designated representative of the Guru, was replaced by *khande di pahul*. Now, the sweetened *amrit* was stirred with a double-edged sword (*khanda*). The usage of a weapon indicated the emphasis on the militaristic requirement of the Panth. All those who were initiated into the Khalsa were to take on the appellation 'Singh', to wear the five K's – *kesh* (long hair), *kangha* (comb), *kirpan* (sword), *kachha* (a type of underwear) and *kara* (steel bracelet).

In the initiation rite of Khalsa, the feminine aspect, which has been overtly emphasized as the importance accorded to women, emerged when Mata Jito added some sugar puffs (*patasha*s) to the consecrated water (*amrit*). Koer Singh, in his *Gurbilas Padshahi Dasvin*, notes that the sacred verses (*bani*) were recited along with the preparation of *pahul* and Mata Jito added some sugar puffs.[45] However, Kesar Singh Chhibar does not accord any role to Mata Jito. He writes that after adding the sugar puffs, the mixture was stirred with a double-edged iron sword and then it was named nectar (*amrit*).[46] Elsewhere, Koer Singh applauds Mata Jito for the act of adding sugar puffs to the already prepared nectar, as it enhanced the power of the nectar in a major way.[47] According to Saroop Das Bhalla, Mata Jito stated that to bear the power of the nectar was not an easy task, nor within the capabilities of everyone. Thus, she ordered the addition of some sweeteners (*misri* or *patasha*s) to the nectar, diluting it and making it appropriate for the use of Sikhs becoming 'Singhs'.[48]

What is of great importance in terms of Khalsa identity construction and gender analysis is that it was solely the male devotee, reborn in the order of the Khalsa as the new warrior-saint, that became the focus of all ritual and symbolism. Exterior symbols – weaponry, steel, and uncut hair – became the signifiers constituting what it meant to be a 'real' Sikh. The double-edged sword (*khanda*), a military implement associated with masculine characteristics, contrasted to the *karad*, a domestic 'feminine' implement. This change was indicative of the process of masculinization that was central to the new order of the Khalsa.[49] The spirituality of the early Gurus, which projected God as the Lord/husband and devotee as a wife/bride and was a metaphor inviting all to a profound relationship with the divine, simply did not fit into the masculine, soldier-saint perception of Guru Gobind Singh. The initial initiation rite *charan ki pahul* had invited all to full participation in the Sikh Panth. With the creation of the Khalsa and the newly mandated rite of *khande ki pahul* as normative, women were symbolically and ritually excluded from the 'brotherhood' and were relegated to a marginal standing. Women, excluded from the Khalsa brotherhood, were inadvertently depreciated as full-fledged followers of the Sikh tradition. An ethos developed, which consistently widened the gulf between the 'true' Khalsa Sikh and those who were either not invited to join, namely women, or those who did not pay heed to the Guru's call. Needless to say, the gulf between males, as possible adherents of the Khalsa military order, and females, as inadvertent adherents of the older Sikh Panth came to the fore in a significant way.

We should not be oblivious to the fact that during the Khalsa initiation, Guru Gobind Singh prohibited any kind of social interaction with the killer of a daughter (*kurri maar*). The fact that this heinous social crime was vehemently criticized by Guru Amar Das, the third Guru, and yet the tenth Guru had to speak against it indicates that this social evil had largely gone unchecked. According to Senapat, the Khalsa code (*rahit*) prohibited the use of tobacco and the company of five ill influences that included the *kurri maar* as well as the *masand*s.[50] In his *Gurbilas Padshahi Dasvin*, Koer Singh prohibited any contact with *kurri maar, masand*s, and Prithi Chand's family, besides forbidding the 'selling of daughters'. Koer Singh also lists the prohibition of gambling and visiting prostitutes in the Khalsa code.

Our discussion on gender during the time of Guru Gobind

Singh will not be complete without a reference to *Charitra Pakhyan*. Also known as *Pakhyan Charitra* or *Triya Charitra*, it has been incorporated into the *Dasam Granth* and forms bulk of the volume. It is a collection of 404 tales of the wiles of women. According to Dharam Pal Ashta, the intent behind these tales was 'moral suggestiveness'.[51] While indirectly, they instructed men in good moral behaviour, they warned the unwary against 'womanly enticements'. The collection also includes stories in which women play no part at all. There were tales of heroic and honourable women, they account for a much lesser number. Even when the woman was portrayed as a victim, the structure of the tale was such that she appeared too powerful over the man. Most of the themes were of love and sexual debauchery, while the women were often the seducers. The thrust of the message, as communicated in the bulk of the stories, fitted well into the framework *stri svabhav*. The woman was portrayed as deceitful, lustful, dishonest, wicked, and disloyal. She wanted the fulfilment of her uncontrolled sexual desire by hook or crook, and the list goes on. The woman was cast as the eternal temptress, the object and the very form of sexual desire, who could ensnare the wisest and the most ascetic man. To make this point clearer, one must recount a popular story in which a beautiful widow attempted to seduce Guru Gobind Singh by disguising herself as a young *sadhu*, who would reveal the goddess Devi to him at a specific spot at midnight. The Guru, caught in an embarrassing situation, was shocked at her intrigue and managed to flee from the area. This was the famous occasion that prompted Guru Gobind Singh to collect and write down these tales on the guiles of women.

The actual authorship of *Charitra Pakhyan* has been an issue of heated debate among scholars. Many historians and theologians have downplayed the importance of the work. Keeping in mind the strong 'masculine' ethos as the main thrust of the Khalsa order initiated by Guru Gobind Singh, it does not seem improbable that he might have viewed women as a distraction. He might have thought that women had the power to turn the warrior-saint away from his true calling. Women, the possessor of innumerable wiles as constructed in the *Pakhyan Charitra*, were a complete antithesis of the kind of male 'brotherhood' ready to face any military challenge as the Guru envisioned.

Even if the Guru did not author this section of the *Dasam Granth*, one cannot deny the fact that the volume is still held as an important Sikh scripture almost at par with the *Adi Granth*. For our purpose of study, *Charitra Pakhyan* was a classic reflection of the general social perceptions about women. Its nuanced study is essential in understanding the construction of gender during the time of the tenth Guru, even if we choose not to read it as his perception. By virtue of it being part of the *Dasam Granth* and being associated with the name of Guru Gobind Singh, it must have sanctified the general derogatory social perception about women. It must have exercised an immense influence on his seventeenth-century followers. It is an attestation of the pervasive influence of a religious leader, testifying to the fact that what was believed to have been the injunctions, utterances, or the images created by the Guru, could commonly be much more important than their actual composition. Regardless of whether or not its authorship could be attributed to Guru Gobind Singh, the work is of considerable importance in understanding gender construction in the immediate post-Guru period.

SOCIAL COMPOSITION OF THE PANTH AND ITS CHANGING CONCERNS

As already noted, the social composition of the Panth had an impact on the perceptions, concerns, and actions of the Gurus. At different points in time, the Panth addressed issues that won over to its fold the people, whose interests coincided with the egalitarian concerns of the Gurus. In other words, the Gurus elicited a distinctive response from the specific constituency of the Panth. All the Gurus were Khatris and Bhai Gurdas' list of the leading members of the early Panth indicates that the Khatri prominence extended beyond the Guru's line. The list covers a sufficient range of castes to suggest that there must have been something resembling a cross-section of Punjabi society in the Panth during the period of its first five or six Gurus. The lowest ranks in the order of Punjabi caste society were perhaps under-represented, but they are not absent. There was enough evidence to show that large recruitments were made not only from among artisan communities of weavers, carpenters, and masons but also from those pursuing such callings as barbers, washermen, leather-workers, sweepers, and scavengers, that is all who were considered low in the Brahmanical caste system. A few of the recruits happened to be Muslims. Moreover, a comparatively light representation in a list of prominent members does not necessarily imply a corresponding proportion of the actual adherents.

At some point, however, the composition of the community radically changed, with the emergence of a new caste group, the Jats, to prominence. From the time of Guru Ram Das and the foundation of Amritsar on a piece of land gifted by Akbar amid fertile lands that had a high concentration of the sturdy Jat peasants, a conscious and concerted drive was made to draw Jats into the fold of the faith. Guru Arjan added strength to this drive by centring around Taran-Taran. The first clear indication of Jat strength in the Panth went back to the later years of Bhai Gurdas' lifetime. The Persian work *Dabistan-i-Mazahib*, which was written during the period of Guru Hargobind, indicates that by the early seventeenth century, the Jats comprised a significant proportion of the Panth.[52]

Though some uncertainty obscures the social composition of the Panth, there are sufficient grounds for supposing that a significant measure of the initial response came from the Jats of central Punjab. The Panth recruited its followers in rural Punjab from its earliest days. Therefore, it was reasonable to suppose that the Jat response to Guru's teachings should be traced to its first beginnings. The Jat response owed much to the egalitarian emphasis of Guru Nanak and his successors. Irfan Habib, contemplating the inclusion of the Jats into the Sikh fold, attributes this influx to a disparity between the economic status of the Jats and their caste status in the sixteenth century. If this theory held true, it meant that there would have been a widening gap separating their ascending economic status and comparatively humble ritual status. He further suggested that the Jats would be strongly attracted to a Panth, which rejected caste as a religious institution.[53]

Another development points to the close connection between the social composition of the Panth and its changing concerns. During the time of Guru Ram Das and Guru Arjan, the popularity of the Panth had been continuously increasing among the Jats. By the time of Guru Hargobind, the transformation of caste constituency from Khatri to Jat dominance had almost completed. The Jats were known for their resistance to authority and would not have been averse to armed resistance. The state oppression would have exacerbated a militant reaction from the Jats. After the Mughals executed Guru Arjan, Guru Hargobind wore arms, and the military concerns of the Panth became apparent. Guru Hargobind used to carry two swords, *miri* and *piri*, one hanging from the right and another hanging from the left, one representing the spiritual and another the temporal authority. He also fortified Amritsar and built the Akal Takht opposite the Harmandir, dispensing justice and temporal order from the former and spiritual guidance from the latter. It was here that the caste composition of the adherents of the Panth would have been pivotal to the change. Guru Hargobind's military stance was likely to have originated with the armed Jat constituency, as opposed to the religious ideology of the young Guru. In sum, the Guru's call to arms under the banner of self-defence took precedence over the transformation of minor (read major) social ills. It is tempting to postulate that the institution of Khalsa towards the end of the seventeenth century was as much the result as the cause of the preponderance of the Jats among his followers.[54]

The early Gurus lived within or near the Majha area of

Punjab, a region that was and is still known for a strong Jat presence. Given the egalitarian nature of the Jats, it is possible that women, in particular, were attracted to the emancipatory message of the Sikh Gurus, as it was women who had a lot to gain from this new ideological current. Several factors point to the full participation of women in the developing Sikh community. First and foremost was Guru Nanak's clear and insistent injunction that the doors to salvation were accessible to both women and men. For the first time in the religious tradition of the area, women were acknowledged as intellectually worthy of the path of spirituality. It sent a strong message that in the eyes of God both sexes were equal. Second, there were strains within the sources pointing to women as having been active participants in the developing community. Third, Guru Amar Das directed his criticism to the oppression in the form of widow burning, veil covering, and female infanticide. It must have managed to win over the hearts of innumerable women. Fourth, the plausibility of the missionary activities of women, also during the time of Guru Amar Das, resulted in an active outreach toward women. Fifth, scriptural indications of an influx of women into the Sikh Panth took place during the time of Guru Ram Das.[55]

Admittedly, women would have had the most to gain from rejecting the restrictions placed upon them by an orthodox Brahmanical system and embracing the egalitarian message of the early Sikh Gurus. The third Guru's criticism of the societal norms pertaining to women would conceivably have encouraged their move into the Sikh fold. Their appointment as religious missionaries was a development, which further corroborates the trend. However, this level of involvement and participation experienced a noticeable downward slide from the time of Guru Ram Das.

One is intrigued by the fact that while Guru Amar Das categorically criticized the practice of female infanticide, it was followed by an astonishing silence by all the Gurus till Guru Gobind Singh, who issued strong injunctions against it. In fact, we do not even get an incidental ruling on the issue.

The silence became more disturbing when the inhumane aspect of the practice had already been hinted at by Guru Amar Das.

With the transformation of the character of the Panth came a shift in the priorities of the Gurus. The patriarchal value system was firmly established during the development of the Sikh community. Already endowed with the cultural and social capital traditionally associated with their gender, men were now placed in powerful hierarchical positions within the new religious community. All the Gurus were male. Though Bibi Bhani, according to Sikh tradition, had won the blessings of her father, Guru Amar Das, she was not considered worthy of Guruship. All sources refer to the unparalleled service and obedience of Bibi Bhani, particularly the episode of her bleeding palm, when she had placed it under a broken bath stool so as to prevent any inconvenience to her father. None mentions the possibility of her being seriously considered for the Guruship. Gyani Gyan Singh's *Tawarikh-i Guru Khalsa* puts it a little differently. According to this version, Guru Amar Das did not happily concede to the wishes of Bibi Bhani. Typical of *triyacharitra*, womanly enticements, and obstinate nature, she insisted on the grant of such a wish. According to the author, Guru Amar Das pointed out that the succession to Guruship was not based on the logic of hereditary possession and warned her that it would only bring about continuous friction within the family.[56] He bestowed the Guruship on the family of Sodhis only, but the succession was only on male lines. Though considered worthy of such blessings, Bibi Bhani could not be the Guru because she was a woman. This trait of succession in male lines prevailed among all the religious traditions in medieval India. Bibi Sharifa, the daughter of Shaikh Farid-ud-din Ganj-i Shakar, has been described as a pious woman. She became a widow in her early youth and did not marry again. She devoted herself to religion in such a way that her father remarked, 'Had it been permitted to give *Khilafat namah* (grant of diploma by a Sufi saint, allowing his disciple to enroll disciples in the order) of the Shaikh and his prayer carpet (*sajjadah*) to a woman,

I would have given them to Bibi Sharifa.' Further, he said, 'if other women would have been like her, women would have taken precedence over men'.[57] This anecdote shows that spiritual authority was not transferred to women not only in Sikhism, but also in Sufism, particularly the Chishti order, which was known to be a more liberal form of Islam. Moreover, the earlier practice of the Panth, where women held some seats of authority, was replaced by *masand*s, so that men came to hold all the positions of prominence and responsibility. The traditional male roles became increasingly valued and female roles devalued, particularly with the institutionalization and politicization of the Sikh Panth.

In the end, one would like to ponder over the reasons that the positive directives of the Gurus towards women were never developed and applied in social ethos. The precepts of the Gurus, concerning the amelioration of the situation of women, remained just precepts. This shortcoming might be attributed to historical and cultural circumstances. The politico-religious relations between the Sikhs and Mughals, dictated by a combination of guile, regional ambitions, and later, survival, led to a scenario where, from Guru Arjan onwards, and specifically under Guru Hargobind, Guru Tegh Bahadur, and Guru Gobind Singh, the threat posed by the Mughals was always central to their concerns and activities. In the initial phase of the Sikh Panth, many contesting claimants existed for the position of the Guru and, to win over the maximum number of adherents, issues appealing to the masses (the social evils) were addressed. It becomes a plausible explanation if we recall that it was only the first three Gurus, particularly the third Guru, who had much to speak in favour of women. It coincided with the phase when women emerged as a prominent component of the new adherents and, thus, women's issues figured prominently. This process must have worked both ways. Very often, it was just the injunctions that did not produce the intended changes. Was it reasonable to even expect religious leaders to address the issue of social evils so majorly or, could it have been that some Gurus themselves accepted the status-quo and endorsed the patriarchal structures? Another explanation for the failure to attain the desired results of the professed reforms could be that the deep-rooted traditional and cultural attitudes towards women proved to be too strong for the Sikh Gurus to eradicate. Unfortunately, there existed a tremendous gap between Sikh precepts and practices, which had been continuously increasing with the passage of time.

NOTES

1. J.S. Grewal, 'A Perspective on Early Sikh History', in *Sikh Studies: Comparative Perspectives on a Changing Tradition*, ed. Mark Jurgensmeyer and N. Gerald Barrier, Berkeley: Graduate Theological Union, 1979, p. 34.
2. Niharranjan Ray, *The Sikhs and the Sikh Society: A Study in Social Analysis*, Delhi: Munshiram Manoharlal, 2nd rev. edn., 1975, p. 32.
3. G.S. Talib, *Sri Guru Granth Sahib*, Eng. tr., 4 vols., Patiala: Punjabi University, 1990 (hereafter referred to as *AG*), p. 17.
4. *AG*, p. 222.
5. *AG*, p. 1288.
6. W.H. McLeod, *The Evolution of the Sikh Community: Five Essays*, New Delhi: Oxford University Press, rpt., 1996, pp. 87-91.
7. Terry Thomas, 'Sikhism: The Voice of the Guru', Units 12-13 of the Open University Series, *Man's Religious Quest*, Milton Keynes: The Open University Press, 1970, p. 63.
8. Irfan Habib, 'Jats of Punjab and Sind', *Essays in Honour of Dr. Ganda Singh*, ed. Harbans Singh and N. Gerald Barrier, Patiala: Punjabi University, 1976, p. 99.
9. Niharranjan Ray, op. cit., pp. 70, 86, 96.
10. Doris R. Jakobsh, *Relocating Gender in Sikh History: Transformation, Meaning and Identity*, New Delhi: Oxford University Press, 2003, p. 26.
11. *AG*, pp. 966-7.
12. *AG*, Var Majh, 27.1, p. 150; two *sloka*s which together summarize the message of Guru Angad are Var Majh, 18: 1-2, *AG*, p. 146.
13. W.H. McLeod, 'The Development of the Sikh Panth', in Karine Schomer (author), ed. W.H. McLeod, *The Sants: Studies in*

a Devotional Tradition in India, Delhi: Motilal Banarsidass, 1987, p. 234.
14. Niharranjan Ray, op. cit., p. 21.
15. *AG*, Ram Kali Ki Var, p. 967.
16. *AG*, p. 787.
17. Ibid.
18. Fauja Singh, 'Guru Amar Das; Life and Thought', *The Punjab Past and Present*, vol. VIII, No. 2, 1979, pp. 300-33; Fauja Singh, *Guru Amar Das: Life and Teachings*, New Delhi; Sterling Publishers, 1979, pp. 116-29.
19. M. K. Gill, *Role and Status of Women in Sikhism*, Delhi: National Book Shop, 1995, p. 69.
20. Surjit Singh Hans, *Reconstruction of Sikh History from Sikh Literature*, Jalandhar: ABS Publications, 1988, p. 142.
21. Ibid., pp. 154-7.
22. *AG*, p. 304.
23. Ganda Singh, 'Nanak panthis: Eng. tr. from *Dabistan-i Mazahib* by Zulfiqar Ardistani', *The Punjab Past and Present*, vol. I, no. 1, 1967, p. 34.
24. Gokul Chand Narang, *Transformation of Sikhism*, Lahore: New Book Society, 1946, pp. 70-1.
25. Ganda Singh, Nanak panthis, p. 34.
26. Niharranjan Ray, op. cit., p. 67.
27. Ganda Singh, Nanak panthis, p. 39.
28. W.H. McLeod, 'The Development of the Sikh Panth', pp. 235-6.
29. Bhai Gurdas, *Varan*, Text, Transliteration and Translation, 2 vols., Jodh Singh, Patiala: Vision and Venture, 1998, Var 26, Pauri 24, pp. 437-8.
30. Saroop Das Bhalla, *Mahima Parkash*, ed. Gopal Singh Lamba and Khazan Singh, Patiala: Languages Department, 1971, p. 159.
31. Gyani Gyan Singh, *Tawarikh-i Guru Khalsa*, ed. K.S. Raju, Patiala: Bhasha Vibhag, 1993, p. 478.
32. Sohan Kavi, *Gurbilas Padshahi Chhevin*, ed. Giani Inder Singh, Amritsar: Jiwan Mandir Pustkala, 1968, p. 278.
33. Swaroop Singh Koshish, *Guru Kian Saakhian*, ed Piara Singh Padam, Amritsar: Singh Brothers, 1995, Saakhi no. 4, p. 42 and Saakhi no. 11, p. 53.
34. Sohan Kavi, *Gurbilas Padshahi Chhevin*, p. 279.
35. Gokul Chand Narang, *Transformation of Sikhism*, pp. 70-1.

The Sikh Panth and Women's Identity

36. Mai Bhago (Mata Bhag Kaur) led a troupe of 40 Sikh soldiers against the Mughals in the Battle of Khidrana, that is Muktsar in 1705. The Sikh soldiers fled from Anandpur Sahib and deserted Guru Gobind Singh in the face of impending loss in battle. She inspired them to rise and fight till the last breath and not act as cowards. She was the only survivor of this battle but the troupe of these brave men succeeded in saving the life of Guru Gobind Singh from the hands of Mughals at this point. Mai Bhago is thus revered as not only a brave Sikh but a person who shook the conscience of the wayward Sikhs and showed them the true path of a Gursikh.
37. Simran Kaur, *Prasidh Sikh Bibiyan*, Amritsar: Singh Brothers, 1991, p. 8.
38. Rattan Singh Bhangu, *Prachin Panth Parkash*, ed. Bhai Vir Singh, New Delhi: Bhai Vir Singh Sahitya Sadan, rpt., 1998, p. 269.
39. Swaroop Singh Koshish, *Guru Kian Saakhian*, Saakhi no. 17, p. 62.
40. Ganda Singh, ed., *Hukum Nameh*, Patiala: Punjabi University, rpt., 1993, No. 13, p. 86.
41. Ibid., No. 23, pp. 106-7.
42. Ganda Singh, ed., *Hukum Nameh*, p. 12.
43. Ibid., Nos. 30 and 31, pp. 122-3.
44. J.S. Grewal and S.S. Bal, *Guru Gobind Singh*, Chandigarh: Punjab University, 1967, p. 115. The term 'Khalsa' was used by the Mughals for revenue collection on lands that were directly supervised by the government, see pp.113-15.
45. Koer Singh, *Gurbilas Padshahi Dasvin*, ed. Shamsher Singh Ashok, Patiala: Punjabi University, 1968, p. 296.
46. Kesar Singh Chhibbar, *Banswalinamah Dasan Padshahi Ka*, ed. Piara Singh Padam, Amritsar: Singh Brothers, 1997, p. 128.
47. Ibid.; Surjit Hans, *A Construction of Sikh History from Sikh Literature*, Jalandhar: ABS Publications, 1988, pp. 129-31.
48. Saroop Das Bhalla, *Mahima Parkash*, p. 826.
49. Doris R. Jakobsh, *Relocating Gender in Sikh History*, pp. 42-3.
50. Senapat, *Sri Gur Shobha*, ed. Ganda Singh, Patiala: Punjabi University, 1967, p. 241.
51. Dharam Pal Ashta, *Poetry of the Dasam Granth*, New Delhi: Arun Prakashan, 1959, p. 156.
52. Ganda Singh, 'Nanakpanthis: Eng. tr. from *Dabistan-i Mazahib* by Zulfiqar Ardistani', *The Punjab Past and Present*, vol. I, no. 1, 1967, p. 57.

53. Irfan Habib, 'Jats of Punjab and Sind', p. 99.
54. J.S. Grewal, 'A Perspective on Early Sikh History', p. 37.
55. Doris R. Jakobsh, *Relocating Gender in Sikh History*, p. 34.
56. Gyani Gyan Singh, *Tawarikh-i Guru Khalsa*, p. 364.
57. Khaliq Ahmad Nizami, *The Life and Times of Shaikh Farid-ud-din Ganj-i-Shakar*, Delhi: Idarah-i-Adabiyat-i-Delli, 1987, p. 65.

Conclusion

The preceding chapters have been conceptualized on the notion that gender is a fluid construct, which is always evolving and transforming. The perceptions of a society, including its social ethos and norms, find their way in varied metaphors and expressions. The notions of gender and allied questions such as the position of women, their role and its value continuously evolve. They emerge and develop with the shifting needs of the region and community within which they unfold. This process is influenced by political, economic, social and cultural factors. Very often, the ideological fermentation of a few individuals or the society at large accompanies these changes in the social understanding. It is a well-accepted conceptual assumption that gender relations cannot be studied in isolation. It has to be looked at in the context of structures and processes in which such relations are embedded. There is a complex interplay between religion and social change. Religious traditions have been important players in the transformation of societies. They have always been important in determining the status of women since such factors exert a powerful influence on the thought, culture and behaviour of the people. The religious ideology plays a crucial role in legitimizing and sustaining the subordination of women. In contrast, it can advocate a more egalitarian society as is the case with Sikhism. For Guru Nanak, men and women were equal not only before God but also before one another. Women are considered an integral part of society and, therefore, they must not be excluded by a ritual or doctrinal consideration.

This study reinstates a basic historical reality that significant cultural differences did not exist in the Punjab. So was the case with perceptions about life on the basis of religion. There existed a fusion of traditions and a composite culture. In the context of the Punjab, multiculturalism is not just a statement of fact, it is also a value. The society of medieval Punjab was marked by the fusion of traditions, where Hindus, Muslims and adherents of the nascent Sikh faith shared the aspirations of their lives and values, besides their social expressions in the form of rituals and rites. The patriarchal psyche of both the major religious communities, Hindus and Muslims, recommended child marriage on the same ideological grounds and both were equally stringent in following it. For any study focusing on social history, conclusive and judgmental generalizations would be oblivious to the multiplicity of traditions and customs. For instance, even if we look at the varied forms of marriages and the underlying logistics behind them, a whole gamut of practices coexisted. It is not only difficult but rather misleading to dub any particular form of marriage as 'ideal'. The commingled culture is evident in the vast similarities between the rituals and customs followed by the Hindus and Muslims.

The survey of the socio-religious and political milieu (the thrust of Chapter 1) has clearly reflected the factors and institutions that facilitated the emergence of Sikhism and its popularity over a substantial section of society. A detailed study of the geographical features underlined the close connection between the geographical features and sociocultural life. To give it a more concrete grounding, an ideological framework has been developed, where the perceptions of the important Bhakti saints, both *sagun* and *nirgun*, have been studied. Obviously, their injunctions were the main area of focus and the baseline for the comparative trajectory. It was quite satisfying to observe that when Guru Nanak's perceptions were compared with that of other Bhakti saints, particularly Kabir who was the most vehement critic of women, it turned out to be much more egalitarian. Guru Nanak's ideological outpourings considered women worthy of spiritual attainments and thus invited her to join the holy congregation (*sangat*). She was considered at par with men in the path of spiritual quest. In the eyes of Guru Nanak, the woman was appreciated for her various traits and procreative capabilities, as often referred to in the course of this study. He acknowledged her social contribution as a mother and wife. In sharp contrast to the Bhakti saints, she was not viewed only as a source of distraction. She was not considered to be the one to bring about the downfall of a man through her maddening sexual lust. It was only Guru Nanak who spoke vehemently against physical pollution (*sutak*) related to the biological functions of the female body. It was only Guru Nanak who viewed the life of a householder as a virtue and recommended the ethos of chastity for both men and women in their marital lives. The Gurus redefined celibacy as marriage to one wife. They taught that the male and the female alike needed to practice conjugal fidelity. They advocated the marriage of two equal partners. Guru Amar Das, the third Guru insisted, 'Only they are truly wedded who have one spirit in two bodies'. He strongly condemned *purdah* and indeed refused to have an audience with women keeping it. He spoke against the custom of *sati* and female infanticide. He established religious centres, where women alongside men were recruited to lead and teach through the *manji* and *peerah* systems. Women worked along with men in maintaining the common kitchen (*langar*), performing various duties and sitting along with the men in the holy congregation (*pangat*). Admittedly, the Gurus' teachings of equality have never been fully realized, which is clearly evident in the treatment of women in present-day Punjab or even in Sikh society. Yet, the contributions of the Gurus, their categorical injunctions condemning the whole gamut of customs and practices against women, cannot be underestimated.

One is inclined to review the critique of a few modern scholars, who held that Guru Nanak did not speak against Sati, polygamy and the condition of widows. It was unreasonable to ignore his contribution to positive positioning and criticism of the sufferings inflicted on women. These were much ahead of the prevailing sociocultural milieu. If the contributions or the positive thrust in Guru Nanak's messages is diluted and he is discredited for using words like *kuchajji*, *kulakhni* and *dohagan* then the supposition that all women are 'good' by virtue of being women is equally misleading. It is like falling into the trap of seeing only the 'black' and the 'white' while turning blind to the 'grey' component of the larger reality, which is often the major part of any society. In medieval times, the general perception (represented by Bhakti saints like Kabir, Tulsidas, Surdas) viewed women as 'black', that is in a negative light. She was seen as a snare, a distraction and a distrustful, dishonest and malicious being driven by sexual lust. In this sense, we are choosing to see only the 'white' and attempt to turn the 'black' into 'white'. Instead, the reality is that, at any point in time, both 'good' and 'bad' people coexisted, whether it was men or women.

The second part of this study focused on marriage, the social sphere, discrimination and women's identity. The system of marriage was an important social institution around which the life of the women revolved. In this context, the social milieu of the medieval period provided rich material on the institution of marriage, caste, ritual purity, widow remarriage, domesticity and seclusion. In view of the intense intermingling of cultures, one cannot presume homogeneity in patterns of social behaviour. In this endeavour one needed to be very sensitive to the nuances caused by caste and class, thus acknowledging the multiplicity of realities. Another factor confronting the study of the institution of marriage was the deep impact of exogamous marriages on the life of women. It was rightly called the 'Second Birth' in a woman's life when she was given a new name to complete this feeling of newness. Cessation of all contacts with her biological family was the general social expectation. One can easily relate to her sense of loss and insecurity when she was almost dropped into the new setup at the mercy of an unknown family, without much hope of emotional or any other kind of support. In sharp contrast to the general social ethos, Guru Amar Das' injunction stressing the compatibility in a marriage must have worked (or at least should have) as a balm to the bruised heart when he said:

Bride and groom are not they who pose as one whole;
Bride and groom are they who are two bodies with one soul.[1]

Here, the Guru advocated the marriage between two equal partners and the sacred institution of marriage aimed at the fusion of two souls into one.

This study would be incomplete without a reference to the family. The family is not only an important primary institution in all civilized societies, it is the most important basic social unit where women have had a formidable role to play. It is this role which emerges as an important yardstick to assess her position in the larger social fabric. Family needs to be studied in its relationship to caste, class, gender and religion. In medieval Punjab, we come across paternalistic dominance within the family, where members had unequal access to material assets and the right to make decisions. Oppression and powerlessness of women coexisted with an underlying ethos of according social respect and honour to her in roles like that of the mother.

The study of rituals and ceremonies brought out the secondary status of women, as reflected by their role and participation in social engagements. The rituals connected the husband and wife but in a clear hierarchical manner, placing the wife in a subordinate position. If these rituals and ceremonies are expected to be clear identity markers of any community, then they are also a tangible reflection of the power equation of different components of the society. It establishes and reinforces the position of men and women, their roles and the existing, largely accepted, gaps in the social order. On one hand, the rituals and ceremonies often reinforced the social order and on the other hand, from a purely systemic viewpoint, rituals were the ceremonies of a mediating institution that shaped the future of a society. They were in effect the vehicles of hope for both individuals and the social order;

rituals helped people overcome indeterminacy in life. Within this conceptual framework, one observed that there was a tension between the ritual and the social order. The secondary (read marginal) status of women was registered by other life-cycle rituals and they revealed the insignificant role played by women, thereby being excluded from the rituals at times.

The Gurus emphatically advocated an egalitarian society, where a woman was awarded the position of equality, respect and dignity. Inspite of this strong condemnation of social customs and practices that discriminated against women, social evils did not cease to exist. Very often, the egalitarian social ethics, values and norms, as preached by the Gurus, religious leaders, and saints, have always been very difficult to implement. To expect the normative preachings to become the operative beliefs and ethos of society with respect to women was still more difficult. The women were not only relegated to their households but were married at a very tender age of eight to nine years so that they would not sexually go astray. They were compelled to observe the veil (*purdah*). A woman was expected to be a Sati at the death of her husband in some castes or observe permanent widowhood in others, even in the case of young widows. Widowhood meant destitution, social rejection and lifelong loneliness. The birth of a daughter was viewed with disdain and sorrow. The birth of the boy was celebrated lavishly, but that of a girl meant scorn and blame from the parents-in-law.

At a social level, the dislike for a girl-child had greater implications for women at large. The woman who failed to produce a male heir was seen as accursed, as one who had failed in her essential duty. In other words, it became clear that a wife's worth came to be crucially determined by her ability to produce male heirs. In the larger social perception, the sons were and are still needed, not only to work on the land (in case of an agricultural set-up) but more importantly, to keep the land within the patriarchal family and to provide support to parents in their old age. In medieval Punjab, the weakness for sons as the desired progeny went to the extent that female infanticide was practised on a significant scale, if not widely. Commendably, Guru Amar Das spoke against it and Guru Gobind Singh prohibited any kind of social contact with the killer of female infant (*kurri maar*).

The Sikh Gurus also spoke against the practice of *sati*. The word *sati* has been used in the *Adi Granth* in different connotations. It implied truth, morality, discipline, virtuousness and generosity. It also referred to the custom of *sati*, whereby a widow burnt herself on the pyre of her dead husband. The practice of *sati* was a question closely linked to widow remarriage. The study of social reform movements in eighteenth-century India impressed upon the fact that widow remarriage had the intent of betterment of widows. However, one is forced to confront the other side of the reality. Among the agriculturist and artisanal classes, widow remarriage was prevalent, so that her procreative capabilities and her physical labour output did not go waste. Though we do not get categorical evidence from the sixteenth and seventeenth centuries, its prevalence in the later period has been recorded. Generally, such social practices did not evolve suddenly. They had their genesis in the remote past. Among the Jats, the practice of widow remarriage was quite common with minor variations under the names of *karewa*, *chadar dalna* or *chadar pauna*. The underlying logic was to transfer whatever little share the widow had inherited in the landed property of her deceased husband. This widow remarriage was to be performed only with the brother, preferably younger, so that the landed property was retained among the male lines only. In case a woman decided against marrying any of her brothers-in-law, then till the time of her last breath she had to remain chaste. Only then she could exercise a little control over her share of land. It was very difficult to assume that she would be able to resist her remarriage against her wishes. Moreover, the precondition of chastity was attached to her right. Looking at the general disempowering mechanism, the family of the parents-in-law and society might have stooped to the level of doubting the chastity of a woman.

Admittedly, it is difficult to assess the impact of the Sikh Gurus in changing the larger social perception, besides partially modifying the dominant patriarchal ideology. The final product of their constructive intervention was a result of the complex interplay of the changing focus of the Sikh Gurus, which was closely related to the development of the Sikh Panth and its existing as well as aspired social base.

The most important contribution of Guru Nanak was that he opened the gates to the path of spirituality for women. In the prevailing sociocultural milieu, it was remarkable that men and women were equal in the eyes of God and the path of salvation was not prohibited for women. Till then, the religious arena was barred for women. They were not even considered worthy of it, because she was considered intellectually inferior, a creation of God just to serve the men. By the act of making the emancipatory goals open to women, they were placed at par with men, just as the Shudras were placed at par with the Brahmins. However, the path of spirituality was open for a woman only after fulfilling her roles of a wife, a mother and so on. Guru Nanak's attitude was not exactly revolutionary. He could refer to the wife as a snare, yet place the householder above the renunciant. In any case, the Sikh Guru advocated the life of a householder with discipline and restraint. One is inclined to agree with J.S. Grewal that Guru Nanak, within the patriarchal framework, created a large space for women much larger than what we find in Kabir or perhaps the whole range of Indian literature springing from devotional theism. Total equality of women with men in the spiritual realm was a radical idea in Indian history, especially because it was not confined to female renouncers (*bikhu*s or *bhakta*s). Guru Nanak's symbolic attack on discrimination against women due to physiological differences carried the idea of equality a long step forward. True, he did not suggest an equal share to the daughter in inheritance. Nor did he say anything in support of inequality of any kind. The principle of equality upheld in one area of life carried important implications for other areas as well. In a social set-up where religion was an important aspect of life, it influenced its varied aspects, both directly and indirectly.

A whole gamut of restrictions and superstitions were attached to childbirth. A woman was considered impure for a certain number of days after delivering a child. Guru Nanak categorically criticized the ritual of menstruation (*sutak*), saying, *jekari sutaku manniyai sabhtai sutaku hoe*.[2] Guru Nanak, on the contrary, highlighted the physiological feminine trait as a quality. He emphasized that without the woman the world could not exist. The Sikh scripture, at large, does not debase the female body. Nor does it place taboos around menstruation, childbirth or any other female physiological functions. There is nothing inferior or abhorrent about feminine sexuality. Female activities and accoutrements were assigned a high value, even a transcendent character. The Sikh affirmation of the feminine as a category of being with essential values and strength was expressed through the symbol of the bride. This thought process extended further in respecting a woman as a 'mother' and went a step further by advocating conjugal relationships in marriage. All the Gurus emphatically stressed the need for chastity and fidelity both for men and women, advocating monogamy. Guru Hargobind called women the 'conscience of men'.

It must be acknowledged that the Gurus contributed positively to the status of women. In the prevailing social ethos, it was creditable to view the role of women as a mother and wives, endowed with varied virtues and able to hold the family together. Her social contribution was immense. The equality of men and women in the spiritual arena acknowledged the intellect of women in contrast to the popular perception that women were stupid and worthy of beating with shoes (*khaley*). There were clear injunctions against the social crimes against women. Guru Amar Das and Guru Gobind Singh categorically prohibited the practice of female infanticide. The Sikh code of conduct at the time of initiation of Khalsa barred any social contact with the killer of daughters (*kurri maar*). Guru Amar Das denounced the practice of wearing the veil (*purdah*). In fact, he even assigned five positions of religious emissaries (*manji*s) to women, which indicated his trust in their intellect and ability propagators of the faith. The Guru vehemently spoke against the practice of Sati. He empathized with women with regard to their disabilities.

The community dining centre (*langar*), which Guru Nanak initiated and other Gurus strengthened, along with the holy congregation (*pangat*), brought down the barriers of caste. The series of social measures – *langar, pangat, manji* and *peerah* – undermined the disabilities the women had suffered, largely owing to the prevalence of the veil. As a consequence, the women made a major contribution to the development of the Panth, with reference to the new institutions.

Last but not the least, Guru Nanak was outspoken in his denunciation of caste. His successors followed him pulling down the cause of social misery. Sometimes, scholars argued that the intention was a denunciation only of those aspects of caste, which accorded the privilege to some and imposed discriminatory penalties on others. It is perplexing to note that even as the validity of caste was questioned, all the marriages in the families of the Gurus were held in strict adherence to the dictates of caste. However, this does not dilute the fact the Gurus were emphatic in their rejection of caste-based pretensions. The membership of the Panth was open to people of all the castes and gender. It must be acknowledged that Guru Nanak was quite articulate in his criticism of practices that touched upon religion. In the initial stages, This insistence on eradication of the caste inequities and gender division was a characteristic feature of the Panthic development. The Sikh Gurus, particularly Guru Nanak, opposed the caste stratification for its disempowering impact on the society at large.

In sum, one would like to conclude that the Sikh Gurus had numerous positive messages that could have gone a long way in awarding fair treatment to women. One must admit that the degree of their effectiveness on the dominant social ethos was limited. It could not bring a radical change in the pervasive patriarchal ideology. One would ponder over the reasons that the positive directives of the Gurus towards women were never developed and applied in fullness. completely. The precepts of the Gurus, concerning the amelioration of the situation of women, remained just precepts. This shortcoming might be attributed to historical and cultural circumstances. The failure to attain the desired results could be attributed to the deep rooted traditional and cultural attitudes towards women, which proved too tenacious for the Sikh Gurus to eradicate. On a positive note, it took much longer for any change to assume a tangible form. Moreover, the Panth was in its infancy, and, as a result, the ideological positions (in the form of injunctions) as well as their responses evolved over time. An assessment of the Sikh Gurus must be made in relation to their social milieu, when patriarchal values were the norm. Guru Nanak questioned the prevailing norms and raised his voice against well-entrenched practices. His contributions to the vital question – the rejection of caste, opening the gateways of spiritual attainments to women, criticizing the pollution (*sutak*) related to childbirth and menstruation, besides emphasizing women's role in procreation – must be appreciated. His tough stance provided a platform for the subsequent Gurus, especially Guru Amar Das, who vehemently opposed the oppressive practices against women. To conclude, we can infer that Guru Nanak was a visionary who, despite living squarely in a patriarchal social framework, contributed significantly by questioning the prevailing norms. His appeal lay in his assertion that salvation was open to all, regardless of gender and caste. He provided a direction to the perceptions of the Sikh Gurus that were effectively followed and extended. In the understanding of J.S. Grewal, Guru Nanak's compositions did not prove a radical departure from the existing order, but a radical departure could be justified on the basis of his compositions.

NOTES

1. G.S. Talib, *Sri Guru Granth Sahib*, Eng. tr., 4 vols., Patiala: Punjabi University, 1990 (hereafter referred to as *AG*), p. 788.
2. If we accept the concept of *sutak*, that is impurities attached with the process of procreation, then these impurities exist everywhere because birth is everywhere.

Glossary

Abhaidan	State/gift of fearlessness as a blessing of God's grace.
Achal, amar	The state of being immortal, i.e. ever stable and everlasting.
Ad Purakh	The primal *purakh*/being, an epithet for God in He being the supreme.
Adi Granth	The Sikh scripture, compiled by Guru Arjan in 1604. It contains the compositions of Guru Nanak Dev along with the first four Sikh Gurus and a number of *bhaktas*, saints and Sufi *shaikh*s shortly afterwards Guru Hargobind added 'Ramkali Ki Vaar'. It was authenticated by Guru Gobind Singh with the compositions of the ninth Guru, Guru Teg Bahadur. Now it is known as *Sri Guru Granth Sahib* and in November AD 1708. Guru Gobind Singh Ji announced that *Sri Guru Granth Sahib Ji* would be the eternal Guru and there will be no physical Guru anymore.
Ahankar	A feeling of pride of materialistic possessions or power.
Ajuni	One who has freed himself from the cycle of birth and death, is immortal. It's an attribute of God.
Akāl Takht	The platform constructed by Guru Hargobind to preside over the temporal affairs of his followers. It was a

	furthered articulation of Guru Hargobind adorning two swords – *piri* and *miri* – indicating his spiritual and temporal responsibilities.
Akal	Immortal; not subject to death, everlasting, eternal, God.
Amrit bani/bachan	Nectar – like sayings and utterances of the Gurus the Guru's *shabad*s.
Amrit	Nectar; a mixture that imparts immortality; used as a metaphor.
Amritsar	The *sarovar* pool of water of *amrit* meaning immortality got constructed by Guru Ram Das. By early nineteenth century its usage was extended to refer to the town of Ramdaspur.
Ashtpadi	A composition of eight *pada*s or verses.
Babur-bani	Four compositions of Guru Nanak, believed to have been composed in connection with the sack of Saidpur (later Eminabad) by Babur. *Babur-bani* captures the physical pain and trauma faced by the common masses at the time of any war.
Baoli	A large masonry or brick well with steps leading to the water.
Bairag	The feeling of renunciant/detachment from the worldly desires and possessions; seen as a marker of spiritual awakening.
Bani	Literally meaning utterance; metaphorically meaning the Word of the Guru; generally equated with Gurbani.
Baraat	Wedding procession of the bridegroom.
Briragi	The person who practices the *bairag* or a renunciate. Perceived as a prerequisite for union with the God by

Glossary

	Hindus in general and Vaishnavs, Nathyogis in specific.
Chandi Bani	Three compositions in the *Dasam Granth*; invocation for Goddess Chandi.
Charanpahul	The *amrit* (nectar) water used at the time of initiation into the Khalsa Panth. Its value lies in it being touched by the Guru's toe/feet (*charan*).
Dakhna	A colloquial word for *dakshina* meaning offerings given to a Brahman for performing a ritual service.
Dasam Granth	The term used for the compilation earlier called the Book of the Tenth Guru (i.e. Dasven Patshan Ka Granth). The authorship of its contents has been a subject of debate.
Deg-tegh	Cauldron and sword, used as symbols of charity (*deg*) and power (*tegh*).
Duhagan	Opposite of *suhagan*, referring to an unhappy, unlucky woman because her spouse no longer loves and cares for her; metaphorically it refers to a person who has not turned towards God.
Durga	One of the eight names of Goddess Devi the consort of Shiva.
Giani	A reputed Sikh scholar, a Sikh theologian.
Got/Gotra	Exogamous caste groupings within the *zat*. Got played a significant role in marital alliances.
Gotra	Subdivision of a caste; subcaste; an endogamous group.
Granthi	A reader of the *Sri Guru Granth Sahib* and thus well respected by the Sikh adherents.
Gurbilas	Works that are panegyric in nature;

	literally *bilas* (description) of the Gurus. This genre of hagiological literature created an image of the Gurus, their pious and heroic qualities. Most of the works of this genre were written in late eighteenth and early nineteenth centuries.
Gurbitas	A panegyrical work written in the praise of Guru(s). They form an important part of hagiographical literature.
Gur mukh marg	The path shown by Guru Nanak and diligently followed by all those who followed the house of Gurus.
Gurudwara	Literally meaning *dwara* (gate) of Guru's house. The Sikh faith's religious place of worship.
Harmandar	'The temple of God'; refers to the Golden Temple of Amritsar.
Haumai	A kind of self-centredness in which everything is centered around one's own ego and God's will is not acknowledged.
Hukamnama	A written order generally giving *hukam* or orders to the *sangat*s. They are written by persons exercising spiritual and moral authority over the adherents of the faith like the Gurus or Gurumahals.
Janamsakhi	Hagiographical works detailing the instances from the life of Guru Nanak. Primarily intended to depict his religious philosophy, doctrines and ethics and thus contributing in the image of his spiritual attainments. There are several traditions of this genre developed in the seventeenth

	and eighteenth centuries, *Puratan-janamsakhi* and *Bale wali janamsakhi* are the two works counted as the most prominent in this genre.
Jap	Repeated incantation, used in connection with the *nam*.
Jogi	Colloquial word for yogi referring to a person who practices *yoga*; a person belonging to any of the twelve orders of the followers of Gorakh Nath.
Kabitt	A poetical form of four lines with a set rhyme structure. *Kabit Sawaiyye* of Bhai Gurdas form an important part of the hagiological literature of the Sikh traditions.
Karah parsad	Sacramental sweet dish prepared of wheat flour, purified butter and sugar (popularly known as *halwa* too), distributed amongst the devotees in the *gurdwara*.
Khalsa	The Sikh order or brotherhood, instituted by Guru Gobind Singh on the Baisakhi of AD 1699.
Khande ki pahul	Literally meaning 'sword initiation' into the Khalsa 'brotherhood'.
Khanqah	A Sufi hospice.
Lagi	Village menials and artisans who also performed the role of matchmaker.
Langar and Pangat	Common kitchen attached to every *gurdwara*. Ideologically the institution/system of *langar* along with *pangat* articulated the egalitarian principle of Sikhism. In a *langar*, the *parshad* (food) was served, sitting in a pangat without any distinction of caste, class, creed, gender, or any other difference.

Lavan	Generally now used as equivalent of *lavan-pherey*. It's a composition of the fourth Guru, Guru Ram Das which used the metaphor of marriage to elaborate on the spiritual goal of union with God. The ceremony of marriage is now referred to as *lavan-pherey* in which each of the four stanzas are recited for each circumbulation of *Sri Guru Granth Sahib* by the bridegroom and the bride. After the performance of the ceremony of *lavan-pherey* they are tied in the pious bond of husband and wife.
Majha	Geographically it refers to the area of central Punjab lying between the Beas and Ravi rivers.
Malwa	Geographically, Malwa region refers to the plain tract extending south and south-east of the Sutlej River. The districts of Ludhiana, Ferozepur and the princely states of Patiala and Nabha are amongst the prominent districts.
Manji and Peerhi	Literally meaning string cot or seat. A *manji* is a Sikh administrative unit founded by the third Guru, Guru Amar Das for the propagation of the faith. The appointed chief was known as the *sangatia*s. It was also known as *peerhi* system.
Manmukh	One who is led by his own inclinations, whims and fancies as opposed to Gurumukhi who follows the disciplined life in accordance to high moral and ethical lives advocated by the Gurus.

Masand	A person appointed by the Gurus for the fulfilment of the administrative responsibilities associated with the affairs of a local *sangat* (congregation) of the Sikhs or a number of *sangat*s.
Mina (micra)	A derogatory epithet used for Prithi Chand, the elder brother of Guru Arjun who refused to accept/acknowledge the succession of Guru Hargobind. As an extension it is used for his successors and their followers.
Misl	*Misl* literally refers to a unit or brigade of the Sikh warriors and refers to twelve sovereign states of the Sikh confederacy.
Moh	*Moh* is often used with *maya* (wealth, world pleasure); refers to affection, love, attachment to kith and kin.
Muhurta	An auspicious time when important rituals are planned to be performed such as marriage.
Mul mantra	The seed or 'root *mantra*' (basic) hymn/chant/saying of the prayer. The *mul mantra* is the essence of the Sikh way of life. *Japji Sahib* and *Sri Guru Granth Sahib* begins with the mul *mantra*.
Muqaddam	The headman of a village; an important position in the administrative hierarchy.
Nai	A barber.
Nain	Wife of the barber who had an important role to play in rituals at the time of the birth of a child in the family.
Nam, dan, isnan	These three terms embody the essential tenets of Guru Nanak for the ideal way of life. *Nam* means worship

	through the name; *dan*, referring to the charity for the welfare of lesser privileged; and lastly *isnan* denoted physical and moral purity.
Nikah	Muslim marriage rites.
Nindak	Literally meaning one who indulges in *ninda*, i.e. criticism. Metaphorically refers to back-biter, a slanderer who talks ill of Guru.
Nirakaar	An attribute to describe the God. Meaning which does not have any *akaar*, i.e. tangible form, shape or size. The God being formless indicates that He is omnipresent.
Nirbhau	Fearless.
Nirvair	One who does not nurture any ill feelings/venom towards anyone.
Nirguna	An adverb to describe God, meaning without attributes.
Pahul	The Khalsa initiation ceremony such as *khande di pahul* and *charan di pahul*.
Panj Kakke	*Panj* means five and *kakke* refers to the first letter of the word. The *panj-kakke*, 'five Ks' refers to the five symbols to be adorned by all the members of the Khalsa. The five symbols are: *kesh* (uncut hair), *kangha* (comb), *kirpan* (dagger), *kara* (steel bangle) and *kachha* (a pair of breeches). Each of these items had a value attached to it and in a nutshell it's the articulation of the principle tenets of Sikhism.
Panth	Literally meaning 'Path', indicates the system of beliefs and practices. Khalsa Panth refers to the Sikh community.
Patshahi/Padshahi	Referring to *badshahi*, i.e. rulership; a metaphor popularly used in the Sikh

Glossary

tradition to the period of the gurudom of the Sikh Gurus.

Pauri — A stanza.

Rahit — The code of conduct/morals to be followed by the Sikhs in their lives. The Sikhs are expected to be leading their lives being in the limits of the *rahitmaryada*.

Rahit-nama — A recorded version of the Khalsa code of discipline.

Sadh-sangat — An association of the pious; used generally for the Sikh congregation gathered for worship.

Sangat — Religious congregation/assembly.

Sarbat Khalsa — *Sarbat* literally means 'one all' thus '*Sarbat Khalsa*' means entire Sikh congregation.

Suba — A geographical unit of empire, the province.

Suchaji — A woman who has good manners and skill and therefore easily wins over the love of her lord, i.e. spouse.

Takht — *Takht* is a Persian word meaning a throne or seat of authority and is a spiritual and temporal center of Sikhism.

Tehsil — An administrative revenue-collecting division within a district.

Tith — An auspicious day in a phase of the moon.

Udasi — A renunciate belonging to an order tracing its origins to Guru Nanak.

Var — A heroic ode of several stanzas; a song of praise.

Zat/jaat — An important category of India's caste system indicating endogamous caste groupings.

A Note on Primary Sources

PUNJABI SOURCES

SRI GURU GRANTH SAHIB

It the first and most important original and contemporary source for the lives of the first five Gurus and Guru Teg Bahadur, the ninth Guru. Several incidents in their lives are reflected in their compositions which are incorporated into the sacred volume. These compositions also reflect the social, religious, and political atmosphere of those days and the views of the Gurus regarding the prevailing social customs, religious rites, and political conditions in the country. The contents of the *Sri Guru Granth Sahib*, also called Adi Granth, contains compositions (5,894 hymns) of the first five Gurus, the ninth guru, fifteen Bhagats (Jai Dev, Nam Dev, Trilochan, Parmanand, Sadna, Ramanand, Beni, Dhanna, Pipa, Sain, Kabir, Ravidas, Farid, Surdas and Bhikhan) and eleven Bhattas (Mathra, Jalap, Harbans, Talya, Salya, Bhai, Kulh, Sahar, Nal, Kirat, Gayand, and Sadrang). Among the 922 hymns of the Bhagats, the highest number of hymns (541) is composed by Kabir.

The compositions of the Gurus are not mere hymns addressed to God since they took a lively interest in the secular welfare of the people. They are outpourings of the heart prompted either by certain historical incidents, discussion with masters of other religions, or advice or admonition to disciples and other enquirers regarding the conduct of their lives.

Nothing excels the description by Guru Nanak on the condition of the people on the occasion of the sack of Saidpur (Eminabad) during the third Indian expedition of Babar in 1520-1. His revolt against established formalism and his protest against people giving up their language and dress just to please the ruling class are reflected in the *Asa di Var*. The *Japuji* and other hymns embody his views on Godhead, the relationship between the One Formless Self-existent Creator and His creation, man, and the conduct of human life in this world.

Similarly, the *shabad*s of the other Gurus and Bhagats, record their views on social and religious subjects, refer to the reforms introduced by them, and trace the gradual growth of Sikh thought and evolution of Sikh *Sangat*s into a distinct community.

The *Ramkali Ki Var* of Satta and Balwand is more historical than religious and is an important contemporary document for students of Sikh history.

The hymns of Guru Amar Das in the *Wadhans Ki Var* point to the jealousy of the anchorite (*tapa*) of Khadur towards Guru Angad. The fourth Guru Ramdas refers, in the *Gauri Ki Var*, to the avarice of a *tapa* of Goindwal on the completion of *bauli* and to the complaint to Khatris of that place against Guru Amar Das (which of course was dismissed as unfounded). In the *Tukhari Chhant*, he describes the visit of Guru Amar Das to Kurukshetra and Haridwar.

The *Sadd of Sundar* is an eyewitness account of the death of the third Guru. It explains the Sikh attitude towards death and points out the futility of the then prevailing ceremonies. The jealousy exhibited by Prithi Chand on the nomination of his younger brother, Arjan to the *gaddi* of Guruship is hinted at and condemned in Rag Suhi and the *Gauri Ki Var*. The admonition of their father, Guru Ramdas, addressed to the quarrelsome son, is given in the Sarang Rag.

In the Majh Rag are to be found the three letters of Guru Arjan addressed to his father from Lahore and a complimentary note composed on his return to Amritsar in 1581, which formed the part of the test placed before him to prove his suitability to the *gaddi*.

Guru Arjan sings in the *Suhi Chhant* of the construction and completion of Hari Mandir and, in the Sorath Rag, he describes the advantages of the *sarovar* or the tank of Ramdas.

There are about a dozen hymns in the Bilawal, Asagaund, Sorath-Gauri, Deva-Gandhari, and Bhairo Rags, referring to the birth and illness of Guru Hargobind and the murderous designs on his life by the agents of Prithia.

The *shloka*s of Guru Teg Bahadur, composed during his confinement in Delhi and incorporated in the *Sri Guru Granth Sahib* by Guru Gobind Singh clearly indicate his detached view regarding his impending death. The 54th *shloka* in this composition is believed to be a courageous reply of Guru Gobind Singh at the age of nine to his father's *shloka* [53], sent to him at Makhowal to test the fitness of his successor.[1]

The inclusion of Bhagat Bani in the *Adi Granth* illuminates the process of scriptural adaptation in the Sikh tradition. The process of the integration of the Bhagat Bani in the Sikh scripture was based on the recognition of two major points. First, there was harmonization in it with the Gurus' thoughts in broad outlines. Second, its differences with the Gurus' thoughts at essential points were highlighted to demonstrate the distinctive Sikh viewpoints. These additional reflections of the Gurus were crucial for shaping the emerging Sikh identity.[2]

There is an ongoing debate about the *Adi Granth* as Guru and the controversy[3] related to its translation, well-represented by two contrasting viewpoints. The intent here is just to touch upon the sharp contrast in the viewpoints and perceptions about the *Sri Guru Granth Sahib* which is well-represented by the following quote:

The Word enshrined in the holy book was always revered by the [Sikh] Gurus as well as by their disciples as of Divine origin. The Guru was the revealer of the Word. One day, the Word was to take the place of the Guru. The line of personal Gurus could not have continued for ever. The inevitable came to pass when Guru Gobind Singh declared the *Sri Guru Granth Sahib* to be his successor. It was only through the Word that the Guruship could be made everlasting.[4]

Since the day of the *Sri Guru Granth Sahib*'s installation in Harimandir, on 3 August 1603, the holy text has been the centre of Sikh life. Ceremonies relating to birth, initiation, marriage, and death take place in the sound and sight of it. The community's ideals, institutions, and rituals derive their meaning from the *Guru Granth*. The other viewpoint, well-represented by scholars like McLeod puts forth that the historian who seeks it as a source for a wider knowledge of the culture of the period must work hard for a limited return.[5]

The second scripture is the *Dasam Granth*, a substantial collection associated with Guru Gobind Singh. The Guru was a prolific writer and went through the whole epic literature of the Hindus. The following are believed to be his important works:

- *Jaap Sahib*
- *Akal Ustat*
- *Bachittar Natak*
- *Chandi Charittar*
- *Chaubis Avtar*
- *Swayyas*
- *Zafar Namah* (Persian)

All the above works constitute the *Dasam Granth*. Although it too bears the title of the Guru, most of it is seldom read. This can be explained partly by the difficult nature of its language and partly by the considerable attention it devotes to tales from the Hindu tradition. The latter feature has produced chronic controversy and largely accounts for the ambivalent attitude towards the *Dasam Granth* which still prevails within the Panth.[6] There are, however, passages from it that command the highest respect and some of these are prominently incorporated in the daily devotional prayers of the Panth. All these works are attributed to Guru Gobind Singh. But the most interesting and important source which requires a little detailed discussion is *Charitro Pakhyan* (vol. IV of *Dasam Granth*), especially in the context of a study on women.

Charitro Pakhyan (Tales of Deceit), also known as *Triya Charitra*, is a collection of 404 tales about the wiles of women.

Charitro Pakhyan, covering 7,555 verses of *Charit Kavya*, is the largest composition in the *Dasam Granth*. The 404 tales may be divided into categories such as tales of bravery, devotion, or intelligence of women (78), of the deceitfulness and unscrupulousness of women (269), and of the deceitfulness of men (26). The sources of the *Charitro Pakhyan* are no fewer than eight ranging from the Mahabharat, the Ramayan, to the Purans. The tales from *Panchtantra* and *Hitopadesh* are included side by side with a few selected from Persian books like *Bagho Bahar* and *Chahar Darvesh*. The inexhaustible treasure of folklore has been used effectively in this compilation by Guru Gobind Singh.[7] It appears that the framework is based on contemporary incidents, anecdotes, or scandals cited in folklore. It is, therefore, presumed that the author reflects the life and the sentiments of his own days.

In this regard, Dharam Pal Ashta observes: 'In most of the tales, however, the themes are love, sex debauchery, violence, crime or poison. They are extremely racy and frankly licentious.'[8] In sexual intrigues, women are often the seducers. Such stories may not be pleasant reading but they do imply lessons of warning to the reader against feminine wiles. Most of them belong to the upper classes among whom the women lead an easy and idle life, for the most part, and few being ill-matched or over-sexed take to sex intrigues to break the monotony of their dull life. The royal harems appear to be the centre of such intrigues which spring from sexual rivalries and jealousies. The mysteries of harem life and the scandals that the slaves whispered about, and persons like Manucci collected and treasured, might have exercised some influence on the commoners and affected their morality adversely.[9] As Dharam Pal Ashta notes, while indirectly they instruct men in good moral behaviour, they warn the unwary against womanly enticements. However, the collection also contains a dozen tales in which women play no part at all, as well as tales of heroic and honourable women. There are still others which relate to men's wiles against women who are the victims of men's high-handedness. One verse sums up their intrigues: 'There is no end to the fancies of these women. Even the Creator after having created them repented. Even He who has created the whole universe accepted defeat after he had probed into the secrets of women.' It is suggested that there is some practical wisdom in these tales. They appear to illustrate perversities of love and sex, which may be traced to the frailty of some and intrigues of others. The chief merit of these tales is moral suggestiveness. While indirectly they instruct men in good moral behaviour, they warn the unwary against womanly enticements.

Further the *Dasam Granth* enjoins the following: 'Whatsoever calamities befall a shrewd man, he will endure facing countless tribulations. But in spite of all this, he will not disclose his secrets to women.'[10]

Many historians and theologians have downplayed the importance of this work; its actual authorship has also been a point of heated controversy. By and large, it has been posited as unlikely to have stemmed from the tenth Guru. This perspective must be traced to the early twentieth century. More importantly, however, Sikhs of the eighteenth and nineteenth centuries held the *Dasam Granth* at par with *Adi Granth*. According to Ashta, while these stories may not be pleasant reading, they do imply lessons of warning to the reader against feminine wiles.[11] These tales also reveal the intellectual level and ethical ideals of society in general and women *sadhu*s in particular. Women are shown capable of doing both good or bad, within human endeavour, and this is no less true of the *sadhu*s.

Thus, regardless of whether its authorship can be attributed to Guru Gobind Singh or not, the work is of considerable importance in understanding gender construction during this period. Its emphasis on women is rare to be found in any other contemporary work and more importantly, the Sikhs of the eighteenth and nineteenth centuries held the *Dasam Granth* at par with *Adi Granth*.

Varan of Bhai Gurdas

Next to the *Sri Guru Granth Sahib*, in authenticity, is the *Varan of Bhai Gurdas* [1551-1629], who was a contemporary of five Gurus [from Guru Angad to Guru Hargobind] and very closely associated with four of them [from 3rd to the 6th]. Moreover, he was one of the few chosen and favoured disciples, next only to Bhai Buddha, who had the unique fortune of anointing as many as five successors of Guru Nanak with the *tilak* of Guruship. He witnessed the peaceful reign of Akbar, the execution of Guru Arjan, the martial response of Guru Hargobind to this event, and his armed conflict with the Mughal *fauzdar*s during the reign of Shah Jahan. Thus, Bhai Gurdas lived in a phase of Sikh history that was marked by crisis and transition as pointed out by J.S. Grewal.[12]

As already noted, the *Vars of Bhai Gurdas*[13] is held in esteem next only to *Sri Guru Granth Sahib*; they are regarded as the key to *Sri Guru Granth Sahib*. Apart from the contents of the *Adi Granth* and the *Dasam Granth*, they are the only compositions traditionally approved for recitation in gurudwaras (4.5[10]). There are thirty-nine *Vars* in all, each consisting of several *pauris*, stanzas of five to ten lines, adding up to approximately nine hundred stanzas of about seven thousand lines. Bhai Gurdas' other important work was *Kabit Sawaiyye*, 556 *kabit*s, which are philosophical.

The *Vars* of Bhai Gurudas contain references to matters connected with political, economic, social, and cultural life during the Mughal period. Besides the general charge of injustice against the rulers and corruption against the *qazi*s, there are references to the *umara*, the *mansabdar*s, the *mir-i-saman*, the *bakshi*, the *dewan*, the *karori*, and many others connected with civil and military affairs of the Mughal government. There are references also to the *bazigar*s, who entertained the common people with their acrobatics, and to *dhadi*s, *bhat*s, and *nai*s, who entertained the common people with their *var*s, *kabit*s, and *sadd*s. The love stories of *Laila Majnun*, *Sassi Punnu*, *Sohni Mahiwal* and *Hir Ranjha* that had already become a part of the Punjabi folklore were also referred to in the *Vars of Bhai Gurdas*. The mythological figures in the *Sri Guru Granth Sahib* like Prahalad, Poodna, and Balmik, among others, have also been highlighted in the *Vars*. In the first and the eleventh *Var of Bhai Gurdas*, we find a lot of information. In the first Var, he depicts the life and travels of Guru Nanak, with his visit to Mecca and Baghdad mentioned for the first time. In the eleventh Var various Sikhs who had been near and dear to the Sikh Gurus are named. The places where the Gurus lived are also named, besides extensive information about the spread of Sikhism and the centres of Sikh faith. Bhai Gurdas was familiar with the Sikhs at Goindwal and Ramdaspur. He refers to several other *sangat*s in the Punjab as well as those of Lahore, Patti, and Sultanpur. But the Sikh *sangat*s were not confined to the province of Lahore; there were eminent Sikhs in Sarhind, Thanesar, Delhi, Agra, Allahabad, Kabul, Kashmir, Bihar, Bengal, Rajasthan, Malwa, and Gujarat. Thus, it is interesting to note that the evidence of Bhai Gurudas on the Sikhs is not confined to the Punjab.

The important ideas and attitudes of Bhai Gurdas appear to be closely linked with his understanding of secular history.[14] The polity and economy of the Mughal empire, which made it possible for the followers of Guru Nanak and his successors to move into distant cities and towns widened the horizons of the contemporary world, and the awareness is reflected in the *Vars of Bhai Gurdas*. He talks not only of Hindus and Muslims but also of Buddhists and Jains, Christians and Jews. Among the Muslims, he refers not only to Mullahs and Sufis or to the Sunnis and the Shias, or the four schools and seventy-two sects of Islam, but also Rafizis, the Mulahida, and the Manafiqa. He refers not only to the Mughals, Pathans, Turks, and the Sayyids but also to Armenians, Rumis, Habshis, and the Firangis.

In the social sphere, there are references to polygamy and polyandry, to divorced and abandoned women. There are references to a large number of sub-castes and occupations. This varied information suggests that Bhai Gurdas was widely aware of the social environment.

Janamsakhis

The word *janam* means 'birth' and *sakhi* literally means 'testimony'. In its literal sense, the composite term accordingly means a 'birth testimony'. While the sacred writings of Guru Nanak offer some information concerning his attitudes towards women, the *janamsakhi* literature of the Sikhs, written during the first half of the seventeenth century, well after Guru Nanak's time, further adds to the picture. There are primarily three traditions of the *janamsakhi*s:

- Puratan Janamsakhis
- Miharban Janamsakhis
- Bala Janamsakhis

Given the nature of the *janamsakhis* they cannot be understood as necessarily biographical but rather as responding to the needs of the later community within which this genre developed.[15] No *janamsakhi*s are close to Nanak in terms of compositions, and their true value is therefore to show how he was perceived by later groups within the Panth. It is an image which testifies to the fact that in history, what is believed to have happened can commonly be more important than what did happen. It is not possible to write a social or economic history of seventeenth-century Punjab from *janamsakhi*s alone, but they do nevertheless provide many useful glimpses. The narrators of the *janamsakhi*s never divorced themselves from their rural context and as a result, there are recurrent references to the village community and its way of life. We are given glimpses of birth ceremonies, naming ceremonies, marriages, and funerals. A child sits with his teacher and is shown how to read. Labourers bring in the harvest for threshing or carry grass to the village for the buffaloes. Women attend to their cooking duties in their well-plastered kitchens. The fact that these features are recorded unconsciously adds considerably to their value as there could be no possible reason for misrepresentation on such points, for any failure to accord with the experience and understanding of the narrator's audience would merely defeat the purpose of anecdotes. In the *janamsakhi*s, rural Punjab speaks with an authentic voice, and although they rarely tell us more than a small part, the *janamsakhi*s provide a valuable supplement to the Persian chronicles and European reports of the same period.[16] However, while claiming full authority on the life and works of Guru Nanak, the *janamsakhi*s give a meagre introduction regarding the female members of the family.

It must also be noted that these *janamsakhi*s cannot be read literally and be treated as authentic. Most scholars admit that it was written at a point in time when *karamat* (miraculous) was taken as a measure of piety; of a superior being. It must also be noted that the information furnished by the *janamsakhi*s should be corroborated with other sources but certainly, these *sakhi*s form an important genre of sources and cannot be dismissed just as a piece of literature. Fauja Singh puts it aptly that the *janamsakhi*s should be placed somewhere between the two genres of literature. One cannot afford to dismiss the fact that the kind of image of Guru Nanak that is presented is historically a reflection of the image people/common masses wanted to perceive of him.[17]

The *Gurbilas* Tradition and Later Historical Works

The eighteenth century provided conditions congenial to an aggressively militant spirit, and for Sikhs this is the heroic period of the Panth's history. As the form and dominant philosophy of the Panth changed, so did its religious perceptions and the literature which gave them expressions. The *janamsakhis* continued to retain considerable measure of their earlier popularity but during the eighteenth and nineteenth century a new approach to the lives of the Gurus appeared. This was the *Gurbilas* or 'Splendour of the Guru' style, a treatment which exalted the courage of the Gurus and lauded their skill in battle. Inevitably, its exponents concentrated their attention on the two great warrior Gurus, on Guru Hargobind and pre-eminently on Guru Gobind Singh.[18] Like the *janamsakhi*s, the *Gurbilas* literature is far more important as a testimony to the beliefs of the writers and their contemporary circumstances than to the actual lives of the Gurus. In a sense, the tradition is an extension of the *janamsakhi*s impulse and style, both forms being clear expressions of devotion to the Guru. It was, however, a very different kind of piety that produced the *Gurbila*s and it shifted the focus from the first Guru to the tenth.[19]

The first example of the *Gurbilas* style to appear was *Shri Gur Sobha* by Sainapat. Three other products of the *Gurbilas* tradition, attributed to the poet Sohan, also deserve to be noted: *Gurbilas Padshahi Dasvin* (Sukha Singh), *Gurbilas Padshahi Dasvin* (Koer Singh), and *Gurbilas Padshahi Chhevin*. Although the latter two claims to be eighteenth-century works, it has been shown that both belong to the mid-nineteenth century. Rattan Singh Bhangu's *Prachin Panth Parkash* deserves a special mention. Three years after Rattan Singh had completed his *Prachin Panth Parkash*, another major work was brought to its conclusion, and this was Bhai Santokh Singh's *Nanak Parkash* and *Gurpartap Suraj Granth*. Other Gurmukhi sources, which deserve a special mention are *Mahima Parkash* (Saroop Das Bhalla), *Panth Parkash*, and *Tawarikh-i-Guru Khalsa* by Giani Gian Singh. We also have *Bansawali Namah Dasan Padshahian Da* by Kesar Singh Chhibbar.

The *Shri Gur Sobha* of Sainapat, one of the rarest contemporary accounts of the life of Guru Gobind Singh, is an admixture of Braj and eastern Punjabi. Its historical importance may be judged by the fact that the author was closely associated with the Guru as the resident poet in his *darbar* at Anandpur and was an eyewitness to most of what he recorded. The main theme of the book as indicated in the invocatory passages is the praise of Guru Gobind Singh. At least six of the twenty *adhyaya*s or chapters, besides several passages in others, are devoted to directly panegyrizing Guru and the Khalsa. This work focuses on the description of different wars fought by Guru Gobind Singh. It also discusses the war of succession among the sons of Emperor Aurangzeb, the Guru's meeting with Emperor Bahadurshah, and the Guru's assassination at

Nanded. Sainapat is the only author who helps us with his rational account to clear, to a large extent, the mystery woven around the death of Guru Gobind Singh. His account of the institution and organization of Khalsa deserves particular attention. It helps elucidate contemporary terminology in at least two instances; Sainapat uses the term *misl* as the military sub-unit and Khalsa is defined as the Sikh community in direct contact/relation with the Guru subsequent to the elimination (effected by him) of the intermediary *masand*s or local community leaders in different parts. In sum, a fairly well-defined outline of Guru Gobind Singh's life emerges from the work as a whole. However; there are a few errors in his description of the Guru's travels in Rajputana on his way to the Deccan which can be easily corrected with the help of other records.

Gurbilas Padshahi Chhevin

This the written collection of all the oral anecdotes about Guru Hargobind; his birth, childhood and early education [Cantos 1-3], and marriage [Canto 5]. It can neither claim to be contemporary nor original. The manuscript preserved in the Punjab University Library, Chandigarh, under accession number 1176, is of anonymous authorship. The contents of the *Gurbilas* are almost identical to those of the other *Gurbilas*, commonly attributed to Kavi Sohan. There are many dates given in the text but most of them do not tally with those commonly accepted in the Sikh tradition. The author nowhere refers to the works he relied upon, though he does state that Guru Hargobind's life has been presented before him in great detail and that he was narrating only in brief. The entire volume is divided into several parts, each part dealing with an important episode from the Guru's life.

Gurbilas Padshahi Dasvin (Koer Singh) and the work by Sukha Singh with the same title give some important pieces of information. *Gurbilas Padshahi Dasvin* by Koer Singh covers the entire span of Guru Gobind Singh's life. It is the first work to record the early years of his career. It also contains references to Guru Gobind Singh passing on the spiritual succession to the *Sri Guru Granth Sahib*, which was deemed to be the Guru after him. It is a poetized account completed in 1751. Out of a total of 2938 *chhand*s, 2901 are written in Braj and the remaining 37 in Punjabi. As for his sources of infor-mation, the poet seems to have had access to two preceding works, Guru Gobind Singh's *Bachitra Natak* and Sainapat's *Shri Gur Sobha*. More than that, he has relied on information personally obtained from Bhai Mani Singh. The *Gurbilas* is, however not free from faults. Its dates are often erroneous; for instance, 1689, instead of 1699 for the creation of the Khalsa, and 1709 instead of 1708 for the death of Guru Gobind Singh at Nanded. A notable feature of the work is the evidence it furnishes about the martyrdom of Bhai Mani Singh and his companions in 1734. Koer Singh seems to have been an eyewitness and mentions the names of some of the Sikhs who were executed along with Bhai Mani Singh. No other contemporary source contains this information.

Sukha Singh's *Gurbilas* was completed in 1797 when he was barely 29. The poetry is more Braj than Punjabi, but the script used is Gurmukhi. Comprising 31 cantos, the work gives a detailed account of the events of the life of Guru Gobind Singh and of the causes which led to the battles he had to fight. His work combines a rare insight into the prevailing political conditions and also into the moral issues involved in the resistance launched by Guru Gobind Singh. *Gurbilas*, however, is not a straight chronological record of events, poetic imagi-nation, and pious adornment predominant over factual nar-ration. Though most of the historical facts of the book are true, the writer has made it an amalgam of history, fiction, and oral tradition. Some of the mythological and fictitious events are also included.

The *Parchian* of Seva Das is an eighteenth-century collection of 50 *sakhis* or anecdotes from the lives of Ten Gurus. Only one *sakhi* each relates to the first eight Gurus, four are con-nected with the ninth Guru Teg Bahadur, and the remaining thirty-eight narrate incidents from the life of Guru Gobind Singh. The work is hagiographical rather than historical, although several episodes agree with similar accounts in other sources such as the *gurbilase*s and *Suraj Granth*. The language is old Punjabi. The *sakhi*s are narrative in style but didactic. Almost all of them convey some tenet or the other of Sikhism.

Mahima Parkash by Saroop Das Bhalla is a versified account in Gurmukhi script of the lives of Sikh Gurus, completed according to inner evidence in AD 1776.[20] The first volume (pp. 348) contains 65 *sakhi*s relating to the life of Guru Nanak, whereas the second volume (p. 900) comprises another 172 *sakhi*s of which 16 deal with the life of Guru Angad, 32 are about Guru Amar Das, 8 about Guru Ram Das, 22 each about Guru Arjan and Hargobind, 22 about Guru Har Rai, 4 about Guru Har Krishan, 19 about Guru Teg Bahadur and 27 about Guru Gobind Singh. At the end of these, there is one more *sakhi* about Banda Singh Bahadur. The main sources utilized by the author according to his testimony were *Puratan Janam Sakhi* and *Adi Sakhian*, and information received from the descendants of the Gurus and some other prominent Sikhs. This is the first work of its kind giving a connected account of the lives of all the Gurus. However, it is not plain history, nor is it free from inaccuracies.

Mahima Parkash Vartak recently published contains anecdotes from the lives of the Gurus.[21] *Mahima Parkash Vartak* contains in all 164 *sakhi*s or anecdotes dealing with the Gurus as follows; Guru Nanak, 20; Guru Angad, 10; Guru Amar Das, 27; Guru Ram Das, 7; Guru Arjan, 15; Guru Hargobind, 20; Guru Har Rai, 17; Guru Har Krishan, 1; Guru Teg Bahadur, 4; and Guru Gobind Singh, 43. With respect to Guru Nanak, the work follows in the main the older *janamsakhi*s such as the *Puratan*. For example, like the *Puratan Janamsakhi*s, it places the birth of Guru Nanak in the month of Baisakh and like the *Puratan*, it does not mention the name of Bhai Bala. The structure of the work is episodic. Each *sakhi* is independent and has its own motive. Some of the stories are didactical; some interpret *Gurbani* in the style of *Miharban*

Janamsakhis, while others deal with historical events. *Mahima Parkash Vartak* is the earliest known work dealing with the lives of all ten Gurus. Its influence is traceable in at least two other accounts, both written in the eighteenth century – Seva Das Udasi's *Parchian* (1741) and Saroop Das Bhalla's *Mahima Parkash* (1776). Some of their stories are apparently drawn from this source.

Prachin Panth Parkash by Rattan Singh Bhangu is a chronicle in homely Punjabi verse relating to the history of the Sikhs from the time of the founder, Guru Nanak to the establishment in the eighteenth century of principalities in the Punjab under *misl sardar*s. The work completed in AD 1841 is owed to the Britisher's curiosity about the Sikhs and their emergence as a political power. Rattan Singh drew upon the available Sikh sources such as *janamsakhi*s and the *Gurbilas* and on the oral tradition that had come down to him from his parents and grandparents. The famous Sikh martyr Matab Singh of Mirankot was his paternal grandfather, and Shyam Singh of Karora Singhia *misl*, his maternal grandfather.[22] The details and sequence of the events here provided have been generally accepted in later Sikh historiography. The earlier period has been dealt with sketchily. The descriptions of Guru Nanak's life is relatively more detailed, but with a miraculous element predominating it as in the *janamsakhis*. The succeeding seven Gurus have been barely mentioned, except Guru Hargobind whose battles against the Mughal forces are briefly touched upon. In his account of Guru Teg Bahadur's martyrdom, Rattan Singh follows Guru Gobind Singh's *Bachittar Natak*. He attributes the fall of the Mughal Empire to the emperor's sinful act of beheading the Guru. S.S. Hans in his article, 'Rattan Singh Bhangu's purpose of writing *Prachin Panth Parkash*' comments that Bhangu is not a mere chronicler of the past, he is deeply involved in the present and he is capable of rising above the contemporary predicament to see that the Sikh kingdoms' only hope lies in the capacity to wage a bitter and unequal struggle against the future enemy, in the ability to convince the enemies of Sikh claims to sovereignty and lastly in their own strength.[23] Rattan Singh Bhangu is probably the greatest historian of the Sikhs, who wrote the kind of history, demanded by the requirements of the age, instead of being a mere chronicler of events leading to the establishment of the Sikh rule on the very eve of its downfall.

Sri Gur Pratap Suraj Granth by Santokh Singh is a voluminous work of the highest literary merit in *Braj* verse portraying in comprehensive detail the lives of the Ten Gurus of the Sikh faith and the career of Banda Singh Bahadur. Notwithstanding certain drawbacks, which scholars with training in modern historiography may point out, it remains the most valuable sourcebook on Sikh history of the period of the Gurus and indeed, on the very roots of the entire Sikh tradition. *Suraj Parkash*, as it is popularly known, is worthy to rank with the classics in this genre. The work is divided into two parts; the first, *Sri Guru Nanak Parkash*, in two sections, is the story of the life of Guru Nanak. The second, *Sri Guru Pratap Suraj* proper, is divided into portions, *ruth* (season), subdivided into chapters called *anshu* (rays). According to Ganda Singh, Bhai Santhokh Singh has not been able to penetrate beyond the crust of prevalent accounts. He considers all the Punjabi works on the subjects, from the *Mahima Parkash* to *Sau Sakhi* and other similar works as equally authentic. The historical accuracy of *Suraj Parkash*, therefore, does not remain unquestioned.[24]

The *Panth Parkash* and *Tawarikh-i-Guru Khalsa* are two of Giani Gian Singh's notable works. He was a theologian and preacher of the Sikh religion belonging to the *Nirmala* sect. *Panth Parkash*, published in 1880, is a history of the Sikhs in verse. As the title suggests, it is an account of the rise and development of the Guru Panth, which is Khalsa or the Sikh community. Scattered throughout the *Panth Parkash* are references to at least 23 different sources that the author consulted or made use of. He has specially mentioned Rattan Singh Bhangu's *Prachin Panth Parkash*, Bute Shah's *Tawarikh-i-Punjab*, and Bhai Santhokh Singh's *Suraj Granth*. Other sources referred to include *Gurbilas Dasvin Padshahi*, *Banswalinamah*, and *Dabistan-i-Mazahib*. Thus, *Panth Parkash* covers a vast span of Sikh history – from Guru Nanak to the annexation of the Punjab by the British and the death of Maharaja Duleep Singh. The last three chapters contain an account of some Sikh sects and cults – Udasis, Nirmalas, Nihangs, Kukas or Namdharis, Gulabdasias, Satkartarias, Niranjanias – and the author's reflection on the contemporary social situation, with some autobiographical details.

His other important work, the *Tawarikh-i-Guru Khalsa*, is divided into five parts. The first, *Guru Khalsa*, deals with the lives of the Ten Gurus. The second, *Shamsher Khalsa* deals with the military exploits of Banda Bahadur and the Sikh struggle against the Mughals and the Afghans. The third, *Raj Khalsa* deals with Maharaja Ranjit Singh and the Anglo-Sikh wars. The fourth, *Sardar Khalsa*, gives information about Sikh rulers, Sikh chiefs and Sikh sects, and the fifth, *Panth Khalsa*, throws light on Sikh *gurdwara*s and Sikh sects.

Giani Gian Singh was a devoted religious scholar but not a critical historian. His approach to history was traditional, and the impulse behind his historical writing was the projection of the glory of the Sikh past. Some of the facts, dates, and sequences of events in the *Panth Parkash* do not bear scientific scrutiny, yet the work enjoys much popularity and prestige, it is expounded formally in Sikh *gurdwara*s and has served to shape the historical imagination of Sikhs over the generations.[25]

Banswalinamah Dasan Padshahian Ka is a poeticized account of the lives of Gurus by Kesar Singh Chibbar. Bhai Kesar Singh Chibbar was the son of Bhai Gurbaksh Singh and the grandson of Bhai Dharam Chand was the great-grandson of Bhai Parag Das (who had embraced martyrdom in the battle of Ruhila in 1621) and cousin of martyrs of Bhai Mati Das and Bhai Sati Das. Thus, Bhai Kesar Singh Chibbar belonged to a family which had been associated with the Guru family for about one century. The term *Banswalinamah* means a genealogy. Another term used in the text is 'Kursi Namah', which is the Persian term for 'genealogy'. However, this work cannot be termed as purely genealogical. It is a rapid account in rather incipient Punjabi verse, of the Ten Gurus and of Banda Bahadur. The book comprising 2,564 stanzas is divided into fourteen chapters. The first ten deal with the Ten Gurus. There is a chapter each on Banda Bahadur and Ajit Singh, adopted son of Guru Gobind Singh. The last chapter of the book alludes to the state of the Sikhs in the early decades of the eighteenth century, and the persecution they faced at the hands of ruling authorities. Although his work leaves out a few important events, there are some details exclusively available in this source – for instance an important event like Guru Gobind Singh awarding *gurugaddi* to *Sri Guru Granth Sahib*. Significantly, the author also tries to prove the superiority of the Brahmins even among the Sikhs which may be due to his own Brahmin ancestry. In any case, this is contrary to the principles of Sikhism which rejects the caste system. Therefore, the work is not free of limitations, the description of historical events and mythological elements occasionally overlap in this work. Its peculiar feature is the wealth of chronological detail it contains about the lives of the Gurus and the members of their families. But the reliability of the dates recorded by the author is not established.

Hukumnamah (ed. Ganda Singh) is a compound of two Persian words. *Hukum*, meaning command or order, and *namah*, meaning letter, refer in the Sikh traditions to letters sent by the Gurus to their Sikhs or *Sangat*s in different parts of the country. This collection includes two *hukumnamah*s from Mata Gujri; nine of Mata Sundri, and nine of Mata Sahib Devi. Thus, it emerges as an important attestation of the power and authority enjoyed by them. Needless to say, *hukumnamah*s are invaluable historical documents. Names of persons and places to which they are addressed provide clues to the composition, of early Sikhism and its spread. They do furnish the missing links and give a contemporary authentic account of the events. Most of these *hukumnamha*s are dated correctly which helps to fix the chronology of certain events. The *hukumnamah*s are important linguistically as well and provide crucial clues for tracing the development of Gurmukhi script and Punjabi prose.

Guru Kian Sakhian (ed. Piara Singh Padam) is based on the references about Gurus appearing in the *Bhatt Vahis*, literally the *vahi* (register of the records) maintained by Bhatts. Before the twentieth century, the records of the genealogies and the specific events of the life of the kings, warriors, and holy men were maintained by the Bhatts in their *vahis*. The same functions were performed by the pandits in Haridwar and Mattan (Kashmir). The Pandits had clients from all sections of the society but the circle of the Bhatts was limited to some elite sections. The Bhatts had preserved precious data about the families of Guru Sahib and some other Sikhs for the seventeenth and eighteenth centuries. *Guru Kian Sakhian*, a collection of 112 *sakhi*s, beginning from Guru Hargobind Singh to Guru Gobind Singh, was written in 1790 by Bhai Saroop Singh. Four of these *sakhi*s relate to Guru Hargobind, nine to Guru Har Rai, four to Guru Har Krishan, sixteen to Guru Teg Bahadur, and seventy-nine to Guru Gobind Singh. It is a Guru history of 73 years of its own kind and gives new pieces of information. However, the extensive use of *Bhattvahis* in the *Guru Kian Sakhian* makes it a little less dependable as the Bhatts were not scholars and they were recording these details primarily to fulfil their roles of *jajmani* and *purohit*. The language of *Guru Kian Sakhian* is a mixture of Punjabi and Hindi. Interestingly, at a couple of places, we find English words. This is plainly anachronistic; it has been so successfully tampered with as to render the authentic portions inseparable from later interpolations. It has, therefore, to be used by scholars with caution.

GURU RATTAN MAL (SAU SAKHI)

It is a collection of approximately 100 *sakhi*s (stories) that deals with the important events in the life of Guru Gobind Singh. Basic tenets of religion, code of conduct, and political events have formed the main contents of these narrations.

This work is probably the first work in Punjabi that criticizes the shrewd diplomatic policies of the English. There is a controversy about the authorship of the work. Some people believe it to be written by Guru Gobind Singh; however, the thrust of the *sakhi*s does not appear to be in line with the ideological thought process of Guru Gobind Singh. Analysing the work, it seems more plausible that it is written by Sahib Singh on the basis of the stories narrated by Ram Koer Singh who used to be always present in the services of Guru Gobind Singh. The work is esoteric and prophetic in nature. The book has some historical value too but has to be used with great caution because of several anachronisms, misstatements, interpolations, and motivated turns given to the text by different scribes.

As is evident from the above discussion, the contemporary or near contemporary Gurmukhi sources focus primarily on the guru period, their ideological formulations and shifting emphasis, principles of Sikhism, institutions, and cultural values. Although these sources primarily focus on guru families providing some information on *guru mahals* and other female members of the Guru families, yet, in the context of their widening appeal, and the composition of *sangats*, we also get valuable references of common women and their position in the religious sphere and household matters.

Apart from this genre of sources, we also have folk literature and folk songs. Folk poetry in regional languages is perhaps the most important expression of feelings and sentiments of the common people or illiterate masses on various themes and subjects. According to Terence Browne, 'Even lyric poems are social facts just as potato crops, tractors, and new industries are.'[26] J.S. Grewal appropriately writes,

> Unfortunately, there is no general awareness among the historians of our country about the value of literature for social and cultural history. Once we learn to treat literary works as the product of history, it is possible to know much more about the past than what the writers wanted us to know.[27]

Around AD 1300, Amir Khusrau observed the people of Lahore province conducting their daily business of life through a language peculiar to the region. He called it 'Lahaurh'. This was one of the several dialects spoken by the people. These dialects were popularized by the people, the most notable among them was the Sufi Sheikh of the Punjab, Sheikh Farid-ud-din-Ganj-i-Shakar, popularly known as Baba Farid. The compositions of Baba Farid were cherished and preserved by his successors at Ajodhan and a large bulk is preserved in *Sri Guru Granth Sahib*. In his verses, we find enshrined the diction and idiom of the new Punjabi language which by this time had come into its own. Although Baba Farid was proficient in Arabic and Persian, yet, his literary command over Punjabi was amazing. A nineteenth-century Punjabi poet refers to him as the first and one of the greatest poets of Punjabi.[28] His imagery comes from the countryside and speaks in a manner that could appeal to the peasant, blacksmith, potter, boatman, and fowler. In sum, the tenor of Baba Farid's poetry was social as well as religious. Grewal rightly comments that in the field of religious poetry, Farid found a great successor in Guru Nanak, but only after two and a half centuries.

Among the Muslim writers of Punjabi, Shah Hussain is regarded as the first major writer after Farid. Shah Hussain was born in AD 1538 at Lahore and died in AD 1601 at the age of 63 years.[29] In the sixteenth century, Shah Hussain wrote *kaafiya*s using some of the metres which were used by popular minstrels, composing in *raga*s in which Guru Nanak and his successors were composing.[30] His *kaafiya*s till date are regarded as matchless for their lyrical excellence in *kaafi* genre. He was followed by Sultan Bahu, Bulleh Shah, and Gulam Farid during the seventeenth, eighteenth, and nineteenth centuries respectively. The most common activity mentioned in the *kaafiya*s is spinning and weaving referred to in 26 of his *kaafiya*s. They also contain interesting references about common women's concerns and their daily routine, enlivening community life. Shah Hussain transformed the entire spirit of Sufi poetry in Punjabi literature. He broadened its sphere from mere philosophical Sufism to encompass the whole gamut of man's feelings.[31]

The secular and oral tradition of Punjabi lore surfaced as a literary phenomenon during the seventeenth century. Most probably Damodar wrote his romance of Heer-Ranjha towards the later times of Akbar's reign and Pilu's *Mirza Sahiban* belongs to the same period. While Damodar wrote the first comedy in Punjabi, Pilu is credited with writing the first tragedy in the language. The first version was written by Damodar. Strangely enough, no subsequent Punjabi poet who composed the *kissa* of *Heer* – Muqbal or Waaris Shah – has mentioned Damodar's name. Damodar has composed his *kissa* in the Jhangi dialect, a sub-variety of Multani. Considering that even Multani did not make much progress as a literary language, Damodar's narrative did not attain literary status. Though much later, his narrative was meant to be sung with musical instruments and thus his literary work was very close to oral tradition. The most popular version of Heer-Ranjha was authored by Waris Shah. Waris Shah was born in AD 1735 at Jandiala Sher Khan, district Shekhu Pura (Pakistan). George Grierson, Usborn, Richard Temple, all appreciated Waris for his supreme command and rich vocabulary of Punjabi language. Amrita Pritam calls Waris 'A Solace for the Sufferers, A Balm for Bruised Hearts'. Waris's *Heer* is the true representation of a Punjabi girl. She has got the same limitations that the Punjabi girl faces during her youth. Characterization of Ranjha sketched by Waris is the true replica of Punjabi young men, he goes deep in the analysis of his character. Apart from describing in detail the farmer's life in Punjab, Waris Shah has given vivid details of nature. Different types of snakes, fruits, trees, and natural remedies are also mentioned by Waris in his verse. Waris Shah's poetry has not left any sphere of life untouched. It turns out to be a great repository of information for the real position of women and the sociocultural customs, or even evils associated with her. Waris Shah's *Heer-Ranjha* saga apart from describing different customs at the time of marriage also describes the various methods used, in the killing of infant daughters which included strangulation, poisoning, drowning, and suffocation. Waris Shah had both the Hindu and Muslim sections of the populace in mind when he talked about the people of Punjab.

In terms of the timeline, Damodar was followed by Hafiz Barkhurdar, who wrote in the times of Shah Jahan. Barkhurdar penned the popular story of Sassi and Punnu. He is also known to have produced the first known Punjabi version of Yusuf and Zulaikha, a popular theme with several Persian poets and based on the Quran. The other story Barkhurdar took up was a purely indigenous tale, the story of Mirza and Sahiban. This story too was placed in the lower Rachna Doab, involving two well-known tribes, the Sials and the Kharals.[32] Barkhurdar knew that Pilu's version of *Mirza Saahiban* was sung by popular minstrels (*dum*s) and that version, in all probability, belonged to the oral tradition. Hafiz Barkhurdar produced the first literary version and recognized Pilu's great merit.

Pilu refers to Raja Rasalu, Dulla and Jaimal, and Fatta, who were all subjects of heroic poetry in the Punjabi oral tradition.[33] There were others too, but no Punjabi writer appears to have taken up a heroic theme for literary treatment in the sixteenth and seventeenth centuries.

Ahmed Gujjar and Muqbal composed still later. Ahmed Gujjar wrote in the reign of Aurangzeb in the late seventeenth century, followed by Muqbal in the reign of Mohamad Shah in the early eighteenth century. Muqbal was the immediate predecessor of Waris Shah, already discussed, who wrote after 1750. Muqbal wrote a *jangnammah* relating to Hasan and Hussain, the tragic heroes of the battle of Karballa along with his *kissa* of Heer-Ranja. In sum, it can be said that largely the themes of literary works were drawn from Punjabi, Indian, and Muslim sources. It must also be noted that these heroes of the popular Punjabi saga formed a respectable reference in the works of Bhai Vir Singh and many others. These characters had become a part of popular culture and were held in high esteem as is evident in the anecdote where Guru

Hargobind visits the Majnu ka Tilla. He explains to his followers that the way Majnu got emotionally annihilated by his love for Laila, similarly, the Guru Sikhs should have the same devotion for the Akal Purakh. This kind of equation of Laila-Majnu to the spiritual quest of a true devotee testifies that Guru Hargobind had approved of such unadulterated, single-minded love and devotion.[34]

The folk songs are also a great treasure of knowledge and address the aspirations of women from their life at large and marital life, in particular. The folk songs sung at the time of marriage ceremonies seem to be giving them a platform to vent out her agonies in an appealing and entertaining manner. Though the value of the oral traditions as a source has great potential which is to date, largely untapped, however, while using popular literature or folk songs, one has to be extra careful and should have sensitivity towards the complex nature of the texts. A straightforward linear reading eliciting certainties is equally problematic. The written texts assembled from oral traditions are part of the collective oeuvre. A whole lot of variations may have been introduced; certain parts must have been reaccentuated, certain potentials in the images actualized, and others allowed to fade over time in the process of writing down oral traditions. Kumkum Sangari, in context of her study on Meera, has aptly observed, 'In this sense, the songs are inscribed in an extended rather than a discreet moment of production.'[35] The folk literature might, in fact, represent the intentions, beliefs, and desires of the period in which they are penned down.

PERSIAN SOURCES

Next comes the category of contemporary Persian sources. Although there are many Persian contemporary sources, they provide very little or rather no information on the position of women in Punjab. However, their corroborative role in weaving the complex picture of society and its values cannot be denied. Furthermore, with the exception of the *Dabistan-i-*

Mazahib, information on Sikhism and the Sikhs before the time of Guru Gobind Singh is rather meagre. Moreover, there is a much greater concentration on Banda Bahadur than even on Guru Gobind Singh.

As may be expected, the bulk of information relates to political history. This by itself is not a limitation. There is little information on political history in contemporary Sikh sources. Therefore, this information from non-Sikh sources is all the more valuable. In conjunction with later Sikh sources, this information forms the bedrock of the political history of the Sikhs during this period.[36] However, not only the *Dabistan* but several other works provide information on the social and religious life of the Sikhs, which can provide useful insights in the light of evidence coming from Sikh sources. In any case, the image of the Sikhs that non-Sikh writers formed from time to time are in itself a form of evidence for a social historian. To substantiate the point it would be useful to briefly analyze the nature and thrust of different sources.

A number of genres are represented in Persian sources throwing light on Punjab. This in itself is a reflection of the intellectual and cultural richness of the period. First of all, there are well-known general works like the *Akbarnama*, the *Kulasat-ut-Tawarikh*, the Tazkiratu's *Salatin-i-Chaghta*, the *Munutakhab-ul-Lubab*, and the *Mirat-i-waridat*. Then there are the histories of short periods or regions, like the *Nuskha-i-Dilkusha*, the *Ibratnamas* of Muhammad Qasim, and Imadu's Sa'adat. There are memoirs of the emperor Jahangir; official and semi-official documents are represented by *Ahkam-i-Alamgiri*, the *Akhbarat-i-Darbar-i-Mulia*, and the reports sent from Delhi by the representatives of other courts.

There are descriptive works like the *Chahar Gulshan* and *Tashribu'l Aqwam*. And then there are works that refuse to be easily categorized like *Dabistan*, the *Tazkira Pir Hassu Teli*, the *Nairang-i-Zaurana*, and the *Jangnama* of Qazi Nur Muhammad.[37]

The contents of the Persian works relate to four phases of Sikh history: the Sikh Gurus and their followers before the time of Guru Gobind Singh, the life of Guru Gobind Singh, the Sikh uprising under Banda Bahadur, and the Sikh resurgence from about 1750 to 1765. However, we will focus on the sources dealing with our period.

Tuzuk-i-Baburi or Babar Nama

This autobiography of Babur throws light on the political, social, economic, and geographical conditions of Punjab and India at the time of Babar's invasion.

Ain-i-Akbari and Akbarnama

The work by Abul Fazl tells us about the historical events from 1556 to 1602 and the Mughal administration. Abul Fazl was the contemporary of Guru Arjan. Abul Fazl is considered to be the official historian of Akbar's reign and no history of Akbar's time is complete without reference to *Akbarnama*. However, Muhammad Akbar in his work *The Punjab Under the Mughals* writes that the account of the Punjab in *Ain-i-Akbari* is meagre and incomplete. In his opinion, the chapter on the Punjab is by far the longest and most important in the *Khulasat-ut-Tawarikh* by Sujan Rai Bhandari. Muhammad Akbar points out that in treatment of the Punjab, Abul Fazl is silent on industries, mines, important cities, holy men, and other points on which he has usually a wealth of information. In the case of other subahs, on the other hand, the author of *Khulasat-ut-Tawarikh*, who was a native of the Punjab, has lovingly recorded every piece of information he could collect about his own province. His account is, therefore, accurate, complete, and up to date and no way inferior to the best descriptive chapter of the *Ain*.[38] Towards the end of the sixteenth century, the Sikh movement was becoming important enough to attract the notice of 'outsiders' including the state.[39] Akbar's visit to Guru Arjan in 1598 is presented by Abul Fazl, in the third part of Akbar Nama, as a matter of imperial grace. But this gesture of goodwill had an inbuilt political dimension too. The term used by Abul Fazl for the religious position of Guru Arjan is 'Brahamanical', which is either an intentional slip or just shows that Abul Fazl had little knowledge of the religious aspect of the Sikh movement.

TUZUK-I-JAHANGIRI

It is variously called *Tarikhi Salim Shahi, Tuzake Jahangiri, Karm Nama Jahangiri, Iqbalnama* and *Maqalate Jahangir*.

This autobiography of Jahangir is full of references to Punjab and contains a clear account of the causes leading to Guru Arjan Dev's martyrdom who was a contemporary of Jahangir. In the *Tuzuk-i-Jahangiri* the emperor claims to have watched the Sikh movement with disapproval. He did not like Guru Arjan converting 'ignorant' Muslims to his own faith. Indeed, we know that the Sikh faith was open to Muslims. Bhai Gurdas mentions Mian Jamal among the prominent Sikhs of Guru Arjan. However, this was not the only professed reason for Jahangir's actions against Guru Arjan, his blessings to the rebel Prince Khusroo become the crowning cause of capital punishment.

DABISTAN-I-MAZAHIB

'School of Religious Doctrine' or more popularly known as 'School of Manners' first came to light in 1787. This manuscript was brought into prominence by Sir William Jones, the founder of the Asiatic Society of Calcutta. Since that time it has been considered the only independent contemporary source of early Sikh history.[40] This book was long believed to have been written by Mohsin Fani but is now believed to be authored by Mubid Zulfikar Ardistani. The author of *Dabistan-i-Mazahib* was a personal friend of the Sixth Guru, Hargobind. He stayed with him for some time and was often in correspondence with him and was present at Kirath Pur on the occasion of his death. In fact, on Guru Hargobind in particular there is no contemporary evidence that is as valuable as that of Dabistan. He was also close to Guru Har Rai, the Seventh Guru. The author of the *Dabistan* does not say much about Guru Angad, Guru Amardas and Guru Ramdas. With the exception of a few minor errors, his account of the earlier Gurus and of the beliefs and practices of the Sikhs, recorded on the authority of the best-informed people, can be safely depended upon. The chapter called the 'Nanak Panthia', which covers some twelve pages of the *Dabistan*,[41] is the first known account of the Sikh people in Persian. The *Dabistan* was translated into English by Shea and Troyer for the Oriental Translation Fund of Great Britain and Ireland in 1843. The translation of 'Nanak Panthia' in Punjabi was published by Sardar Umrao Singh Majithia in the June 1930 issue of the *Khalsa Review* and by Ganda Singh in Phulwari of Phagan Chet, 1987 Bikrami.

The *Dabistan* gives not only comprehensive information but is also extremely significant for our understanding of the pre-Khalsa panth. The author provides extremely useful evidence on the change in the attitude of the Mughal Emperors towards the Gurus and the change in the attitude of Guru Hargobind towards the state. *Dabistan* becomes still more significant when combined with the evidence of Bhai Gurdas who wrote mostly in the early decades of the seventeenth century. The *Dabistan* does not provide information on all the dimensions covered by Bhai Gurdas. The evidence of the Dabistan re-inforces the suggestive evidence of Bhai Gurdas who was acutely conscious of the change after the martyrdom of Guru Arjan. The *Dabistan* also contains extremely useful information on the organization of the Sikh community which indicates in several ways that the Sikhs had a religious identity of their own. The Gurus appointed their representatives, called *masands*, for the twin purpose of initiating others into the Sikh faith and collecting offerings from the Sikhs. The author of the *Dabistan* gives information on some of the important *masands* of the Gurus. He also indicates at several places that the Sikhs were not much concerned about caste distinctions.

KHULASAT-UL-TAWARIKH

Sujan Rai was nearing completion in the 22nd year of the spiritual reign of Guru Gobind Singh (AD 1696), as mentioned by the author on page 70 of Zafar Hasan's edition of 1918. This would make him a contemporary of the last four at least, if not five, Gurus, from Guru Har Rai to Guru Gobind Singh. There has been varied opinion on the importance of the work. As the author belonged to Punjab, he was greatly impressed by the Sikh movement and gives some important information about the Sikhs and Sikh Gurus.[42] Muhammad Akbar in his work, 'Punjab Under the Mughals' considers *Khulasat* a more important work concerning Punjab than *Ain-i-Akbari*. According to him, Sujan Rai's account is accurate, full, and up to date, and in no way inferior to the best descriptive chapters of *Ain*. According to Muhammad Akbar in the century that intervened between the *Ain* and the *Khulasat*, changes occurred in the Mughal Empire. The names of the Sarkars, the numbers of the *mahal*s, the amount of the revenue, and the description of the towns, as given by the author of the *Khulasat*, enable us to institute an interesting comparison with the *Ain*. Both *Ain* and *Khulasat* tell us about the existence of a number of mines as well as the weather in the area. According to Ganda Singh,[43] Sujan Rai's description of the religious life of the Sikhs of those days and their deep-rooted devotion to Gurus is significant.[44] Other important Sikh topics dealt with in this work are the religious position of Guru Nanak and his successors, Akbar's visit to Guru Arjan, the death of Guru Teg Bahadur in Delhi in 1081 AH (AD 1675), and brief notes on historical places like Nanak Mata, Guru Ka Chak (the present Amritsar), Makhowal (Anand Pur), and Kirat Pur.

According to J.S. Grewal, although Sujan Rai, a Bhandari Khatri, belonging to Batala, a place associated with the marriage of Guru Nanak, could have been expected to have reliable information on the Sikhs, he does not seem to have been a close observer or a meticulous researcher. His account of the Gurus is not only brief but full of mistakes. He refers to Guru Nanak's Gnosticism and his verses. Guru Nanak, he says was born in 1469 at Talwandi Rai Bhuna. He showed miracles from a very young age. He travelled widely before he got married at Batala and settled in a village on the Ravi. He died at the age of 70-80 years in the reign of Salim Shah. This date is wrong like several other dates in Sujan Rai's account of the Gurus. Grewal further points out, that writing in 1695, Sujan Rai remains silent on the martyrdom of Guru Arjan and the martial activity of Guru Hargobind and Guru Gobind Singh. Sujan Rai is the only historian, who refers to Guru Har Rai's association with Dara Shikoh in his flight to Punjab.[45] Sujan Rai supports the statement of the Sikh writers that Guru Har Rai came to the assistance of Dara Shukoh on the banks of the Beas with the object of retarding the progress of his brother Aurangzeb against him.

Muntakhib-Ul-Lubab

Khafi Khan throws light on the history of the Mughal emperors from the beginning till AD 1722. Khafi Khan has described the rise of Sikhs under Banda and he has furnished great details, though in the usual abusive language often used for the Sikhs in those days. A careful study of the writings of Khafi Khan will yield valuable details and information about the Sikhs. About the early Sikh history that is 1469 to AD 1708, Khafi Khan has not written much. About Guru Gobind Singh, Khafi Khan has written only the following lines:

> During those days when Bahadur Shah had set out on his march towards the Deccan a person named Gobind, one of the leaders of the notorious sect, came to his presence and accompanied him with two or three hundred horse men, lancers and footmen and two or three months later, he died from a wound of a daggers though his murderer remained unknown.[46]

The procession of Banda and his companions entering Delhi is also graphically described by Khafi Khan.

Guru Gobind Singh receives considerable attention from non-Sikh writers but almost entirely for the post-Khalsa phase of his life, that is, the last eight or nine years. Even the institution of Khalsa does not receive much attention. What gets emphasized in non-Sikh sources is the political activity of Guru Gobind Singh and his followers. By far the most important evidence on Guru Gobind Singh comes from *Ahkam-i-Alamgiri* and the *Akhbarat-i-Darbar-i-Muolla*.

A Note on Primary Sources

Ahkam-i-Alamgiri is a very important source of information of Aurangzeb's reign and a significant document for the study of Guru Gobind Singh's last phase of life. It was written by Inayat Ullah Khan. He had been a newswriter in Aurangzeb's reign and later he was appointed teacher of Zeb-un-nissa, daughter of Aurangzeb who recommended him to her father for employment. The extracts from the *Ahkam-i-Alamgiri* have an importance of their own. The first one refers to the destruction of the Sikh temple in the town of Burya in accordance with imperial orders. The mosque built in its place was destroyed by the follower of Guru Nanak, who killed the custodian too. The primary concern of the emperor was with the conduct and the appointment of *qazi* and the *muhtasib*. The spirit of aggression against the Mughal authorities and even more so the confession of murder, strongly suggests the reaction of Khalsa against the aggressive action of Wazir Khan, the *faujdar* of Sarhind, who had already provided support against Guru Gobind Singh. The second extract from *Ahkam-i-Alamgiri* leaves no doubt that a detailed report of Wazir Khan's action against Guru Gobind Singh was sent to the emperor and was seen by him. The third extract from the *Ahkam* is an order addressed to Munim Khan, the Deputy Governor of Lahore in which he is told that on a petition from Guru Gobind Singh to be allowed to see the emperor in person. These extracts from the *Ahkam* are useful in themselves what is even more important; they add a new dimension to the evidence of Zafar Namah and the *Gurshobha*.

The newsletters called *Akhbar-i-Darbar-Muolla* were not exclusively news of the imperial court as the title would suggest but were generally the summary of the news submitted to the emperor by the official news writers, *Waqia-Nawis, Waqai-i-Nigar*, etc. The representatives of various states and provinces of the country stationed at the capital passed on these news to their respective masters. Such collection of letters was available at Pune and Jaipur. Late Ganda Singh examined these letters from AD 1707 to 1718 for Sikh History Research Department, Khalsa College, Amritsar. These letters relate to the last years of Guru Gobind Singh and Banda Singh Bahadur. English translation of Ganda Singh's selection had been done by Bhagat Singh, which was published in *Punjab Past and Present*.[47]

Other important sources include Abdu'r Rasul's *Nairang-i-Zamana* is an account of his journey through Rajasthan. Among other things, he describes an armed conflict between the followers of Guru Gobind Singh and the Rajput garrison of the fort of the Chittor. Writing in 1759-60, Rai Chaturman takes notice of 'Hindu Sects' in his *Chahar Gulshan*. Nanak Panthis are included in this section of work. In his view, Guru Nanak was a Vaishnava who worshipped Ram. But his followers held that he was opposed to the Vedas. Sikhism had become a separate faith, whether because Guru Nanak himself established a new path or because his successors introduced innovations. In any case, it was necessary to give an account of the Nanak Panthis because in every country and city they were found in thousands. Rai Chatturman's account of Gurus, from Guru Nanak to Guru Teg Bahadur is based on Sujan Rai Bhandari's work. He tries to improve upon his source but without any success. According to Rai Chatturman, Guru Gobind Singh ascended the spiritual seat of his father in the reign of Bahadur Shah in 1710-11 (actually 1675). J.S. Grewal questions Rai Chatturman's chronology. If it is presumed that Guru Gobind Singh guided his disciples for twenty-one years (which would place his death in 1731-32!). He himself instigated an Afghan to take revenge for the death of his father in the hand of Guru Teg Bahadur, and the Afghan killed him. Rai Chatturman goes on to talk of Ajit Singh, Hathi Singh, Mata Sundari, and Mata Sahib Deva as the surviving members of Guru Gobind's family. Ajit Singh, who had been recognized by the Guru as his son after the death of all his three sons, was enthroned on the spiritual seat with permission from the imperial court. The other contemporary Sikh writer Sainapat states explicitly that Guru Gobind Singh did not select any specific person to be his successor. Instead, he declared that Guruship henceforth was vested in Khalsa and the scripture.

Thus, J.S. Grewal concludes that Rai Chatturman's evidence on Guru Gobind Singh is grossly wrong.[48]

Bhim Sen's *Nuskha-i-Dilkusha* does not take much notice of Guru Gobind Singh who is stated to be 'a descendant of Guru Nanak' after his decisive victory over Prince Azam. The work says that 'Guru Gobind Singh obtained the good fortune of presenting himself before the emperor'. The reference to Guru Gobind Singh's meeting with Bahadur Shah is found in both Persian and Punjabi sources. What is interesting about Bhim Sen's notice is that it was not based on information emanating from Sikh sources. His account was based on what he had heard about the Sikhs. For instance, he states that Guru Gobind Singh did not follow the ways of religious men and was proud of his soldierly profession. Bhim Sen refers to Guru Nanak's service (*naukari*), his association with religious men, his disciples in the territory of Lahore and Multan, his compositions, and his deputies. No country, city, township, or village was there without his followers. Offerings were carried to 'his descendants' who are his 'successors'. They spent their lives in splendour and some of them took to the path of rebellion. Guru Teg Bahadur was among them. He called himself Padshah and a large number of people gathered around him. When Aurangzeb came to know of his activities, he summoned the Guru to the court and he was executed. As Grewal states, we may be sure that Bhim Sen relied on what he had heard from some people who had only a general, rather vague idea of the early Sikh movement. Nevertheless, Bhim Sen's reference to the cause of Guru Teg Bahadur's execution is significant. Most of the non-Sikh sources mention Guru Teg Bahadur's militancy as the reason for Aurangzeb's action. By contrast, Sikh sources like the *Bachittar Nattak* and the *Gurshobha* dwell exclusively on the religious dimension of the Sikhs.

Mirza Muhammad in his *Ibartnama* looks upon Guru Gobind Singh as introducing some new 'customs' of Guru Nanak and his successors who are seen more or less as Hindu recluses. The Sikhs who accepted Guru Gobind Singh's core group of disciples came to be known as Khalsa. With their support, he began to establish his power over the *zamindar*s of the neighborhood through warlike means. Wazir Khan repeatedly sent forces against him and the Guru lost two of his sons in battles. When Bahadur Shah was marching from Peshawar to Delhi, Guru Gobind Singh in fact, accompanied the imperial camp to win over the grace of Bahadur Shah. Guru Gobind Singh was in Rajasthan at that time. Mirza Muhammad rightly says later that the Guru accompanied the emperor to the Deccan. There he was killed by an Afghan who bore enmity toward him. He was cremated according to the customs of Hindus. Although Mirza Muhammad's *Ibartnama* contains derogatory language for Banda Bahadur and the Sikhs, his account is important as a contemporary witness.

FOREIGN TRAVELOGUES

In addition, we also have contemporary Spanish and French sources such as Father Guerreiro's Spanish Account (letter dates 25 September 1606 and 8 August 1607) and Father Du Jarrics French Account AD 1614.[49] Their works are of great value as they throw light on the condition of the people, the state of trade and industry. In a way, their observations have freshness and weight of their own. But apart from the events in which they participated or which they personally witnessed, their report merely reproduced bazaar rumors and the stories current among the populace, and cannot be set against the contemporary works. Eugenia Vanina puts it more succinctly when she points out the limitations of the approach where some scholars base their studies of medieval India entirely on European records, which of course, are very useful as sources. She says that

during the period under review [sixteenth to eighteenth centuries is the focus of her work] European travellers were more interested in cloth and spice prices than in the spiritual riches of India. Even those who were interested in this subject were, in spite of their wisdom and insight, separated from Indian culture by a huge wall of religious superstitions, ignorance and arrogance of the representatives of the 'highest' culture and most true religion.[50]

NOTES

1. Ganda Singh, 'The Major Sources of Early Sikh History', in *History and Ideology: The Khalsa Over 300 years*, ed. J.S. Grewal and Indu Banga, New Delhi: Tulika Books and Indian History Congress, 1999, p. 11.
2. Pashaura Singh, *The Guru Granth Sahib: Canon, Meaning and Authority*, New Delhi: Oxford University Press, 2003.
3. Verne A. Dusenbery, 'The Word as Guru: Sikh Scripture and the Translation Controversy', *History of Religions*, vol. 31, no. 4, May 1992.
4. Harbans Singh, 'Guru Granth Sahib: Guru Eternal for the Sikhs', *Sikh Courier* 12, number 14 (Summer 1986), p. 8.
5. W.H. McLeod, *The Evolution of the Sikh Community: Five Essays*, New Delhi: Oxford University Press, 1976 (rpt., 1996), p. 20.
6. W.H. McLeod, *Textual Sources for the Study of Sikhism*, Chicago: University of Chicago, 1984, p. 2.
7. Dharam Pal Ashta, *Poetry of the Dasam Granth*, New Delhi: Arun Prakashan, 1959, p. 151.
8. Ibid., pp. 151-3.
9. Ibid., p. 151.
10. Ibid., pp. 154, 156, 418.
11. Ibid., p. 153
12. J.S. Grewal, 'The Sikh Panth in the Vars of Bhai Gurdas', in *History and Ideology: The Khalsa Over 300 years*, ed. J.S. Grewal and Indu Banga, New Delhi: Tulika Books and Indian History Congress, 1999, p. 26.
13. For biographical information see Rattan Singh Jaggi, *Bhai Gurdas: Jiwan Te Rachna*, Patiala: Punjabi University, 1974; Trilochan Singh, *Guru Tegh Bahadur*, Delhi: Gurdwara Parbandhak Committee, 1967, pp. 16, 19, 23, 30, 41, 54, 58-9, 65, 162, 200-201; W.H. McLeod, *Guru Nanak and the Sikh Religion*, Delhi: Oxford University Press, 1996, pp. 14-15, 19, 28-30.
14. Grewal, 'The Sikh Panth in the Vars of Bhai Gurdas', p. 29.

15. W.H. McLeod, *The Sikhs: History, Religion, and Society*, New York: Columbia University Press, 1989.
16. For a detailed discussion see W.H. McLeod, *Early Sikh Tradition: A Study of Janam-Sakhis*, Oxford: Clarendon Press, 1980; McLeod, *The Evolution of the Sikh Community: Five Essays*; W.H. McLeod, 'Cries of Outrage: History Versus Tradition in the Study of Sikh Community', in *Exploring Sikhism Aspects Of Sikh Identity, Culture And Thought*, W.H. McLeod Delhi: Oxford University Press, 2000.
17. For a thought-provoking discussion on the nature and value of the *janamsakhi*s see *Janamsakhi Adhyayan*, ed. Kripal Singh Komal, pubd. by Principal, Brijendra College, Faridkot and Guru Nanak Foundation, District Bhatinda, 1970.
18. McLeod, *Textual Sources for the Study of Sikhism*, p. 1.
19. Ibid., p. 11.
20. Saroop Das Bhalla, *Mahima Parkash*, 2 vols., ed. Gobind Singh Lamba and Khazan Singh, Patiala: Languages Department, 1971.
21. Saroop Das Bhalla, *Mahima Parkash Vartak*, ed. Kulvinder Singh Bajwa, Amritsar: Singh Brothers, 2004.
22. For details see Harbans Singh, *The Encyclopaedia of Sikhism*. Patiala: Punabi University, 1995.
23. S.S. Hans, 'Rattan Singh Bhangu's Purpose of Writing Prachin Panth Parkash', Punjab History Conference Proceedings, 9th session, 1975.
24. Ganda Singh, 'The Major Sources of Early Sikh History', p. 18.
25. Bhagat Singh, *Giani Gian Singh*, Patiala: Punjabi University, 1978 and an article by Bhagat Singh, 'Giani Gian Singh', Punjab History Conference Proceedings, 9th Session, 1975.
26. Terence Brown, *Ireland: A Social and Cultural History, 1922-79*, London: Fontana, 1981, p. 9.
27. Ibid., p. 338, J.S. Grewal, 'Literary Evidence: The Case of Waris Shah', PIHC 43rd Session, 1982, p. 388.
28. J.S. Grewal, 'Punjabi Literature (1750-1850)', in *Sikhisim and Secularism: Essays in Honour of Professor Harbans Singh*, ed. Dharam Singh, Delhi: Harnam Publishing House, p. 152.
29. Sant Singh Sekhon, *A History of Punjabi Literature*, vol. II, Publication Bureau, Punjabi University, Patiala, 1996, p. 23.
30. Grewal, 'Punjabi Literature (1750-1850)', p. 153.
31. Shah Hussain, 'A Notice', in *Biographical Encyclopedia of Sufis of South Asia*, ed. N. Hanif, Delhi: Sarup & Sons, 2000, pp. 140-1.

A Note on Primary Sources

32. Grewal, 'Punjabi Literature (1750-1850)', p. 154.
33. For further information see R.C. Temple, *The Legends of the Panjab*, Patiala: Languages Department, 1884.
34. Sohan Kavi, *Gurbilas Padshahi Chhevin*, ed. Giani Inder Singh, Amritsar: Jiwan Mandir Pustkala, 1968, p. 315.
35. Kumkum Sangari, 'Mirabai and the Spiritual Economy of Bhakti', *Occasional Papers on History and Society* (Second Series, Number XXVIII), New Delhi: Nehru Memorial Museum and Library, 2001, p. 27.
36. J.S. Grewal and Irfan Habib, ed., 'Introduction' in *Sikh History from Persian Sources*, Delhi: Tulika Books and the Indian History Congress, 2001, p. 2.
37. Ibid., p. 18.
38. Muhammad Akbar, *Punjab Under the Mughals*, Lahore: Ripon Printing Press, 1948, pp. 15-17.
39. Ibid., p. 3.
40. *Dabistan-i-Mazahib*, Kanpur: Munshi Nawal Kishore, 1904.
41. Kirpal Singh, 'Perspectives of Sikh Gurus', *The Punjab Past and Present*, vol. XVIII-II, October 1984, Sr. no. 36, Punjabi University, Patiala, p. 35.
42. Akbar, *Punjab Under the Mughals*, pp. 15-17.
43. Ganda Singh, 'The Major Sources of Early Sikh History', p. 14.
44. Ibid., p. 12.
45. Ibid., p. 37.
46. Khafi Khan, *Muntakhib-Ul-Lubab*, 2 vols, Part 1, Calcutta: Asiatic Society, 1870; also see Kirpal Singh, 'Perspectives of Sikh Gurus', *The Punjab Past and Present*, vol. XVIII-II October 1984 Sr. no. 36, Punjabi University, Patiala.
47. Ganda Singh, *The Panjab Past and Present*, Patiala: Punjabi University, April 1967, pp. 133-5.
48. J.S. Grewal, 'Khalsa of Guru Gobind Singh: A Problem in Historiography', Punjab History Conference Proceedings, First Session, 1968, p. 18.
49. C.H. Payne, Scenes and Characters, from Indian History: As Described in the Works of Some Old Masters, London; New York: H. Milford, Oxford University Press, 1925.
50. Eugenia Vanina, *Ideas and Society: India Between the Sixteenth and Eighteenth Centuries*, New Delhi: Oxford University Press, 1996, p. 12.

Bibliography

PRIMARY SOURCES

Barkhurdar, Ranjha, *Sassi Ate Hor Qisse Rachit Ranjha Barkhurdar*, ed. Piara Singh Padam and Gobind Singh Lamba, Amritsar: Guru Nanak Dev University, 1977.

Bhai Bala, *Guru Nanak Dev Ji Ki Janamsakhi*, M.S.Rattan, Amritsar: Bhai Chattar Singh Jiwan Singh, n.d.

Bhai Gurdas, *Kabit Sawaiyye*, tr. Shamsher Singh Puri, Amritsar: Singh Brothers, 2007.

——, *Varan*, Text, Transliteration and Translation, 2 vols., Jodh Singh, Patiala: Vision and Venture, 1998.

Bhalla, Saroop Das, *Mahima Parkash Vartak*, ed. Kulvinder Singh Bajwa, Amritsar: Singh Brothers, 2004.

——, *Mahima Parkash*, 2 vols., ed. Gobind Singh Lamba and Khazan Singh, Patiala: Languages Department, 1971.

Bhangu, Shahid Rattan Singh, *Prachin Panth Parkash*, ed. Bhai Vir Singh, New Delhi: Bhai Vir Singh Sahitya Sadan, rpt., 1998.

——, *Prachin Panth Parkash*, ed. Jeet Singh Sital, Amritsar: Sikh Itihas Research Board, Shiromani Gurdwara Prabandhak Committee, 1994.

Chhibbar, Kesar Singh, *Banswalinamah Dasan Padshahi Ka*, ed. Piara Singh Padam, Amritsar: Singh Brothers, 1997.

Dasam Granth, Amritsar: Chattar Singh and Jeewan Singh, n.d.

Kaushish, Bhai Swaroop Singh, *Guru Kian Saakhian*, ed. Piara Singh Padam, Amritsar: Singh Brothers, 1995.

McLeod, W.H., *The B-40 Janamsakhi*, Amritsar: Guru Nanak Dev University, 1980.

Meharbaan Ji Sodhi, *Janamsakhi Shri Guru Nanak Dev Ji*, ed. Kripal Singh and Shamsher Singh Ashok, Amritsar: Sikh History Research Department, Khalsa College, 1962.

Muqbal, *Qissa Hir Ranjha*, ed. Shamsher Singh Ashok, Patiala.

Nayyar, Gurbachan Singh, ed. *Gur Rattan Mal: Sau Sakhi*, Patiala: Punjabi University, rpt., 1995.

Peelu, *Qissa Mirza Sahiban*, Ms., Manuscript Section, Central Library, Patiala: Central Library, Punjabi University, n.d.
Sainapat, *Sri Gur Sobha*, ed. Ganda Singh, Patiala: Punjabi University, rpt., 1967.
Shah, Fazal, *Sohni Mahiwal*, ed. Diwan Singh and Roshan Lal Ahuja, Jalandhar: 1979.
Shah, Hashim, *Hashim di Kav Rachna*, ed. Gurdev Singh, Ludhiana, 1969.
——, *Qissa Sohni Mahiwal: Hashim Rachnavali*, ed. Piara Singh Padam, Patiala, n.d.
Shah, Waris, *Qissa Heer Waris Shah*, ed. Shamsher Singh Ashok, Patiala, 1976.
Singh, Bhai Sukha, *Gurbilas Padshahi Dasvin*, ed. Giani Inder Singh, Patiala: Bhasha Vibhag, Punjab, 1979
Singh, Bhai Vir, ed. *Puratan Janamsakhi Guru Nanak Dev Ji*, New Delhi: Bhai Vir Singh Sahitya Sadan, rpt., 2004.
Singh, Ganda, ed. *Hukum Nameh*, Patiala; Punjabi University, rpt., 1993.
Singh, Gopal, *Sri Guru Granth Sahib*, Eng. tr., Delhi: Gurdas Kapoor & Sons, 1964.
Singh, Guru Gobind, *Thus Spake the Tenth Master*, Eng. tr. Gopal Singh, Patiala: Punjabi University, 1978.
Singh, Gyani Gyan, *Suraj Parkash*, ed.Churaman Bhai Santokh Singh, Amritsar: Bhai Chattar Singh Jeevan Singh, 1997.
——, *Tawarikh Guru Khalsa*, ed. K.S. Raju, Patiala: Bhasha Vibhag, 1993.
——, *Sri Guru Panth Parkash*, Patiala: Bhasha Vibhag, 1970.
Singh, Koer, *Gurbilas Padshahi Dasvin*, ed. Shamsher Singh Ashok, Punjabi University, Patiala, rpt., 1997.
Singh, Sahib, ed. *Bhattande Sawayye*, Amritsar: Singh Brothers, 2001.
Singh, Santokh, *Sri Guru Partap Suraj Granth*, ed. Bhai Vir Singh, Amritsar: Khalsa Samachar, 1931.
Singh, Shamsher, ed. *Guru Khalsa de Nishan te Hukam Nameh*, Amritsar: Sikh Itihas Research Board, 1967.
Sitta,Y.S., *Shah Hussain: Jiwani te Rachna*, Patiala: Punjabi University, n.d.
Sohan Kavi, *Gurbilas Padshahi Chhevin*, ed.Giani Inder Singh, Amritsar: Jiwan Mandir Pustkala, 1968.
Talib, G.S., *Sri Guru Granth Sahib*, Eng. tr., 4 vols., Patiala: Punjabi University, 1990.
Trumpp, Ernest, *The Adi Granth*, London,W.H. Allen, 1877, rpt., New Delhi: Munshiram Manoharlal, 1970.

Yaar, Ahmad, *Qissa Sassi Punnu*, ed. Nihal Singh Ras, Amritsar: Kitab Trinjan, 1963.
Yaar, Qadir, *Puran Bhagat*, ed. Gurcharan Singh, Patiala, 1969.
Yaar, Qadir, *Puran Bhagat*, in *Punjab Dian Lok Gathawan*, ed. Richard Temple, Patiala: Bhasha Vibhag, rpt., 1970.

WORKS IN PERSIAN

Ahmad, Nizamuddin, *Tabaqat-i-Akbari*, 3 vols., Eng, tr. Brajendranath De and Baini Prashad, Calcutta: The Asiatic Society, rpt., 1996.
Alberuni, Abu Raihan, *Alberuni's India (Tahqiq-ul-Hind)*, Eng. tr. E.C. Sachau, New Delhi: S. Chand and Co., rpt., 1964.
Ardistani, Mubid Zulfiqar, *Dabistan-i-Mazahib*, Eng. tr. Ganda Singh, entitled 'Nanakpanthis', *The Punjab Past and Present*, vol. 1, 1967.
Babur, Zahir-ud-din Muhammad, *Baburnama*, vol. II, Eng. tr. A.S. Beveridge, New Delhi: Munshiram Manoharlal, rpt., 1970.
Badauni, Abdul Qadir, *Muntakhab ut-Tawarikh*, ed. Ali Ahmad and Lees, Bib. Ind., Calcutta, 1864-69.
——, *Muntakhab ut-Tawarikh*, Eng. tr., vol. I, George S. Ranking; vol. II, W.H. Lowe, vol. III, Wolseley Haig; all three volumes edited by B.P. Ambashthya, Patna: Academica Asiatica, 1973.
Battuta, Ibn, *Travels in Asia and Africa*, Eng. tr. H.A.R. Gibb, London: Routledge & Kegan Paul, 1929.
Begum, Gulbadan, *Humayun Namah*, Eng. tr. Annette S. Beveridge, New Delhi: Atlantic Publishers & Distributors, rpt., 2018.
Bhandari, Sujan Rai, *Khulasat-ut-Tawarikh*, ed. Zafar Hasan, Delhi: J. & Sons Press, 1918; partly Eng. tr. Jadunath Sarkar, *India of Aurangzib*, Calcutta: Bose Bros, 1901.
Fazl, Abul, *Ain-i Akbari*, vol. I, Eng. tr. H. Blochmann and D.C. Phillot, Calcutta: The Asiatic Society, rpt., 1977.
——, *Ain-i Akbari*, vols. II and III, Eng. tr. H.S. Jarrett, Corrected and Annotated by Jadunath Sarkar, Calcutta: The Asiatic Society, 1949.
——, *Ain-i-Akbari*, vol. III, ed. Ahmad Ali and Abdur Rahim, Bib. Ind., Calcutta, 1873-87.
——, *Akbarnama*, 3 vols., Eng. tr. H. Beveridge, New Delhi: Atlantic Publishers & Distributors, rpt., 2019.
Haqq, Maulvi Abdul, *The Role of the Sufis in the Early Development of Urdu*
Isami, Abdul Malik, *Futuh us-Salatin*, vol. II, Eng. tr. Agha Mahdi Husain, Aligarh: Centre of Advanced Study, Department of History,

Aligarh Muslim University and Bombay: Asia Publishing House, 1976.

———, *Futuh us-Salatin*, vol. II, Eng. tr. Agha Mahdi Husain, Aligarh: CAS in History, Aligarh Muslim University and Bombay: Asia Publishing House, 1976.

Khan, Saqi Mustad, *Maasir-i-Alamgiri*, Eng. tr., Jadunath Sarkar, New Delhi: Oriental Reprint Corporation, rpt., 1986.

Meharban, *Janam Sakhi Shri Guru Nanak Dev Ji*, ed. Kirpal Singh and Shamsher Singh Ashok, Amritsar: Sikh History Research Department, Khalsa College, 1962.

Muqbal, *Kissa Hir Ranjha*, ed. Dilbara Singh Bajwa, Chandigarh: Unistar Books, 2013.

Nihala, 'Sakhi Sarwar Di Shaadi' in *Punjabi Lok Gathawan*, vol. II, ed. Richard Temple, Patiala: Languages Department Punjab, 1970.

Nijatu ur-Rashid, ed. S. Moinul Haq, Lahore, 1972.

Nuruddin Jahangir, *Tuzuk-i Jahangiri*, Eng. tr. Alexander Rogers and HenryBeveridge, New Delhi: Low Price Publications, rpt., 1989.

Qadir Yar, 'Puran Bhagat', in *Punjab Dian Lok Gathawan*, vol. II, ed. Richard Temple, Patiala: Languages Department Punjab, 1970.

Sarwar, Mufti Ghulam, *Tarikh-I Makhzan-i Punjab*, Lucknow: Nawal Kishore Press, 1877.

Sethi, Agra, *Var Haqiqat Rai*, ed. Ganda Rai, Amritsar: Kitab Trinjan, n.d.

Shah, Bulleh, *Kalaam Bulleh Shah*, ed. Shah Chaman, Agra: Chetna Prakashan, 2010.

Shah, Lakh, *Kissa Sassi Punnu*, ed. Hazura Singh, Amritsar: Kitab Trinjan, n.d.

Shah, Waris, *Hir*, Agra: Chetna Prakashan, rpt. 2010.

Sijzi, Amir Hasan, *Fawaid ul-Fuad*, Eng. tr. Bruce B. Lawrence (entitled, *Nizam al-Din Awliya: Morals for the Heart*), New York: Paulist Press, 1992.

Singh, Ganda, ed. *Makhiz-i Tawarikh-i-Sikhan*, Amritsar: Sikh History Society, 1949.

Singh, Sri Sant Kirpal, *Asa di Var Steek*, Amritsar: Chhatr Singh, Jeevan Singh, rept. 2007.

Singh, Tulsa, *Jhagra Jatti Te Khatrian Da*, Ms 800, A.C. Joshi Library, Panjab University, Chandigarh.

Sirhindi, Yahya Ahmad, *Tarikh-i Mubarak Shahi*, Eng. tr. H.M. Elliot and John Dowson, entitled *History of India as Told by its Own Historians*, vol. IV, Allahabad: Kitab Mahal, rpt., n.d.

Talib, G.S., *Sri Guru Granth Sahib*, Eng. tr., 4 vols., Patiala: Punjabi University, 1990.
Thanvi,Ashraf Ali, *Behishti Zewar*, Eng. tr. Mohammad Masroor Khan Saroha, Delhi: Urdu Bazaar, 1979.
Vadera,Ganesh Das, *CharBagh-i Punjab*, ed. Kirpal Singh, Amritsar: Sikh History Research Department, Khalsa College, 1965.
Yaar, Ahmad, *Ahsan ul-Kasis*, ed. Piara Singh, Patiala: Languages Department Punjab, 1962.
Yaar,Ahmed, *Qissa-i-Kamrup*, Lahore: Qadiri Press, 1881.

WORKS IN HINDI

Das, Shyam Sundar, ed. *Kabir Granthavali*, Varanasi: Kashi Nagari Prachar in Sabha, VS 2034.
Dayal, Sant Dadu, *Sri Dadu Vani*, ed. Narayan Das, Jaipur, 2nd edn. VS 2026.
Jaisi, Malik Muhammad, *Padmavat*, ed. V.S. Aggarwal, Chiragaon, Jhansi: Pitambar Books, 2nd ed. n.d.
Jones, Rev. William, ed. *Manava Dharma Shastra*, Eng. tr. G.C. Haughton, Delhi: Asian Educational Services, rpt., 1982.
Linda, Hess and Sukhdev Singh, *The Bijak of Kabir*, Delhi: Motilal Banarsidas, 1986.
Machwe, Prabhakar, *Kabir*, New Delhi: Sahitya Academy, 1968.
Mirabai, *Mira Bai Ki Padavali*, ed. Acharya P.R. Chaturvedi, Prayag: Hindi Sahitya Sammelan, 1976.
——, *Mirabai Ki Padavali*, ed. Krishna Deva Sharma, New Delhi: Regal Book Depot, 1992.
Surdas, *Sur Sagar*, ed. Nand Dulare Vajpai, Kashi: Kashi Nagari Pracharini Sabha, 4th edn. 2 vols., 1916.
Tewari, Parasnath, *Kabir*, New Delhi: National Book Trust, rpt., 1981.
Tulsi Das, *Ram Charit Manas*, 8th edn., No. 6/16/2, Gorakhpur: Gita Press, VS 2027; M.P. Gupta, ed., *Tulsi's Sri Ramacharita-manas*, Allahabad: Hindustani Academy, n.d.; Ram Naresh Tripathi, *Ram Charit Manas: Tulsi Das's Ramayan*, Allahabad: Hindi Mandir Press, 1935.

FOREIGN TRAVELOGUES

Bernier, Francois, *Travels in the Mogul Empire: AD 1656-68*, Eng tr. Archibald Constable and Vincent A. Smith, Delhi: Low Price Publications, rpt., 1994.

Commissariat, M.S., ed., *Mandelslo's Travels in Western India*, London: Oxford University Press, 1931.
Foster, William, ed. *Early Travels in India*, New Delhi: Low Price Publications, rpt. 2012.
Linschoten, Jan Huyghen van, *The Voyage of Jan Huyghen van Linschoten to the East Indies, 1874-75*, New Delhi: Asian Educational Services, rpt., 2004.
Manucci, Niccolao, *Storia Do Mogor*, 4 vols., Eng. tr. William Irvine, Calcutta: Indian Text Series, rpt., 1965.
Pelsaert, Francisco, *Jahangir's India: The Remonstrantie of Francisco Pelsaert*, Eng. tr. W.H. Moreland and P. Geyl, Delhi: Idarah-i-Adabiyat-i-Delli, 1972.
Tavernier, Jean Baptiste, *The Six Voyages of Jean Baptiste Tavernier*, vol. II, London: Robert Littlebury and Moses Pitt, 1678.
Teltscher, Kate, *India Inscribed: European and British Writing on India, 1600-18*, New Delhi: Oxford University Press, 1995.
Thevenot, Jean de, *The Indian Travels of Thevenot and Careri*, Eng. tr. S.N. Sen, New Delhi: National Archives of India, 1949.
Valle, Pietro Della, *The Travels of a Noble Roman into East Indies and Arabian Deserta*, vol. I, ed. Edward Grey, London: The Hakluyt Society, 1892.

SECONDARY SOURCES

Aggarwal, Ashwini, 'Sati-How Old? How Indian?', *Haryana Sahitya Akademi Journal of Indological Studies*, vol. III, 1991.
Ahluwalia, Jasbir Singh, 'Gender Equality', in *Doctrinal Aspects of Sikhism and Other Essays*, Patiala: Punjabi University, 2001.
Ahmad, Aziz, *Studies in Islamic Culture in the Indian Environment*, Oxford: Oxford University Press, 1964.
Ahuja, Jasbir Kaur, 'Mata Gujri: Consort and Mother', *Sikh Review*, vol. 4, no. 5, 1993; also in *Sikh Courier*, vol. 35, 1995.
Akbar, Muhammad, *The Punjab Under the Mughals*, Delhi: Idarah-i-Adabiyat-i-Delli, rpt., 1974.
Alam, Ishrat, 'Textile Tools as depicted in Ajanta and Mughal Paintings', in *Technology in Ancient and Medieval India*, ed. Aniruddha Ray and S.K. Bagchi, Delhi: Sundeep Prakashan, 1986.
Alam, Muzaffar, 'Politics under the Later Mughals', *in Five Punjabi Centuries: Polity, Economy, Society and Culture c.1500-c.1900*, ed. Indu Banga, New Delhi: Manohar, 1997.

Bibliography

Ali, Meer Hasan, *Observations on the Mussulmauns of India*, London: Humphrey Milford and Oxford University Press, 1917.

Ali, S.A., *Islamic History and Culture*, Delhi: Idarah-i-Adabiyat-i-Delli, 1978.

Altekar, A.S., *The Position of Women in Hindu Civilization*, Delhi: Motilal Banarsidas, 16th edn. 2016.

Anand, Mulk Raj, *Folk Tales of Punjab* (Folk Tales of India Series), New Delhi: Sterling, 1978.

Anand, Surinder Kaur, 'Women in the Punjab during Eighteenth and Nineteenth Centuries', *Proceedings of the Punjab History Conference*, 13th Session, 1979.

Arora, Harjit Kaur, 'Sikhism and the Status of Women', *Sikh Spirit*, 51. http://www.bsingh.dsl.pipex.com/khalsa/news51.htm

Ashraf, Kanwar Muhammad, *Life and Conditions of the People of Hindustan, 1200-1550*, New Delhi: Munshiram Manoharlal, rpt., 1970.

Ashta, Dharam Pal, *Poetry of the Dasam Granth*, New Delhi: Arun Prakashan, 1959.

Bala, Shashi, 'The Idea of Society as Reflected in Guru Nanak Bani', *Proceedings of the Punjab History Conference*, 26th Session, 1994.

Ballantyne, Tony, 'Framing the Sikh Past', *International Journal of Punjab Studies*, vol. 10, nos 1 & 2. January-December 2003, pp. 1-24.

Balwinder Jeet, 'Social Evils During the Reign of Maharaja Ranjit Singh: A Contemporary Perspective', *Proceedings of the Punjab History Conference*, 37th Session, March 2005.

Balwinderjit, 'Social Evils During the Reign of Maharaja Ranjeet Singh: A Contemporary Perspective', Proceedings of the Punjab History Conference Proceedings, 37th Session, 2005.

Banerjee, Anil Chandra, *Guru Nanak and His Times*, Patiala: Punjabi University, Patiala, 1971.

Banerjee, Indubhushan, *Evolution of the Khalsa*, 2 vols., Calcutta: A Mukherjee & Co., rpt. 1979.

Banga, Indu, ed. *Five Punjabi Centuries: Polity. Economy, Society and Culture, c.1500-1900*, New Delhi: Manohar, 1997.

Barrier, N. Gerald, *Sikhs and their Literature*, Delhi: Manohar, 1970.

Basarke, Alice, *Her Story: Women in Sikh Religion and History*, Amritsar: Singh Brothers, 2002.

Basu, Aparna and Anup Taneja, eds., *Breaking out of Invisibility: Women in Indian History*, ICHR Monograph Series VII.

Bedi, Sohinder Singh, 'Women in the Folk Sayings of Punjab', *Women in Indian Folklore*, ed. S. Sengupta, Calcutta: Indian Publications, 1969.

———, *Folklore of Punjab*, Delhi: National Book Trust, 1971.

Bhandar, Ramkumar Verma, *Hindi Sahitya Ka Alochanatmak Itihas*, 4th edn. Allahabad: Ramnarayan Benimadhav, 1958.

Bhatia, Shyamala, 'Indian Society in the Medieval Times as Depicted in Guru Granth Sahib', *Proceedings of the Punjab History Conference*, 36th Session, 2004.

Bhattacharya, Niladri, 'Pastoralists in a Colonial World', in *Nature, Culture and Imperialism: Essays on the Environmental History of South Asia*, ed. David Arnold and Ramachandra Guha, New Delhi: Oxford University Press, 1995

Bingley, A.H., *Sikhs*, Patiala: Department of Languages, rpt., 1970.

Bosch, Mineke, 'Women's Culture in Women's History; Historical Notion on Feminist Vision?', in *Historiography of Women's Cultural Tradition*, ed. Maaike Meijer and Jetty Schapp, Dordrecht: Foris Publication, 1987.

Bose, Mandakranta, ed. *Faces of Feminine in Ancient, Medieval and Modern India*, New York: Oxford University Press, 2000.

Bose, Mandakranta, ed. *Faces of the Feminine in Ancient, Medieval and Modern India*, New Delhi: Oxford University Press, 2000.

Bose, Mandakranta, ed. *Visions of Virtue: Women in the Hindu Tradition*, Vancouver: MBose, 1996.

Bourdieu, Pierre, 'Social Space and Symbolic Power', *Sociological Theory*, vol. 7, no. 1, Spring 1989.

Brown, John Cave, *Indian Infanticide: Its Origins, Progress and Suppression*, London: W.H. Allen & Co., 1857.

Buhler, George, *The Laws of Manu*, rpt. Charleston, South Carolina: Biblio Life, April 2009.

Butalia, Urvashi, 'Community, State and Gender on Women's Agency during Partition', *Economic and Political Weekly*, 24 April 1993.

Census of India, *Punjab and Delhi, 1911*, vol. 17, pt 1, p. 219, Karnal District Gazetteer, 1976.

Chakarvarty, Uma, 'Conceptualizing Brahmanical Patriarchy in Early India: Gender, Caste, Class and State', *The Economic and Political Weekly*, 3 April 1993.

Chakravarty, Uma, 'Conceptualising Brahmanical Patriarchy in Early India: Gender, Caste, Class and State', *Economic and Political Weekly*, 3 April 1993.

——, 'The World of the Bhaktin in South Indian Traditions: The Body and Beyond', *Manushi*, nos. 50, 51, 52, 1989.

——, 'Whatever Happened to Vedic Dasi?: Orientalism, Nationalism and Script for Past', in *Recasting Women: Essays in Indian Colonial History*, ed. Kumkum Sangari and Sudesh Vaid, New Jersey: Rutgers University Press, 1997.

——, 'Reconceptualising Gender: Phule, Brahmanism and Brahmanical Patriarchy', *Women in Indian History: Social, Economic, Political and Cultural Perspectives*, ed. Kiran Pawar, Patiala and Delhi: Vision & Venture, 1996.

Chanana, Karuna, 'Partition and Family Strategies: Gender-Education Linkages among Punjabi Women in Delhi', in *Economic and Political Weekly*, 24 April 1993.

Chattopadhyaya, B.D., 'Geographical Perspectives, Culture Change and Linkages: Some Reflections on Early Punjab', Presidential Address (Ancient Section), Proceedings of the *Punjab History Conference*, 27th Session, 1995.

Chaturvedi, Parshuram, *Kabir Sahitya Ki Parakh*, Allahabad: Bharti Bhandar, 1955.

——, *Uttar Bharat Ki Sant Parampara*, 2nd edn. Allahabad: Bharti Bhandar, 1965.

Chhabra, G.S., *Advanced Study of Punjab*, Jullundur: New Academic Publishing Company, 1968.

——, *Social and Economic History of Punjab (1849-1901)*, New Delhi: Sterling Publishers, 1971.

Chopra, P.N., *Some Aspects of Society and Culture during the Mughal Age, 1526-1707*, Agra: Shiva Lal Agarwala, 1963.

Chowdhry, Prem, 'Contesting Claims and Counter-Claims: Questions of the Inheritance and Sexuality of Windows in a Colonial State', in *Social Reform, Sexuality and the State*, ed. Patricia Uberoi, Delhi: Sage, 1996.

——, 'Popular Perceptions of Widow-Remarriage in Haryana: Past and Present', in *From the Seams of History: Essays on Indian Women*, ed. Bharati Ray, Delhi: Oxford University Press, 1995.

——, 'Customs in a Peasant Economy: Women in Colonial Haryana', in *Recasting Women: Essays in Indian Colonial History*, ed. Kumkum Sangari and Sudesh Vaid, New Jersey: Rutgers University Press, 1997.

Clifford Geertz, 'Religion as a Cultural System', in *Anthropological Approaches to the Study of Religion*, ed. Michael Banton, London: Tavistock Publications, 1966.

Cole, Owen W., 'Status of Women in Sikhism and Christianity', in *Sikhism and Secularism: Essays in Honour of Prof. Harbans Singh*, ed. Dharam Singh, Harman Publishing House, 1994.

Coryat, Thomas, *Early Travels in India, 1583-1619*, ed. William Foster, Delhi: Low Price Publications, 2012.

Cossman, Brenda and Ratna Kapur, 'Communalising Gender/Engendering Community Women, Legal Discourse and Saffron Agenda', in *Economic and Political Weekly*, 24 April 1993.

Cunningham, J.D., *A History of the Sikhs*, Delhi: S. Chand & Company, rpt., 1966.

Customary Law of the Main Tribes in the Gurdaspur District, Lahore: Punjab Government Press, 1913.

Das, Veena, 'Indian Women: Work, Power and Status', in B.R. Nanda, *Indian Women: From Purdah to Modernity*, New Delhi: Vikas, 1976.

——, 'On Female Body and Sexuality', *Contributions to Indian Sociology*, (N.S.), vol. 21, no. 1, 1987.

de Beauvoir, Simone, *The Second Sex*, Eng. tr. H.M. Parshley, New York: Vintage, 1974

de Laet, Joannes, *The Empire of the Great Mogol*, ed. J.S. Hoyland and S.N. Banerjee, Delhi: Idarah-i-Adabiyat-i-Delli, 1975.

de Thevenot, Jean, *The Indian Travels of Thevenot and Careri*, Eng tr. S.N. Sen, New Delhi: National Archives of India, 1949.

DeLong-Bas, Natana J., *Oxford Encyclopedia of Islam and Women* (2 vols.), USA: Oxford University Press, 1st edn. October 2013.

Dhillon, Dalbir Singh, 'Socio Religious Change in the Punjab during Sixteenth Century Punjab', *Proceedings of the Punjab History Conference*, 15th session, 1981.

Dhillon, Gurdarshan Singh, 'Review of Construction of Religious Boundaries in Sikh Past (Harjot Oberoi)', *Sikh Review*, vol. 42, no. 7, July 1994.

Dhindsa, Balvinder Kaur, 'Some Aspects of the Society of 18th Century Punjab', *Proceedings of the Punjab History Conference*, 24th session, 1991.

District Gazetteer of Rawalpindi, 1883-4.

Duggal, S.L., *Agricultural Atlas of Punjab*, Ludhiana: Punjab Agricultural University, 1966.

Dunning, Stephen, 'The Sikh Religion: An Examination of Some of the Western Studies', *The Journal of Religious Studies*, vol. II, no. 1, Autumn 1970.

Dusenbery, Verne, 'A Word as Guru: Sikh Scripture and its Translation Controversy', *History of Religions*, vol. 31, no. 4, 1992.

Dwyer, William J., *Bhakti in Kabir*, Patna: Associated Book Agency, 1981.

Eaton, Richard M., 'The Political and Religious Authority of the Shrine of Baba Farid', in *Essays on Islam and Indian History*, New Delhi: Oxford University Press, 2000.

Eliade Mircea, *The Encyclopaedia of Religion*, New York: Macmillan Publications, 1987.

Falcon, R.W., *Hand book on Sikhs for the Use of Regimental Officers*, Allahabad: Pioneer Press, 1896.

Falk, Nancy and Rita M. Gross, eds., *Unspoken Worlds: Women's Religious Lives in Non-Western Cultures*, San Francisco: Harper and Row, 1980.

Fenn, Richard K., 'The Sociology of Religion: A Critical Survey', in *Sociology: The State of the Art*, ed. Tom Bottomore et al., London: Sage, 1982.

Foster, William, ed. *Early Travels in India, 1583-1619*, London: Oxford University Press, 1921; (rpt., Delhi: Low Price Publications, 2012).

Foucault, Michel, *The History of Sexuality*, vol. 1: *An Introduction*, NewYork: Vintage, 1980.

French, Louis E., 'The Taunt in Popular Martyrologies', in *The Transmission of Sikh Heritage in the Diaspora*, ed. Pashaura Singh and N. Gerald Barrier, Delhi: Manohar, 1996.

Garg, Balwant, 'It's God and Gurudwara now for Punjab's Unwanted Girl Child', *The Times of India*, Bangalore edn., 18 November 2007.

Gazetteer of Rohtak District, 1883-4, Calcutta: compiled and published under the authority of the Punjab Government, Calcutta, n.d.

Gazetteer of the Ferozepur District, 1915, Lahore: Civil and Military Gazette Press, 1916.

Gazetteer of the Ferozepur District, 1915, Printed by the Superintendent, Government Printing, Punjab, 1916, Relied Sale Agents: Rama Krishna & Sons (Lahore, 1916), Tracker Spine & Company, Calcutta & Shimla.

Geertz, Clifford, 'Religion as a Cultural System', in *Anthropological Approaches to the Study of Religion*, ed. Michael Banton, London: Tavistock Publications, 1966.

Gill, M.K., *The Role and Status of Women in Sikhism*, Delhi: National Book Shop, 1995.

Gill, Tejwant Singh, 'Guru Nanak's View of Women', *Journal of Sikh Studies*, vol. 20, no. 2, 1996.

Ginzburg, Carlo, *The Cheese and the Worms: The Cosmos of a Sixteenth-Century Miller*, Baltimore, MD: Johns Hopkins University Press, 1992.

Grewal, J.S., 'Khalsa of Guru Gobind Singh: A Problem in Historiography', *Proceedings of the Punjab History Conference*, 2nd Session, 1966.

——, 'The Prem Sumarg: A Theory of Sikh Social Order', *Proceedings of the Punjab History Conference*, 1st Session, 1968.

——, *From Guru Nanak to Maharajah Ranjit Singh*, Amritsar: Guru Nanak Dev University, 1972.

——, ed. *Studies in Local and Regional History*, Amritsar: Guru Nanak Dev University, 1974.

——, 'The Historian's Punjab', in *Miscellaneous Articles*, J.S. Grewal, Amritsar: Guru Nanak University, 1974.

——, *Guru Nanak in History*, Chandigarh: Panjab University, rpt., 1979.

——, 'A Perspective on Early Sikh History', in *Sikh Studies: Comparative Perspective on a Changing Tradition*, ed. Mark Jurgensmeyer and N. Gerald Barrier, Berkeley: Graduate Theological Union 1979.

——, 'Dissent in Early Sikhism', *Proceedings of the Punjab History Conference*, 14th session, 1980.

——, 'Literary Evidence: The Case of Waris', *Proceedings of the Indian History Congress*, 43rd Session, 1982.

——, *The Sikhs of the Punjab*, New Delhi: Cambridge University Press, 1990.

——, *Guru Nanak and Patriarchy*, Simla: Indian Institute of Advanced Study, 1993.

——, 'Punjabi Literature, 1750-1850', *Sikhism and Secularism: Essays in Honour of Prof. Harbans Singh*, ed. Dharam Singh, Harman Publishing House, 1994.

——, 'The Hir of Ahmed', *Proceedings of the Punjab History Conference*, 26th Session, 1994.

——, 'Inaugural Address', *Proceedings of the Punjab History Conference*, 27th Session, 1995.

——, *Sikh Ideology, Polity and Social Order*, New Delhi: Manohar, 1996.

——, 'The Prem Sumarg: A Theory of Sikh Social Order', in *Essays in Honour of Dr. Ganda Singh*, ed. Harbans Singh and N. Gerald Barrier, Patiala: Punjabi University, 1996.

―, 'A Gender Perspective on Guru Nanak', in *Women in Indian History: Social, Economic, Political and Cultural Perspectives*, ed. Kiran Pawar, Patiala & Delhi: Vision & Venture, 1996.

―, 'The Sikh Panth in the Vars of Bhai Gurdas', in *History and Ideology: The Khalsa over Three Hundred Years*, ed. J.S. Grewal and Indu Banga, New Delhi: Tulika Books and Indian History Congress, 1999.

―, 'Foundation of the Sikh Faith', in *Five Centuries of Sikh Tradition, Ideology, Society, Politics and Culture*, ed. Reeta Grewal and Sheena Pall, Delhi: Manohar, 2005.

―, 'Guru Nanak and his Panth', in *The Sikhs: Ideology, Institutions and Identity*, New Delhi: Oxford University Press, 2009.

―, *Recent Debates in Sikh Studies: An Assessment*, New Delhi: Manohar, 2011.

Grewal, J.S. and Indu Banga, *Early Nineteenth Century Panjab: From Ganesh Das'Char Bagh-i-Panjab*, Amritsar: Guru Nanak Dev University, 1975.

―, eds. *History and Ideology: The Khalsa Over 300 Years*, New Delhi: Tulika Books and Indian History Congress, 1999.

Grewal, J.S. and Irfan Habib, eds. *Sikh History from Persian Sources*, Delhi: Tulika Books and Indian History Congress, 2001.

Grewal, J.S. and S.S. Bal, *Guru Gobind Singh*, Chandigarh: Punjab University, 1967.

Grewal, Rita and Sheena Pall, eds. *Five Centuries of Sikh Tradition, Ideology, Society, Politics and Culture: Essays for Indu Banga*, New Delhi: Manohar, 2005.

Gross, Rita M., 'Studying Women in Religion: Conclusions Twenty Five Years Later', in *Today's Woman in World Religions*, ed. Arvind Sharma, Albany: SUNY Press, 1994.

―, ed. *Beyond Androcentrism: New Essays on Women and Religion*, Montana: Scholars Press, 1977.

Gulati, G.D., 'Anecdotal Account of Medieval Punjab, The Evidence of *Fawaid-al-Fuad*', *Proceedings of the Punjab History Conference*, 34th Session, 2002.

Gulati, Saroj; *Women and Society in North India in 11th & 12th Centuries*, Delhi: Chanakya Publications, 1985.

Gupta, Hari Ram, *History of the Sikhs*, 6 vols., New Delhi: Munshiram Manoharlal, 1980.

Gupta, Susheel, *The Sikh Religion: A Symposium*, Calcutta: 1958.

Gurevich, Aron Y., *Categories of Medieval Culture*, Oxfordshire: Routledge & Kegan Paul, 1984.

Gustafson, W. Eric and Kenneth W. Jones, eds., *Sources on Punjab History*, New Delhi: Manohar, 1975.

Habib, Irfan, 'Akbar and Social Inequities A Study of the Evolution of His Ideas', *Proceedings of Indian History Congress*, vol. 53 (1992), published by Indian History Congress.

——, 'Caste in Indian History', in *Essays in Indian History: Towards a Marxist Perception*, New Delhi: Tulika Books, 1995.

——, 'Jats of Punjab and Sind', *Essays in Honour of Dr. Ganda Singh*, ed. Harbans Singh and N. Gerald Barrier, Patiala: Punjabi University, 1976.

——, *An Atlas of the Mughal Empire*, New Delhi: Oxford University Press, 1982.

——, *Essays in Indian History: Towards a Marxist Perception*, New Delhi: Tulika Books, 1995.

——, *The Agrarian System of Mughal India, 1556-1707*, 2nd edition, New Delhi: Oxford University Press, 1999.

Hans, Surjit Singh, *A Reconstruction of Sikh History from Sikh Literature*, Jalandhar: ABS Publications, 1988.

Hardy, Peter, 'Islam in Medieval India', in *Sources of Indian Tradition*, ed. W.M. Theodore de Barry, New York: Columbia University Press, 1958

Hasan, S. Nurul, 'Medieval Punjab', in *Essays in Honour of Dr. Ganda Singh*, ed. Harbans Singh and N. Gerald Barrier, Patiala: Punjabi University, 1976.

Hawley, John Stratton, *Sati, the Blessing and the Curse: the Burning of Wives in India*, New York: Oxford University Press, 10th edn. 1994.

Hershman, Paul and Hilary Standing, eds. *Punjabi Kinship and Marriage*, Delhi: Hindustan Publishing Corporation, 1981.

Hess, Linda and Shukdev Singh, *The Bijak of Kabir*, Delhi: Motilal Banarsidas, 1986.

Hobsbawm, Eric and Terence Ranger, eds., *The Invention of Tradition*, Cambridge: Cambridge University Press, 1983.

Holm, Jean and John Bowker, eds., *Women in Religion*, London: Pinter.

Horowitz, Berny and Madhu Kishwar, 'Family Life – The Unequal Deal: Women's Condition and Family Life among Agricultural Labourers and Small Farmers in a Punjab Village', in *Search of Answers: Indian Women's Voices from Manushi*, eds. Madhu Kishwar and Ruth Vanita, London: Zed Books, 1984.

Hugo, F., *A Dictionary of the Social Sciences*, Delhi: Ambica Publications, 1977.

Ibbetson, D.C., *Census of the Punjab: 1881*, Calcutta: Superintendent of Government Printing, 1883.

——, *Punjab Castes*, rpt., Delhi: Low Price Publications, 1993.

——, *The Religion of the Punjab*, Calcutta: Government Printing Press, 1883.

Ikram, S.M., *Muslim Civilization in India*, ed. Anslie T. Embree, New York & London: Columbia University Press, 1965.

Jafferey, Patricia, *Frogs in a Well: Indian Women in Purdah*, New Delhi: Manohar, 2000.

Jafri, S.Z.H., ed. *Recording the Progress of Indian History: Symposia Papers of the Indian History Congress, 1992-2010*, Delhi: Primus Books, 2012.

Jain, Sharda, et al., 'Deorala Episode: Women's Protest in Rajasthan', *Economic and Political Weekly*, 22: 45, 7 November 1987.

Jakobsh, R. Doris, 'Gender Issues in Sikh Studies: Hermeneutics of Affirmation or Hermeneutics of Suspicion', in *The Transmission of Sikh Heritage in the Diaspora*, ed. Pashaura Singh and N. Gerald Barrier, New Delhi: Manohar, 1996.

——, 'Where are the Women? Making Room for Women in Sikh Studies: A North American Perspective', *Proceedings of the Punjab History Conference*, 29th Session, 1997.

——, 'Construction of Gender in History and Religion: The Sikh Case', in *Faces of Feminine in Ancient Medieval & Modern India*, ed. Mandakranta Bose, New York: Oxford University Press, 2000.

——, *Relocating Gender in Sikh History: Transformation, Meaning and Identity*, New Delhi: Oxford University Press, 2003.

——, 'What's in the Name? Circumscribing Sikh Female Nomenclature', *Sikhism and History*, New Delhi: Oxford University Press, 2004.

Jamison, Stephanie W., *Sacrificed Wife/Sacrificer's Wife: Women, Ritual, and Hospitality in Ancient India*, New York: Oxford University Press, 1996.

Jammu, Parkash Singh, 'The Development of Dowry System in Punjab', *Proceedings of the Punjab History Conference*, 11th Session, 1976.

Johal, Daljinder Singh, 'Institution of Marriage in Medieval Punjabi Literature', *Proceedings of the Punjab History Conference*, 16th Session, 1982.

——, 'Evidence on Religion & Religious Groups in Heer Waris Shah', *Proceedings of the Punjab History Conference*, 14th Session, 1980.

Jones, Kenneth W., 'Changing Gender Relationships Among Hindus in Early Punjab', in *Five Punjabi Centuries: Polity, Economy, Society, & Culture, c. 1500-1990*; ed. Indu Banga, Delhi: Manohar, 2000.
Joseph, E.,*Customary Law of the Rohtak District: 1910*, Lahore: Superintendent of Government Printing, 1911.
Joshi, L.M., 'Religion and Society in Indian Civilization', *The Journal of Religious Studies*, vol. VIII, no. 2, Autumn 1980.
——, ed. *History and Culture of Punjab*, vol. I, Patiala: Punjabi University, 2000.
Juergensmeyer, Mark and N. Gerald Barrier, eds., *Sikh Studies: Comparative Perspectives on a Changing Tradition*, Berkeley: Graduate Theological Union, 1979.
Kane, Pandurang Vaman, *History of Dharma Shastra*, 8 vols., Poona: Bhandarkar Oriental Research Institute, 1962.
Kannabiran, V. and K. Kannabiran, 'Caste and Gender: Understanding Dynamics of Power and Violence', *Economic and Political Weekly*, 14 September 1991.
Kaul, Hari Kishan (Superintendent of Census Operations), 'Note on Female Infanticide, Home Police', in Stracey T.P. Russell, *History of the Muhiyals: The Militant Brahman Race of India*, Lahore: Civil and Military Gazette, 1911.
Kaur, Bhupinder, *Status of Women in Sikhism*, Amritsar: Shiromani Gurdwara Prabandhak Committee, 2000.
Kaur, Gurnam, ed. *Sikh Value System and Social Change*, Patiala: Punjabi University, 1995.
Kaur, Iqbal, 'Mata Gujri', in *Eminent Sikh Women*, ed. Mohinder Kaur Gill, New Delhi: Vijay Publications, 1999.
Kaur, Jagjit Singh, 'Women in Punjabi Folk Songs', in *Women in Indian Folklore*, ed. S. Sengupta, Calcutta: Indian Publications, 1969.
Kaur, Jasbir, 'Mata Gujri: Consort & Mother', *Panchbati Sandesh*, January-March 1999.
Kaur, Jasdeep, 'The Role and Position of Women in Sikh Religion', *Studies in Sikhism and Comparative Religion*, vol. 12, no. 2, July-December 1993.
Kaur, Kanwaljit, 'Sikh Women', in *Fundamental Issues in Sikh Studies*, ed. Kharak Singh et al., Chandigarh: Institute of Sikh Studies, 1992.
Kaur, Sahib, 'Role of Women in Sikhism', *Sikh Review*, vol. 42, no. 10, 1994.
Kaur, Simran, *Prasidh Sikh Bibiyan*, Amritsar: Singh Brothers, 1991.

Kaur, Sukhjit, 'Mata Jeeto', in *Eminent Sikh Women*, ed. Mohinder Kaur Gill, New Delhi: Vijay Publications, 1999.

——, 'Mata Maha Devi', in *Eminent Sikh Women*, ed. Mohinder Kaur Gill, New Delhi: Vijay Publications, 1999.

——, 'Mata Sahib Kaur', in *The Guru's Consorts*, ed. Mohinder Kaur Gill, New Delhi: Radha Publications, 1992.

Kaur, Surjit, 'Place of Women in Sikhism: Unequal Partners', *Sikh Review*, vol. 44, no. 4, April 1996.

Kaur, Tajinderpal, 'Bibi Bhani', in *The Guru's Consorts*, ed. Mohinder Kaur Gill, New Delhi: Radha Publications, 1992.

Kaur, Upinderjit, 'Role and Status of Women in Sikhism', *The Journal of Religious Studies*, vol. 19, no. 1, 1991.

——, 'Women and Sikh Religion', *Sikh Religion and Economic Development*, New Delhi: National Book Organisation, 1990.

Keene, H.G., *A Sketch of the History of Hindustan*, Delhi: Idarah-i-Adabiyat-i-Delli, rpt., 1972.

Kesar, Zinat, *Muslim Women in Medieval India*, Delhi: Janaki Prakashan, 1992.

Khan, Ahsan Raza, 'The Problem of the North-Western Frontier of Hindustan in the First Quarter of the Sixteenth Century', *Proceedings of the Indian History Congress*, vol. 28, Mysore, 1966.

Kinsley, David, *Hindu Goddesses*, Berkeley: University of California Press, 1986.

Kishwar, Madhu and Ruth Vanita, eds., *In Search of Answers: Indian Women's Voices from Manushi*, 2nd rev. edn. New Delhi: Horizon India Books, 1991.

Kohli, Surender Singh, *Position of Women in Sikhism*, New Delhi: Harman Publishers, 1994.

Kohli, Yash, ed. *The Women of Punjab*, Bombay: Chic Publications, 1983.

Kumar, Nirmal, 'Guru Granth Sahib: An Ideological Discourse in Connection with Social and Religious Reforms', *Proceedings of the Punjab History Conference*, 36th Session, 2004.

Kumar, Nita, 'Introduction', in *Women as Subjects: South Asian Histories*, ed. Nita Kumar, Charlottesville: University Press of Virginia, 1994.

Lal, Muni, *Babur, Life and Times*, Delhi: Vikas Publishing House, 1977.

Latif, Syad Muhammad, *History of the Panjab: From the Remotest Antiquity to the Present Time*, New Delhi: Kalyani Publishers, rpt., 1994.

Leslie, Julia, *The Perfect Wife*, New Delhi: Oxford University Press, 1989.

Lewis, Gilbert, *Day of Shining Red: An Essay on Understanding Ritual*, Cambridge University Press, 1988.
Lewis, Oscar, *Village Life in Northern India*, New York: Vintage Books, 1958.
Lorenzen, David N., 'Introduction', 'The Historical Vicissitudes of Bhakti Religion', in *Bhakti Religion in North India: Community, Identity and Political Action*, ed. David Lorenzen, Delhi: Manohar, 1996.
——, 'The Lives of Nirguni Saints', in *Bhakti Religion in North India: Community Identity and Political Action*, ed. David N. Lorenzen, Albany: Suny Press, 1995.
——, ed. *Bhakti Religion in North India: Community Identity and Political Action*, Albany: Suny Press, 1995.
Luthra, P.S., 'Sikhism', in *Religions and the Status of Women*, ed. Jyotsna Chatterji, New Delhi: Uppal Publishing House, 1990.
Lyall, Sir Alfred, *Asiatic Studies: Religious and Social*, London: John Murray, 1884.
Macauliffe, Max Arthur, *The Sikh Religion: Its Gurus, Sacred Writings and Authors*, 6 vols., Delhi: Low Price Publications, 1990.
Macauliffe, Max et al., *The Sikh Religion: A Symposium*, Calcutta: Susil Gupta (India) Private Ltd., 1958.
Majumdar, R.C., *The Classical Accounts of India*, Calcutta: Firma K.L. Mukhopadhyay, 1960.
Malhotra, Anshu, *Gender, Caste and Religious Identities: Restructuring Class in Colonial Punjab*, New Delhi: Oxford University Press, 2002.
Malhotra, Anshu and Farina Mir, ed. *Punjab Reconsidered: History, Culture and Practice*, New Delhi: Oxford University Press, 2012.
Mani, Lata, *Contentious Traditions: Debate on Sati in Colonial India*, Berkeley, Calif.: University of California Press, December 1998.
Mansukhani, Gobind Singh, 'The Origin and Development of Sikh Studies', *Fundamental Issues in Sikh Studies*, ed. Kharak Singh et al., Chandigarh: Institute of Sikh Studies, 1992.
Mayer, A.C., *Caste and Kinship in Central India*, London: Routledge and Kegan Paul, 1960.
McCrindle, *The Invasion of India by Alexander the Great*, New Delhi: Cosmo Publications, rpt., 1983.
McLeod, W.H., 'Sikhism and Gender', *Sikhism*, London: Penguin Books, 1997.
——, *Exploring Sikhism: Aspects of Sikh Identity, Culture and Thought*, New Delhi: Oxford University Press, 2000.

———, *Guru Nanak and the Sikh Religion*, New Delhi: Oxford University Press, 1996.
———, *Historical Dictionary of Sikhism*, London: Scarecrow Press, 1995.
———, *Sikhism*, New Delhi: Penguin, 1997.
———, *Textual Sources for the Study of Sikhism*, Chicago: University of Chicago, 1984.
———, *The B40 Janam-Sakhi*, Amritsar: Guru Nanak Dev University, 1980.
———, *The Chaupa Singh Rahit-Nama*, Dunedin: University of Otago, 1987.
———, *The Evolution of the Sikh Community: Five Essays*, New Delhi: Oxford University Press, rpt., 1996.
———, *The Sikhs: History, Religion and Society*, New York: Columbia University Press, 1989.
———, *Who is Sikh? The Problem of Sikh Identity*, Oxford: Oxford University Press, 1992.
McMullen, Clarence O., *Religious Beliefs and Practices of the Sikhs in Rural Punjab*, New Delhi: Manohar, 1989.
Menon, Ritu and Kamla Bhasin, 'Recovery, Rupture, Resistance: Indian State and Abduction of Women during Partition', *Economic and Political Weekly*, 24 April 1993.
Minault, Gail, 'Others Voices, Other Rooms: The View from Zenana', in *Women as Subjects: South Asian Histories*, ed. Nita Kumar, Charlottesville: University Press of Virginia, 1994.
Minault, Gail, ed. *The Extended Family: Women and Political Participation in India and Pakistan*, Delhi: Chanakya, 1981.
Misra, Rekha, *Women in Mughal India (AD 1526-1748)*, Delhi: Munshiram Manoharlal, 1967.
Misra, Satish Chandra, 'The Medieval Reality: An Approach', Presidential Address (Medieval Section), *Proceedings of the Punjab History Conference Proceedings*, 11th Session, 1976.
Mohinder Singh, ed. *History and Culture of Panjab*, New Delhi: Atlantic, 1989.
Montgomery, R., *Minute on Infanticide in Punjab*, Lahore; Chronicle Press, 1853.
Moosvi, Shireen, 'The World of Labour in Mughal India (*c*.1500-1750)', *Proceedings of the Indian History Congress*, vol. 71 (2010-11).
———, *People, Taxation and Trade in Mughal India*, New Delhi: Oxford University Press, 2010.
Mukhiya, Harbans, 'The Conversion to Islam in the Punjab during the

16th-17th Centuries: A Preliminary Draft', *Proceedings of the Punjab History Conference*, 7th Session, 1972.

Myerhoff, Barbara and Sally Falk Moore, eds., *Secular Ritual*, Amsterdam: Van Gorcum, 1977.

Nabha, Bhai Kahn Singh, *Gurshabad Ratnakar Mahankosh*, Delhi: National Book Shop, rpt., 1995.

Nadvi, Maulana Syeed Hasan Ali, *Hindustani Musalman Ek Nazar Mein*, Urdu, 2nd edn. Lucknow: Majlis-e-Tahqiqat o-Nashriyat-e-Islam, 1974.

Nandy, Ashis, 'The Sociology of Sati', *Indian Express*, 5 October 1987.

Narang, Gokul Chand, *Transformation of Sikhism*, Lahore: New Book Society, 1946.

Nayyar, Gurbachan Singh, 'The Historic Decision of Abolishing Personal Guruship', Proceedings of the Punjab History Conference, 21st Session, 1987.

Nicholas, R. and R. Inden, *Kinship in Bengali Culture*, Chicago: University of Chicago Press, 1977.

Nijjar, Bakhshish Singh, 'Amusement and Sports in the Punjab under the Sultans (AD 1000-1526)', *Proceedings of the Punjab History Conference*, 2nd Session, 1966.

——, *Punjab Under the Sultans AD 1000-1526*, Delhi: Sterling Publishers, 1968.

Nizami, Khaliq Ahmad, ed. *Politics and Society during the Early Medieval Period: Collected Works of Professor Mohammad Habib*, vol. I, Aligarh: Centre of Advanced Study, Department of History and New Delhi: People's Publishing House, 1974.

Nizami, Khaliq Ahmad, *Religion and Politics in India during the Thirteenth Century*, New Delhi: Oxford University Press, 2002.

——, *Studies in Medieval Indian History and Culture*, Allhabad: Kitab Mahal, 1966.

——, *The Life and Times of Shaikh Farid-ud-din Ganj-i-Shakar*, rpt., Delhi: Idarah-i Adabiyat-i Delli, 1973.

O'Connell, Joseph T., *Religious Movements and Social Structure: The Case of Chaitanya's Vaishnavas of Bengal*, Shimla: Indian Institute of Advanced Studies, 1993.

O'Hanlon, Rosalind, 'Recovering the Subject: Subaltern Studies and Histories of Resistance in Colonial South Asia', *Modern Asian Studies*, vol. 22, 1988.

Oberoi, Harjot, 'Brotherhood of the Pure: The Poetics and Politics of Cultural Transgression', *Modern Asian Studies*, vol. 26, no. 1, 1992.

―――, 'From Ritual to Counter Ritual: Rethinking the Hindu-Sikh Question, 1884-1915', in *Sikh History and Religion in the Twentieth Century*, ed. Joseph T. O'Connell et al., Toronto: Center for South Asian Studies, University of Toronto, 1988.

―――, 'Popular Saints, Goddesses and Village Sacred Sites: Re-reading Sikh Experience in the Nineteenth Century', *History of Religions*, vol. 31, no. 4, 1992.

―――, *The Construction of Religious Boundaries: Culture, Identity and Diversity in the Sikh Tradition*, Delhi: Oxford University Press, 1994.

Ojha, P.N., *Aspects of Medieval Society and Culture*, Delhi: B.R. Publishing Corporation, 1978.

Oman, J. Camphell, *Cults, Customs and Superstitions of India*, London: T. Fisher Unwin, 1908.

Oman, J. Camphell, *The Mystics, Ascetics and Saints of India*, Delhi, Oriental Publishers, rpt., 1973.

Pawar, Kiran, ed. *Women in Indian History: Social, Economic, Political and Cultural Perspectives*, Patiala and Delhi: Vision & Venture, 1996.

Prinsep, Henry T., *Origin of Sikh Power in Punjab*, Patiala: Languages Department, Punjab, rpt., 1970.

Pruthi, Raj and Bela Rani Sharma, *Trends in Women Studies*, New Delhi: Anmol Publications, 1995.

―――, eds., *Sikhism and Women*, New Delhi: Anmol Publications, 1995.

Punjab District Gazetteers, published in the years stated and for the following districts: Dera Ghazi Khan (1883-4), Ferozepur (1883-4), Gurdaspur (1884), Jalandhar (1884), Lahore (1883-4), Ludhiana (1888-89), Rawalpindi (1883-4), Kalsia (1904), Nabha (1904).

Punjab State Gazetteers: Phulkian States (Patiala, Jind and Nabha), Lahore: The Civil and Military Gazette Press, 1901.

Qanungo, Kalika Ranjan, *Dara Shukoh*, vol. I, Calcutta: S.C. Sarkar, 1952.

Quotes about women in Granth Sahib, http://allaboutsikhs.com/articles/womenquotes.htm.

Qureshi, Ishtiaq Husain, *The Administration of the Sultanate of Delhi*, New Delhi: Oriental Books Reprint Corporation, rpt., 1971.

Radin, Paul, *Primitive Religion: Its Nature and Origin*, New York: Dover Publications, 1937.

Rajan, Rajeshwari S., 'Subject of Sati: Pain and Death in the Contemporary Discourse on Sati', *Yale Journal of Criticism*, 3:2 (1990).

Rattigan, W.H. *A Digest of Civil Law for the Punjab*, 13th edn. revised by Om Prakash Aggarwal, Allahabad: University Book Agency, 1953.

Ray, Bharati, ed., *From the Seams of History: Essays on Indian Women*, New Delhi, Oxford University Press, 1995.

Ray, Niharranjan, *The Sikhs and Sikh Society: A Study in Social Analysis*, Munshiram Manoharlal, 2nd rev. edn. 1975.

Ricoeur, Paul, *Freud and Philosophy*, New Haven: Yale University Press, 1970.

Roe, Charles A., *Tribal Law in the Punjab*, Lahore: Civil and Military Gazette Press, 1895.

Rogers, Susan Carol, 'Female Forms of Power and Myth of Male Dominance', *American Ethnologist*, vol. II, no. 4, 1975.

Rosaldo, M.Z. and L.L. Lamphere, edn. *Women, Culture and Society*, Stanford: Stanford University Press, 1974.

Rose, H.A., *A Glossary of the Tribes and Castes of the Punjab and North-West Frontier Province*, 3 vols., Lahore: The Civil and Military Gazette Press, 1911.

Roy, Kumkum, *Women in Early Indian Societies: Series in Early Indian History*, General Editor B.D. Chattopadhyaya, New Delhi: Manohar, 1999.

Sagoo, Harbans Kaur, 'Position of Women in Indian Society as Reflected in Guru Nanak's Hymns', *Studies in Sikhism and Comparative Religion*, vol. 16, no. 2, July-December 1997.

——, *Guru Nanak and the Indian Society*, New Delhi: Deep & Deep, 1993.

Sangari, Kumkum, 'Consent, Agency and Rhetorics of Incitement', *Economic and Political Weekly*, 28.18, 1 May 1993.

——, 'Mirabai and the Spiritual Economy of Bhakti', *Occasional Papers on History and Society*, (Second Series, Number XXVIII), New Delhi: Nehru Memorial Museumand Library, 2001.

——, 'Consent and Agency: Aspects of Feminist Historiography', in *Women in Indian History: Social, Economic, Political and Cultural Perspectives*, ed. Kiran Pawar, Patiala and Delhi: Vision &Venture, 1996.

Sangari, Kumkum and Sudesh Vaid, eds., *Recasting Women: Essays in Colonial History*, New Jersey: Rutgers University Press, 1990.

Sardar Singh Bhatia, 'Bibi Sahib Kaur (1771-1801)', in *Encyclopedia of Sikhism*, vol. 4, ed. Harbans Singh, Patiala: Punjabi University, 1998.

Schlingloff, D., 'Cotton-Manufacture in Ancient India', *Journal of Economic and Social History of the Orient*, vol. XVII, no. 1, March 1974.

Schomer, Karine, 'Kabir in the Guru Granth Sahib: An Exploratory Essay', in *Sikhs Studies: Comparative Perspective on a Changing Tradition*, ed. Mark Juergensmeyer and N. Gerald Barrier, Berkeley: Graduate Theological Union, 1979.

Schomer, Karine (author), and W.H. Mcleod (eds.), *The Sants: Studies in a Devotional Tradition in India*, Delhi: Motilal Banarsidass, 1987.

Scott, David C., 'Women and Patriarchy in World Religions', *The Journal of Religious Studies*, vol. XXI, no. 1, Spring 1992.

Scott, James C., *Weapons of the Weak: Everyday Forms of Peasant Resistance*, New Haven: Yale University, 1985.

Scott, Joan W., 'Gender: A Useful Category of Historical Analysis', *The American Historical Review*, vol. 91, no. 5, December 1986.

———, 'Gender: Still a Useful Category of Analysis?', *Diogenes*, vol. 57, Issue 1, October 2010.

———, *History of Gender and Politics*, New York: Columbia University Press, 1988.

Sekhon, Harinder Kaur, 'Sikhs and Rights of Women', *Nishaan*, vol. 4, 2002.

———, 'Women in Sikhism', *Seminar*, 476, April 1999.

———, 'Status of Women in Sikhism', http://www.sikhwomen.com/equality/social/history/statusofwomeninsikhism.htm.

Sekhon, Sant Singh, *A History of Punjabi Literature*, vol. II, Patiala: Punjabi University, 1996.

Selections from the Records of the Government of India, *Papers Relating to Infant Marriage and Enforced Widowhood in India*, India, Home Department, January 1886, Superintendent of Government Print, India.

Selvidge, Marla J., 'Powerful and Powerless Women in the Apocalypse: A Conflict of Passions', *The Journal of Religious Studies*, vol. 19, no. 1, 1991.

Shampotra, Mohan Lal, *Kuriti Nivaran*, Lahore, 1890.

Shankar, Raj Kumari, 'Women in Sikhism', in *Women in Indian Religions*, ed. Arvind Sharma, New Delhi: Oxford University Press, 2002.

Sharma, G.N., *Social Life in Medieval Rajasthan*, Agra: Lakshmi Narayan Aggarwal, 1968.

Sharma, Radha and Harish C. Sharma, 'The Position of Women in the Society of Punjab as Reflected in the Customary Laws', *Proceedings of the Punjab History Conference*, 30th Session, 1998.

Shea, David and Anthony Troyer, *The Dabistan or School of Manners*, Paris: Oriental Translation Fund, 1843.
Shobha, Savitra Chandra, *Medieval India and Hindi Bhakti Poetry: A Socio-Cultural Study*, Delhi: Har Anand Publications, 1996.
Singer, Milton, *When a Great Tradition Modernizes*, New York: Praeger Publishers, 1972.
Singh, Baghat,'Giani Gian Singh', *Proceedings of the Punjab History Conference*, 9th Session, 1975.
——, 'Condition of Women in the Punjab in the Early Nineteenth Century', *The Punjab Past and Present*, October 1981.
——, 'Mata Kishan Kaur', *The Guru's Consorts*, ed. Mohinder Kaur Gill, New Delhi: Radha Publications, 1992.
——, 'The Role of Sangat in the Development of Sikh Community', *Proceedings of the Punjab History Conference*, 3rd Session, 1968.
——, *Giani Gian Singh*, Patiala: Punjabi University, 1978.
Singh, Bhai Jodh, 'Sri Guru Amar Das Ji', *The Punjab Past and Present*, vol. 8, no. 2, 1979.
——, ed., *Bani Bhagat Kabir Ji Steek*, Patiala: Punjabi University, rpt., 2016.
Singh, Bhai Vir, *Satwant Kaur*, Eng. tr. Ujagar Singh Bawa, New Delhi: Bhai Vir Singh Sahitya Sadan, 1988.
——, *Sundri*, Eng. tr. Gobind Singh Mansukhani, New Delhi: Bhai Vir Singh Sahitya Sadan, 1988.
Singh, Bhajan, 'Mata Damodri', *Eminent Sikh Women*, ed. Mohinder Kaur Gill, New Delhi: Vijay Publications, 1999.
Singh, Chetan, 'Interaction Between Divergent Social Formations: Possible Explanation for Some Instances of Unrest in the 17th Century Punjab', *Proceedings of the Punjab History Congress*, 30th Session, 1998.
——, 'Polity, Economy and Society Under the Mughals', in *Five Punjabi Centuries*, ed. Indu Banga, New Delhi: Manohar, 1997.
——, 'Region, Realm and Rule: Aspects of Politics and Governance in Punjab under Akbar', Presidential Address (Medieval Section), *Proceedings of the Punjab History Conference*, 34th Session, 2002.
——, *Region and Empire: Punjab in the Seventeenth Century*, New Delhi: Oxford University Press, 1991.
Singh, Daljeet, 'Nathism, Vaishnavism and Sikhism: A Comparative Study', in *Perspectives on the Sikh Tradition*, ed. Gurdev Singh, Chandigarh: Siddharth Publishers, 1986.
Singh, Daljeet, *Punjab Socio-Economic Condition (AD 1501-1700)*, Delhi: Common Wealth, 2004.

———, 'Sri Guru Granth Sahib: The Concept of God, Universe, Shabad, Ego and Guru', *Proceedings of the Punjab History Conference*, 36th Session, 2004.

Singh, Darshan, 'The Su Dharam Marg Granth: A Little Known Source of the Sikh Code of Conduct', *Proceedings of the Punjab History Conference*, 12th Session, 1978.

Singh, Dharam, 'The Social Dimensions of Sikh Theology', in *Sikhism and Secularism Essays in Honour of Prof. Harbans Singh*, ed. Dharam Singh, Harman Publishing House, 1994.

Singh, Diwan, *The Revolution of Guru Nanak*, Chandigarh: People's Publishing House, 1993.

Singh, Fauja, 'Guru Amar Das: Life and Thought', *The Punjab Past and Present*, vol. 8, no. 2, 1979.

———, *Guru Amar Das: Life and Teachings*, New Delhi: Sterling Publishers, 1979.

———, *History of the Punjab, (AD 1000-1526)*, vol. III, Patiala: Punjabi University, 1972.

———, ed. *Historians and Historiography of the Sikhs*, New Delhi: Oriental Publishers, 1978.

Singh, G.B. and D.R. Narang, 'Correct Date of Birth of Guru Gobind Singh', *Proceedings of the Punjab History Conference Proceedings*, 24th Session, 1991.

Singh, Ganda, 'Major Sources of Early Sikh History', in *History and Ideology: The Khalsa over Three Hundred Years*, ed. J.S. Grewal and Indu Banga, New Delhi: Tulika Books and Indian History Congress, 1999.

———, 'Nanakpanthis: Eng. tr. from *Dabistan-i Mazahib* by Zulfiqar Ardistani', *The Punjab Past and Present*, vol. I, no. 1, 1967.

———, 'Presidential Address: Medieval Section', *Proceedings of the Punjab History Conference*, 3rd Session, 1968.

Singh, Gopal, *Thus Spake The Tenth Master*, Patiala: Punjabi University, 1978.

Singh, Gulcharan, 'Mata Gujri: A Life of Travail and Sacrifices', *Spokesman Weekly*, vol. 26, nos. 16-17, 1979.

———, 'Mata Gujri', *Khera: Journal of Religious Understanding*, vol. 5, no. 4, March 1984.

———, 'Women's Lib in Sikh Scriptures & Sociology', *The Sikh Review*, vol. 36, no. 411, 1998.

Singh, Gurbux, 'Society in the Punjab under Ranjit Singh: Mufti Ali-Ud Din's Analysis', *Proceedings of the Punjab History Conference*, 10th Session, 1976.

Singh, Gurcharan, *Studies in Punjab History and Culture*, New Delhi: Enkay Publishers, 1990.
Singh, Gurdeep, 'Homage to Mata Gujri', *Sikh Review*, 23 (259), July 1975.
Singh, Harbans, 'Guru Granth Sahib:Guru Eternal for the Sikhs', *Sikh Courier*, vol. 12, no. 14, Summer 1986.
——, 'Place of Women in Sikhism', *Khera: Journal of Religious Understanding*, vol. 9, no. 3, 1990.
——, 'Status of Women in Sikh Religion', *Sikh Courier*, vol. 9, No. 3, Sum-August 1978.
——, 'Status of Women in Sikhism', ed. Yash Kohli, *The Women of Punjab*, Bombay: Chic Publications, 1983.
——, 'Status of Women in Sikhism', *Sikh Messenger*, August 1985.
Singh, Hari, *Mata Sahib Kaur 1681-1747*, Patiala: Punjabi University, 1988.
Singh, Harjinder Dilgeer, *The Sikh Reference Book*, Denmark: Sikh Educational Trust, 1997.
Singh, Jagjit, 'Caste System and the Sikhs', in *Perspectives on the Sikh Tradition*, ed. Gurdev Singh, Chandigarh: Siddharth Publications; Patiala: Academy of Sikh Religion and Culture, 1986; Amritsar: Singh Brothers, 1996.
Singh, Jaspal, 'Mata Khivi', in *The Guru's Consorts*, ed. Mohinder Kaur Gill, New Delhi: Radha Publications, 1992.
Singh, Jaswant, 'Status of Women in Sikhism', *Sikh Courier*, 41(91), Spr-Sum 2001; also in *Abstracts of Sikh Studies*, vol. 3, no. 4, 2001.
Singh, Joginder, 'Mata Nanki', in *The Guru's Consorts*, ed. Mohinder Kaur Gill, New Delhi: Radha Publications, 1992.
Singh, Kanwaljit Kaur, 'Sikh Women', *Sikh Messenger*, Spr-Sum, 1990.
Singh, Kanwaljit Kaur, 'Sikhism', in *Women in Religion*, ed. Jean Holm and John Bowker, London: Pinter Publishers, 1994.
Singh, Kartar and Gurdial Singh Dhillon, *Stories from Sikh History*, Book II, New Delhi, Hemkumt Press, 1975.
Singh, Kharak et al., *Fundamental Issues in Sikh Studies*, Chandigarh: Institute of Sikh Studies, 1992.
Singh, Khushwant, *A History of Sikhs*, 2 vols., Delhi: Oxford University Press, 1991.
Singh, Kirpal, 'Condition of Women as Depicted in Adi Guru Granth', *Journal of Sikh Studies*, vol. 20, no. 2, 1996; also in *Proceedings of the Punjab History Conference*, 24th Session, 1991.
——, 'The Adi Granth as a Source of Social History and Culture', *Proceedings of the Punjab History Conference*, 36th session, 2004.

Singh, Maheep, 'The Status of Women in Hindu and Sikh Societies', *Studies in Sikhism and Comparative Religion*, vol. 9, no. 1, April 1990.
Singh, Mohinder, ed. *Prof. Harbans Singh: Commemoration Volume*, Delhi: Prof Harbans Singh Commemoration Committee, 1988.
Singh, Mohinder, *History and Culture of Punjab*, New Delhi, Atlantic, 1989.
Singh, Narenderpal,'Outstanding Women in Sikhism', in *The Women of Punjab*, ed. Yash Kohli, Bombay: Chic Publications, 1983.
Singh, Nikky-Guninder Kaur, 'Bridal Symbol in Sikh Literature', *Khera: Journal of Religious Studies*, vol. 18, no. 2, 1990.
——, 'Mother in the Guru Granth: A Literary Resource for the Emerging Global Society', *Khera: Journal of Religious Understanding*, vol. 13, no. 1, 1993.
——, 'Poetic Rhythm and Historical Account: The Portrait of Guru Nanak Through Bhai Gurdas', *International Journal of Punjab Studies*, vol., 5, no. 2, New Delhi, Thousand Oaks, London: Sage Publications, 1998, pp. 142-3.
——, 'Sikh Bridal Symbol: An Epiphany of Interconnections', *Journal of Feminist Studies in Religion*, vol. 8, no. 2, Fall 1992.
——, 'Sikhism (Women)' in *Encyclopedia of Women and World Religion*, vol. 2, ed. Serenity Young, New York: Macmillan Reference, 1999.
——, 'The Significance of Guru Gobind Singh Recalling Durga', *Sikh Review*, vol. 37, no. 7, 1989.
——, *The Feminine Principle in the Sikh Vision of the Transcendent*, Cambridge [England]; New York, NY, USA: Cambridge University Press, 1993.
Singh, Nirbhay, 'Folkloric Perspective of Cultural Plurality and National Identity,' *The Sikh Viewpoint*, vol. XXIV, no. 1, Spring 1994.
Singh, Pashaura, *The Guru Granth Sahib: Canon Meaning and Authority*, New Delhi: Oxford University Press, 2000.
Singh, Pashaura and N.G. Barrier, eds., *The Transmission of Sikh Heritage in the Diaspora*, New Delhi: Manohar, 1996.
Singh, Sudershan,'Status of Women under the Sikh Gurus',in *Sikh Religion*, New Delhi: Orient Publishers, 1979.
Singh, Sukhmander, 'A Work of Scholarly Indulgence', in *Invasion of Religious Boundaries: A Critique of Harjot Oberoi's Work*, ed. Jasbir Singh Mann et al., Vancouver: Canadian Sikh Study & Teaching Society.

Singh, Sulakhan,'Some Problems of Udasi History Upto 1849', *Punjab History Conference Proceedings*, Patiala: Punjabi University, 1979, pp. 138-43; Sulakhan Singh, 'Literary Evidence on the Udasis: Sant Rein's Udasi Bodh', *Proceedings of Indian History Congress*, vol. 44 (1983), pp. 292-7, published by Indian History Congress.

Singh, Surinder, *The Making of Medieval Panjab: Politics, Society and Culture, c.1000-c.1500*, New Delhi: Manohar, 2020.

Singh, Teja,'Women in Sikhism', in *Essays in Sikhism*, New Delhi: Siddhartha Publishers, 1989.

——, *Essays in Sikhism*, Lahore: Sikh University Press, 1944.

——, *What Sikhism did for Womankind?* Amritsar: Sikh Tract Society, 1921.

Singh, Teja and Ganda Singh, *Short History of the Sikhs*, vol. I, *1469-1765*, Patiala: Punjabi University, rpt., 1989.

Sinha, Narender Krishna, *Rise of the Sikh Power*, Calcutta: University Press, 1946.

Sirhindi, Shaikh Ahmad, *Maktubat-i-Imam-i-Rabbani*, vol. I, Letter no. 192, Munshi Nawal Kishore, Lucknow, quoted in Irfan Habib, *Exploring Medieval Gender History*, Symposia Paper No. 23, Indian History Congress, 2000.

Smart, Ninian, *Man's Religious Quest: Hindu Patterns of Liberation*, Milton Keynes: Open University, 1981.

Sobha, Savitri Chandra, 'Social Life As Reflected in the Works of Surdas', in *Surdas; A Revaluation*, Nagendra, ed. National Publishing House, New Delhi, 1979.

——, *Medieval India and Hindi Bhakti Poetry: A Socio-Cultural Study*, Delhi: Har-Anand Publications, 1996

Sodhi, N.S.,'Religion and Society', *The Journal of Religious Studies*, vol. XIII, Spring, 1985.

Srinivas, M.N., *Caste in Modern India and Other Essays*, Bombay: Asia Publishing House, 1962.

Steel, F.A., *The Garden of Fidelity: Being the Autobiography of Flora Annie Steel. 1847-1929*, London: MacMillan and Co. Limited, 1929.

Strabo, Bk. XV Chap 30 cited in Women's UN Report Network, 8 September 2008, http://wunrn.wpengine.com, (5.3, Ancient Travellers' Accounts).

Suri, Pushpa, 'Mata Gujari', in *The Guru's Consorts*, ed. Mohinder Kaur Gill, New Delhi: Radha Publications, 1992.

Suri, Surindar S., 'The Impact of Religion on Punjab's Culture', *The Journal of Religious Studies*, vol. XIV, no. 1, Spring 1986.

——, 'Position of Women in Sikhism', in *The Authority of the Religions and the Status of Women*, ed. Jyotsna Chatterji, Delhi: Uppal Publishing House, 1990.

Suri, V.S., *Punjab through the Ages: Historical Survey of Political, Territorial and Administrative Changes in North Western India from the Earliest Times upto 1966*, Chandigarh: Punjab Itihas Prakashan, 1971.

Talib, Gurbachan Singh, 'Guru Nanak Dev's Vision of History', *The Journal of Religious Studies*, vol. VIII, no. 1, Spring 1980.

——, 'Women in Sikhism', in *Encyclopaedia of Sikhism*, vol. 4, ed. Harbans Singh, Patiala: Punjabi University, 1998.

Temple, Richard, ed. *Punjab Dian Lok Gathawan*, Patiala: Bhasha Vibhag, 1970.

Thomas, Terry, 'Sikhism: The Voice of the Guru', Units 12-13 of the Open University Series, *Man's Religious Quest*, Milton Keynes: The Open University Press, 1970.

Thapar, Romila, 'In History', *Seminar*, vol. 342, February 1988.

——, *The Penguin History of Early India*, New Delhi: Penguin Books, 2002.

Tharu, Susie and K. Lalita, eds., *Women Writings in India: 600 BC to the Present*, vol. 1, New York: Feminist, 1991.

The Gazetteer of Punjab, Provincial, 1888-9.

Thomas, Frederick William, *Mutual Influence of Mohammedans and Hindus in India*, Cambridge: Deighton, Bell & Co., 1892.

Thomas, Terry, 'Sikhism; The Voice of the Guru', in *Man's Religious Quest*, Milton Keynes: Open University Press, 1970.

Titus, Murray, *Islam in India and Pakistan*, Calcutta: YMCA Publishing House, 1959.

Tod, James, *Annals and Antiquities of Rajasthan*, vol. II, ed. William Crooke, Delhi: Motilal Banarsidass, rpt., 1971.

Tripathi, R.P., *Rise and Fall of the Mughal Empire*, Allahabad: Central Book Depot, 1957.

Tupper, Charles Lewis, *Punjab Customary Law*, Calcutta: Superintendent of Government Printing, 1882.

Upadhyay, Vasudeva, *Socio-Religious Condition of North India, AD 700-1200*, Varanasi: Chowkhamba Sanskrit Series Office, 1964.

Vanina, Eugenia, *Ideas and Society in India from 16th to 18th Centuries*, Oxford University Press, Delhi: 1996.

Verma, Ramkumar, *Hindi Sahitya Ka Alochnatamak Itihas*, 4th edn. Allahabad: Ramnarayan Benimadhav, 1958.

Wahi, Tripta, 'Evidence from the Adi Granth from the Changing Social Base and Message of the Sikh Panth: Some Reflections', *Proceedings of the Punjab History Conference*, 36th Session, 2004.
Weber, Max, 'The Social Psychology and the World Religion', in *From Max Weber: Essays in Sociology*, ed. H.H. Gerth and C. Wright Mills, New York, Oxford University Press, 1946.
Webster, John C.B., 'Modern Historical Scholarship and Sikh Religious Traditions: Some Exploratory Remarks', in *Studies in Local and Regional History*, ed. J.S. Grewal, Amritsar: Guru Nanak University, 1974.
Webster, John C.B., 'Sikh Studies in the Punjab', in *Comparative Perspective on a Changing Tradition*, Mark Juergensmeyer and N. Gerald Barrier, Berkeley: Graduate Theological Union, 1979.
Wikley, J.M., *Punjabi Musalmans*, New Delhi: Manohar, rpt., 1991.
Williams, L.F. Rushbrook, *An Empire Builder of the Sixteenth Century*, London: Longmans, Green & Company, 1918.
Yalmen, Nur, 'On the Purity of Women in Castes of Ceylon and Malabar', *Journal of the Royal Anthropological Institute of Great Britain and Ireland*, vol. 93, 1962.
Yang, Anand, 'The Many Faces of Sati in the Early Nineteenth Century', *Manushi*, vol. 42-3, 1987.
Young, Katherine K., 'Hinduism', in *Women in World Religions*, ed. Arvind Sharma, Albany, N.Y.: Suny Press, 1987.
Young, Katherine K., 'Women in Hinduism', in *Today's Woman in World Religions*, ed. Arvind Sharma, Albany: Suny Press, 1994.

Index

Ain-i Akbari 166, 251, 287
Adi Granth 26, 120, 122, 132, 166, 168, 170, 174, 175, 224, 230, 237, 240, 244, 278, 283, 294, 325, 341: caste distinctions and differences, practice of 174; how to win over the love of her husband (*shauh*) 169
Advanced Studies in Sikhism 32
Akbar 60-1, 63, 64, 66, 71, 74, 86, 84, 111, 113, 187-91, 251, 274, 276, 280, 282, 287, 289, 326: favoured and commended monogamy 190-1; policy, non-interference helped the Sikh Gurus and the Sikh community 94; prohibited forced *sati* in or before 1583 287; province of Lahore had five *doab*s 63; viewed prostitution as a social evil 280; was against practice of child marriage 187-8
Akbarnama 63
Alberuni 76-7, 81, 89, 105, 199
Anglo-Sikh War (1845-6) 26
Avadhutas 88
Aziz Ahmad 83

Babur 37, 66, 68-70, 72, 93-4, 126, 133, 291
Babur-bani verse 126, 133-4
Ballantyne, Tony 29, 32
Banerjee, Indubhushan 27, 70
Banga, Indu 31
Bansavalinamah 17
bathing ceremony (*gharigharoli*) 216

Bedi *got* 180
Bedi, Dharam Chand 38, 273: practice of female infanticide 273
Bengal Vaishnavism 116
Bhai Gurdas 75, 161, 162, 163, 165, 174, 176, 189, 193-6, 221, 231, 236, 238-40, 242-4, 249, 252, 270, 279-80, 283, 293, 316, 325-6
Bhai Jodh Singh 27
Bhai Kahan Singh Nabha 27
Bhai Vir Singh 27, 28
Bhakti movement (800-1700) 41, 95, 102, 107-8, 117, 149: principal innovations of 149
Bhakti poets 103, 108, 112-13
Bhakti *sant*s (saints) 15, 43, 44, 95, 103, 108, 111, 113, 117, 136, 336-8
Bhakti *sant*s, views on women 107-17: Dadu Dayal 111; *Dadu Dayal ki Bani* 112; Dadu's period, growing stability and political unification under Akbar 111; illusion of duality 112; Jaisi's portrait of women's position 110-11; Kabir classified women into two categories 109-10; Kabir's period, social unrest 111; Malik Muhammad Jaisi 110; *Padmavat* 111; phenomenal world (*maya*) and sexual urge (*kama*) 112; political, sociocultural, and economic realities of the time 109; sexual urge (*kama*) 110;

Surdas, attitude towards sex and carnal love 114; Surdas, lived during a period of rapid change 113; Tulsidas, society and politics, degree of stability 114; *varnashram* 114
'Bhakti' in Sanskrit 108
Bhandari, Sujan Rai 77
birth of a child 225-6: Hindu pregnant women, *ritan* 225; Jat Sikhs, *chatthi* 225; Muslims, custom of reciting *azaan* and *iqamat* 226; Muslims, largely incorporated the customs of Hindus 226; post-natal phase, mother considered polluted 225-6; *sutak* 225-6
boundaries, transgression of 154
Brahmanical caste system 95, 326, 328: mild control of 95
Brahmanical customs 177
Brahmanical Hindu social set-up 146
Brahmanical *jati* hierarchy 78
Brahmanical patriarchal system 46, 146
Brahmanical religion 88
Brahmanical system 48
Bride: given seven bites of *churi* and *khichri* 224; home, bathing ceremony (*gharigharoli*) 216; price or *wattasatta* 159
bride's family 221
bridegroom's family 216, 220, 221, 223
Brown, John Cave 272

Caste and marriage 171-1: caste and gender, complex relationship between 172; caste structure, safeguarding of 173; Indian caste system 172; marital alliances 176; puberty, appearance of 172-3; purity of caste 172; *varna* system 173; *zat* or *jati* 171-2
caste system 24, 43, 102, 105, 110, 111, 113, 147-8, 171-81, 198, 199, 253, 304-7, 309: clutches of 180; influence in Punjab 176-7; linked to gender relations 172
caste system, influence in Punjab 176-7: caste and kinship 177; fusion of traditions, plurality of sociocultural customs 177; hierarchical status 178; inter and intra-caste differences 179; ritual purity and social relations 177; Sikh Gurus, rejected status distinctions between castes and their relevance to salvation 179; Sikh Panth, persistent existence of 'the caste diversity' 179; social fluidity 177
celibate 165
chadar dalnaa/pauna 16, 47, 341
Chaitanya's Bhakti movement, Bengal 116-17
chappan bhannana 216
Char-Bagh-i-Punjab 80
Charitra Pakhyan 323-5: general social perceptions about women 325
Charitro Pakhyan 46
Cheese and Worms 154
Child marriage 186-8: adultery 188; dual ceremony, patriarchal rationale 188; female sexuality, pervasive view of 188; woman's consent in the choice of spouse, immaterial 188; woman's supposedly uncontrollable sexual desire 188; women as instrument of procreation 188; women as

object of sexual gratification for their husbands 188
Childbirth: restrictions and superstitions 343
Chishti fame, Sufi movement of 108
Christian ideology 40
Chundawand 250
citizenry 151
Civil and Religious Institutions of the Sikhs 25
common culture 15, 16, 20, 212
consecrated dessert (*karha prasad*) 176
corrective histories 28
cultural change 57
cultural fusion 23-4
cultural interaction 57-8
cultural practices 24, 46, 152, 159, 177, 182: multiplicity of 152, 159
Cunningham, J.D. 25-6, 27: treatment of Sikh history 26

Das, Veena 146-7
Dasam Granth 17, 324-5: general derogatory social perception about women 325
Dasnamis 89
Dhillon, G.S. 40
Digby, Simon 21, 39
disinheritance 247

early Indo-Islamic period: egalitarian nature of the Jats 48
Eka nari jati hoi par nari dhi bhain vakhanai 165
endogamous group 181
Essays in Sikhism 28
Evolution of the Sikh Community, The 32
Exogamous marriage, impact on women 47, 193-8: adjusting to her husband's family 196; *andar baithi lakh di; bahar nikli kakh di* 197; compatibility or sharing 197; daughter, thought alien wealth (*paraya dhan*) 194; exclusion from the community 198; faithful wife, behavior of 196-7; female labour, recognized as a wage earner 197; folk songs, anguish experienced by women 194; *Gurbilas Padshahi Chhevin* 194; impact on the life of women 338; intelligent daughter-in-law of a good family 195-6; *Kabit Swayye* 195; Kulwadhu' *sati* 195; marriage, sacramental aspect of 193; segregation, forms of 197; *sikhiya* 194; social expectation from newly wedded daughter-in-law 195; strict restrictions on women's freedom of movement 196

families of Gurus: marital alliances in 180; family histories 187, 192-204
Family 44, 47, 88, 109-11, 113, 115-16, 127, 132, 145, 147, 152-3, 159, 161-3, 165, 172, 177, 183-5, 187, 220, 225, 227-30, 232-3, 235, 236, 240, 242, 245-8, 250, 252, 256-8, 270-1, 276, 280, 282-3, 286, 292, 295, 307, 314, 316, 319-20, 329, 338-41, 343: brother-sister bonding 228-9; daughter-in-law's social fate, at the hands of her mother-in-law 230-1; hierarchical structuring of relations 230; Hindu family 212; patriarchal structure 230; power relations built into the family 232; relations within the household

230; Sikh history, norms of behavior, exemplary conduct of the Gurus 229; veneration and caring attitude for women 233; women's freedom and rights, restricted within the prevailing family structure 232
Family priests 79-80, 225
Family life 229, 232, 295: for women, ideology of seclusion and domesticity 229-30
fault-lines 24, 45
Fazl, Abul 166, 189, 191, 251, 282, 286, 287: *Ain-i Akbari* 166-7, 251
female infanticide 37, 38, 45, 47-8, 107, 225, 244, 254, 269, 271-4, 292-4, 302, 306, 310-11, 328, 337, 341, 343
feminine *bani* 132
Five Punjabi Centuries: Polity, Economy, Society and Culture 31
fusion of traditions 16, 19-20, 24, 104-5, 150, 177-8, 336

gand ceremony 215
gand pherna 215
Geertz, Clifford 104
gender egalitarianism 21
gender equality 130
gender negotiations 16
gender perspective 17, 21, 33
gender relations 14, 17, 19, 24, 102, 159, 172, 258, 302, 335
gender studies 16, 21
Gender 14-15, 17, 33, 49-50, 136, 152, 172, 255, 260, 304, 307, 335, 339, 344, 345: as a primary category of analysis 14; category of 13; symbolization of religious traditions 14
geographical region 59
Geography: key concepts of 57

girl-child 44: birth of 274; dislike for 274, 340; and female infanticide 269-75; great economic and social burden 183
got 177-8
Grewal, J.S. 26, 30, 31, 32, 63, 64, 65, 70, 74, 75, 86, 94, 118-20, 123, 128, 134, 136, 164, 301, 342, 345: *sant* tradition of northern India 134
Growth of Responsibility in Sikhism 28
gur gaddi 58, 229
Gurbilas Padshahi Chhevin 17, 163, 194, 215, 218, 222
Gurbilas Patshahi Dasvin 17
Gurdev Singh's *Perspectives on the Sikh Tradition* 32
Gurditta 187, 214, 215, 218, 244, 269, 270, 315: marital alliance of 187
gurdwara reform 28
Gurevich, Aron Y. 21
Gurmukh 165: practices *raj yog* (highest *yog*) 165
Guru Amar Das 37-8, 45, 48, 163, 171, 174, 175, 189, 193, 229, 271, 277-8, 289-90, 292, 302, 305, 307-11, 312, 314, 323, 328-9, 337-8, 341, 343-5: criticism of the societal norms pertaining to women 48; denounced the custom of *purdah* 37, 292, 310, 337; highly critical of female infanticide 45; inclusion of women in the Sikh Panth 37; *manji* system, transformed into order of *masand*s 49; quincentenary celebrations 30; opposed the sociocultural practices stacked against women 307; spoke against the

prevalence of female infanticide 271; was a Bhalla 180; women taught *manji* and *peerah* systems 336
Guru Angad 180, 307-8, 310: followed the teachings of Guru Nanak 308; Khatri of a Trehan *got* 180; stressed the need to strive for spiritual attainment 308
Guru Arjan Dev 71, 166, 175, 192, 223, 227, 235, 246, 280, 303, 314-16, 320, 326-7, 330: sixteen embellishments of women (*solah kiya singar ki anjan payai*) 166
Guru Gobind Singh 22, 26-9, 31, 35, 45, 162, 164, 171, 176, 192, 199, 215, 217, 218, 221, 235, 271, 290, 292, 302, 320-1, 323-5, 328, 330, 341, 343: ascendancy of militancy among the Sikhs peaked 320-1; ideological perceptions of the Sikh Gurus into practical reality 176; inclination toward Puranic-Brahmanical culture, perceptions of women 321; initiated Khalsa order 321-5; marriage, graphic description of *vatna* 215-16; strict prohibition of the killing of female infants 45; wedding procession, introduction (*milni*) ceremony 218
Guru Gobind Singh Foundation 27
Guru Hargobind 20, 163, 187, 192, 194, 214, 222-4, 236, 244, 246, 269, 292, 315-20, 326, 327, 330, 343: faith in prayer recitation and listening to devotional hymns 316; military stance, likely originated with the armed Jat constituency 327; vision and understanding of his mission 317-18, 319; wish for a daughter 269-70
Guru Harkrishan 180
Guru Har Rai 318-19
Guru Mahals 34
Guru Nanak 15, 18, 22, 26-9, 31-2, 35-8, 40-1, 44, 58, 63, 70-3, 75-6, 86-7, 89, 91-5, 103-10, 117-36, 161-2, 164-5, 168-9, 173-4, 180, 187, 189, 216, 223, 228-9, 231, 234-8, 244, 273, 277, 280, 291, 303-10, 312, 321, 326, 328, 335-8, 342-5: acknowledged women's social contribution as a mother and wife 337; and Kabir, comparative trajectory between 108; appreciates women only for procreative qualities 135; attitude towards Islam and Hinduism 92-3; attitude towards the *ulema* and the Sufis 92-3; conception of a good wife 131-2; contemporary social order 86; God's creation, dimension to 130-1; ideological formulation of 58; Khatri by *zat* 180; initiated community dining centre (*langar*) 308-9; opening the gates to the path of spirituality for women 303; outspoken in his denunciation of caste 344; path of spirituality for women 342; perceptions against modern perceptions of gender equality 130; political milieu 71-3; position on women 18; positive evaluation of womanhood 129-30; relationship with the *sant* tradition 118-19; religious songs and *shabad*s (hymns)

305; *shabad* and *guru*, concepts of 119-20; symbolic attack on discrimination against women 135; woman, potential temptresses of worldly illusion (*maya*) 304

Guru Nanak, attitude towards the *ulema* and the Sufis 92-3: cycle of 'action-reaction' 93; *qazi* 92-3; towards the *pandit* and *yogi* 92

Guru Nanak, conception of a good wife 131-2: abandoned woman 132; life of a bad wife (*dohagun*) 132

Guru Nanak, emancipation being open to women 128-9: state of attributelessness (*sunn mandal*) 128-9; *sangat* (holy congregation), concept of 129

Guru Nanak, God's creation, dimension to 130-1: intoxicating *maya* as poison (*bikh*) 131

Guru Nanak, political milieu 71-3: Afghan rulers, politico-administrative arrangements 72; direct denunciation of contemporary rule 72; extorting *jaziya* and pilgrimage tax, non-Muslim subjects discriminated 72; ideological fermentation 71; *maya-sanch rajai ahankari maya sath na challai piari* 73; ruler's order was against justice and equity 73; Turko-Afghan rule 72

Guru Nanak, positive evaluation of womanhood 129-30: *Brihaspatisutras* 130

Guru Nanak's ideological position: useful role played by women 165-6

Guru Nanak's verses 72, 119, 136, 164, 169, 237: nuanced analysis 164; refer to conjugal relationships 169

Guru Nanak and His Mission 28

Guru Nanak Dev, marriage of: bride's home, bathing ceremony (*gharigharoli*) 216-17; hagiography of Meharbaan 216

Guru Nanak in History 86, 125

Guru Ram Singh 273: censored the practice of female infanticide 273

Guru Teg Bahadur 22, 220, 229, 270

Guru Teg Bahadur, marriage of 220-1: giving away of dowry (*daaj*) 220-1

Guru Tegh Bahadur's martyrdom: tercentenary of 29-30

Habib, Irfan 81, 167, 250-1, 253, 274, 287-8, 305, 327: Gurus' focus on marriage 167; normative and operative beliefs, wide gap between 168

hath-yoga 89, 121, 134: woman in 134

Hau tisu gholi ghumaia par nari de neri na javai 165

Hindu Gujjars of Lahore: converted to Islam by Hujwiri 85

Hindu *sants* 117

Hindus, marriage rituals: emanated from the girl's family 213; *gand pauna* 215; girl's parents announced their readiness for marriage 213; Guru directed the *lagi*s to Mata Ganga 213; important for both the parties to consult a Brahmin astrologer 213; *lagi*s (girl's parents' representatives) 213-14;

sahasudharna 214-15; *shagun* or *roqna* for the chosen bridegroom 213
Hindus: female infanticide 272
Hir-Ranjha 17, 271, 273
History of the Sikhs 25
homogeneity 19, 23, 31, 39, 59, 151, 338: in patterns of social behavior 151
horizontal linkages 178
Hukum Namah 164
Hum Hindu Nahin 28
Human culture 57-8
Hypergamy 273-4

ideal women 37, 130, 149, 154
ideological homogeneity 31-2
Ideology 16, 33, 36, 58-9, 104, 154, 159, 313: of hierarchical deference 230; of seclusion 277; of seclusion and domesticity 229; of the Gurus 38, 39, 42, 43; of the Panth 308; of the privileged classes 104
Imperfect woman (*kuchajji*) 223
Indian Muslims 85, 226
Inheritance laws, women's economic contribution 246-53: adopting a child, certain limits 249; adoption, unknown among Muslims 249; agnates, had the right to succeed to property 248; devaluation of women on family land and household 247; extinction of male lineage, specific customs for succession 248; geographical features and economic requirements 252-3; Hindu women, appeared as *zamindar*s 250; identification of the right of inheritance 248; Muslim women in seventeenth-century, possession of land rights 250; Muslim women, revenue grants from the Mughal government 250-1; powerlessness of women 247; property rights in land, near-total disinheritance 247; Shariat 250; spinning, done almost by women 251; succession to landed property 250; widows' proprietary rights 251; woman, economic status as an individual 247; women from lower echelons of society, independence among 253; women, engaged in pastoral activities and processing 252; women, performed labour-intensive and rigorous tasks 252; women's labour, not limited to the domestic industry 251-2
inherent gender bias 22
institutionalized religion 14

Jain *sannyasi*s 88
Jakobsh, Doris 32, 33, 36, 49, 129, 135, 166, 310
Jamison, Stephanie 149
janamsakhi 17, 32-3; tradition 40, 305
janj dhukni 218
Jats 48, 66, 81-2, 177, 181, 184, 190, 193, 200-1, 273, 305, 313, 326-8, 341: practice of widow remarriage 341
jodi-ralein (meaning, may God bless this son with a sister) 269
Judaeo-Christian frame-work 33

Kabir and Guru Nanak, comparative trajectory

between 121-36: *Adi Granth* 122; attributeless *nirgun* God 127; *Babur-bani* 126; *Guru Nanak in History* 125; Guru Nanak rejects both asceticism and renunciation 125; Guru Nanak, use of the *hukam* 124-5; Guru Nanak's concept of the *shabad* and *guru* 125; Guru Nanak's emphasis on the *nam*(name) 125; Hindu and Muslim revelatory scriptures 123; *hukam*, concept of 124; Kabir, denounced religious beliefs and practices of his times 123; Kabir, egalitarian concepts 126-7; Kabir, familiarity with the tenets and practices of the *yogi*s 124; Kabir, no emancipation without Rama-*nam* 125; Kabir's attitude towards women 126; Kabir's three sorts of femaleness 127; Kabir's tolerance of mendicancy and renunciation 125; *nirgun bhakti* or *sant* tradition 121-2; *sant* movement, fountainhead of 122; Sikh religious community, moods and motivations of 122

Kabir, egalitarian concepts: attributeless *nirgun* God 127; *bhakti*, higher femaleness of 127; *nirgun* God 126-7; *stri dharma* 127; *stri svabhav* 127

Kabir, notions of *maya* 127-8: *dohagin* 127; patriarchal values, family as an institution 127; *shringara* 127; *sohagin* as the model of *stri dharma* 127; woman equated with *maya* 127; women and *maya*, identical

obstacles to *bhakti* and salvation 128

Kabir 18, 43-4, 103-4, 107-13, 117-28, 131-4, 136, 175, 336, 338, 342: attitude towards women 117; held women in low esteem 43; opposition for the system of *purdah* 277; three sorts of femaleness 127

Kabit Sawaiyye 270, 279
kanyadaan 159
Kapalikas 88
karewa 16, 47, 183, 200-3, 281, 341
Kaul, Hari Kishan 274
Khalsa 27-8, 29, 76, 173, 176, 271, 290, 292, 302, 316, 321-4, 327, 329, 343
Khan, Saadullah 64
Khatri *got*s 180
Khatris of Lahore 186
Khatris of Punjab 75, 77, 82, 91, 95, 177, 179-81, 185, 325, 358: allegiance to the elevated rank of Kshatriya 180
Khatris of the Chopra section 190
Khazan Singh's *History and Philosophy of the Sikh Religion* 27
Khusrau, Amir 64, 69, 105, 282, 377: refers to Lahauri as common language 64
Kirtan 120
Kokash, Sharad 154
kuar dhoti da suhagan 218
Kumar, Nita 45

Lahore *suba* 60
lassi-mundari, game of 224
left-handers (*vamachari*s) 90
Lodhi, Alam Khan 69, 93-4
Lodhi, Daulat Khan 93-4
Lodhi, Sikandar 93
low-grade Khatris 200

Index

M.K. Gill's *Role and Status of Women in Sikhism* 34
Mahima Parkash 229
Mai Bhago 34, 318
maian pauna or *tel charhauna* 216
Malhotra, Anshu 60
manji system 48-9, 311, 313
*manji*s 49
marital alliances 148, 176-82, 187, 189: classical hierarchy of all four *varna*s 177; caste and kinship 177; of the Sikh Gurus 176
marital bond 159
marital practices: coexisted in societies 159-60
Marriage 106: ceremonies and rituals 212; equal partnership of love and sharing 38; ideological basis of 160; within one's *zat* (caste/subcaste) but outside of one's *got* (exogamous clan) 177
marriage rites: departure (*doli*) of the bride for her parents-in-law's place 221-2
marriage songs 217: impart practical knowledge to the would-be bride of her life ahead 217
Married life 38
married woman: useful role in society, maintaining sexual discipline 166
Maryada Purushottam Ram 146
Mata Damodari 192, 223, 244, 269: advised daughter, never seek bad company 223
Mata Gujri 22, 222, 320: *doli* 222-3, *hukamnama*s of 22
Max Arthur Macauliffe 26-7
McLeod, W.H. 32
McMullen, Clarence 23, 39, 152
medieval chronicles 21
medieval Hinduism 88

medieval India: caste system 24
Medieval Indian Hindi Bhakti poetry 102-3
medieval Punjab: paternalistic dominance within the family 228
men-women equality 38
Mir, Farina 60
Mirabai 113, 115-16, 126: life and writings 115-16
Mohammedan Khojas of Bhera (in Shahpur) 190
moh-mahi 47
Mughal policy of non-interference 94
muh dikhai 224
multiculturalism 16, 336
Muslim society in the Punjab 84-5: Hindu Gujjars of Lahore, converted to Islam by Hujwiri 85; horizontal stratification 84; Indian Muslims 85; Individual Muslims 85; Indo-Muslim culture 86; influx of Muslims into the land 85; Islam through material inducement 85; Islamic society 84; middling class 84-5; native Muslims, proportion of 85; religious dignitaries 84; sectarian differences 84; Shaikh Ali bin Usman Hujwiri 85; socio-economic facts 84; Sufi Shaikhs 85
Muslims, marriage ritual: betrothal ceremony 213-14; *gand nikah* 215; proposal initiated by the boy's side 213
Muslims: early marriage was the norm 187; system of *purdah* 275-6

N. Lorenzen, David 58-9
N.K. Sinha 27

Naata 44
Nath *yogis* 18
Nath, Yogi Bhangar 162
Nathpanthi *yogis* 88
Nathyogis: *hatha-yoga* of 118; theories and practices of 120
Nikah ceremony 219-20: *akad niqah* 220; Islamic law, mutual consent to marriage 219-20; *qazi* invoked the blessings of God (*niyatkhair*) 219; *qazi* recited *Sifai-i-Imam* 219; *qazi* recited the prophecy of faith (*kalma*) five times 219
non-Vedic origin: heterogeneous sects of 88
normative beliefs and practices 23
north Indian *sants* 117
northern India: saintly tradition (*sant parampara*) of 118

Pagwand 250
Pakhyan Charitra 324, 325: women, the possessor of innumerable wiles 325
pandit 92, 123
Pandnama-i Jahangiri 274
pani varna 223-4
Panjaban 64
pativrata dharam 160
patriarchal family 116, 193, 233, 275, 340
patriarchal ideology 15, 152, 160, 218, 255, 342, 345
patriarchal religion: contemporary critics of 152-3
patriarchy: adverse effects of 153
patrilineal/patrilocal social organizations 106
Philosophy of Sikhism 28
Polygamy 107
Polygamy 44, 47, 48, 105, 107, 110, 168, 189-93, 337: Abul Fazl 191; Bhai Sheetal Singh's *Rahit Namah* 192; existence of harems of the kings 189; Guru Hargobind, wives of 192; *gurugaddi* (Guru's seat) 192; harems 189; high-class aristocracy, among Hindus and Muslims as well as lower classes 190; *hukammamah* issued by Mata Sahib Deva 192; implications for women 191; Kesar Singh Chibber's *Bansawalinamah* 192; marrying by *chaadar pauna* 190; Mata Sundari and Mata Sahib Deva, relations of 192-3; matrimonial alliances 189; Muslim tradition, Sunnis and Shias could have four wives 189-90; practised largely due to the practice of widow remarriage 190; sixth Sikh Guru, three wives 192

position and rights of women, customary practices 46
power ideology 154
Prachin Panth Parkash 17
prevalent ideology, role of 147
Principal Teja Singh 27
property rights 44, 105, 172, 228, 242, 247, 248, 249, 283: inheritance by women 250, 283; of the widows 183, 200, 201, 204, 249, 250, 286, 288, 341
Prostitution 278-81: *Adi Granth*, references to prostitutes 278; Bhai Gurdas, general social attitude towards prostitutes 279; economic dependence and the wretched conditions of widows 279-80; *Kabit Sawaiyye* 279; *khari swalio vesua jia bajha itaia* 280; people who visited the prostitutes, bear social

disapproval 280; prostitutes, social attitude towards 279; whore 279-80; women drawn into, in a variety of situations 280-1
Punjab hills—pockets of Tantric Buddhism in 88
Punjab: as a geographical entity, vagueness of 60; derivation of 59-60; ethnicities 18; five *doab*s 60; home to people of many ethnicities 43; Indo-Muslim culture 86; multiculturalism 16; multiple religious faiths 88; patrilineal and patri-virilocal systems 177-8
Punjabi, cultural category of 64
Punjabi University 27
Punjab, girl child marriage: *Bansawalinamah* 187; parents made earliest provision for their daughter's marriage 187; premature liaison for a girl 187; Sikh Gurus, no direct or indirect injunction criticizing child marriage 187; Sikh history 187
Punjab, marriage rituals 212-13
Punjab, political conditions in 65-71: Achaemenians 66; Babur made five attempts to conquer India 68; Babur's first expedition 68; Banerjee, Indubhushan 70-1; Buddhists and Hindushahis of Afghanistan 66-7; Guru Nanak, emergence of 70; Humayun's recovery of his lost kingdom 66; Ibrahim Lodhi 69; Jahangir's accession to the throne 71; western *doab*s 67-8
Punjab, types of marriages 181-6: *chaadar andazi* or *chaadar dalna* or *karewa* 183; Class I *Dharamnata (Pun)* 183, 184; Class II *Wattasatta* (Marriage by exchange) 183, 184; Class III *Takka* (On payment of money) 183, 185; cultural practices 181-2; *golat* or *golavat* 184; *haakri* 186; Hindu scriptures, eight forms of marriage 183; ideality of marriage customs, notions of 182; Jat population of Punjab, marriages involving bride wealth 185; Khatris, custom of selling girls 185-6; marital alliances, role of caste 182; marriage with dowry 183; *Qissa*s, evoked indigenous aspect of Punjabi countryside 182; rituals 181-2; selling a daughter in marriage 183; *watta*, custom of 185
Punjab, geographical understanding 59-65: Bari Doab 61-2; Bist-Jalandhar Doab 61-2; Chaj Doab 61; cultural characteristics of the people 63; differentiated sub-regions 62; Indus River system 61; intra-regional and inter-regional interactions 63; Khushwant Singh's list, Punjabi names for different regions 61; Majha (or middle tract) 61; Phulkian states 61; politico-geographical criterion, primacy of 65; Pothuhar plateau 62; Punjab in the Mughal times 60-1; Rachna Doab 61; regional identity, consciousness of 63; S. Nurul Hasan's perception 65; *Saptsindhu*, or *Madra Desh*, or *Panchnad* 63; Sindh-Sagar Doab 61, 62; *Tuzuki-Baburi* or

Baburnama 63; upper Bari Doab 62
Puran Bhagat 186
Puratan Janam Saakhis 173
purdah 275-7: did not permit women to mix freely with other members of the clan 276; *ghunghat* 275; Hindus adopted *purdah* as a protective measure 275; *manji* and *peerah* systems, active involvement of women 277; measure of respectability among higher classes 275; *panihari* 277; peasants and working women, free from hostage of *purdah* 276-7
purush svabhav or *purush dharam* 146

qualitative or quantitative change 57

radical feminist epistemology 13
Rahit 29
Raja Todar Mal: pride humbled by the birth of a female child 274
Ram Kali Raga 163: practice of offering women in charity at the places of pilgrimage 163
Ramcharitmanas 173: marriage party of Sri Ram as Tulsidas 173
Ray, Niharranjan 88
regional articulations 59
religion and society, complex interplay between 145
religion: as a source of power for women 145-6
religious and societal norms, close connection between 14
religious authorities 146
religious beliefs 146
religious ideology 15, 327, 335
Religious milieu 87-95: Abdul Quddus Gangohi 88; Bu Ali Qalandar of Panipat 87; Chishtis and Suhrawardis 87; Chishtis of Hansi 87; Haidar Shaikh 88; Punjab, ethnic plurality in 87; Sabiri branch of the Chishtis 87-8; Shaikh Ahmad Sirhindi 88
religious sphere 116-17
religious traditions 19, 335
Ricoeur, Paul: hermeneutics of suspicion 50; transformative 'power of affirmation' 50
Ritual charities 92
rituals and ceremonies 339-40: role and participation in social engagements 339
Rule of exogamy 177-8

saguni sants 43, 44
Sahaj 124, 132
saha sudharna 214-15
Sakhi 34, 120, 235, 271: urge of a woman to serve the faith 170
Sandhu Jats 249
samskar 228
sant belief 118: essence of 119
sant doctrines 118
Sant in Sikh Usage 119
Sant Nanak 118
sant parampara 118
sant synthesis 118
sant tradition 107, 108, 118, 120, 121, 134
Sant Tulsidas 18
Sarin Khatris 272
Sarkar-i-Punjab 60
Sati 37, 38, 41, 44, 47-8, 105, 107, 110, 112, 134, 168, 199, 243, 247, 254, 281-90, 291-3, 306, 309-11, 337, 340, 341, 344: Abdul Qadir Badauni's view 282; Abraham Roger's view 288-9; *Adi Granth*, custom of *sati*, quite common in medieval

Index

Punjab 283; Amir Khusrau's view 282; Bernier's view 287-8; *Dabistan-i-Mazahib* 283; Diodorus Siculus' view 284-5; fates of unfortunate widows, centrifugal and centripetal forces 285-6; general social attitude 282; Guru Amar Das, condemned the custom of *sati* 289-90; Ibn Battuta's view 284; in Taxila and among the Kathians (Madra) in ancient Punjab 284; *jauhar* 284; Mandakranta Bose's view 289; Megasthenes, silent on this issue 285; P.V. Kane, views on 287; primarily confined to the upper classes among the Hindus 281; restricted to high castes like Brahmins and Kshatriyas 284; *Sahmarana* or *sahagamana* 281-2; social pressure on the widow to burn herself 288; status of the 'only *dharm*' for the widow 286; Strabo's views 284-5; *Tawarikh-i Guru Khalsa* 290; widow's right to property 286; women were forced to perform *sati*, pressure from relatives or public opinion 286
satsang 120
Sau Sakhi 17
Savitri Chandra Sobha 102
Scott, Joan Wallach 13, 49-50, 152
Scripture: ritual reading of 92
Secondary literature 24-5: Sikh history, equated with the history of the Punjab 25; Sikh studies, sub-discipline of 24-5
sexes, segregation of 106
sexual desires: self-restraint and self-control in 161
Shah Muhammad 64

Shah, Waris 17, 20, 64, 181, 182, 185, 186, 215, 219-1, 224, 271: marriage, link between the domain of caste and kinship 186; methods employed in the killing of infant daughters 271-2
Shaikh Ahmad Sirhindi: efforts to bring about an Islamic revival 88
Shaikh Ali bin Usman Hujwiri 85
Shaikh Daud 85
Shaiva Brahmins 89
Shaiva *sannyasi*s 89
Shaivism 88-90
Shaktas 90, 124, 126: Ambala 90; Chandigarh 90; Kalka 90; left-handers (*vamachari*s) 90; Panchkula 90; Shakti cult, Puranic version of 90; Simla 90; worshipped the Goddess in her various forms 90
Shaktism 51, 88
Shampotra, Mohan Lal 184
shraddh ceremonies 227
Sikh Bibiyan by Simran Kaur 34
Sikh faith 17, 26, 83, 122, 174, 243, 336
Sikh faith, cardinal institutions of: community kitchen (*langar*) and the holy congregation (*pangat*) 174-5
Sikh Gurus 33: as ardent advocates of women's liberation 36; castigated *yogi*s 161; condemned female infanticide 38; economic interests of 49; egalitarian ideas of 175; female infanticide 272-3; followed the same practices as Hindus 212; histories of 22; inclusivity 133; influenced the dominant patriarchal ideology 152; instances of polygamy 44;

marital alliances in the families 180; oft-quoted sayings about marriage 160, 167; patriarchal ideologies 16-17; perceived gender 15; recommended the monogamous ideal of marriage 163; redefined celibacy as marriage to one wife 163, 337; religious injunctions of 152; spoke against the practice of *sati* 341; views on women's condition 290-5; wives and sisters of 35

Sikh historiography 29, 136

Sikh history 22, 25, 26, 27, 29, 31-4, 39-40, 187, 229, 244, 290

Sikh identity 28, 182, 315: and practice, diversity in 28

Sikh ideology 32, 181: equalities in the religious, social, and political spheres of the Sikh Panth 181

Sikh Jats 273: female infanticide 273

Sikh men and women, egalitarianism between 34

Sikh movement 35: Guru Mahals 35

Sikh Panth 15, 26, 31, 35-8, 42, 48-9, 119-20, 179, 181, 236, 300-1: gender differences within 49; in the sixteenth century, socio-religious evolution of 31; social composition and its changing concerns 325-31

Sikh Panth and Women's Identity 300-1: accession to Guruship (*gaddi*), family-centric feature 314; Amro, Bibi 310; Anandpur Sahib, surrounded by the enemy's army, help by women 318; *charan di pahul* 322, 323; *Charitra Pakhyan* 324-5; *Dabistan-i-Mazahib* 314; *Dasam Granth* 324; double-edged sword (*khanda*) 322-3; early phase of 306; early phase of the Panth 306; emergence of the pilgrimage site, Goindwal 311; evaluating Guru Nanak's perception of women 306-7; existing sociocultural values 303-4; expansion of 310; female perspective towards the body of the Guru 311; five 'potent thugs' 304; five K's 322; Guru Amar Das, practice of veil (*purdah*) 310; Guru Arjan, declared as *Sacha Padshah* 314-15; Guru as *Sacha Padshah* 313; Guru Gobind Singh, militaristic concerns of 321; Guru Tegh Bahadur 320; Guru, institutionalization of the position 301; *hukamnamah* to the Patna *sangat*, reference to Bebe Per Bai 319-20; initiation rite of Khalsa, the feminine aspect 322; *janamsakhi* tradition 305; *karad*, a domestic 'feminine' implement 323; Khalsa code (*rahit*) 323; Khalsa identity construction and gender analysis 322-3; *khande di pahul* 322; *khande ki pahul*, newly mandated rite 323; Koer Singh, *Gurbilas Padshahi Dasvin* 322; Koer Singh, prohibited any contact with *kurri maar, masand*s 323; Langar, Mata Khiwi, participated in the preparation of food in the common kitchen 309; *langar-pangat* system, egalitarian values of 309; *Mahima Parkas* 308; *Mahima Parkas Vartak* 308; Mai Bhago's episode 318; *manji* system 310; *manji* system, transformed into the order of *masnads* 313; *manjis* and *peeris*, expanding Sikh community 314; *Masnad-i-Ali* (or high dignitaries) during the Afghan rule 313; *masands* 313-14; messages and ideological perception 301; militaristic ethos of the Panth, women adherents almost invisible 317; *Pakhyan Charitra* or *Triya Charitra* 324; Panth and the Lahore administration, relations between 316; Panthic development in its initial stages 304-5; presence of women in the *sangat* 312-13; *Ramkali ki Var* 308; Saroop Das Bhalla, *Mahima Parkash* 310; seventy-two cradles were established 310; Sikh Gurus and the Mughals, relations between 315; Sikhism, distinctive features and the general outline of 303; socio-political Sikh Panth 301-2; *stri svabhav* 324; *Tawarikh-i-Guru Khalsa* 316; warned the unwary against 'womanly enticements' 324; women as temptresses 304; women, influx into the young Sikh tradition 313

Sikh Panth, social composition and its changing concerns 325-31: Bibi Sharifa 329-30; *Dabistan-i-Mazahib* 326; Gyani Gyan Singh's *Tawarikh-i Guru Khalsa* 329; inclusion of Jats into Sikh fold 327; Jat response to Guru's teachings 326-7; Khatri prominence, extended beyond the Guru's line 325-6; participation of women in the developing Sikh community, factors of 328; recruited its followers in rural Punjab 326; shift in the priorities of the Gurus 329; *triyacharitra* 329; women, embracing the egalitarian message of the early Sikh Gurus 328

Sikh stories: *janj* and *janj dhukni*, description of 218

Sikh Studies 24, 27, 28, 29, 32, 33

Sikh tradition 17, 34, 35, 37, 41, 130, 135, 176, 236, 277, 294, 309, 313, 323, 329: anti-caste cardinal principle of Khalsa 176; gender egalitarianism of 34

Sikhism 15, 18, 19, 26-34, 36, 38, 40, 42-4, 48, 58, 66, 70, 71, 75, 81, 82, 93, 94, 121, 148, 152, 161, 168, 171, 176, 301, 303, 312, 318, 330, 335, 336: better position for women 148; monogamy as an ideal form of marriage 168; position of women in 33; regional identity 30

Sikhs per se 178

Singer, Milton 42

Singh, Chetan 60

Singh, Daljeet 32, 121: *Sikhism* 32

Singh, Ganda 22, 27, 28, 29, 31, 320

Singh, Gopal 166: translation of *Sri Guru Granth Sahib* 166

Singh, Jagjit 179

Singh, Nikky-Guninder Kaur: principles of femininity in the *Adi Granth* 132

Singh, Sukhmander 40

Singh, Teja 28

Sri Guru Granth Sahib 17, 20, 44, 46, 166, 168, 269, 309: 32 virtues (*battigunni*) in a woman 46; inclusion of poetry of Baba Farid 19; relationship between man and woman 168-9

Sita, chastity of 146
Sketch of the Sikhs 25
social evils 45, 47-8, 102, 108, 110, 134, 184, 254, 306, 311, 330, 340
social ideology 59, 103, 301
Social milieu 15, 16, 73-87, 107, 148, 153, 162, 169, 203, 214, 245, 254, 294, 304, 306, 312, 313, 338, 345: Baloch and Pathan clans 76; Brahmanical *jati* hierarchy 78; Brahmins (*ahl-i-brahmana*) 77; Brahmins as a priestly class 80; *Char-Bagh-i-Punjab* 80; cultural comingling, era of 83; *Dabistan-i-Mazahib* 81; four-*varna* order 77-8; Guru Nanak castigates the Khatris 75-6; Guru Nanak to the social situation 75; Hadi and Dom, engaged in 'unclean work' 77; *haumai* (self-centredness) 76; headmen (*muqaddam*s), hypocrisy of 75; Hindu craftsmen, condition of 82-3; Hindu society in the rural Punjab 81; Hindu society, ideal norm of 76-7; Hindus of the Punjab, did not fit completely into four-*varna* order 77-8; Jats had their landed headmen (*zamindar*s, *chaudhri*s, and *muqaddam*s) 82; Jats, history of 81-2; Jats, *zamindari* rights 81; Khatris of Punjab 80; *Khulasat-ut-Tawarikh* 80; Kshatriyas of north India 80; Kshatriyas of the Punjab, social prestige 80; Kshatriyas, important constituent of the Nanak Panth 80-1; loss of the position of the Rajputs 78; Mahayana Buddhism 78; Malik Muhammad Jaisi 74; Muhammad bin Qasim, Hindu kingdoms of India 74; Muslim society in the Punjab 84; Niharranjan Ray's opinion, *Smarta Pauranik* 78; people below the Shudras 77; priests (*ahl-i-dharm*) among the Hindus 79; *qazi*s 76; Rais 79; Rajput ruling class 78; Rajput sovereignty, loss of 79; Shaikh Farid 74; social situation in the Punjab 73; socio-economic stage in 1699 76; sub-castes in each *varna* 77; Sufi Shaikhs 76; Sufis (*auliya*) 76; Sufis, evolution of the 'syncretic culture' 83; *Tarikh-i-Mubarak Shahi* 75; untouchables, conditions of 83; *varna* concept, Kshatriyas of 78-9; *varna* system 77, 79
social reality 14, 91, 111, 148, 150, 237, 243, 246, 275, 319
sociocultural formations, spatial variations in 58
socio-religious milieu 95
Sodhis 272, 329: female infanticide 272
Sri Guru Panth Parkash 164, 215, 218, 220-1: references to the marriage of Suraj Mal 215
Sri Raag 189, 238, 304
stri dharam 146, 154-7, 160
stri svabhav 127, 134, 160, 188, 200, 229, 251, 281, 324
Suba-i-Lahore 60
Sufi Shaikhs 76, 85, 126

Tabaqat-i-Akbari 86
Tawarikh-i Guru Khalsa 271, 290, 316, 329

Index 441

Thapar, Romila 105
The Baisakhi of Guru Gobind Singh 28
The Religion of the Sikhs 27
The Sikh Ideology 32
The Sikh Religion: Its Gurus, Sacred Writings and Authors 26
The Sword and Religion 28
The-Shahnameh-i-Maharaja Ranjit Singh 64
traditional Hindu marriage 186-7: *garbhadhaan* or *muklawa* 186, 187; married girl child, inauspicious (*shanee*) 186-7; wedding ceremony, binding, performed before girl reached puberty 186
true abstinence or renunciation 161
Trumpp, Ernest 26
Tulsidas 114: held women in low esteem 43; overriding concerns for social stability 114; propriety (*maryada*), observance of 115; traditional views about women 114; women of high qualities (*uttam*) 114; women of low quality (*neech*) 114
Turko-Afghan rule 107

Udasi Bodh of Sant Rein 199
untying *gana*s, ceremony of 224
Upadhyay, Vasudeva 79

Vadera, Ganesh Das 65
vagpharai 218
Vaishnava *bhakti* 108
Vaishnava Brahmins 89
Vaishnava texts 89
Vaishnavism 88, 90-1, 116, 121: Bhakti 91; Rama Bhakti, cult of 91; Vaishnava Bhakti 91
Var 1, Pauri 38 of *Varan* 162
Var 6, Pauri 18 162
Vasudeva Upadhyaya 105
Vedic wedding ceremony 220: bride's house, display of her dowry 220; *chauk pauna* 220; *gand chitarna* 220; *lavan pheran* 220; *phere lena* 220
Weapons of the Weak: Everyday Forms of Peasant Resistance 253-60: dissociative behaviour or rebellious attitudes as spirit-possession 256-7; ideal' female role emphasized humility and submissiveness 256; *jhagrra*s and *kissa*s as a 'popular' literary form 259-60; latent forms of deviant behavior 256; Moh-Mahi 258; public abuse 257-8; spirit-possession behaviour among women 256; viewing women as objects 258; women couldn't resist any act of domination 254; women sang folk songs at the time of marriage and associated occasions 258-9
wedding procession/ *janj charhni* 217-18
Widow remarriage, patriarchal guardianship 198-204: Hindu widow, constantly reminded of her misfortune 204; Ibbetson, Denzil 199; *iddat*, Islamic rules of 202; *iddat*, period of 202; *karewa* among the landowning classes 201; *karewa*, system of 200-2; lower down the caste system 199-200; marriage through *karewa* 201; Muslim widow, property rights 204; patriarchal social psychology 201; practice among

the Jats 201; *stri svabhav*, general perception of 200; Tara Bai 199; widow's right as to whom she could marry 201-2
Widowhood 198-9, 280, 288, 340
Wife, *ardhangani* or burden 236-46: ability to produce male heirs 274; *Adi Granth*, conjugal relationship 237; *Adi Granth*, image of a wife, complies with the social reality 237-8; bad wife called *kuchaji*, *dohagan* and *kulakhanni* 237; Bhai Gurdas, expressed social expectation for the wife 238; birth of a daughter, unwelcome event 244; deceit-filled love 240; faithful and loyal wife, solely interested in serving her husband 241-3, 245; humble position in relation to her husband 240; love for the spouse in marital life 238; *pativrata*, conception of 240; procreative abilities 243; queen, who is blessed with a son in the harem of the king 244-5; required to control her aggressive and sexual urges 237; sexual control of women 239-40; shameless woman 239; Sikh history, preference for a son 244; *suchajj* (doer of good deeds) 237; *suhagan* (wedded) 237; *sulakhani* (virtuous or an ideal woman) 237
Wismad 28
Woman who failed produce a male heir: accused 274; forced to accept a *saut* 274

Women: appreciated for their procreative capabilities 168; in Sikh society, roles and status of 35; in the social sphere 212-60; intrinsically defective nature 147; missionaries 49; repression of 147; respectable position of 150; social space of 47
Women as mothers 233-6: domestic affairs, women consulted 235; Guru Matas, anecdotes of 236; Guru Nanak's maternal images 235-6; Punjab, position of the mother 234; Sikh scripture, affirms the centrality of menstrual blood 234
Women's condition, Gurus' views on 290-5: *Adi Granth*, images of the mother, of the bride and of 'feminine roles' 294; Bhai Gurdas, blissfully happy life of a wife (*suhagin*) 293; Bhai Gurdas, life of love and affection of an unmarried girl 293; Guru Amar Das, spoke against the practice of *sati* 292; Guru Nanak, emphasis on conjugal relationship, fidelity, and chastity 291; Guru Nanak's attitude 291; Gurus frowned upon certain practices 293; negative attitudes towards women 293; Sikh scripture, does not debase the female body 292
women's duty or *stri dharam* 160
Women's nature or *stri svabhav* 160

zat 177